GERMAN
LEARNER'S DICTIONARY
ENGLISH–GERMAN / GERMAN–ENGLISH

Revised & Updated

GERMAN

LEARNER'S DICTIONARY

ENGLISH–GERMAN / GERMAN–ENGLISH

Revised & Updated

REVISED BY WALTER KLEINMANN

Coordinator of Language Programs
Sewanhaka Central High School District

◆

Based on the original
by Genevieve A. Martin and Theodor Bertram

This work was previously published under the title *Living Language™ Common Usage Dictionary—German* by Genevieve A. Martin and Theodor Bertram, based on the dictionary developed by Ralph Weiman.

Published by Living Language, A Random House Company, New York, New York.

Living Language is a member of the Random House Information Group.

Random House, Inc., New York, Toronto, London, Sydney, Auckland

www.livinglanguage.com

LIVING LANGUAGE and colophon are registered trademarks of Random House, Inc.

If you're traveling, we recommend **Fodor's Guides.**

This book is available for special discounts for bulk purchases for sales promotions or premiums. Special editions, including personalized covers, excerpts of existing books, and corporate imprints, can be created in large quantities for special needs. For more information, write to Special Markets/ Premium Sales, 1745 Broadway, MD 6-2, New York, NY, 10019 or e-mail specialmarkets@randomhouse.com.

Printed in the United States of America

ISBN 1-4000-2138-3

10   9   8   7

CONTENTS

INTRODUCTION

The *Living Language® German Dictionary* lists more than 15,000 of the most frequently used German words, gives their most important meanings, and illustrates their use. This revised edition contains updated phrases and expressions as well as many new entries related to business, technology, and the media.

1. More than 1,000 of the most essential words are capitalized to make them easy to find.

2. Numerous definitions are illustrated with phrases, sentences, and idiomatic expressions. If there is no close English equivalent for a German word, or if the English equivalent has several meanings, the context of the illustrative sentences helps to clarify the meanings.

3. Because of these useful phrases, the *Living Language® German Dictionary* also serves as a phrase book and conversation guide. The dictionary is helpful both to beginners who are building their vocabulary and to advanced students who want to perfect their command of colloquial German.

4. The German expressions (particularly the idiomatic and colloquial ones) have been translated into their English equivalents. However, literal translations have been

added to help the beginner. For example, under the entry *Kuh,* cow, you will find: *Er ist bekannt wie eine bunte Kuh.* He is well-known everywhere. ("He's known as well as a colorful cow.") This dual feature also makes the dictionary useful for translation work.

EXPLANATORY NOTES

Literal translations are in parentheses. Colloquial is abbreviated to *coll.*

Gender is indicated by *m.* for masculine, *f.* for feminine, and *n.* for neuter.

Case is indicated by *nom.* for nominative, *gen.* for genitive, *dat.* for dative, *acc.* for accusative.

Possessive is abbreviated to *poss.,* pronoun to *pron.,* adjective to *adj.,* preposition to *prep.*

THE GERMAN
SPELLING REFORM OF 1998

The educational ministries of all German states agreed upon a spelling reform in the 1990s. This was supposed to make German spelling a little easier on students and natives alike. The spelling reform became mandatory in the year 2000. The following are the most important rules.

- After short vowels *ß* becomes *ss*. *ß* remains *ß* after long vowels, if the stem of the word shows no more consonants. *Fass* (keg) but *Straße* (street).

- Double consonants after a stressed short vowel: *nummerieren* (to number). *Ass* (ace), *Tipp* (tip).

- Always write as two separate words: verb combinations with *sein* such as *pleite sein* (to be destitute), combinations of two verbs such as *kennen lernen* (to get to know), combinations of verb and participle such as *gesagt haben* (to have said), combinations of verb plus noun such as *Rad fahren* (to ride a bicycle), combinations of verb and adverb such as *beiseite legen* (to set aside), combinations of verb plus adjective such as *gut lesen* (to read well), and verb + *-ig, -isch, -lich,* such as *lastig fallen* (to be a burden).

- Capitalize all nouns and derivatives of nouns: *Trimm-dich Pfad* (fitness trail), *Leid tun* (to be sorry), *das Dutzend* (the dozen), *im Deutschen* (in German), *Schweizer Käse* (Swiss cheese).

- Write out all letters that meet: *Schiff + Fahrt = Schifffahrt* (boat ride).

- In letters, *du* (you), *dir* (to you), *dein* (your), *eure* (your [pl.]), etc., are written in lowercase.

- Many foreign words receive a "Germanized" spelling: *Fotograf* (photographer).

- Words separate after spoken syllables: *Fens-ter* (window), *Ba-der* (bathroom), *A-bend* (evening).

- Commas are no longer necessary before *und* or *oder*.

German-English

A

AB 1. *adv. off, down, away from, from.*
  ab heute   *from today.*
  ab und ab   *now and then.*
  ab und zu   *to and fro, now and then.*
  von hier ab   *from here (on).*
  von nun ab   *henceforth.*
  2. *separable prefix (implies a movement down or away, imitation, appropriation, deterioration, destruction).*
  Das Flugzeug stürzte ins Meer ab.   *The plane fell into the sea.*
  Einige alte Häuser werden abgerissen.   *Some old houses will be demolished.*
  Er hat ihm tausend Euro abgeschmeichelt.   *He got a thousand euros from him by flattery.*
  Ich schreibe meine Aufgabe ab.   *I copy my homework.*
Abart *f. variety; variation of species.*
abbeißen *to bite off.*
  sich die Nägel abbeißen   *to bite one's nails.*
abbezahlen *to pay off.*
abbiegen *to turn off.*
Abbild *n. copy, image.*
abbinden *to unbind.*
Abbitte *f. apology; forgiveness.*
abbrechen *to break up, interrupt, deduct, gather.*
  Blumen abbrechen   *to gather flowers.*
  die Arbeit abbrechen   *to cease work.*
abdanken *to dismiss, abdicate.*
  Der Fürst hat abgedankt.   *The prince has abdicated.*
abdrehen *to turn off, switch off.*
  Drehen Sie das Radio ab!   *Turn off the radio!*
abdrucken *to print*
ABEND *m. evening.*
  Es wird Abend.   *It is getting dark.*
  heute Abend.   *tonight.*
Abenteuer *n. adventure.*
  auf Abenteuer ausgehen   *to look for adventure.*
abenteuerlich *adventurous.*
Abenteurer *m. (-in f.) adventurer.*
ABER *but, however, anyway.*
  Ich wollte ausgehen aber das Wetter war zu schlecht.   *I wanted to go out but the weather was too bad.*
  Das Kind wollte spielen, die Mutter aber wollte nicht.   *The child wanted to play but the mother did not want to.*
  Der König aber . . .   *The King, however, . . .*

  Nein aber!   *I say!*
  Nun aber!   *But now!*
  tausend und aber tausend   *thousands and thousands.*
abermals *again, once more.*
abfahren *to set off, depart.*
  Der Zug fährt um drei Uhr ab.   *The train leaves at three.*
  Sie fuhr übel ab.   *She got the worst of it.*
Abfahrtsort *m. place of departure.*
abfinden *to settle, come to an agreement.*
abführen *to lead away, carry away.*
Abführung *f. removal.*
Abgabe *f. tax, tribute, delivery.*
  abgabenfrei   *tax free.*
  abgabenpflichtig   *taxable; accessible.*
Abgang *m. departure, exit.*
ABGEBEN *to give, supply, deliver, pay taxes.*
  sich mit etwas abgeben   *to occupy oneself with a matter.*
  Wir können die Waren zu diesem Preis nicht abgeben.   *We cannot supply the merchandise on these terms (at this price).*
abgehen *to depart, go off.*
  Er lässt sich nichts abgehen.   *He denies himself nothing.*
  von seinem Vorhaben nicht abgehen   *to persist in one's plans.*
abgemacht *agreed.*
abgewinnen *to win from.*
abgewöhnen *to disaccustom, give up.*
  Ich habe mir das Rauchen abgewöhnt.   *I have given up smoking.*
Abgrund *m. abyss, precipice.*
abhalten *to hold off, restrain.*
  Lassen Sie sich nicht abhalten!   *Don't let me stop you!*
abhängen *to unhang, hang up (phone), disconnect.*
abhängig *sloping, dependent on.*
abheben *to lift off, uncover, become detached.*
  Die helle Gestalt hebt sich auf dem dunklen Hintergrund vorteilhaft ab.   *The light figure is brought into relief against the dark background.*
Abhilfe *f. relief.*
abholen *to get, collect.*
  Das Taxi wird mich abholen.   *The taxi will pick me up.*
Abkunft *f. descent, origin.*
ablenken *to divert, distract.*
ablesen *to pick up, read from.*
abliefern *to deliver.*
ABMACHEN *to remove, loosen, agree, settle.*
  Abgemacht!   *Agreed!*
abnehmen *to take off, gather, pick up (phone), to lose weight.*

Er nimmt seinen Hut ab. *He takes off his hat.*

Er hat zehn Pfund abgenommen. *He lost ten pounds.*

Abneigung f. *dislike, antipathy.*

Abort m. *lavatory; W.C.*

abräumen *to take away, remove.*

ABREISE f. *departure.*

eine unvorhergesehene Abreise *an unexpected departure.*

Absage f. *refusal.*

absagen *to refuse, to cancel, call off.*

eine Gesellschaft absagen lassen *to call off a party.*

Falls Sie mir nicht absagen, komme ich. *Unless you call it off, I'll come.*

Abscheu m. *aversion, horror.*

abscheulich *horrible, abominable, atrocious.*

Das war abscheulich von ihm. *It was very horrible of him.*

ABSCHIED m. *departure.*

Abschied nehmen *to take leave.*

Ich werde Abschied von Ihnen nehmen. *I am going to leave you.*

den Abschied bekommen *to be dismissed.*

Der Offizier hat seinen Abschied genommen. *The officer has been placed on the retired list.*

abschreiben *to copy, to deduct.*

abseits prep. (gen.) *aside, apart, away from.*

ABSICHT f. *intention, purpose, view.*

in der Absicht *with the intention.*

Er tat es in böser Absicht. *He did it with a malicious intention.*

absichtlich *on purpose.*

(sich) abspielen *to occur, to take place.*

Abstand m. *distance, interval.*

Er nahm Abstand von seiner Erbschaft. *He gave up his inheritance.*

Er nahm Abstand von dem schnell vorbeifahrenden Zug. *He stood back from the fast passing train.*

Absturz m. *fall, crash.*

Er wurde bei einem Flugzeugabsturz getötet. *He was killed in a plane crash.*

ABTEIL n. *compartment, division, section.*

Abteil erster Klasse n. *first-class compartment.*

Nichtraucherabteil *nonsmoking compartment.*

Abteilung f. *department (in a store).*

Schuhabteilung f. *shoe department.*

abtrocknen *to dry off, wipe.*

das Geschirr abtrocknen *to dry the dishes.*

abwärts *downward.*

abwechseln *to vary, change, alternate.*

abwesend *absent.*

Abwesenheit f. *absence.*

abzahlen *to pay off.*

abziehen *to retain, take off, subtract, deduct.*

Der Arbeitgeber zieht die Steuer vom Einkommen ab. *The employer deducts taxes from the salary.*

ach! *Ah! Oh!*

ACHT *eight.*

heute in acht Tagen *A week from today.*

achtmal *eight times.*

ACHT (-ER, -E, -ES) *eighth.*

achten *to esteem, regard, respect.*

ACHTUNG f. *esteem.*

Achtung! *Beware! Attention!*

achtungsvoll *respectfull.*

ACHTZEHN *eighteen.*

ACHTZEHNT (-ER, -E, -ES) *eighteenth.*

ACHTZIG *eighty.*

ACHTZIGST (-ER, -E, -ES) *eightieth.*

ACKER m. *field, soil.*

Ackerbau m. *agriculture.*

ackern *to plough.*

Ackersmann m. *ploughman*

addieren *to add up.*

Adel m. *nobility, aristocracy.*

Ader f. *vein.*

Adjektiv n. *adjective.*

adelig *noble.*

ADRESSE f. *address.*

Hier ist meine Adresse. *Here is my address.*

adressieren *to address.*

Adverb n. *adverb.*

Affe m. *monkey.*

Affekt m. *excitement.*

affektiert *affected.*

Agent m. *agent.*

ahnen *to have a premonition.*

Es ahnt mir Unglück. *I have a premonition of evil.*

Ich habe keine Ahnung. *I don't have the slightest idea.*

ähnlich *similar, like.*

ähnlich sehen *to look alike.*

Ähnlichkeit f. *similarity, resemblance.*

Akademie f. *academy, university.*

Akten pl. *deeds, documents.*

Aktie f. *share, stock.*

aktiv *active.*

Akzent m. *accent, stress.*

Alarm m. *alarm.*

Alkohol m. *alcohol, liquor.*

ALL (aller, alle, alles) *entire, whole, every, each, any.*

all die Leute *all the people.*

all und jeder *each and every.*

alle Tage *every day.*

auf alle Fälle *in any case.*

ohne allen Grund *for no reason at all.*

ALLEIN *alone, single, solitary, apart, lonesome.*

Ich bin allein. *I am alone.*

Sie lebt allein. *She lives alone.*

allerart *diverse.*

allgemein *universal.*

Alphabet *n. alphabet.*

ALS *when, than, as, like.*

Als Bismarck starb, gab es noch keine Flugzeuge. *When Bismarck died, they still didn't have any airplanes.*

Sie ist größer als ihr Bruder. *She is taller than her brother.*

als ob *as if, as though.*

Er tut, als ob er die Antwort kenne. *He acts as if he knew the answer.*

so bald *as soon as.*

ALSO *so, thus, in this way.*

"Also sprach Zarathustra . . ." *"Thus spoke Zarathustra . . ."*

ALT *old, aged, ancient.*

alte Sprachen *ancient languages (classics).*

altehrwürdig *venerable.*

altgläubig *orthodox.*

altmodisch *old-fashioned.*

eine alte Jungfer *an old maid.*

ALTER *n. age, old age, antiquity.*

Mittelalter *n. Middle Ages.*

älter *older, elder, senior.*

Altertum *n. antiquity.*

Altertumshändler *m. antique dealer.*

älteste *oldest.*

am (an dem) *on, at.*

Amerikaner *m.* (**-in** *f.*) *American.*

amerikanisch *American.*

AMT *n. office, charge, board. In compound words, the suffix amt designates a government office:*

das Auswärtige Amt *the Foreign Office.*

Polizeiamt *n. police station.*

Zollamt *n. customs.*

in Amt und Würden stehen *to be a person of position.*

amüsant *amusing.*

AMÜSIEREN *to amuse.*

sich amüsieren *to enjoy oneself.*

Ich habe mich bei der Gesellschaft sehr amüsiert. *I enjoyed myself at the party.*

AN 1. *prep. (dat. when answering the question Wo? acc. when answering the question Wohin? and depending on the idiom).*

an die Arbeit gehen *to go to work.*

an der Arbeit sein *to be at work.*

an der Donau *on the Danube.*

an und für sich *in itself.*

Er starb an seinen Wunden. *He died of his wounds.*

Es ist an mir. Ich bin dran. *It is on me. It is my turn.*

Ich gehe an die Tür. *I go to the door.*

Ich weiß, was an der Geschichte dran ist. *I know what the story is.*

2. *separable prefix (implies movement closer to the speaker, proximity, contact, attraction, climbing, beginning).*

Der Hund ist angebunden. *The dog is tied.*

Der Tag bricht an. *The day begins.*

Er behielt seine Schuhe an. *He kept his shoes on.*

Er zieht seine Jacke an. *He puts his coat on.*

anbehalten *to keep on.*

Ich will meinen Mantel anbehalten. *I want to keep my coat on.*

anbieten *to offer, volunteer.*

Anblick *m. sight, view.*

Andenken *n. memory, souvenir.*

zum Andenken an meine Eltern *in memory of my parents.*

ANDER *other, another, different, next.*

am anderen Morgen *the next morning.*

anderer Meinung sein *to be of a different opinion.*

ein andermal *another time.*

einen Tag um den andern *every other day.*

etwas anderes *another thing, something else, something different.*

nichts anderes als *nothing but.*

unter anderem *among other things.*

anderenfalls *otherwise.*

andererseits *on the other side.*

andeuten *to indicate.*

Anerbieten *n. offer, proposal.*

Anfall *m. attack, fit.*

Herzanfall *m. heart attack.*

Anfang *m. beginning, start.*

anfangen (*to*) *begin, start.*

von Anfang bis Ende *from beginning to end.*

Anfrage *f. inquiry.*

anfragen *to inquire.*

anfreunden (**sich**) *to become friends.*

angemessen *suitable, accurate.*

Angesicht *n. face, countenance.*

von Angesicht zu Angesicht *face to face.*

angesichts *considering, in view of.*

Angewohnheit *f. habit, custom.*

angrenzen *to border.*

Angriff *m. attack.*

in Angriff nehmen *to set about.*

Angst *f. anxiety.*

ängstigen *to frighten.*

sich ängstigen vor *to be afraid of.*

sich ängstigen um *to feel anxious about.*

anhaben *to wear, have on.*

Er hat einen neuen Anzug an. *He's wearing a new suit.*

anhalten *to stop, pull up.*
anhören *to listen to.*
Anker *m. anchor.*
anklagen *to accuse.*
ankleiden *to dress.*
anklopfen *to knock at.*
ANKOMMEN *to arrive, approach, reach.*
  Es kommt darauf an, ob Sie Zeit haben.
    It depends on whether you have time.
  Der Zug ist um 15.00 Uhr angekommen.
    The train arrived at 3:00 P.M.
ANKUNFT *f. arrival.*
anmelden *to announce, notify, report.*
Anmut *f. grace, charm.*
anmutig *graceful, charming.*
Annahme *f. acceptance, assumption.*
annehmen *to accept, receive, assume, take care of.*
anpassen *to fit, suit, adapt.*
anprobieren *to try on.*
anrechnen *to charge.*
  zu viel anrechnen   *to overcharge.*
  Ich rechne Ihnen Ihre Hilfe hoch an.
    I appreciate your help very much.
Anrede *f. address.*
anreden *to address, accost.*
  Der Polizist redete mich an.
    The policeman spoke to me.
anregen *to incite, stimulate, excite.*
Ansage *f. announcement, notification.*
ansagen *to announce, notify.*
anschauen *to look at, contemplate.*
anschaulich *evident, clear.*
Anschrift *f. address (letter).*
anschuldigen *to accuse.*
ANSEHEN *to look at, consider, regard.*
  dem Ansehen nach   *to all appearances.*
  im Ansehen stehen   *to be esteemed.*
  vom Ansehen kennen   *to know by sight.*
Ansicht *f. view, sight, opinion.*
  nach meiner Ansicht   *according to my opinion.*
Ansichtskarte *f. picture postcard.*
Ansprache *f. speech, address.*
Anspruch *m. claim, pretension.*
  Anspruch haben auf   *to be entitled to.*
Anstand *m. manners, decency, etiquette.*
  ohne Anstand   *without hesitation.*
anständig *decent, respectable.*
ANSTATT (statt) 1. *prep. (gen.) instead of;* also *conj.*
  Anstatt eines Regenschirms nahm er einen Hut.   *Instead of an umbrella, he took a hat.*
anstrengen (sich) *to strain, exert.*
anstrengend *tiring, trying, exacting.*
ANTWORT *f. answer.*
ANTWORTEN *to answer.*
anvertrauen *to entrust, confide.*

Anwalt *m. lawyer, attorney.*
anwesend *present.*
Anwesenheit *f. presence.*
Anzahl *f. quantity, amount.*
anzahlen *to pay on account.*
Anzeige *f. notice, advertisement.*
anzeigen *to notify, report, announce.*
  Ich halte es für angezeigt.   *I consider it advisable.*
(sich) anziehen *to put on (clothes); to dress oneself.*
ANZUG *m. suit, dress.*
Anzüglichkeit *f. suggestive remark.*
anzünden *to light the fire, set fire to.*
APFEL *m. apple.*
  in den sauren Apfel beißen   *to swallow a bitter pill.*
APFELSINE *f. orange.*
Apotheke *f. pharmacy.*
Apotheker *m. pharmacist.*
Apparat *m. apparatus, appliance, telephone.*
  Bleiben Sie am Apparat!   *Hold the phone!*
Appetit *m. appetite.*
applaudieren *to applaud.*
APRIL *m. April.*
Äquator *m. equator.*
ARBEIT *f. work, job.*
ARBEITEN *to work, manufacture.*
  arbeitsfähig   *able-bodied.*
  arbeitsunfähig   *unfit for work.*
Arbeiter *m. (-in f.) worker, laborer.*
  Arbeiterstand *m.*   *working class.*
Arbeitgeber *m. employer.*
Arbeitnehmer *m. employee.*
arbeitsam *industrious, diligent.*
Architekt *m. architect.*
Architektur *f. architecture.*
arg *bad, mischievous.*
  Sie dachte an nichts Arges.   *She meant no harm.*
Ärger *m. annoyance, anger, worry.*
ärgerlich *annoying, angry.*
ärgern *to annoy, irritate, bother.*
  sich ärgern   *to be angry.*
Argument *n. argument.*
Aristokrat *m. aristocrat.*
Aristokratie *f. aristocracy.*
aristokratisch *aristocratic.*
ARM *m. arm.*
ARM *poor.*
Armband *n. bracelet.*
Armbanduhr *f. wristwatch.*
Ärmel *m. sleeve.*
Armlehne *f. arm of chair.*
Armut *f. poverty.*
Arrest *m. arrest.*
ART *f. kind, manner, way, type.*
artig *good, well-behaved.*
Artikel *m. article.*

Arznei *f. medicine (drug).*

Arzneikunde *f. pharmacy (profession of).*

Ast *m. branch (tree).*

Atem *m. breath.*

Dieser Kriminalroman hält uns in Atem. *This detective story keeps us in suspense.*

atemlos *breathless.*

atemraubend *breathtaking.*

Der Film war atemraubend. *The movie was breathtaking.*

Athlet *m. (-in f.) athlete.*

atmen *to breathe.*

AUCH *also, too, even.*

was auch immer *whatever.*

wer auch immer *whoever.*

wo auch immer *wherever.*

Was auch geschieht, Sie sind verantwortlich. *Whatever happens, you are responsible.*

Wer auch immer kommen mag, ich bin nicht zu Hause. *Whoever comes, I am not home.*

Wo auch immer er auftauchen mag, man wird ihn erkennen. *Wherever he appears, he will be recognized.*

AUF 1. *prep. (dat. when answering the question Wo? acc. when answering the question Wohin? and depending on the idiom). on, upon, at, in, to, for, during.*

Er kommt auf die Straße hinab. *He comes down to the street.*

Ich kaufe Gemüse auf dem Markt. *I buy vegetables at the market.*

Ich traf sie auf dem Ball. *I met her at the ball.*

Ich fahre auf das Land. *I drive to the country.*

Sie wohnen auf/in diesem Schloss. *They live in that castle.*

Die Jäger gehen auf die Jagd. *The hunters go hunting.*

Der Tag folgt auf die Nacht. *The day follows the night.*

alle bis auf einen *all except one.*

auf der Rückfahrt von Wien *during the return from Vienna.*

auf Deutsch *in German.*

auf einmal *suddenly.*

auf keinen Fall *in no case.*

auf Wiedersehen! *Good-bye!*

Liebe auf den ersten Blick *love at first sight.*

2. *adv. up, upward.*

auf und ab *up and down.*

3. *Separable prefix (implies motion upward or outward, opening, completion).*

Ich setze meinen Hut auf. *I put my hat on.*

Die Sonne geht auf. *The sun is rising.*

Bitte, machen Sie das Fenster auf. *Please open the window.*

aufbewahren *to keep, preserve, stock.*

Aufbewahrung *f. preservation, storage.*

aufbrauchen *to use up.*

aufeinander *one on top of the other.*

Aufenthalt *m. stay, residence.*

aufessen *to eat up.*

Auffassung *f. conception, interpretation.*

Aufgabe *f. task, duty, problem.*

aufgeben *to commission, order, lose, give up, resign, check, send.*

die Hoffnung aufgeben *to lose hope.*

ein Telegramm aufgeben *to send a telegram.*

aufhängen *to hang up.*

aufheben *to pick up, rise, abolish.*

aufheitern *to cheer up.*

aufklären *to clear, explain.*

Aufklärung *f. explanation.*

aufmachen *to open, unlock, undo.*

aufmerken *to pay attention, attend.*

aufmerksam *attentive.*

Aufmerksamkeit *f. attention.*

Aufnahme *f. taking up, admission, enrollment, snapshot.*

aufnahmefähig *receptive.*

Aufnahmeprüfung *f. entrance examination.*

aufnehmen *to lift, take up, admit, photograph, record (a voice).*

aufpassen *to adapt, fix, pay attention.*

Aufgepasst! *Attention!*

Aufpasser *m. watcher, spy.*

aufräumen *to arrange, put in order, clean.*

aufrecht *upright, straight.*

aufregen *to stir up, excite.*

aufregend *exciting, seditious.*

Aufregung *f. excitement, agitation.*

Aufsatz *m. main piece, top, ornament, article (newspaper); composition.*

aufschließen *to unlock.*

Aufschluss *m. opening up, explanation, information.*

Aufschluss über eine Sache geben *to give some information about something.*

aufschreiben *to write down.*

Aufsehen *n. sensation, attention.*

Er erregt Aufsehen. *He attracts attention.*

Aufstand *m. tumult, revolt.*

AUFSTEHEN *stand up, rise, get up.*

aufstehen gegen *to rebel against.*

Stehen Sie auf! *Get up!*

aufstellen *to set up, erect, draw up, nominate.*

Eine Behauptung aufstellen *to make a statement.*

Auftrag *m. commission, instruction.*

im Auftrage von *by order of.*

einen Auftrag ausführen *to execute an order.*

auftragen to carry up, serve up, draw, charge.

Er hat mir viele Grüße an Sie aufgetragen.
    He sends you his regards. ("He charged me with many greetings for you.")

aufwachen to awaken.

aufwachsen to grow up.

Aufwand m. expenditure, expense.

aufwärts upward.

Er schwimmt ein Fluss aufwärts. *He swims upstream.*

aufwecken to wake someone up.

aufziehen to bring up, raise, wind a watch, pull up, tease.

Aufzug m. procession, parade, attire, outfit, act (play), elevator.

AUGE n. eye.

Er versuchte mir Sand in die Augen zu streuen. *He tried to deceive me ("throw dust into my eyes").*

gute Augen haben to have good eyesight.

große Augen machen to look very surprised.

Ich habe kein Auge zugemacht. *I did not sleep a wink.*

unter vier Augen privately ("among four eyes").

Wir haben ihn aus den Augen verloren.
    We lost sight of him.

Augenarzt m. oculist, eye doctor.

Augenblick m. moment.

im Augenblick for the moment.

augenblicklich immediately, at the moment.

Augenbraue f. eyebrow.

Augenlid n. eyelid.

Augenwimper f. eyelash.

AUGUST m. August.

Auktion f. auction, sale.

AUS 1. prep. (dat.) out, out of, for, from, in, upon.

Aus den Augen, aus dem Sinn. *Out of sight, out of mind.*

Er kommt aus dem Theater. *He comes out of the theater.*

Er hat es aus Liebe getan. *He did it for love.*

Meine Uhr ist aus Gold. *My watch is made of gold.*

Sie stammt aus Paris. *She is a native of Paris.*

2. adv. out, over, up.

von hier aus from here.

von mir aus for my part.

3. separable prefix. (Implies the idea of motion out; in this case also combines with hin or her), achievement.

Die Vorstellung ist aus. *The performance is over.*

Ich gehe aus dem Speisezimmer hinaus.
    I leave (go out of) the dining room.

ausbilden to form, develop, cultivate, educate, train.

ausbleiben to stay away, fail to appear, escape.

Ihre Strafe wird nicht ausbleiben. *You will not escape punishment.*

Ausblick m. outlook, prospect.

ausbrechen to break out.

in Tränen ausbrechen to burst into tears.

Ausbruch m. outbreak, eruption, escape.

Ausdauer f. perseverance, assiduity.

ausdauern to hold out, outlast, endure.

ausdehnen to expand, prolong.

ausdenken to invent, conceive, imagine.

Ausdruck m. expression, phrase.

ausdrücken to squeeze, express.

sich kurz und klar ausdrücken to express oneself briefly and to the point.

auseinander apart, separately.

ausführen to take out, export, realize.

ausführlich adj. detailed, full; in detail, fully.

Erzählen Sie mir alles ausführlich. *Tell me everything in detail.*

ausfüllen to fill out, stuff.

Ausgabe f. delivery, edition, issue, publication.

Ausgang m. way out, exit, end.

ausgeben to give out, deliver, issue, deal (cards).

ausgehen to go out, come out, run out, proceed, start from, end.

Ihm geht die Geduld aus. *He is losing his patience.*

Wie wird diese Sache ausgehen? *How will this matter end?*

AUSGEZEICHNET excellent, distinguished.

ausgleichen to make even, equalize, settle, arrange, compensate.

aushalten to bear, suffer, support, hold out, last.

Aushang m. notice (posted); poster.

aushängen to post a notice.

Aushilfe f. aid (temporary); assistant.

auskleiden to undress.

auskommen to manage, get along.

Es ist schwer mit ihm auszukommen. *It is difficult to get along with him.*

Ich komme nicht mit dem Papier aus. *I can't manage with the paper. (I don't have enough of it.)*

Auskunft f. information.

Auskunftei f. information bureau.

auslassen to leave out, omit, let out.

Auslese f. choice, selection.

auslesen to select, choose, read through.

ausmachen to put out, constitute, come to, settle, amount.

Das macht nichts aus. *It does not matter.*

Ausmaß n. measurement, scale, proportion.

mit solchem Ausmaß to such an extent.

ausmessen to measure, survey.
Ausnahme f. exception.
  ohne Ausnahme without exception.
auspacken to unpack.
Ausrede f. excuse, pretense.
ausreden to finish speaking, excuse.
  einem etwas ausreden to dissuade
    somebody from something.
ausrichten to execute, deliver, obtain.
  Haben Sie es ihm ausgerichtet? Did you
    give him the message?
Ausruf m. cry, exclamation.
ausrufen to cry out, admonish, proclaim.
ausruhen to rest.
  sich ausruhen to rest oneself.
Aussage f. statement, assertion, declaration,
    evidence.
aussagen to affirm, declare, give evidence.
ausschalten to cry out, switch off.
  Schalten Sie den Motor aus! Switch off
    the motor!
ausscheiden to separate, withdraw.
ausschiffen to disembark, land.
ausschließen to exclude.
ausschließlich exclusive (of).
ausschmücken to decorate, adorn.
ausschneiden to cut out, snipe.
AUSSEHEN to look out, appear.
Aussehen n. look.
außen on the outside, abroad, without.
  von außen from the outside.
aussenden to send out.
AUSSER 1. prep. (dat.) out of, out, besides.
  außer der Jahreszeit out of season.
  außer sich beside oneself.
  2. conj. except, unless, but.
  Außer Sonntags, gehe ich jeden Tag in die
    Schule. I go to school every day
    except Sunday.
außerdem besides, moreover.
äußerlich external; on the outside.
äußern to express.
äußerst utmost.
aussetzen to set out, put out, offer, bequeath.
  auszusetzen haben to find fault with.
Aussicht f. view, prospect.
aussöhnen to reconcile.
aussondern to separate, select.
Aussprache f. pronunciation, accent.
aussprechen to pronounce, express.
aussuchen to seek out, search.
Austausch m. exchange.
austauschen to exchange.
Auster f. oyster.
austragen to deliver, distribute.
austreten to tread under, trample, retire.
Ausverkauf m. clearance sale.
ausverkaufen to sell off, clear out (a shop).
Auswahl f. choice, assortment, selection.

auswählen to choose, select.
Auswanderer m. emigrant.
auswandern to emigrate.
Auswanderung f. emigration.
auswärtig foreign, abroad.
Ausweg m. way out.
ausweichen to avoid, evade, shun.
Ausweis m. certificate, document, identity card.
ausziehen to undress, pull out, extract, move,
    remove.
Auszug m. departure, extract, removal.
Auto n. automobile, car.
Autobahn f. parkway.
Autobus m. bus.
Axt f. axe.

B

Bach m. brook.
BACKEN to bake, fry.
Bäcker m. baker.
Backobst n. dried fruit.
Backofen m. oven.
Backpulver n. baking powder.
BAD n. bath, spa.
Badeanstalt f. baths, swimming pool.
Badeanzug m. bathing suit.
Badehose f. swim trunks.
Bademantel m. bathrobe.
Badeort m. spa.
Badetuch n. bath towel.
Badewanne f. bathtub.
Badezimmer n. bathroom.
BAHN f. track, road, way, railway.
Bahnarbeiter m. railway worker.
Bahnbeamter m. railroad official.
Bahngleis n. track.
BAHNHOF m. train station.
Bahnsteig m. platform.
Bahnübergang m. railroad crossing.
Balance f. balance, equilibrium.
balancieren to balance.
BALD soon, shortly.
  bald . . . , bald . . . sometimes . . . ,
    sometimes . . .
  bald darauf soon after.
Balkon m. balcony.
Ball m. ball, dance.
Ballett n. ballet.
Ballon m. balloon.
Band n. ribbon.
Bande f. band, gang.
bändigen to tame, to break.
Bandmaß n. tape measure.
BANK f. 1. bench, seat.
  auf die lange Bank schieben to postpone,
    delay.

2. *bank*.
Geld auf der Bank haben   *to have money in the bank*.
Bankangestellter *m. bank clerk*.
Bankanweisung *f. bank transfer*.
BAR *bare, naked, devoid of, pure*.
barfuss   *barefoot*.
die bare Wahrheit   *the bare truth*.
bar bezahlen   *to pay in cash*.
Bär *m. bear*.
Bargeld *n. cash*.
bar zahlen   *to pay cash*.
barmherzig *merciful*.
Barmherzigkeit *f. mercy*.
Baron *m.* (**-in** *f.*) *Baron(ess)*.
Bart *m. beard, whiskers*.
BAU *m. building, construction, edifice, frame*.
Bauch *m. belly, stomach*.
BAUEN *to build, construct, cultivate*.
Luftschlösser bauen   *to build castles in the air*.
Bauer *m. peasant*.
Bauernhof *m. farm*.
Bauernvolk *n. country folk*.
baufällig *dilapidated*.
BAUM *m. tree, pole*.
Baumschule *f. nursery (trees)*.
Baumwolle *f. cotton*.
Baustein *n. brick*.
beabsichtigen *to intend*.
beachten *to observe, notice*.
Beachtung *f. consideration, attention*.
beachtenswert *noteworthy*.
Beamter *m. official, civil servant*.
Zollbeamter *m.*   *customs officer*.
beängstigen *to alarm*.
beanspruchen *to claim, demand*.
beantworten *to answer, reply*.
beaufsichtigen *to supervise*.
beben *to tremble*.
vor Angst beben   *to tremble with fear*.
Becher *m. cup, goblet*.
bedacht *thoughtful, considerate*.
bedanken *to thank*.
Bedarf *m. need, requirement*.
bedauerlich *deplorable, regrettable*.
bedecken *to cover*.
Der Himmel ist bedeckt.   *The sky is overcast*.
bedenken *to think, think over, reflect, ponder*.
sich eines andern bedenken   *to change one's mind*.
bedenklich *doubtful, questionable*.
Bedenkzeit *f. time for reflection*.
(sich) bedienen *to help oneself*.
Bedienung *f. service*.
einschließlich der Bedienung   *service included*.
bedürfen *to need, require*.

Bedürfnis *n. need, want, necessity*.
(sich) beeilen *to hurry oneself*.
beeindrucken *to impress*.
beerdigen *to bury*.
Beerdigung *f. funeral*.
befassen *to touch*.
sich befassen mit   *to concern oneself with, to deal with*.
Er befasst sich mit Politik.   *He is concerned with politics*.
Befehl *m. order, command*.
befehlen *to order, command*.
befestigen *to fasten, fortify*.
befolgen *to obey (someone)*.
befreien *to free, liberate*.
Befreier *m. liberator*.
Befreiung *f. liberation*.
befreunden *to befriend*.
sich befreunden mit   *to become friends with*.
befriedigen *to satisfy, content*.
befriedigend *satisfying*.
Befriedigung *f. satisfaction, gratification*.
befürchten *to fear*.
Befürchtung *f. fear, apprehension*.
befürworten *to recommend*.
begabt *gifted*.
begeben (sich) *to set about*.
begegnen *to meet, encounter*.
begeistern *to inspire, fill with enthusiasm*.
begeistert *inspired, enthusiastic*.
Begeisterung *f. inspiration, enthusiasm*.
Beginn *m. beginning*.
BEGINNEN *to begin, start*.
beglaubigen *to attest, certify, to authenticate*.
begleiten *to accompany*.
nach Hause begleiten   *to see (someone) home*.
begründen *to found, to prove*.
Behaglichkeit *f. comfort*.
behalten *to keep, retain, remember*.
Behalten Sie das Kleingeld!   *Keep the change!*
behandeln *to handle, deal with*.
behaupten *to maintain, assert, affirm*.
Behelf *m. help, expedient*.
behelfen (sich) *to manage, do without*.
BEI 1. *prep. (dat.) at, by, near, with, because of, in case of*.
bei der Hand   *by hand*.
Bei Feuer müssen wir die Feuerwehr rufen.   *In case of fire, we must call the fire department*.
Bei ihrem Charakter wird sie unglücklich werden.   *With (because of) her character, she will be unhappy*.
bei Tage   *by day*.
bei weitem   *by far*.
beim Arzt   *at the doctor's*.

Er arbeitet bei Licht. *He works by light.*

Hast du Geld bei dir (*or* dabei)? *Do you have any money on you?*

Ich kaufe meine Kleider bei Engels. *I buy my clothes at Engels.*

Meine Schwester wohnt bei mir. *My sister lives with me.*

Beichte *f. confession.*

beichten *to confess.*

BEIDE *both.*

   wir beide *both of us.*

   einer von beiden *one of the two.*

   keiner von beiden *neither of them.*

   beiderseits *on both sides, mutually.*

BEIFALL *m. approval, approbation, applause.*

beifolgend *herewith, enclosed.*

beiläufig *accidental, casual; incidentally.*

beilegen *to add, enclose.*

Beileid *n. sympathy.*

   Beileid bezeigen *to console somebody.*

beim (bei dem) *at, by.*

BEIN *n. leg, bone.*

   sich kein Bein ausreissen *to take it easy.*

   Er ist immer auf den Beinen. *He's always on his feet.*

beinahe *nearly, almost.*

beisammen *together.*

beiseite *aside, apart.*

BEISPIEL *n. example.*

   zum Beispiel *for example.*

   Das ist ein schlechtes Beispiel. *This is a bad example.*

beispiellos *unheard of, without example.*

beißen *to bite.*

   Der Hund beißt nicht. *The dog does not bite.*

beistehen *to help, stand by.*

beistimmen *to agree with.*

Beitrag *m. contribution, subscription.*

bejahen *to answer in the affirmative, assent, accept.*

bejammern *to lament.*

bejammernswert *deplorable, lamentable.*

bekämpfen *to combat, fight, struggle.*

BEKANNT *well-known, acquainted.*

   bekannt machen mit *to introduce to.*

Bekannter *m. & f. acquaintance, friend.*

Bekanntmachung *f. publication, announcement, notice.*

bekennen *to confess, admit, profess.*

   sich schuldig bekennen *to plead guilty.*

beklagen *to complain, lament.*

BEKOMMEN *to get, receive, catch, agree with.*

   Das ist nicht mehr zu bekommen. *You can't get that any more.*

   Es bekommt mir nicht. *It does not agree with me.*

bekräftigen *to confirm, corroborate.*

belächeln *to smile at.*

belachen *to laugh at.*

belästigen *to molest, trouble.*

beleben *to animate, revive.*

Beleg *m. proof, evidence, illustration.*

BELEGEN *to cover, reserve.*

   Ich möchte einen Platz belegen. *I want to reserve a seat.*

   belegte Brötchen *sandwiches.*

   eine Vorlesung belegen *to enroll for a course.*

belehren *to enlighten, instruct.*

   eines Besseren belehren *to correct.*

beleidigen *to offend, insult.*

beliefern *to supply.*

belohnen *to reward.*

Belohnung *f. reward.*

belügen *to lie (falsify).*

belustigen *to amuse, entertain.*

Belustigung *f. amusement.*

bemerkbar *noticeable, perceptible.*

bemerken *to notice, observe, remark.*

bemerkenswert *noticeable, noteworthy.*

Bemerkung *f. remark, observation.*

bemitleiden *to pity, be sorry for.*

bemitleidenswert *deplorable.*

benachrichtigen *to inform, advise.*

Benachrichtigung *f. information, advice.*

benachteiligen *to prejudice.*

Benachteiligung *f. prejudice, injury.*

(sich) benehmen *to behave oneself.*

   Benimm dich nicht wie ein kleines Kind! *Don't behave like a child!*

beneiden *to envy.*

benötigen *to require.*

benutzen *to use, employ, utilize.*

beobachten *to observe, watch.*

   heimlich beobachten *to shadow.*

BEQUEM *comfortable, convenient, lazy.*

   Sei nicht so bequem! *Don't be so lazy!*

   Wir sitzen bequem. *We are seated comfortably.*

bequemen *to condescend, comply, submit.*

Bequemlichkeit *f. convenience.*

beraten *to advise.*

Berater *m. adviser.*

beratschlagen *to deliberate.*

berechnen *to calculate, estimate.*

bereden *to talk over, persuade.*

Beredsamkeit *f. eloquence.*

Bereich *m. & n. reach, range, area, zone, domain.*

BEREIT *ready, prepared.*

   bereit halten *to keep ready.*

   bereitwillig *willing, ready.*

Bereitwilligkeit *f. willingness.*

bereuen *to repent, regret.*

BERG *m. mountain, hill.*

über alle Berge sein   *to be out of the woods.*

Mir standen die Haare zu Berge.   *My hair stood on end.*

Bergmann *m. miner.*

berichten *to report.*

berichtigen *to correct, amend, settle (a bill).*

Berichtigung *f. correction, amendment.*

berücksichtigen *to consider.*

Berücksichtigung *f. consideration, regard.*

BERUF *m. profession, occupation.*

beruflich *professional.*

berufstätig *working, employed.*

beruhigen *to quiet, calm.*

Beruhigung *f. reassurance, comfort.*

BERÜHMT *famous, celebrated.*

Berühmtheit *f. fame, celebrity.*

besänftigen *to soften, appease, soothe.*

beschädigen *to damage, injure, harm.*

beschäftigen *to occupy, engage, employ.*

sich beschäftigen   *to occupy oneself.*

Beschäftigung *f. occupation.*

beschäftigungslos *unemployed, out of work.*

Bescheid *m. answer, information.*

Bescheid geben   *to inform.*

Ich habe ihm gehörig Bescheid gesagt.   *I told him off.*

bescheiden *modest, moderate.*

Bescheidenheit *f. modesty.*

bescheinen *to shine upon.*

bescheinigen *to certify, attest.*

Bescheinigung *f. certificate, receipt.*

beschleunigen *to hasten, accelerate.*

beschränken *to limit, confine, restrict.*

Beschränkung *f. limitation, restriction.*

beschreiben *to write upon, describe.*

Beschreibung *f. description.*

beschuldigen *to accuse.*

Beschuldigung *f. accusation.*

Beschwerde *f. complaint, hardship, trouble.*

(sich) beschweren *to complain.*

Beschwerdebüro *m.*   *complaint department.*

Besen *m. broom.*

besetzen *to occupy, trim, set.*

Es ist alles besetzt!   *All seats are occupied.*

Besetzt!   *Occupied! Busy!*

Besetzung *f. occupation, cast (theater).*

Die Besetzung ist aussergewöhnlich gut.   *The cast is outstanding.*

besichtigen *to view, inspect, visit.*

Besichtigung *f. view, inspection.*

besiegen *to conquer, beat, defeat.*

besinnen *to consider, reflect.*

sich besinnen   *to remember.*

sich eines Besseren besinnen   *to think better of.*

besinnlich *contemplative, thoughtful.*

Besitz *m. possession, property, estate.*

besorgen *to take care of, fetch, procure, provide.*

Besorgnis *f. fear, alarm.*

Besorgung *f. care, management.*

Besorgungen machen   *to go shopping.*

besprechen *to discuss, talk over, criticize, review.*

BESSER *better.*

umso besser   *so much the better.*

bessern *to improve, recover.*

sich bessern   *to improve oneself.*

Besserung *f. recovery, improvement.*

Gute Besserung!   *Get well soon!*

best(-er, -es) *best.*

beständig *constant, permanent, steady; constantly, all the time.*

Beständigkeit *f. constancy, stability.*

bestätigen *to confirm, ratify.*

bestechen *to bribe, corrupt.*

bestechlich *corruptible.*

Bestechung *f. bribery, corruption.*

Besteck *n. silverware.*

bestellen *to arrange, order, tell, cultivate.*

Waren bestellen   *to order goods.*

zu sich bestellen   *to send for.*

BESTIMMEN *to decide, fix, intend, define, induce.*

bestimmen über   *to dispose of.*

Bestimmt!   *Agreed!*

Bestimmtheit *f. certainty, precision.*

bestrafen *to punish.*

Bestrafung *f. punishment.*

BESUCH *m. visit, company, attendance.*

BESUCHEN *to visit, attend.*

Besucher *m. visitor, spectator, audience.*

(sich) beteiligen *to give a share, take part, take an interest.*

beteiligt sein   *to participate.*

Beteiligung *f. share, participation.*

betonen *f. to stress, accent, emphasize.*

Betonung *f. stress, emphasis.*

beträchtlich *considerable.*

(sich) betragen *to behave.*

betreffen *to concern.*

was mich betrifft   *so far as I am concerned.*

betreten *to tread on.*

Betreten des Rasens verboten!   *Keep off the grass!*

Betrieb *m. management, plant, factory.*

in Betrieb sein   *to be working.*

außer Betrieb   *not working, closed.*

in Betrieb setzen   *to set in motion.*

(sich) betrinken *to get drunk.*

betrüben *to grieve, distress.*

Betrug *m. deception, fraud, swindle.*

betrügen *to deceive, defraud, trick.*

BETT *n. bed.*

das Bett hüten   *to be confined in bed.*

früh zu Bett gehen   *to go to bed early.*

Bettdecke *f. blanket, bedspread.*

betteln *to beg.*

Bettlaken *n. sheet.*

Bettler *m. beggar.*

Bettwäsche *f. bed linen.*

beugen *to bend, bow.*

beunruhigen *to disturb, alarm, upset.*

beurlauben *to grant leave, take leave.*

beurlaubt   *absent on leave.*

Beutel *m. bag, purse.*

bevollmächtigen *to empower, authorize.*

BEVOR *before.*

bewachen *to watch over.*

bewältigen *to master.*

bewegen *to move, stir.*

Beweggrund *m. motive.*

Was war der Beweggrund des Verbrechens?
  What was the motive for the crime?

beweglich *movable, mobile, quick, lively.*

BEWEGUNG *f. movement, agitation, motion.*

einer politischen Bewegung angehören   *to belong to a political party.*

Beweis *m. proof, evidence.*

beweisen *to prove, demonstrate.*

Beweisführung *f. demonstration.*

bewerben *to apply for, compete.*

sich bewerben um   *to apply for a position.*

Er bewarb sich um eine neue Stellung.
  He applied for a new job (position).

Bewerber *m. applicant, candidate.*

Bewerbung *f. application, candidacy.*

bewilligen *to consent, concede.*

bewusst *conscious.*

sich einer Sache bewusst sein   *to be conscious or aware of something.*

bewusstlos *unconscious.*

BEZAHLEN *to pay.*

sich bezahlt machen *to pay for itself (be lucrative).*

bezaubernd *charming.*

Bezug *m. covering, cover, case.*

in Bezug auf   *in regard to.*

Bezug nehmen auf   *to refer to.*

unter Bezugnahme auf   *with reference to.*

Bibel *f. Bible.*

Bibliothek *f. library.*

Bibliothekar *m. librarian.*

Biene *f. bee.*

Bier *n. beer.*

BIETEN *to offer.*

sich alles bieten lassen   *to put up with everything.*

BILD *n. image, picture, illustration, portrait, likeness.*

BILDEN *to form, shape, educate.*

Der Präsident hat ein neues Kabinett gebildet.   *The president has formed a new cabinet.*

die bildenden Künste   *fine arts.*

Bildseite *f. face, head (coin).*

Bildschirm *m. screen, monitor.*

Bildung *f. formation, constitution, education.*

billig *just, reasonable, fair, moderate.*

binden *to bind, tie.*

BIS *until, as far as, about.*

zwei bis drei Pfund   *about two or three pounds.*

bis an *(acc.)*   *up to.*

bis in alle Ewigkeit   *till the end of time.*

bis dann/dahin   *until then.*

bis auf *(acc.)*   *except for.*

Mir gefällt der Film bis auf das Ende.
  I like the film except for the ending.

bis auf weiteres   *until further notice.*

bis zu *(dat.)* *(down) to.*

von dem Kopf bis zu den Füßen   *from head to foot.*

bis jetzt   *so far.*

bisher   *till now.*

bisweilen   *sometimes.*

Bischof *m. bishop.*

bisschen *a bit, a little, awhile.*

Das ist ein bisschen stark.   *That's going a bit too far.*

Er kam ein bisschen spät.   *He came a little late.*

Bissen *m. bite, mouthful.*

Bitte *f. request, prayer.*

BITTE *please.*

bitte, bitte schön, bitte sehr.   *(In response to a request: Here you are. In response to thanks: You are welcome; don't mention it.)*

Wie, bitte?   *I beg your pardon?*

BITTEN *to ask, beg, implore.*

Ich bitte um Entschuldigung.   *I beg your pardon.*

bitter *bitter.*

blamieren *to expose to ridicule.*

sich blamieren   *to make a fool of oneself.*

BLATT *n. leaf, petal, blade, sheet.*

kein Blatt vor den Mund nehmen   *to speak plainly.*

blättern *to leaf through the pages of a book.*

BLAU *blue.*

Blech *n. tin.*

Blei *n. lead.*

BLEIBEN *to stay, remain, keep, last.*

bleiben lassen   *to leave alone.*

Das bleibt unter uns.   *That's between you and me.*

Es bleibt dabei.   *Agreed.*

sich gleich bleiben   *to remain the same.*

stehen bleiben   *to stop, stand still.*

bleibend *permanent, lasting.*

bleich *pale, faded, faint.*

bleichen *to bleach.*

Bleistift m. pencil.
blenden to blind, dazzle.
BLICK m. glance, look, gaze.
　auf den ersten Blick　at first sight.
　Er warf ihm einen bösen Blick zu.
　　　He gave him a dirty look.
blind blind, false.
　ein blinder Alarm　a false alarm.
Blindheit f. blindness.
blinken to glitter, glimpse, twinkle, signal.
Blitz m. lightning, flash.
blitzen to lighten, flash, sparkle.
Block m. block, log, pad, stocks.
blond blond, fair.
BLOß bare, naked, uncovered; merely, only.
　Ich tue es bloß Ihnen zu gefallen.　I am
　　　only doing it to please you.
blühen to bloom.
BLUME f. flower.
　Lasst Blumen sprechen!　Say it with
　　　flowers!
Blumenkohl m. cauliflower.
Bluse f. blouse.
BLUT n. blood, race, parentage.
blutarm anemic.
Blutdruck m. blood pressure.
bluten to bleed.
Blutprobe f. blood test.
Blutvergiftung f. blood poisoning.
Boden m. floor, ground, soil, attic.
Bogen m. bow, curve, arch.
BOHNE f. bean.
　grüne Bohnen　string beans.
　weiße Bohnen　dried beans.
Bombardement n. bombardment.
bombardieren to bomb.
Bombe f. bomb.
　Atombombe f.　atomic bomb.
Bonbon m. & n. candy.
BOOT n. boat.
　Bootsfahrt f.　boat ride.
Börse f. purse, stock exchange.
Börsenmakler m. stockbroker.
bösartig ill-natured, wicked, malicious.
BÖSE bad, angry, evil.
boshaft malicious, nasty.
Bote m. messenger.
Botschaft f. news.
Botschafter m. ambassador.
boxen to box.
Brand m. burning, fire, conflagration.
　in Brand geraten　to catch fire.
Brandschaden m. damage by fire.
BRATEN m. roast.
　Brathuhn n.　roast chicken.
　Bratkartoffeln pl.　fried potatoes.
　Bratapfel m.　baked apple.
BRATEN to roast, grill, fry.
Brauch m. usage, use, custom.

brauchbar useful, practicable.
BRAUCHEN to use, employ, need.
　Wie lange werden Sie noch brauchen?
　　　How much more time will it take you?
Brauhaus n. brewery, tavern.
BRAUN brown.
Brause f. shower, douche, spray.
brausen to storm, rage, roar, rush.
　sich abbrausen　to take a shower.
Braut f. fiancee.
　Brautführer m.　best man.
　Brautjungfer f.　bridesmaid.
　Brautkleid n.　wedding dress.
　Brautpaar n.　engaged couple.
Bräutigam m. bridegroom.
brav good, honest, excellent.
BRECHEN to break, pick.
　Er spricht ein gebrochenes Deutsch.
　　　He speaks broken German.
BREIT broad, wide, flat.
　weit und breit　far and wide.
Breite f. breadth, width, latitude.
Bremse f. brake.
bremsen to put the brakes on.
BRENNEN to burn, brand, bake, roast.
　darauf brennen　to be anxious.
　Es brennt in der Stadt.　There is a fire in
　　　town.
Brett n. board, plank, shelf, stage.
　am schwarzen Brett　on the blackboard.
BRIEF m. letter.
Briefkasten m. mailbox.
Briefmappe f. attaché case.
Briefmarke f. stamp.
Briefpapier n. stationery.
Brieftasche f. wallet, pocketbook.
Briefträger m. mailman.
Briefumschlag m. envelope.
Brille f. eyeglasses.
BRINGEN to bring, fetch, carry, put, take.
　dazu bringen　to induce to.
　Er hat sich ums Leben gebracht.　He has
　　　committed suicide.
　es zu etwas bringen　to achieve something.
　Ich werde das in Ordnung bringen.　I'll
　　　straighten that out.
　Sie hat es auf neunzig Jahre gebracht.　She
　　　turned ninety years old.
britisch British
BROT n. bread.
　sein Brot verdienen　to earn one's living.
Brötchen n. roll.
Bruch m. break, fracture, fraction.
Bruchteil m. fraction
BRÜCKE f. bridge (also dental).
　Er hat alle Brücken hinter sich abgebrochen.
　　　He has burnt his bridges behind him.
BRUDER m. brother.
　Bruderschaft f.　brotherhood.

Brunnen m. spring, well, fountain.
Brust f. breast, chest, bosom.
Bube m. boy, jack of cards.
BUCH n. book.
Buchdeckel m. cover, binding.
Buchführung f. bookkeeping.
Buchhaltung f. bookkeeping.
Buchhändler m. bookseller.
Buchhandlung f. bookshop.
Büchse f. can.
Büchsenöffner m. can opener.
Buchstabe m. letter, character.
Buchumschlag m. jacket (book).
Bügelbrett n. ironing board.
Bügeleisen n. iron (for pressing).
bügeln to press.
Bühne f. stage, platform.
Bund m. league, confederation.
Bündel m. bundle.
bunt colored, lively, gay.
   Das ist mir zu bunt.   *I'm fed up with it.*
Burg f. castle, citadel, fortress.
Bürge f. bail.
bürgen to guarantee, vouch for.
Bürger m. citizen, townsman.
Bürgerkrieg m. civil war.
Bürgermeister m. mayor.
Bürgersteig m. pavement.
BÜRO n. office.
bürokratisch bureaucratic.
Bursche m. youth, lad, fellow.
Bürste f. brush.
bürsten to brush.
Busch m. bush.
Buße f. penitence, repentance.
   Buße tun   *to do penance.*
büßen to suffer for, expiate.
Büste f. bust.
Büstenhalter m. brassiere, bra.
BUTTER f. butter.
Butterbrot n. slice of bread and butter.

C

Café n. café.
Cello n. cello.
Cellist m. cellist.
Cent m. cent ($^1/_{100}$ euro).
Champagner m. champagne.
Charakter m. character, disposition.
charakteristisch characteristic.
Chauffeur m. chauffeur.
Chef m. head, boss, chief.
Chemie f. chemistry.
chemisch chemical.
Chinese m. (**-in** f.) Chinese (person).
chinesisch Chinese.

Chirurg m. surgeon.
Chor m. choir, chorus.
Choral m. chorale.
Chorgesang m. choir singing.
Choristin f. chorus girl.
Chorknabe m. choirboy.
Christ m. Christian.
Christenheit f. Christendom.
Christentum n. Christianity.
Chronik f. chronicle.
Cousin m. (**Vetter**) cousin (man).
Cousine f. (**Kusine**) cousin (woman).
Creme m. cream (cosmetic).

D

DA 1. adv. there, here.
   2. conj. when, because, as, since.
   da sein   to be present.
   da stehen   to stand near, stand by.
DABEI near, near by, close to, along,
   moreover.
   Dabei bleibt es.   *There the matter ends.*
   Er hat kein Geld dabei.   *He has no money
     on him.*
dableiben to stay, remain.
Dach n. roof.
   unter Dach und Fach   to be safe.
Dachkammer f. attic.
DADURCH through it, by it, thereby.
   dadurch dass   through the fact that.
   Er ist dadurch berühmt geworden.   *That
     made him famous.*
DAFÜR for that, for it, instead of it.
   dafür sein   to be in favor of.
   Ich kann nichts dafür.   *It is not my fault.*
DAGEGEN 1. adv. against it.
   nichts dagegen haben   to have no
     objection.
   2. conj. on the other hand.
DAHEIM at home.
DAHER from there.
   Ich komme gerade daher.   *I am coming
     straight from there.*
DAHIN to there.
   bis dahin   by then.
   Ich gehe sofort dahin.   *I am going there
     right now.*
dahinten behind.
damalig then, of that time.
Dame f. lady, queen (cards), checkers.
   eine Partie Dame spielen   to play a game
     of checkers.
DAMIT 1. adv. with it, by it.
   Was wollte er damit sagen?   *What does he
     mean by that?*
   2. conj. so that, in order to.

Ich sage es noch einmal, damit Sie es nicht vergessen. *I'll say it once more so that you won't forget it.*

damit nicht *for fear that.*

Dämmerlicht *n. dusk.*

Dämmerung *f. twilight, dawn.*

Dampf *m. vapor, steam.*

Dampfbad *n. steam bath.*

dämpfen *to dampen, tone down, extinguish, steam (cooking).*

Dampfer *m. steamer.*

DANACH *afterward, after that, thereafter.*

Es sieht danach aus. *It looks like it.*

daneben 1. *adv. near it, next to it, close by.* 2. *conj. besides, moreover, at the same time, also.*

DANK *m. thanks, gratitude, reward.*

Gott sei Dank! *Thank God!*

zum Dank *as a reward.*

DANKBAR *grateful, thankful.*

DANKE *thank you.*

Danke schön! *Thank you very much!*

DANKEN *to thank.*

Nichts zu danken. *Not at all, don't mention it.*

DANN *then, thereupon.*

dann und wann *now and then.*

DARAN (dran) *at it, of that, in it, in that.*

Ich glaube daran. *I believe in it.*

nahe daran sein *to be near, on the point of.*

Wer ist dran? *Whose turn is it?*

DARAUF (drauf) *on, upon it, after that, thereupon.*

Es kommt darauf an. *It all depends.*

Ich lege keinen Wert darauf. *I'm not interested in it.*

DARAUS (draus) *of it, of that, from this, from that.*

Daraus ist nichts geworden. *Nothing came of it.*

darbieten *to offer, present.*

Darbietung *f. entertainment, offering.*

DAREIN (drein) *into it, therein.*

DARIN (drin) *in it, in that.*

Es ist nichts darin. *There is nothing to it.*

darlegen *to explain.*

Darlegung *f. explanation, exposition.*

Darlehen *n. loan.*

DARÜBER (drüber) 1. *adv. over it, above it, about it.*

Darüber besteht kein Zweifel. *There is no doubt about that.*

darüber hinaus *beyond that.*

2. *conj. meanwhile.*

DARUM (drum) *round it, for it, about it.*

Ich kann mich nicht darum kümmern. *I can't take care of that.*

DARUNTER (drunter) *under it, underneath, among them, by that.*

Was verstehen Sie darunter? *What do you mean by that?*

DAS 1. *neuter article (nom. and acc.), the.*

2. *demons. pron. that.*

3. *rel. pron. which, that.*

dasjenige das *the one which.*

dasselbe *the same.*

da sein *to exist, be present.*

Dasein *n. existence, life.*

Der Kampf um das Dasein *struggle for life.*

DASS *conj. that.*

dass doch *if only.*

Datei *f. file (computer).*

Datenverarbeitung *f. data processing.*

Datum *n. date.*

Dauer *f. length, duration.*

auf die Dauer *for long.*

DAUERN *to last, continue.*

lange dauern *to take a long time.*

Dauerwelle *f. permanent wave.*

Daumen *m. thumb.*

DAVON *for it, from this, from that, of it, of that.*

Was halten Sie davon? *What do you think of it?*

Geben Sie mir ein Paar davon. *Give me a pair of them.*

Das hängt davon ab. *It depends.*

DAVOR *in front of it, of it, of that.*

Sie stehen direkt davor. *They stand right in front of it.*

DAZU *to it, for it, for that purpose.*

Es ist schon zu spät dazu. *It is already too late for that.*

dazu gehören *to belong to it.*

dazwischen *in between.*

Decke *f. cover, blanket, ceiling.*

Deckel *m. cover, lid.*

DECKEN *to protect, cover, guard, secure.*

Deckung *f. cover, shelter, protection.*

in Deckung gehen *to take cover.*

Defekt *m. defect, deficiency.*

Degen *m. sword.*

DEIN *(poss. adj. fam. form) your.*

DEIN (-er ,-e, -es) *(poss. pron. fam. form) yours.*

DEM *dat, sing of der and das to the, to this, to whom, to which.*

demnach *then.*

demnächst *soon, shortly.*

demzufolge *accordingly.*

Wie dem auch sei *be that as it may.*

Demokrat *m. democrat.*

Demokratie *f. democracy.*

Demut *f. humility.*

demütig *humble.*

demütigen *to humiliate.*

Demütigung *f. humiliation.*

DEN *acc. sing. of der; dat. pl. of die the, this, to them, whom, that.*

DENEN *dat. pl. of die (rel. pron.) to whom, to which.*

DENKEN *to think, intend, mean.*
Was denken Sie zu tun? *What do you intend to do?*
denken an *to remember, think of.*
sich denken *to imagine.*
Das kann ich mir schon denken. *I can well imagine.*

Denker *m. thinker.*

DENN *for, because, then.*
es sei denn, dass *unless.*

dennoch *nevertheless.*

deponieren *to deposit.*

DER 1. *masc. article (nom.) the; fem. (gen. & dat.) of the, to the; pl. (gen.) of the.*
2. *demons. pron. this.*
3. *rel. pron. which, who, that.*
derjenige der *the one who, he who.*
derselbe *the same.*

DEREN *gen. fem. and pl. of die (rel. pron.) whose.*

DES *gen. sing. of der and das of the.*

DESHALB *therefore, for that reason.*

DESSEN *gen. sing. of der and das pron. whose.*

Detektiv *m. detective.*

deuten *to point out, explain, interpret.*

deutlich *distinct, clear; distinctly, clearly.*

Deutlichkeit *f. distinctness, clearness.*

DEUTSCH *German.*

DEUTSCHE *m. & f. German (person).*

DEUTSCHLAND *n. Germany.*

Deutung *f. interpretation, explanation.*

Devise *f. foreign bill, motto.*

DEZEMBER *m. December.*

Dialekt *m. dialect.*

Diamant *m. diamond.*

Diät *f. diet.*
Diät leben *to diet.*

DICH *acc. of du (fam. form) you.*

DICHT *thick, dense, tight, close.*

dichten *to compose, write poetry, invent.*

DICHTER *m. poet.*

Dichtung *f. poetry, fiction.*

DICK *thick, stout, fat.*
Er ist dick geworden. *He got fat.*

Dickkopf *m. blockhead.*

DIE 1. *fem. article (nom. and acc.), the pl. article (nom. and acc.), the.*
2. *demons. pron. this.*
3. *rel. pron. who, which, that.*
diejenige die *she who, the one which.*
dieselbe *the same.*

DIEB *m. thief, burglar.*
Halten Sie den Dieb! *Stop the thief!*

Diebstahl *m. theft.*

DIENEN *to serve.*
Womit kann ich dienen? *Can I help you?*

Diener *m. servant.*

Dienerin *f. maid.*

dienlich *serviceable.*

Dienst *m. service, duty, situation, employment.*
ausser Dienst *off duty.*
zu Diensten stehen *to be at a person's disposal.*

DIENSTAG *m. Tuesday.*

diensteifrig *zealous.*

Dienstmädchen *n. maid.*

Dienststelle *f. headquarters.*

DIES (-er, -e, -es) *this, that.*

DIESMAL *this time.*

DIESSEITS *(gen.) on this side.*

Diktat *n. dictation, treaty.*

DING *n. thing, object.*
guter Dinge sein *to be in high spirits.*
vor allen Dingen *first of all.*

Diplom *n. diploma, certificate.*

Diplomatie *f. diplomacy.*

diplomatisch *diplomatic.*

DIR *dat. of du (fam. form) you, to you.*

direkt *direct.*

Direktor *m. director.*

Dirigent *m. conductor.*

dirigieren *to conduct, direct.*

Diskette *f. floppy disk.*

diskret *discreet, tactful.*

Diskretion *f. discretion.*

diskutieren *to discuss.*

Distanz *f. distance.*

DOCH *however, anyway, nevertheless, but, still, yet; surely, of course, yes (in answer to a negative question); indicates a well-known fact.*
Willst du nicht kommen? Doch. *Won't you come? Of course.*
Ich habe doch gewusst, dass er schwer krank war. *I knew (very well) he was very ill.*
Ich werde doch gehen. *I will go anyhow.*
Ja doch! *Of course.*
Sie werden doch zugeben, dass er recht hatte. *But you will admit he was right.*
Und doch ist es nicht so traurig, wie Sie denken. *And still it is not as sad as you think.*

DOKTOR *m. doctor.*
den Doktor machen *to take the degree of doctor.*

Doktorarbeit *f. thesis for doctorate.*

Dokument *n. document.*

dokumentieren *to prove, to document.*

Dolch *m. dagger.*

dolmetschen *to interpret.*

Dolmetscher *m. interpreter.*

Dom *m. cathedral.*
Donner *m. thunder.*
   vom Donner gerührt *thunderstruck.*
donnern *to thunder.*
Donnerschlag *m. thunderbolt.*
DONNERSTAG *m. Thursday.*
Donnerwetter *n. thunderstorm.*
   Donnerwetter! *Good heavens!*
doppeldeutig *ambiguous.*
Doppelpunkt *m. colon.*
doppelt *double.*
   Doppelbett *n. double bed.*
   Doppelzimmer *n. room with twin beds.*
DORF *n. village.*
Dorn *m. thorn.*
DORT *there, yonder.*
   dorther *from there.*
   dorthin *there, that way, over there.*
Dose *f. box, can, dose.*
DRAHT *m. wire, cable; line.*
Drängen *to push, press, hurry, urge.*
   Nicht drängen! *Do not push!*
draußen *outside, outdoors, abroad.*
drehen *to turn, rotate, revolve.*
DREI *three.*
Dreieck *n. triangle.*
DREIßIG *thirty.*
DREIßIGSTE *thirtieth.*
DREIZEHN *thirteen.*
DREIZEHNTE *thirteenth.*
dringen *to enter, get in, penetrate.*
   dringen auf *to insist on.*
dringend *urgent.*
DRITTE *third.*
Droge *f. drug.*
Drogerie *f. drugstore.*
drüben *over there, yonder.*
Druck *m. pressure, compression.*
   in Druck gehen *to go to press.*
drucken *to print.*
Druckknopf *m. push button.*
Druckfehler *m. misprint.*
Dschungel *f. jungle.*
DU *pers. pron. fam. form you.*
Duft *m. scent, smell, fragrance.*
DUFTEN *to smell sweet, be fragrant.*
duftig *sweet-smelling, fragrant.*
dulden *to endure, bear, suffer.*
dumm *stupid, dull, ignorant.*
   Sei nicht so dumm! *Don't be so stupid!*
   Es wurde mir zu dumm. *I got sick and
   tired of it.*
Dummheit *f. stupidity, blunder.*
Dummkopf *m. idiot, dunce.*
düngen *to fertilize.*
Dünger *m. fertilizer, manure.*
dunkel *dark, gloomy, vaguely.*
   Ich erinnere mich dunkel . . . *I vaguely
   remember . . .*

Dunkelheit *f. darkness, obscurity.*
dunkeln *to get dark.*
dünn *thin, weak, rare.*
DURCH 1. *prep. (acc.) through, across, by, by
   means of, because of.*
   Ich ging durch den Wald. *I walked
   through the forest.*
   Durch den Krieg wurden viele Städte
   zerstört. *Many cities were destroyed
   because of the war.*
   Er bestand die Prüfung durch viel Arbeit.
   *He passed the examination by working
   hard (through much work).*
   Er schickt es durch die Post. *He sends it
   by mail.*
   die ganze Zeit durch *all the time.*
   durch and durch *through and through.*
   2. *prefix*
   a) *inseparable, through, across, around.*
   Die Milchstraße durchzieht den Himmel.
   The Milky Way goes across the sky.
   b) *separable (implies the idea of
   accomplishment).*
   Ich lese das Buch durch. *I read the book
   to the end.*
durcharbeiten *to work through, study
   thoroughly.*
durchaus *thoroughly, absolutely.*
   durchaus nicht *not at all, not in the least.*
durcheinander *confusedly, in disorder.*
durchfahren *to drive through (without
   stopping).*
Durchfahrt *f. thoroughfare, passage.*
   Keine Durchfahrt! *No thoroughfare!*
durchfechten *to fight out.*
durchfinden *to find one's way through.*
durchführbar *to carry out, accomplish,
   execute.*
Durchführung *f. accomplishment, execution,
   performance.*
Durchgang *m. passageway.*
   Kein Durchgang! *No trespassing!*
durchgehen *to go through, pass through, run
   away.*
durchhalten *to hold out, carry through.*
durchmachen *to go through, suffer.*
   Sie haben viel durchgemacht. *They have
   gone through a lot.*
Durchmesser *m. diameter.*
durchnehmen *to work through, go over.*
Durchreise *f. journey through, passing
   through, transit.*
durchreisen *to travel through, cross.*
Durchreisevisum *n. transit visa.*
durchschauen *to look through.*
Durchschlag *m. colander, strainer, carbon
   copy.*
durchschlagend *powerful.*
durchschneiden *to cut through.*

durchsetzen *to achieve, carry out, bring about.*

durchsuchen *to search through.*

Durchsuchung *f. search, police raid.*

Durchzug *m. march through, passage through.*

DÜRFEN *to be allowed to, be permitted.*
Darf ich, bitte? *May I, please?*
Darf ich um den nächsten Tanz bitten? *May I have the next dance?*
Darf man hier rauchen? *Is smoking allowed here?*

dürftig *poor, needy, indigent.*

DÜRR *dry, parched, dried, lean, skinny.*
dürres Holz *dry wood.*

DÜRRE *f. dryness, drought.*

Durst *m. thirst.*
Das macht Durst. *That makes (one) thirsty.*

dürsten *to be thirsty, long for, crave.*

durstig *thirsty.*

Dusche *f. shower bath.*

duschen (sich) *to take a shower.*

Düsenflugzeug *n. jet plane.*

Dutzend *n. dozen.*
dutzendmal *dozens of times.*

E

Ebbe *f. ebb, low tide.*
die Ebbe und die Flut *the ebb and flow.*

EBEN *even, flat, smooth, just.*
eben erst *just now.*
eben deshalb *for that very reason.*
ebenfalls *likewise, too, also.*
ebenmäßig *symmetrical, proportional.*
ebenso *just as, just so, quite as.*
Es geschieht dir eben recht. *It just serves you right.*

Ebene *f. plain.*

ebnen *to level, smooth.*

Echo *n. echo.*

ECHT *genuine, true, real, legitimate.*

Echtheit *f. legitimacy.*

Ecke *f. corner, angle.*

eckig *triangular, cornered.*

edel *noble, well-born, generous.*

Efeu *n. ivy.*

Effekt *m. effect, stocks.*

Effekthascherei *f. showing off.*

effektvoll *effective.*

Egoismus *m. egoism.*

Egoist *m. egoist.*

egoistisch *egoistic.*

egozentrisch *egocentric.*

EHE *before, until.*
ehemals *formerly.*
eher *sooner, rather.*

Ehe *f. matrimony, marriage.*

Ehefrau *f. wife, spouse.*

Ehegatte *m. husband.*

Ehepaar *n. married couple.*

ehelich *matrimonial, conjugal.*

Ehescheidung *f. divorce.*

Ehescheidungsklage *f. divorce suit.*

Eheschließung *f. marriage.*

EHRE *f. honor, reputation, respect.*
Meine Ehre steht auf dem Spiel. *My honor is at stake.*

ehren *to honor.*

ehrenamtlich *honorary.*

Ehrenbezeigung *f. mark of respect.*

Ehrenwort *n. word of honor.*

ehrerbietig *respectful.*

Ehrerbietung *f. deference, respect.*

Ehrfurcht *f. respect, awe, reverence.*

Ehrgefühl *n. sense of honor, self-respect.*

Ehrgeiz *m. ambition.*

ehrlich *honorably.*
ehrlich gesagt *to tell the truth.*
Ehrlich gesagt, glaube ich ihm nicht. *To tell (you) the truth, I don't believe him.*

ehrgeizig *ambitious.*

Ehrlichkeit *f. honesty.*

Ehrlosigkeit *f. dishonesty, infamy.*

Ei *n. (pl. Eier) egg.*
Eigelb *n. egg yolk.*
Eiweiß *n. egg white.*
Rühreier *scrambled eggs.*
Spiegeleier *fried eggs.*
weiche Eier *soft-boiled eggs.*

Eiche *f. oak.*

Eichhörnchen *n. squirrel.*

Eifer *m. zeal, ardor.*

Eifersucht *f. jealousy.*

eifersüchtig *jealous.*

eifrig *eager, keen, zealous.*

EIGEN *own, proper, particular, special, choosy.*
Er ist sehr eigen im Essen. *He is very fussy about his food.*

eigenartig *odd, peculiar, strange, queer.*

eigensinnig *stubborn, obstinate.*

eigentlich *real, actual; actually, really, exactly, just, as a matter of fact, indeed.*
Was heißt das eigentlich? *What does it actually mean?*

Eigentum *n. property.*

eigentümlich *strange, odd, peculiar.*

(sich) eignen *to be suited, qualified.*

EILE *f. hurry, haste, speed.*
Es hat keine Eile. *There's no hurry about it.*
Eile mit Weile. *Haste makes waste.*

EILEN (sich) *to hurry.*
Das eilt sehr. *This is very urgent.*
Das eilt nicht. *There's no hurry.*

eilig *fast, hasty.*
  es eilig haben   *to be in a hurry.*
Eilzug *m. fast train, express.*
EIN, eine, ein 1. *indefinite article, a, an.*
  2. *number, one.*
  3. *pron. one.*
  eines Tages   *some day.*
  ein für allemal   *once and for all.*
  4. *separable prefix (implies the idea of*
    entrance or reduction in volume).
  Die Lehrerin trat in das Schulzimmer ein.
    The teacher (fem.) entered the
    classroom.
  Läuft dieser Stoff ein?   *Does this material*
    shrink?
EINANDER *each other, one another.*
  Wir haben einander jahrelang nicht gesehen.
    We have not seen each other for years.
einarbeiten *to get used to, familiarize with.*
einatmen *to inhale.*
Einbahnstraße *f. one-way street.*
einbiegen *to turn onto.*
  Biegen Sie in diese Straße ein!   *Turn onto*
    this street.
(sich) einbilden *to imagine; fancy, think,*
  believe.
Einbildung *f. imagination, conceit,*
  presumption.
einbrechen *to break open, through.*
  Heute Nacht ist ein Dieb bei ihm
    eingebrochen.   *Last night a thief*
    broke into his house.
Einbrecher *m. burglar.*
Einbruch *m. housebreaking, burglary.*
EINDRUCK *m. impression.*
  Er tut es bloß, um Eindruck zu machen.
    He does it only to show off.
EINFACH *simple, plain, single; simply,*
  plainly, elementary.
  einfache (Fahrt)   *one-way (ticket).*
Einfall *m. idea, collapse, whim.*
  Wie kommen Sie auf den Einfall?   *What*
    gave you the idea?
einfältig *simple.*
Einfluss *m. influence.*
einflussreich *influential.*
Einfuhr *f. importation, import.*
einführen *to introduce, import.*
Einführung *f. importation.*
Einfuhrzoll *m. import duty.*
Eingabe *f. petition, memorial, input.*
EINGANG *m. entrance.*
  Kein Eingang.   *No entrance.*
  Verbotener Eingang!   *Keep out!*
Eingemachtes *n. preserves.*
eingebildet *conceited.*
Eingebung *f. inspiration.*
eingestehen *to admit, confess.*
eingewöhnen *to accustom.*

Einhalt *m. stop.*
  Einhalt gebieten   *to put a stop to.*
einhalten *to observe, follow, keep to, meet.*
  Wird er den Termin einhalten?   *Will he*
    meet the deadline?
Einheit *f. unity, union, unit.*
einheitlich *uniform.*
einholen *to bring in, collect, gather, make up.*
  einholen gehen   *to go shopping.*
einig *in agreement, united, unanimous.*
einigemal *several times.*
einigen *to unite, unify.*
  sich einigen   *to come to terms, agree.*
einig (-er, -e, -es) *some, any, a few.*
einigermaßen *to some extent, somewhat.*
Einigkeit *f. harmony.*
Einigung *f. agreement.*
einjagen *to alarm, frighten.*
EINKAUF *m. purchase, buying.*
EINKAUFEN *to buy, purchase, shop.*
  Einkaufspreis *m.*   *price of purchase.*
Einkommen *n. income.*
Einkommensteuer *f. income tax.*
einladen *to invite.*
EINLADUNG *f. invitation.*
Einlass *m. entrance, admission.*
einlassen *to admit, let in.*
einleben *to settle down, familiarize oneself.*
einleiten *to begin, initiate, introduce, institute.*
Einleitung *f. introduction.*
einmachen *to preserve.*
Einmachglas *n. preserves jar.*
EINMAL *once, formerly.*
  auf einmal   *all at once.*
  Es war einmal . . .   *Once upon a time*
    there was . . .
  noch einmal   *once more.*
(sich) einmischen *to interfere, to meddle.*
einmütig *unanimous.*
Einnahme *f. occupation, capture, conquest.*
einnehmen *to collect, engage, occupy, receive,*
  captivate.
einnehmend *captivating.*
einordnen *to arrange, classify, file.*
einpacken *to wrap up.*
einpflanzen *to plant, inculcate.*
einrahmen *to frame.*
einreden *to persuade, talk someone into.*
einreichen *to hand in, deliver, present.*
einreihen *to insert, include, arrange.*
Einreise *f. entry into a country.*
Einreiseerlaubnis *f. permit to enter a country.*
einrichten *to arrange, prepare, manage,*
  furnish.
  sich einrichten   *to plan.*
Einrichtung *f. furniture, layout.*
EINS *one, the same.*
  Es kommt auf eins hinaus.   *It comes to the*
    same thing.

EINSAM *lonely, solitary, lonesome.*
Einsamkeit *f. loneliness, solitude.*
einschläfern *to lull to sleep.*
einschalten *to insert, put in.*
einschenken *to pour in.*
einschlafen *to fall asleep.*
einschlagen *to drive in (nail), break, wrap up.*
    Schlagen Sie mir das bitte ein. *Will you please wrap that for me?*
einschließen *to lock up, enclose.*
einschließlich *inclusive.*
Einschreibebrief *m. registered letter.*
einschreiben *to enter, note down, register.*
einschüchtern *to intimidate.*
EINSEITIG *one-sided, partial.*
einsetzen *to put in, insert.*
    sich einsetzen für *to speak on behalf of.*
Einspruch *m. protest, objection.*
    Einspruch erheben *to object to, protest against.*
EINST *once, one day.*
    einstmals *once, formerly.*
    einstweilen *meanwhile, for the present.*
    einstweilig *temporary.*
einsteigen *to get in.*
    Nach Düsseldorf einsteigen! *(Passengers) to Düsseldorf, all aboard!*
einstellen *to put on, adjust, stop, cease.*
    Arbeit einstellen *to strike.*
    Betrieb einstellen *to close down.*
    sich einstellen auf *to be prepared.*
Einstellung *f. adjustment, enlistment, attitude.*
    Ich verstehe Ihre Einstellung nicht. *I don't understand your attitude.*
einstimmen *to join in.*
einstimmig *unanimous.*
einstudieren *to study, rehearse.*
einteilen *to divide, plan, distribute.*
Einteilung *f. division, distribution, arrangement.*
eintönig *monotonous.*
Eintönigkeit *f. monotony.*
Eintracht *f. harmony, union, concord.*
(sich) eintragen *to register.*
eintreffen *to arrive, happen.*
    Was ich befürchtete, ist eingetroffen. *What I was afraid of has happened.*
EINTRETEN *to go in, enter.*
    Bitte, treten Sie ein! *Won't you come in, please!*
    eintreten für *to intercede.*
    eintreten in *to join.*
EINTRITT *entrance, entry.*
    Eintritt verboten! *No admission!*
    Eintritt frei! *Admission free!*
Eintrittsgeld *n. admission fee.*
Eintrittskarte *f. admission ticket.*
EINVERSTANDEN *agreed.*
    einverstanden sein *to agree.*

Einverständnis *n. agreement, consent.*
Einwand *m. objection, protest.*
einwandfrei *faultless, perfect.*
Einwanderer *m. immigrant.*
einwandern *to immigrate.*
Einwanderung *f. immigration.*
einwechseln *to change money.*
einwenden *to object.*
einwilligen *to consent.*
Einwilligung *f. consent.*
Einwurf *m. slit, slot.*
Einzahl *f. singular.*
einzahlen *to pay in.*
Einzahlung *f. payment, deposit.*
EINZELN *individual, particular, separate, single.*
    Kann man jeden Band einzeln kaufen? *Can I buy each volume separately?*
    jeder einzelne *each and every one.*
einziehen *to pull in, draw, move in.*
    Sie sind schon in ihre neue Wohnung eingezogen. *They have already moved into their new apartment.*
EINZIG *only, sole, unique.*
    einzig und allein *solely, entirely.*
    Er ist das einzige Kind. *He is the only child.*
Einzug *m. entry, entrance, moving in.*
EIS *n. ice, ice cream.*
    Eisbahn *f. rink.*
    Eisschrank *m. refrigerator.*
    eisig *icy.*
EISEN *n. iron.*
    zum alten Eisen werfen *to junk.*
    Eisenbahn *f. railway.*
    Eisenbahnwagen *m. railway car.*
    Eisenwaren *pl. hardware.*
    eisern (-er, -e, -es) *of iron, inflexible.*
    der eiserne Vorhang *the iron curtain.*
    Er hat einen eisernen Willen. *He has an iron will.*
eitel *vain, conceited, idle.*
Eitelkeit *f. vanity, conceit.*
Elefant *m. elephant.*
elegant *elegant.*
Eleganz *f. elegance.*
Elektriker *m. electrician.*
elektrisch *electric.*
elektrisieren *to electrify.*
Elektrizität *f. electricity.*
elektronische Post *f. electronic mail (e-mail).*
elektronischer Briefkasten *m. e-mail address.*
Element *n. element.*
elementar *elementary.*
Elend *n. misery, misfortune, distress.*
elend *miserable, ill; miserably.*
Elfenbein *n. ivory.*
ELFTE *eleventh.*
Ellenbogen *m. elbow.*

elterlich *parental.*
ELTERN *pl. parents.*
elternlos *orphaned.*
Emigrant *m. emigrant.*
Empfang *m. receipt, reception.*
EMPFANGEN *to receive, welcome.*
Empfänger *m. receiver, addressee.*
empfänglich *receptive.*
Empfangsnahme *f. receipt (paper).*
empfehlen *to recommend.*
empfinden *to experience, feel, perceive.*
empfindlich *sensitive; susceptible.*
Empfindlichkeit *f. sensitivity.*
empören *to rouse, excite, shock.*
sich empören *to be furious; rebel.*
Empörung *f. rebellion.*
ENDE *n. end, result, conclusion, extremity.*
   am Ende   *in the end, after all.*
   Ende gut, alles gut.   *All is well that
      ends well.*
   letzten Endes   *finally.*
   zu Ende führen   *to finish.*
   zu Ende gehen   *to come to an end.*
ENDEN *to end, finish, stop, die.*
Endergebnis *n. final result.*
endgültig *final, definite.*
endlos *endless.*
Endstation *f. terminus.*
Energie *f. energy.*
energisch *energetic, vigorous.*
ENG *narrow, tight, close, intimate.*
   engherzig   *narrow-minded.*
engagieren *to engage.*
Engel *m. angel.*
Engländer *m. Englishman.*
Engländerin *f. Englishwoman.*
Englisch *n. English.*
   auf Englisch   *in English.*
Enkel *m. 1. ankle. 2. grandson.*
Enkelkind *n. grandchild.*
Enkeltochter *f. (Enkelin) granddaughter.*
entbehren *to be without, lack, miss.*
entbehrlich *superfluous, spare.*
Entbehrung *f. privation, want.*
entdecken *to discover, find out, detect.*
Entdecker *m. discoverer.*
Entdeckung *f. discovery.*
Ente *f. duck.*
entehren *to dishonor.*
enteignen *to expropriate, dispossess.*
Enteignung *f. expropriation.*
enterben *to disinherit.*
entfalten *to unfold, develop, display.*
entfernen *to remove, take away, depart.*
   sich entfernen   *to leave.*
entfernt *far off, far away, distant.*
Entfernung *f. distance.*
entfliehen *to run away, escape.*
entfremden *to estrange, alienate.*

Entfremdung *f. estrangement, alienation.*
entführen *to carry off, elope, to abduct.*
Entführung *f. abduction, elopement,
   kidnapping.*
entgegen *toward, opposed to, contrary to.*
entgegen arbeiten *to work against,
   counteract.*
entgegengehen *to go to meet, face.*
entgegengesetzt *opposite.*
entgegenhalten *to object, contrast.*
entgegenkommen *to come to meet.*
   auf halbem Weg entgegenkommen   *to meet
      halfway.*
entgegenkommend *obliging, kind, helpful.*
entgegennehmen *to accept, receive.*
entgegensetzen (entgegenstellen) *to oppose,
   contrast.*
entgegentreten *to advance toward, oppose.*
entgegnen *to reply, answer.*
Entgegnung *f. reply.*
entgehen *to escape, elude.*
enthalten *to contain, hold, include.*
   enthalten sein   *to be included.*
   sich enthalten   *to refrain.*
entkommen *to escape.*
entladen *to unload, discharge.*
Entladung *f. discharge.*
entlassen *to dismiss.*
Entlassung *f. dismissal.*
entmutigen *to discourage, dishearten.*
entnehmen *to take from, gather, understand.*
enträtseln *to solve, decipher.*
entrüsten *to provoke, irritate, make angry.*
Entrüstung *f. anger, indignation.*
entsagen *to renounce, abandon.*
   dem Thron entsagen   *to abdicate.*
Entscheid *m. answer.*
entscheiden *to decide, make up one's mind.*
   Entscheiden Sie das.   *You decide that.*
entscheidend *decisive, critical.*
Entscheidung *f. decision, judgment, sentence,
   award.*
entschieden *decided, firm, resolute.*
Entschiedenheit *f. determination, certainty.*
entschließen *to decide, make up one's mind.*
   Ich habe mich anders entschlossen.   *I've
      changed my mind.*
Entschlossenheit *f. determination.*
Entschluss *m. resolution, decision.*
entschuldbar *excusable.*
ENTSCHULDIGEN *to excuse.*
   Entschuldigen Sie, bitte!   *Please excuse
      me!*
   Ich bitte vielmals um Entschuldigung.
      I am awfully sorry.
   sich entschuldigen   *to apologize.*
entschwinden *to vanish, disappear.*
entsetzen *to frighten, dismiss from, relieve.*
entsetzlich *terrible, dreadful.*

(sich) entsinnen *to remember, recollect, recall.*

entspannen *to relax.*

Entspannung *f. relaxation, rest, recreation.*

entstehen *to arise, originate.*

Entstehung *f. origin, formation.*

entstellen *to distort, misrepresent.*

enttäuschen *to disappoint.*

Enttäuschung *f. disappointment.*

ENTWEDER ... ODER *either ... or.*

entwerfen *to draw up, design.*

entwerten *to depreciate.*

ENTWICKELN *to develop, explain.*

   einen Film entwickeln *to develop a film (photographic).*

Entwicklung *f. development.*

Entwicklungsjahre *pl. adolescence.*

entwürdigen *to degrade, disgrace.*

Entwurf *m. sketch, draft.*

entziehen *to deprive of, take away from, withdraw.*

entzücken *to delight, charm, enchant.*

entzückend *charming, delightful.*

entzwei *in two, torn, broken.*

Episode *f. episode.*

Epoche *f. epoch, era.*

ER *he.*

   er selbst *himself.*

(sich) erarbeiten *to obtain through hard work.*

erbarmen *to feel pity, have mercy.*

erbärmlich *pitiful, miserable.*

erbarmungslos *merciless, pitiless.*

Erbe *m. heir.*

Erbe *n. heritage.*

erben *to inherit.*

Erbfolge *f. succession.*

(sich) erbieten *to offer, volunteer.*

erblassen *to turn pale.*

erblicken *to catch sight of, perceive.*

erbrechen *to break open.*

   sich erbrechen *to vomit.*

Erbschaft *f. inheritance, legacy.*

Erbse *f. pea.*

Erbstück *n. heirloom.*

Erbteil *n. portion of inheritance.*

Erdbeben *n. earthquake.*

Erdbeere *f. strawberry.*

Erdboden *m. ground, soil, earth.*

ERDE *f. earth, ground, soil.*

   auf der Erde *on earth.*

Erdgeschoss *n. ground floor.*

   zu ebener Erde *on the ground floor.*

Erdkunde *f. geography.*

erdolchen *to stab.*

Erdteil *m. continent.*

(sich) ereignen *to happen, occur, pass.*

   Wann hat sich das ereignet? *When did that happen?*

Ereignis *n. event, occurrence, incident.*

erfahren *to learn, experience.*

   Wo kann ich das erfahren? *Where can I get this information?*

Erfahrung *f. experience, information.*

   aus Erfahrung *by experience.*

   erfahrungsgemäss *from experience.*

erfinden *to find out, discover, invent.*

Erfinder *m. inventor.*

Erfindung *f. invention.*

Erfolg *m. success, result, outcome.*

erfolgen *to result, follow.*

erfolglos *unsuccessful, fruitless.*

erfolgreich *successful.*

erforderlich *necessary, requisite.*

erforschen *to explore, investigate.*

Erforschung *f. exploration, investigation.*

ERFREUEN *to give pleasure, gladden, be pleased, rejoice.*

   sich erfreuen *to enjoy.*

erfreulich *delightful, gratifying, satisfactory.*

ERFREUT *glad, pleased, delighted.*

   Sehr erfreut *(in social introductions). How do you do? (Delighted.)*

erfrieren *to die of cold, freeze to death.*

erfrischen *to refresh.*

Erfrischung *f. refreshment.*

ergänzen *to complete, restore.*

Ergänzung *f. completion, restoration.*

ergeben *to produce, yield, result in.*

ergeben *devoted.*

   Ihr ergebener *yours faithfully.*

ergreifen *to seize, take hold of.*

ergreifend *moving, touching.*

Ergriffenheit *f. emotion.*

erhalten *to receive, obtain, preserve.*

Erhalter *m. supporter, preserver.*

erhältlich *obtainable.*

Erhaltungszustand *m. condition, state of preservation.*

erheben *to raise, lift up, collect.*

erhebend *elevating, impressive.*

erheblich *considerable.*

Erhebung *f. raising, elevation, revolt.*

erhitzen *to heat, warm.*

(sich) erholen *to recover, get better.*

Erholung *f. recovery, rest, recreation.*

ERINNERN *to remind.*

   Erinneren Sie mich später daran. *Remind me about it later.*

   sich erinnern an *to remember, recall.*

   Ich kann mich nicht mehr daran erinnern. *I can't remember it any more.*

Erinnerung *f. remembrance, recollection, memory.*

   Erinnerung wachrufen *to evoke memories.*

   zur Erinnerung an *in memory of.*

erkälten *to chill.*

   sich erkälten *to catch a cold.*

erkämpfen *to win by fighting.*

23

erkennbar *recognizable.*

ERKENNEN *to recognize, perceive, realize.*
  zu erkennen geben   *to show, indicate.*

erkenntlich *recognizable, grateful.*

Erkenntnis *f. knowledge, perception, understanding.*

ERKLÄREN *to explain, account for, declare.*

ERKLÄRUNG *f. explanation, interpretation, declaration.*

erkranken *to fall ill, be taken ill.*

Erkrankung *f. illness.*

(sich) erkundigen *to inquire, make inquiries.*

Erkundigung *f. inquiry.*

ERLAUBEN *to allow, permit, presume.*
  Erlauben Sie, bitte!   *Allow me, please!*

Erlaubnis *f. permission, leave, license.*

erleben *to experience.*

Erlebnis *n. event.*

erledigen *to carry through, wind up, dispatch.*
  erledigt sein   *to be dead tired.*

erleichtern *to facilitate, ease, relieve.*

Erleichterung *f. facilitation, relief.*

erlogen *false, untrue, fabricated.*

erlösen *to save, redeem, deliver.*

Erlösung *f. redemption, release, deliverance.*

ermächtigen *to empower, authorize.*

Ermahnung *f. exhortation, admonition.*

ermäßigen *to reduce, abate.*
  ermäßigte Preise   *reduced prices.*

ermöglichen *to make possible, enable.*

ermorden *to murder, assassinate.*

Ermordung *f. murder, assassination.*

ermüden *to tire out, weary.*

Ermüdung *f. fatigue, weariness.*

ermutigen *to encourage.*

ernähren *to nourish, feed, support.*

Ernährung *f. nourishment, food, support, maintenance.*

ernennen *to nominate, appoint.*

Ernennung *f. nomination, appointment.*

erneuern *to renew, renovate, replace.*

Erneuerung *f. renewal, renovation.*

erniedrigen *to humiliate, depress.*

Erniedrigung *f. humiliation, degradation.*

ERNST *serious, severe, grave, seriously.*
  Sie nimmt die Sache ernst.   *She takes the matter seriously.*
  ernst meinen   *to be serious about something.*

Ernst *m. seriousness, earnestness, gravity.*
  Ernst machen mit   *to put into practice.*
  Ernstfall *m. emergency.*

Ernte *f. harvest, crop.*

Erntearbeit *f. harvesting.*

ernten *to harvest.*

erobern *to conquer, capture.*

eröffnen *to open, start, disclose.*

erörtern *to discuss.*

Erörterung *f. discussion.*

erpressen *to extort, blackmail.*

Erpressung *f. extortion, blackmail.*

erraten *to guess.*

erregbar *excitable, irritable.*

erregen *to excite, stir up.*

Erregung *f. excitement, agitation.*

erreichbar *attainable, within reach.*

erreichen *to reach, attain, get.*

ERSATZ *m. substitute, equivalent, spare.*
  Ersatzreifen m.   spare tire.
  Ersatzteil m.   spare part.

erscheinen *to appear, come out.*

Erscheinung *f. appearance, figure, apparition.*

erschießen *to shoot; to kill by shooting.*

Erschießung *f. execution by gunfire.*

erschöpfen *to exhaust.*
  erschöpfend   *exhaustive.*

Erschöpfung *f. exhaustion.*

erschrecken *to frighten.*

erschrocken *frightened.*

erschüttern *to shake, upset, shock.*
  Die Nachricht hat uns erschüttert.   *We were shocked by the news.*

erschweren *to make more difficult, aggravate.*

ersetzen *to replace, compensate, restore.*

ersparen *to save, economize.*

ERST *first, at first, only.*
  der erste beste   *the first that comes.*
  eben erst   *just now.*
  erst als   *not until.*
  erst recht nicht   *certainly not.*
  Erst die Arbeit, dann das Spiel.   *Business before pleasure.*

Erstaufführung *f. opening night.*

erstaunen *to astonish.*

erstaunlich *astonishing.*

ersten Mal (zum) *for the first time.*

erstens *firstly.*

erstgeboren *firstborn.*

ersticken *to suffocate.*

erstmalig *first, for the first time.*

Ertrag *m. produce, yield, profit, returns.*

erträglich *bearable, endurable.*

ertränken *to drown.*

ertrinken *to be drowning.*

erübrigen *to save, spare.*

erwachen *to awake.*

erwachsen *to grow up.*
  die Erwachsenen   *the grown-ups, adults.*

erwägen *to consider, weigh.*

erwähnen *to mention.*

ERWARTEN *to wait for, await, expect.*

Erwartung *f. expectation, hope.*
  in Erwartung Ihrer Antwort   *looking forward to your reply.*

erwartungsvoll *expectant, full of hope.*

erweitern *to widen, expand.*

Erweiterung *f. widening, expansion.*

Erwerb *m. acquisition, gain, profit.*

erwerben to acquire, gain.
erwerbslos unemployed, out of work.
Erwerbslosenunterstützung f. unemployment
   relief.
ERZÄHLEN to tell, relate, narrate.
Erzählung f. story, tale, narrative.
erzeugen to breed, produce, procreate.
Erzeugnis n. product.
   Deutsches Erzeugnis.   Made in Germany.
Erzeugung f. procreation, production.
erziehen to raise, educate, train.
erzieherisch educational.
Erziehung f. education, upbringing.
Erziehungswesen n. educational system.
erzwingen to force, extort.
ES it.
essbar edible.
ESSEN to eat, dine.
Essen n. food, dinner, meal.
Essenszeit f. mealtime.
Essig m. vinegar.
Esslöffel m. tablespoon.
Esswaren pl. provisions, victuals.
Esszimmer n. dining room.
Etage f. floor.
ETWA nearly, about, by chance.
ETWAS some, something, any, anything, a bit,
   somewhat.
EUCH acc. and dat. of ihr (fam. pl. form) you,
   to you.
EUER poss. adj. (fam. pl. form) your.
EUER (-ER, -E, -ES) poss. pron. (fam. pl.
   form) yours.
eurerseits on your part.
euresgleichen like you, of your kind.
euretwegen for your sake, on account
   of you.
Euro m. euro (currency).
Europa n. Europe.
evakuieren to evacuate.
evangelisch Protestant.
Evangelium n. Gospel.
EWIG eternal, forever, all the time.
Ewigkeit f. eternity.
exakt exact.
Examen n. examination.
examinieren to examine.
Exemplar n. sample.
Existenz f. existence.
existieren to exist, live.
Experiment n. experiment.
experimentieren to experiment.
Export m. export.
Exporteur m. exporter.
exportieren to export.
Extrablatt n. special edition.
Extrakt m. extract.
Exzellenz f. excellency.
exzentrisch eccentric.

F

Fabel f. fable, story, plot.
fabelhaft fabulous.
Fabrik f. factory, mill, plant.
Fabrikanlage f. plant.
Fabrikant m. manufacturer.
Fabrikarbeiter m. factory worker.
Fabrikat n. product (manufactured).
Fabrikation f. making.
fabrizieren to manufacture.
Fach n. compartment, shelf, drawer.
   Was ist Ihr Fach?   What's your line?
Fachkenntnis f. technical knowledge.
Fachmann m. expert, specialist.
Fackel f. torch.
Faden m. thread.
   an einem Faden hängen   to hang by a
    thread.
FÄHIG able.
   fähig sein   to be able, capable.
Fähigkeit f. capability.
Fahne f. flag, banner.
Fahrbahn f. road, track.
fahrbar passable, navigable.
Fähre f. ferry.
FAHREN to drive, ride, go, travel.
   Fahren Sie rechts!   Keep to the right!
   mit dem Schiff fahren   to sail.
   spazieren fahren   to go for a ride.
Fahrer m. driver.
Fahrgast m. passenger.
Fahrgeld n. fare.
Fahrkarte f. ticket (transportation).
Fahrkartenschalter m. ticket window.
fahrlässig careless, negligent.
Fahrlässigkeit f. carelessness, negligence.
Fahrplan m. timetable.
Fahrrad n. bicycle.
Fahrschein m. transportation ticket (bus).
Fahrspur f. lane.
Fahrstuhl m. lift, elevator.
   Fahrstuhlführer m.   elevator boy, attendant.
FAHRT f. ride, journey, trip.
   Hin- und Rückfahrt   round-trip.
   in voller Fahrt   at full speed.
   Was kostet die Fahrt, bitte?   How much is
    the fare, please?
Fahrzeug n. vehicle.
Fakultät f. faculty.
FALL m. fall, drop, case, accident.
   auf jeden Fall, auf alle Fälle   in any case.
   auf keinen Fall!   On no account!
Falle f. trap.
FALLEN to fall.
   fallen lassen   to let fall, drop.
   im Krieg fallen   to be killed in action.
   in den Rücken fallen   to attack from behind.

in Ohnmacht fallen   *to faint.*
Das Fest fällt auf einen Sonntag.   *The holiday falls on a Sunday.*
Das fällt nicht weiter ins Gewicht.   *That is of no further consequence.*
falls *in case, in the event.*
Fallschirm *m. parachute.*
FALSCH *wrong, incorrect, false.*
  Sie hat falsche Zähne.   *She has false teeth.*
  Das Geld ist falsch.   *The money is counterfeit.*
  falsch verstehen   *to misunderstand.*
fälschen *to falsify, forge.*
Fälscher *m. forger.*
Falschheit *f. falseness, falsehood.*
Falschspieler *m. cheat (at cards).*
Fälschung *f. forgery.*
Falte *f. pleat, fold, wrinkle.*
falten *to fold.*
familiär *familiar, intimate.*
FAMILIE *f. family.*
Familienname *m. last name.*
Fanatiker *m. fanatic.*
Fang *m. catch, capture, prey.*
fangen *to catch, capture.*
FARBE *f. color, paint.*
  farbenblind   *color-blind.*
färben *to color, dye.*
  sich die Haare färben   *to dye one's hair.*
farbig *colored.*
farblos *colorless, pale, boring.*
Fasching *m. carnival.*
Fass *n. barrel, cask.*
  Das schlägt dem Fass den Boden aus.   *That's the last straw.*
Fassade *f. front (of a building), facade.*
FASSEN *to catch, seize, hold, apprehend, grasp, comprehend.*
  Fassen Sie sich kurz!   *Make it short!*
  ins Auge fassen   *to consider, to keep in mind.*
  einen Entschluss fassen   *to make a decision.*
Fassung *f. setting, composure.*
  aus der Fassung bringen   *to upset, disconcert.*
fast *almost, nearly.*
faul *lazy, rotten.*
  Das ist eine faule Sache.   *This is a shady business.*
faulen *to rot.*
Faulheit *laziness.*
Faulpelz *m. idler, lazybones.*
Faust *f. fist.*
  auf eigene Faust   *on one's own responsibility.*
  faustdick hinter den Ohren haben   *to be sly.*
Fausthandschuh *m. mitten, boxing glove.*
fax *m. fax.*

faxen *to fax.*
FEBRUAR *m. February.*
FEDER *f. feather.*
  Federhalter *m.   fountain pen.*
  federleicht   *light as a feather.*
fegen *to sweep.*
FEHLEN *to miss, make a mistake, lack, be absent.*
  es an nichts fehlen lassen   *to spare no pains.*
  Sie werden mir sehr fehlen.   *I'll miss you very much.*
  Was fehlt Ihnen?   *What's the matter with you?*
FEHLER *m. fault, defect, mistake, blunder.*
  Das ist mein Fehler.   *That is my fault.*
Fehlschlag *failure.*
Feier *f. festival, celebration, ceremony, party.*
Feierabend *time for the workday to end.*
  Wir machen jetzt Feierabend.   *Let's call it a day.*
feierlich *solemn, festive, ceremonious.*
Feierlichkeit *f. solemnity, ceremony.*
feiern *to celebrate.*
  Sie feiern ihre goldene Hochzeit.   *They are celebrating their golden anniversary.*
Feierstunde *f. leisure hour, festive hour.*
Feiertag *m. holiday.*
feige *cowardly.*
Feigheit *f. cowardice.*
feil *for sale, mercenary.*
  feil bieten   *to offer for sale.*
  feil halten   *to have for sale.*
FEIN *fine, thin, delicate, refined, distinguished, elegant.*
Feind *m. enemy.*
feindlich *hostile.*
feinfühlig *sensitive.*
Feingefühl *n. sensitivity.*
Feinheit *f. fineness, grace, elegance, refinement, subtlety.*
Feinschmecker *m. gourmet.*
FELD *n. field, plain, ground, square.*
  Schlachtfeld *n.   battlefield.*
Feldstecher *m. binoculars.*
Feldzug *m. campaign.*
Fell *n. skin, hide, coat, fur (animals).*
  Diese Katze hat ein schönes Fell.   *This cat has beautiful fur.*
Fels *m. rock, cliff.*
  felsenfest   *firm as a rock.*
felsig *rocky, craggy.*
FENSTER *n. window.*
Fensterbank *f. windowsill.*
Fensterrahmen *m. window frame.*
Fensterscheibe *f. windowpane.*
Ferien *pl. holidays, vacation.*
  in die Ferien gehen   *to go on vacation.*
FERN *far, distant, remote.*

von fern *from afar, from a distance.*
Ferne *f. distance.*
ferner *further, furthermore, besides.*
Ferngespräch *n. long-distance phone call.*
Fernglas *n. binoculars, field glass.*
fernmündlich *by telephone, over the telephone.*
Das Telegramm wurde mir fernmündlich durchgegeben. *The telegram was given to me over the phone.*
Fernsehen *n. television.*
Fernsprechbuch *n. telephone directory.*
Fernsprecher *m. telephone.*
Fernsprechstelle *f. telephone booth.*
FERTIG *ready, ready-made, finished, done.*
fertigbringen *to bring about, accomplish.*
sich fertig machen *to get ready.*
Werden Sie damit fertig werden? *Will you be able to manage this by yourself?*
FEST *n. festival, feast.*
FEST *firm, hard, rigid, steady, solid, stiff, stable, firmly, stiffly, fully.*
eine feste Stellung *a permanent post.*
fester Schlaf *sound sleep.*
festbinden *to tie, bind, fasten.*
Festessen *n. banquet.*
festfahren *to get stuck.*
Festhalle *f. banqueting hall.*
festhalten *to hold tight.*
sich festhalten an *to hold on to.*
festigen *to make firm.*
Festigkeit *f. solidity, firmness.*
festlegen *to fix, lay down.*
festlich *festive, solemn.*
Festlichkeit *f. festivity.*
festmachen *to fasten, attach, fix, settle.*
Festnahme *f. arrest, seizure.*
Festplatte *f. hard drive.*
festsetzen *to fix, set, settle.*
Der Preis wird auf hundert Mark festgesetzt. *The price has been fixed at one hundred marks.*
festsitzen *to be stuck, fit tightly.*
Festspiel *n. festival performance.*
Feststellung *f. statement, determination, identification.*
Festtag *m. holiday, feast.*
Festung *f. fortress, stronghold.*
FETT *fat, plump, fertile, rich, greasy.*
Fett *n. grease, fat.*
fettig *fatty, greasy.*
FEUCHT *damp, humid, muggy.*
FEUER *n. fire, firing, bombardment.*
Feuer! *Fire!*
Feuer fangen *to catch fire.*
Feuer geben *to give a light.*
feuerfest *fireproof.*
Feuergefahr *f. danger of fire.*
feuergefährlich *inflammable.*

Feuerlöscher *m. fire extinguisher.*
Feuerung *f. fuel.*
Feuerversicherung *f. fire insurance.*
Feuerwache *f. fire station.*
Feuerwerk *n. firework.*
Feuerzeug *n. lighter.*
Fieber *n. fever, temperature.*
Fieber messen *to take one's temperature.*
fieberhaft *feverish.*
fiebern *to be feverish, have a temperature.*
Fieberthermometer *n. clinical thermometer.*
Fieberwahn *m. delirium.*
Figur *f. figure, form, shape.*
Filiale *f. branch.*
FILM *m. film, picture, movie.*
Filmaufnahme *f. shooting of film.*
filmen *to film.*
Filmstreifen *m. filmstrip.*
Filter *m. filter.*
filtern *to filter, strain.*
Filz *m. felt.*
filzig *stingy.*
Finanz *f. finance.*
Finanzamt *n. revenue office.*
finanziell *financial.*
finanzieren *to finance, support.*
FINDEN *to find, discover, meet with, think, consider.*
Finder *m. finder.*
findig *clever, ingenious.*
Findigkeit *f. cleverness.*
FINGER *m. finger.*
Fingerabdruck *m. fingerprint.*
Fingerfertigkeit *f. dexterity, skill.*
Fingerhut *m. thimble.*
Fingerspitze *f. tip of the finger.*
Fingerspitzengefühl *n. instinct; intuition.*
Fingerzeig *m. hint, tip.*
finster *dark, gloomy, obscure.*
Finte *f. feint, trick.*
Firma *f. firm, business.*
FISCH *m. fish.*
FISCHEN *to fish.*
Fischer *m. fisherman.*
Fischerei *f. fishing, fishery.*
Fischgräte *f. fish bone.*
Fischhändler *m. fishmonger.*
FLACH *flat, plain, level.*
Fläche *f. surface, plain, area.*
Flachland *n. flat country, plain.*
Flagge *f. flag.*
flaggen *to deck with flags.*
Flamme *f. flame.*
FLASCHE *f. bottle.*
Flaschenbier *n. bottled beer.*
Flaschenöffner *m. bottle opener.*
flatterhaft *fickle, inconsistent.*
flattern *to flutter; wave.*
FLECK *m. place, spot, stain.*

vom Fleck kommen   *to get on, make headway.*
Flecken *m. spot, stain.*
fleckenlos *spotless.*
fleckig *spotted, stained.*
Flegel *m. boor, impertinent person.*
flegelhaft *rude, insolent.*
Flegeljahre *pl. teenage years.*
flehen *to implore, beseech.*
FLEISCH *n. flesh, meat, pulp.*
Fleischbrühe *f. meat broth.*
Fleischer *m. butcher.*
fleischig *fleshy, plump.*
fleischlos *meatless.*
FLEIß *m. diligence, industry.*
  mit Fleiß   *on purpose.*
fleißig *diligent, industrious.*
flicken *to patch, mend, repair.*
Fliege *f. fly.*
FLIEGEN *to fly, rush.*
  in die Luft fliegen   *to blow up.*
Flieger *m. airman, aviator, pilot.*
fliehen *to run away, flee.*
fließen *to flow, run.*
  fließendes Wasser   *running water.*
  fließend sprechen   *to speak fluently.*
flink *quick, agile, nimble.*
Flinte *f. shotgun, rifle.*
  die Flinte in das Korn werfen   *to give up.*
Flirt *m. flirtation.*
flirten *to flirt.*
Flitterwochen *pl. honeymoon.*
Floh *m. flea.*
Flöte *f. flute.*
flöten *to play the flute.*
flott *afloat, floating.*
Flotte *f. fleet, navy.*
Fluch *m. curse, imprecation.*
fluchen *to curse, swear.*
Flucht *f. flight, escape.*
flüchten *to flee, escape.*
flüchtig *careless, passing, superficial.*
  Er ist nur ein flüchtiger Bekannter.   *He is only a passing acquaintance.*
Flüchtling *m. fugitive.*
FLUG *m. flight (aerial).*
Flugblatt *n. pamphlet.*
Fluggast *m. air passenger.*
Flughafen *m. airport.*
Flugplatz *m. airfield, airport.*
Flugzeug *n. airplane*
Flugzeugträger *m. aircraft carrier.*
Flur *f. field, meadow.*
Flur *m. hall, corridor.*
FLUSS *m. river.*
flüssig *liquid, fluid.*
Flüssigkeit *f. fluidity.*
Flusslauf *m. course of a river.*
flüstern *to whisper.*

Flut *f. tide, flood.*
fluten *to stream, flow.*
FOLGE *f. sequence, succession.*
  Folge leisten   *to comply with.*
Folgeerscheinung *f. consequence, effect.*
FOLGEN *to follow, succeed, obey, mind.*
  daraus folgt   *hence follows.*
folgendermaßen *as follows.*
folgern *to infer, conclude, deduce.*
Folgerung *f. inference, conclusion, deduction.*
folglich *consequently.*
folgsam *obedient, docile.*
Folgsamkeit *f. obedience, docility.*
foltern *to torture.*
fordern *to demand, ask, claim, require.*
Forderung *f. demand, claim, challenge.*
Form *f. form, shape.*
Formalität *f. formality.*
Format *n. size, weight, importance.*
Formel *f. formula.*
formell *formal.*
formen *to form, shape.*
förmlich *formal, ceremonious, regular.*
Formlosigkeit *f. formlessness, shapelessness.*
Formular *n. form.*
formulieren *to formulate, define.*
formvollendet *perfect in form.*
forschen *to investigate, search.*
Forschung *f. inquiry, investigation.*
Förster *m. forester, gamekeeper.*
FORT *adv. and separable prefix (implies movement away from speaker, or continuation). away, off, gone, on (going on).*
  und so fort   *and so forth.*
fortan *henceforth, from this time.*
Fortbildung *f. further study.*
fortfahren *to drive away, remove, continue.*
  Er ist gestern fortgefahren.   *He left yesterday.*
fortführen *to lead away, go on, continue.*
fortgehen *to go away.*
fortgesetzt *continuous, incessant.*
fortschreiten *to advance, proceed, make progress.*
Fortschritt *m. progress.*
fortschrittlich *progressive.*
fortsetzen *to continue, carry on, pursue.*
Fortsetzung *f. continuation, pursuit.*
  Fortsetzung folgt   *to be continued.*
Fracht *f. freight.*
Frachtdampfer *m. freighter.*
FRAGE *f. question, inquiry, problem.*
  Das ist noch die Frage.   *That remains to be seen.*
  eine Frage stellen   *to ask a question.*
  ohne Frage   *undoubtedly.*
FRAGEN *to ask, inquire.*
  fragen nach   *to ask for.*

sich fragen *to wonder.*
Es fragt sich, ob es der Mühe wert ist. *The question is whether it is worth the trouble.*
Fragezeichen *n. question mark.*
fraglich *in question, questionable, doubtful.*
fraglos *unquestionable.*
Franzose, -n *n. Frenchman.*
Französin, -nen *f. Frenchwoman.*
französisch *French.*
FRAU *f. woman, wife, Mrs.*
gnädige Frau *Madam.*
Ihre Frau (Gemahlin) *your wife.*
Frauenarzt *m. gynecologist.*
FRÄULEIN *n. young lady, girl, Miss.*
fraulich *womanly.*
frech *impudent, insolent, fresh.*
Frechheit *f. impudence, insolence.*
FREI *free, vacant, open, liberal, spontaneous, frank; freely, frankly, at ease.*
die freie Zeit *leisure, spare time.*
Es ist mein freier Tag. *This is my day off.*
Ist dieser Platz frei? *Is this seat taken?*
unter freiem Himmel, im Freien *outside, in the open air.*
Freibillet *n. complimentary ticket.*
Freidenker *m. freethinker.*
freigeben *to set free, release, open (to the public).*
freigebig *liberal, generous.*
Freigebigkeit *f. liberality, generosity.*
Freigeist *m. freethinker.*
freihalten *to hold, treat.*
Freiheit *f. freedom.*
freilassen *to release, set free.*
Freilassung *f. release.*
Freimut *m. frankness, candor.*
freimütig *frank, candid.*
freisprechen *to acquit, absolve.*
Freispruch *m. acquittal.*
Freistelle *f. scholarship.*
FREITAG *m. Friday.*
Freizeit *f. leisure time.*
freiwillig *voluntary, spontaneous.*
Freiwillige *m. volunteer.*
FREMD *strange, foreign, unknown, exotic.*
fremdes Gut *other people's property.*
fremdartig *strange, odd.*
FREMDE *m. foreigner, tourist, foreign country.*
in der Fremde (im Ausland) *abroad.*
Fremdenführer *m. tourist guide.*
Fremdenverkehr *m. tourist traffic.*
Fremdsprache *f. foreign language.*
Fremdwort *n. foreign word.*
Fressen *n. animal food, feed.*
fressen *to eat (animals), feed.*
FREUDE *f. joy, delight, pleasure, cheer.*
Freude haben an *to enjoy, delight in.*

freudestrahlend *beaming with joy.*
freudelos *joyless, cheerless.*
freudig *joyful, cheerful.*
freuen *to please, delight.*
sich freuen *to be pleased, rejoice.*
Es freut mich sehr, Sie kennenzulernen. *I am very glad to meet you.*
sich freuen auf *to look forward to.*
FREUND *m. (-in f.) friend.*
FREUNDLICH *friendly, kind, obliging, pleasant.*
Freundlichkeit *f. friendliness.*
Freundschaft *f. friendship.*
freundschaftlich *friendly, serviceable.*
FRIEDE *m. peace.*
Friedensbruch *m. breach of peace.*
Friedensvertrag *m. peace treaty.*
Friedhof *m. churchyard, cemetery.*
friedlich *peaceful.*
friedliebend *peace-loving.*
frieren *to freeze, be cold, get cold.*
Die Füsse frieren mir. *My feet are freezing.*
Mich friert (es). *I am cold.*
FRISCH *fresh, bright, lively, new.*
frisch gestrichen *wet paint.*
frische Eier *fresh eggs.*
frische Wäsche *clean linen.*
FRISÖR *m. barber, hairdresser.*
Friseuse *f. hairdresser (female).*
frisieren *to fix one's hair.*
sich frisieren lassen *to have one's hair done.*
Frisur *f. hairdressing, hairdo.*
froh *glad, happy.*
frohgemut *cheerful.*
FRÖHLICH *merry, happy.*
Fröhliche Weihnachten! *Merry Christmas!*
Fröhlichkeit *f. cheerfulness.*
Frohsinn *m. cheerfulness.*
fromm *pious, religious, godly.*
Front *f. front (military).*
Frosch *m. frog.*
Frost *m. frost, cold, chill.*
frösteln *to shiver, feel chilly.*
FRUCHT *f. fruit, crop, produce.*
fruchtbar *fruitful, fertile.*
Fruchtbarkeit *f. fruitfulness, fertility.*
Frucht bringend *fruit-bearing, productive, fertile.*
fruchten *to bear fruit, to have effect.*
Fruchtsaft *m. fruit juice.*
FRÜH *early in the morning.*
heute früh *this morning.*
morgen früh *tomorrow morning.*
Frühe *f. morning, dawn.*
in aller Frühe *very early.*
früher *earlier, sooner, former.*
früher oder später *sooner or later.*

frühestens *at the earliest.*
FRÜHLING *m. spring.*
FRÜHSTÜCK *n. breakfast.*
frühstücken *to eat breakfast.*
Fuchs *m. fox.*
fügen *to join, put together, add, submit.*
fügsam *yielding, submissive.*
Fügung *f. dispensation, coincidence.*
fühlbar *tangible, perceptible.*
FÜHLEN *to feel, sense, be sensitive to.*
   sich gut fühlen   *to feel well.*
FÜHREN *to lead, conduct, direct, handle,*
   carry.
   ein Gespräch führen   *to have a*
     conversation.
   Wer führt?   *Who is ahead?*
   Er führt immer das große Wort. *He is*
     always bragging.
   Er führt etwas im Schilde. *He is up to*
     something.
Führer *m. leader, driver, pilot, guidebook.*
Führerschein *m. driving license.*
Führung *f. leadership, command, direction,*
   management, behavior, conduct.
FÜLLEN *to fill, stuff.*
   sich füllen   *to fill up.*
   Das Stadion füllt sich langsam. *The*
     stadium is slowly filling up.
Fund *m. finding.*
Fundament *n. foundation.*
fundieren *to lay a foundation.*
FÜNF *five.*
FÜNFTE *fifth.*
FÜNFZEHN *fifteen.*
FÜNFZEHNTE *fifteenth.*
FÜNFZIG *fifty.*
FÜNFZIGSTE *fiftieth.*
Funk *m. radio (communications medium).*
Funke *m. spark.*
funkeln *to sparkle.*
FÜR *prep. (acc.) for, by, to.*
   ein für allemal   *one for all.*
   Er geht Schritt für Schritt vorwärts. *He*
     walks forward step-by-step.
   Ich arbeite für mich. *I work for myself.*
   Ich habe Karten für das Theater. *I have*
     tickets for the theater.
   Stück für Stück   *piece by piece.*
   Tag für Tag   *day by day*
   Was für ein?   *what kind of?*
FURCHT *f. fear, fright, dread, anxiety.*
furchtbar *awful, horrible, terrible; awfully,*
   terribly.
fürchten *to fear.*
fürchterlich *terrible, horrible, frightful.*
furchtlos *fearless, intrepid.*
Furchtlosigkeit *f. fearlessness, intrepidity.*
furchtsam *timid, nervous.*
Furchtsamkeit *f. timidity.*

Fürst *m. (-in f.) prince(ss).*
Fürwort *n. pronoun.*
FUẞ *m. foot, base, bottom.*
   auf eigenen Füßen stehen   *to be*
     independent.
   auf freien Fuß setzen   *to set at liberty.*
   Er lebt auf grossem Fuß. *He is living in*
     grand style.
   Ich stehe mit ihm auf gutem Fuß. *I am on*
     good terms with him.
   zu Fuß   *on foot.*
Fußball *m. soccer.*
Fußbank *f. footstool.*
Fußgänger *m. (-in f.) pedestrian.*
   nur für Fußgänger   *for pedestrians only.*
Fußspur *f. footprint.*
Fußstapfen *m. footstep.*
Fußtritt *m. kick.*
Futter *n. 1. food, feed (animals). 2. sheath,*
   lining.
Futterseide *f. silk for lining.*

G

Gabe *f. present, gift, talent.*
Gabel *f. fork.*
gähnen *to yawn, gape.*
GANG *m. walk, stroll, aisle, course, gear,*
   hall, errand.
   in Gang setzen   *to start, set.*
   in vollem Gang   *in full swing.*
   die Sache nimmt ihren Gang *the matter*
     takes/runs its course.
Gans *f. goose.*
Gänseblümchen *n. daisy.*
ganz *all, whole, entire, complete; in full,*
     wholly, entirely, thoroughly, altogether.
   die ganze Stadt   *the whole town.*
   ganz anders   *quite different.*
   ganz besonders   *more especially.*
   ganz gleich   *all the same, no matter.*
   ganz und gar   *wholly.*
   ganz und gar nicht   *not at all.*
   im Ganzen   *on the whole.*
   im Grossen und Ganzen   *for the most part.*
   von ganzem Herzen   *with all my heart.*
gar *done, cooked through; fully, very, quite,*
     even.
   gar kein . . .   *no . . . whatsoever.*
   gar nicht   *not at all.*
   gar nichts   *nothing at all.*
Garage *f. garage.*
Garderobe *f. wardrobe, cloakroom.*
Garderobenmarke *f. check (cloakroom).*
Garderobennummer *f. check (cloakroom).*
Gardine *f. curtain.*
Garn *n. yarn, thread.*

garnieren *to trim, garnish.*
Garnitur *f. trimming, outfit.*
garstig *nasty, ugly.*
GARTEN *m. garden, yard.*
Gartenhaus *n. summerhouse.*
Gartenlaube *f. garden house (pavilion).*
Gärtner *m. gardener.*
Gas *n. gas.*
Gashahn *m. gas valve.*
Gasleitung *f. gas pipes, gas supply.*
Gasse *f. narrow street, alley.*
GAST *m. visitor, guest.*
gastfreundich *hospitable.*
Gastfreundschaft *f. hospitality.*
Gastgeber *m. host.*
Gasthaus *n. inn, hotel.*
Gasthof *m. inn, hotel.*
gastlich *hospitable.*
Gastspiel *n. guest performance.*
Gastwirt *m. innkeeper.*
Gasuhr *f. gas meter.*
Gatte *m. husband.*
Gattin *f. wife.*
Gaumen *m. palate.*
Geächteter *m. outlaw.*
Gebäck *n. pastry, cookie.*
Gebärde *f. gesture, movement.*
(sich) gebärden *to behave, conduct oneself.*
Gebäude *n. building, structure, edifice.*
GEBEN *to give, present, produce, yield.*
   Das gibt mir zu denken.   *That makes me*
     wonder.
   es gibt *there is, there are.*
   Was gibt es zum Mittagessen? *What are*
     they having for lunch?
   gegeben werden *to perform, act (in*
     theater).
   Was wird heute im Theater gegeben?
     What's playing tonight at the theater?
Gebet *n. prayer.*
Gebiet *n. district, territory, area, field.*
gebieten *to order, command.*
Gebirge *n. mountain chain.*
gebirgig *mountainous.*
Gebiss *n. set of teeth, denture.*
Gebot *n. order, command, law.*
Gebrauch *m. use, customs, rites.*
gebrauchen *to use, make use of.*
gebräuchlich *usual, in use.*
Gebühr *f. duty, tax, fee, rate.*
gebühren *to be due.*
   sich gebühren *to be proper.*
gebührenfrei *tax free*
gebührenpflichtig *taxable.*
gebührlich *suitable, proper.*
GEBURT *f. birth, origin, extraction.*
Geburtshelferin *f. midwife.*
Geburtsjahr *n. year of birth.*
Geburtsschein *m. birth certificate.*

Geburtstag *m. birthday.*
Gedächtnis *n. memory, remembrance.*
   aus dem Gedächtnis *from memory.*
GEDANKE *m. thought, idea.*
   sich Gedanken machen *to worry.*
   Wie kommen Sie auf den Gedanken?
     What gives you that idea?
gedankenlos *thoughtless.*
Gedankenlosigkeit *f. thoughtlessness.*
Gedeck *n. cover (a table), set of table linens.*
gedeihen *to grow, develop, succeed.*
gedenken *to intend, think of, commemorate.*
Gedenkfeier *f. commemoration.*
Gedicht *n. poem.*
Gedränge *n. crowd, throng.*
gedruckt *printed.*
Geduld *f. patience, endurance.*
(sich) gedulden *to have patience.*
geduldig *patient.*
Gefahr *f. danger, risk.*
gefährden *to endanger, expose to danger.*
gefährlich *dangerous, perilous.*
gefahrlos *safe, secure, without danger.*
gefahrvoll *dangerous, perilous.*
GEFALLEN *to please, suit.*
   Das gefällt mir. *I like that.*
   sich gefallen lassen *to submit, put up with.*
gefällig *pleasant, agreeable.*
Gefangener *m. prisoner, captive.*
   Kriegsgefangener m. *prisoner of war.*
Gefangenschaft *f. captivity, confinement.*
Gefangensetzung *f. capture, arrest.*
Gefängnis *n. prison, jail.*
Gefäß *n. container, receptacle.*
gefasst *composed, collected, calm.*
   sich gefasst machen auf *to be prepared for.*
Geflügel *n. birds, poultry, fowl.*
Geflüster *n. whispering.*
Gefolge *n. suite, entourage.*
GEFÜHL *n. feeling, sentiment, sense,*
     emotion, sensation.
gefühllos *numb, heartless.*
Gefühllosigkeit *f. numbness, heartlessness.*
gefühlvoll *tender, sentimental.*
GEGEN *prep. (acc.) against, about, around,*
     toward, for, to, compared with.
   Die Soldaten kämpfen gegen den Feind.
     The soldiers fight against the enemy.
   Er schwamm gegen den Strom. *He swam*
     against the current.
   Es ist gegen neun Uhr. *It is about nine*
     o'clock.
   gegen voriges Jahr *compared with last*
     year.
   gegeneinander *against each other.*
   waren gegen Geld tauschen *to exchange*
     goods for money.
GEGEND *f. country, region, district.*
Gegenseite *f. opposite side.*

gegenseitig *reciprocal, mutual.*
Gegenstand *m. subject.*
gegenstandslos *pointless.*
Gegenteil *n. contrary, opposite.*
  im Gegenteil   *on the contrary.*
gegenüber *opposite.*
Gegenwart *f. present, presence.*
gegenwärtig *present.*
Gegenwert *m. equivalent value.*
Gegner *m. opponent, adversary, enemy.*
Gehalt *m. content.*
Gehalt *n. salary.*
gehaltlos *worthless.*
gehaltvoll *valuable, substantial.*
gehässig *spiteful, malicious.*
Gehässigkeit *f. spite, malice.*
geheim *conceal, hidden, clandestine.*
GEHEIMNIS *n. secret, mystery.*
geheimnisvoll *mysterious.*
Geheimpolizei *f. secret police.*
GEHEN *to go, walk, pass, move, leave; run,*
  work (machinery).
  an die Arbeit gehen   *to go to work.*
  Das geht nicht.   *That won't do.*
  Es geht mir gut, danke.   *I am fine, thank*
    you.
  Es geht nichts über gutes Bier.   *There is*
    nothing like good beer.
  Es geht um Tod und Leben.   *It is a matter*
    of life and death.
  gehen auf (nach)   *to face on, look out on.*
  Das Fenster geht auf den Hof.   *The*
    window faces the courtyard.
  gehen lassen   *to let go, give up.*
  sich gehen lassen   *to let oneself go.*
  Wie geht es Ihnen?   *How are you?*
Gehilfe *m. assistant, clerk, helper.*
Gehirn *n. brain.*
GEHÖR *n. hearing; ear (mus.).*
gehorchen *to obey.*
GEHÖREN *to belong to, be owned by.*
  Es gehört ihm.   *It belongs to him.*
  Das gehört nicht zur Sache.   *That's beside*
    the point.
  Dazu gehört Zeit.   *That takes time.*
gehorsam *obedient.*
Geige *f. violin.*
geigen *to play the violin.*
GEIST *m. spirit, genius, mind.*
geistesabwesend *absentminded.*
Geistesgegenwart *f. presence of mind.*
geisteskrank *of unsound mind, insane.*
geistesschwach *feebleminded.*
geistig *spiritual, intellectual, mental.*
geistlich *religious, spiritual.*
geistlos *spiritless, lifeless, dull.*
geistreich *ingenious, spiritual, witty.*
Geiz *m. stinginess, avarice.*
geizig *avaricious, stingy.*

Gelände *n. country, countryside.*
Geländer *n. railing, banister.*
gelangen *to reach, arrive, attain to.*
gelassen *calm, collected.*
Gelassenheit *f. calmness, composure.*
geläufig *fluent, familiar, current.*
gelaunt *disposed.*
  gut gelaunt   *in good humour.*
  schlecht gelaunt   *cross, bad-tempered.*
Geläute *n. chime, ringing of bells.*
GELB *yellow.*
gelblich *yellowish.*
Gelbsucht *f. jaundice.*
GELD *n. money.*
  Bargeld *n. cash.*
  Kleingeld *n. change.*
Geldentwertung *f. inflation, devaluation.*
Geldschein *m. paper money, bill.*
Geldschrank *m. safe.*
Geldstück *n. coin.*
Geldtasche *f. purse.*
Gelee *m. jelly.*
gelegen *1. situated. 2. convenient.*
  Er kam gerade zu gelegener Zeit.   *He came*
    just at the right time.
Gelegenheit *f. opportunity, occasion, chance.*
Gelegenheitskauf *m. bargain.*
gelegentlich *occasional, accidental.*
gelehrig *docile, teachable.*
Gelehrsamkeit *f. learning, erudition.*
gelehrt *learned, scholarly, erudite.*
Gelehrter *m. scholar, savant.*
Geleise *n. track.*
Geleit *n. escort, convoy.*
geleiten *to accompany, escort.*
Geleitwort *n. motto.*
Gelenk *n. joint, articulation.*
Geliebte *m. & f. lover, mistress, beloved.*
gelingen *to succeed, manage.*
gelten *to matter, mean, be worth, have*
  influence, be valid.
  Das gilt nicht.   *That does not count.*
  gelten als   *to be considered as.*
Geltungsdauer *f. period of validity.*
gemächlich *comfortable.*
Gemahl *m. husband.*
Gemahlin *f. wife.*
gemäß *suitable.*
GEMEIN *ordinary, general, low, vulgar,*
  common.
  Es war gemein von ihm.   *It was mean*
    of him.
  gemein haben mit   *to have in common with.*
Gemeinde *f. community, congregation, parish,*
  municipality.
Gemeinheit *f. vulgarity, baseness, bad trick.*
gemeinnützig *beneficial to the community.*
Gemeinschaft *f. community.*
  in Gemeinschaft mit   *together with.*

GEMÜSE n. vegetables.
Gemüsehändler m. greengrocer.
Gemüt n. soul, mind, heart, feelings.
Gemütlich good-natured, cozy.
Gemütlichkeit f. comfort, coziness.
GENAU close, tight, exact, accurate.
　Er nimmt es sehr genau.　He is very
　　particular.
　Nehmen Sie es nicht zu genau!　Don't take
　　it too literally!
Genauigkeit f. exactness, accuracy, precision.
General m. general.
genesen to recover, get better.
Genesung f. recovery, convalescence.
genial highly gifted, brilliant.
Genialität f. genius, originality.
Genick n. nape (of neck).
Genie n. genius.
genieren to trouble, inconvenience, bother.
genießbar edible, drinkable.
genießen to eat, enjoy, have the benefit of.
Genosse m. companion, colleague.
GENUG sufficient, enough.
Genugtuung f. satisfaction, compensation.
Geographie f. geography.
GEPÄCK n. luggage, baggage.
Gepäckabfertigung f. luggage dispatch office.
Gepäckannahme m. luggage counter.
Gepäckaufbewahrung f. luggage checkroom.
Gepäckausgabe f. luggage office.
Gepäckschein m. receipt for registered
　　luggage.
Gepäckstück n. bag, parcel.
Gepäckträger m. porter.
GERADE direct, upright, straight, honest;
　　just, exactly, directly.
　nun gerade　now move than ever.
　geradeus　straight on.
Gerät n. tool, implement, utensil.
geraten to succeed, turn out well.
　sich in die Harre geraten　to come to
　　blows.
　Ihm gerät nichts.　He never succeeds in
　　anything.
　in Brand geraten　to catch fire.
geräumig roomy, spacious.
Geräusch n. noise.
geräuschvoll noisy.
GERECHT just, fair, equitable.
Gerechtigkeit f. justice, righteousness,
　　fairness.
Gerede n. talk, rumor, gossip.
Gereiztheit f. irritation.
Gericht n. dish, course, judgment.
　Jüngstes Gericht　Last Judgment.
　vor Gericht　in court.
Gerichtshof m. court of law.
gering small, little, unimportant.
　nicht im geringsten　not in the least.

geringfügig unimportant.
Gerippe n. skeleton.
GERN gladly, with pleasure, readily, easily.
　gern essen　to like (to eat something).
　Gern geschehen!　Don't mention it!
　gern haben　to like (a person or object).
　gern tun　(or any verb of action) to like (to
　　do something).
　Ich esse gern Eisbein mit Sauerkraut.
　　I like pig's knuckles with sauerkraut.
　Sie hat ihn gern.　She likes him.
　Tanzen Sie gern?　Do you like to dance?
Geruch m. smell, scent, odor.
geruchlos odorless.
Gerücht n. rumor, report.
Gerüst n. scaffold, stage.
GESANG m. song, singing.
　Gesanglehrer　m. singing teacher.
GESCHÄFT n. business, transaction,
　　commerce, commercial firm, store:
geschäftlich commercial.
Geschäftsführer m. manager.
Geschäftsmann m. businessman.
Geschäftsfrau f. businesswoman.
geschäftsmäßig commercial.
Geschäftsviertel n. shopping district.
Geschäftszeit f. office hours; **Sprechzeit** f.
　　doctor's office hours.
GESCHEHEN to happen, occur, be done.
　Es geschieht ihm recht.　It serves him
　　right.
　Es ist um mich geschehen.　I am done for.
　geschehen lassen　to allow, permit, let
　　happen.
gescheit clever, intelligent, sensible.
Geschenk n. present, gift.
GESCHICHTE f. story, history.
Geschichtsbuch n. history book.
Geschick n. fate, destiny.
geschickt clever, capable.
Geschirr n. crockery, dishes, china, tableware.
GESCHLECHT n. sex, gender, kind, species,
　　race, family, stock.
geschlechtlich sexual.
GESCHMACK m. taste, flavor.
　Geschmack finden an　to like.
geschmacklos insipid, in bad taste.
Geschmacklosigkeit f. bad taste.
geschmackvoll tasteful.
Geschrei n. shouting, screaming, clamor.
Geschwätz n. idle talk.
geschwätzig talkative, verbose.
geschwind quick, fast, swift, prompt, speedy.
Geschwindigkeit f. quickness, rapidity.
　Geschwindigkeitsgrenze 60 km　speed
　　limit 60 kilometers.
Geschwister pl. brother(s) and sister(s).
Geselle m. fellow, companion, journeyman.
Geselligkeit f. sociability, social life.

GESELLSCHAFT *f. society, association, company.*
  (jemandem) Gesellschaft leisten   *to keep (someone) company.*
  in Gesellschaft   *socially.*
Gesellschafter *m. partner.*
Gesellschaftsanzug *m. evening clothes.*
Gesellschaftskleidung *f. evening dress.*
  Gesellschaftskleidung erwünscht.   *evening dress requested.*
Gesellschaftsspiel *n. party game.*
Gesetz *n. law, statute.*
Gesetzbuch *n. code.*
gesetzlich *legal, lawful.*
gesetzwidrig *unlawful, illegal.*
GESICHT *n. vision, sight, hallucination, appearance, face.*
  Das steht Ihnen gut (zu Gesicht).   *It is very becoming to you.*
  Gesichter schneiden   *to make faces.*
  Sie lachte übers ganze Gesicht.   *She was all smiles.*
Gesichtszug *m. feature.*
Gesinnung *f. mind, way of thinking.*
gesinnungslos *unprincipled.*
gesinnungstreu *loyal.*
Gesinnugswechsel *m. change of opinion.*
gesittet *well-mannered.*
gespannt *stretched, strained.*
Gespenst *n. ghost.*
gespenstig *ghostly.*
Gespött *n. mockery, derision.*
GESPRÄCH *n. talk, conversation, discourse.*
gesprächig *talkative.*
Gesprächsstoff *m. topic of conversation.*
Gestalt *f. form, figure, shape, build, frame, manner, fashion.*
gestalten *to form.*
Geständnis *n. confession.*
  ein Geständnis ablegen über   *to make a confession.*
gestehen *to confess, admit.*
Gesträuch *n. shrubs, bushes, shrubbery.*
Gesuch *n. application, petition, request.*
GESUND *healthy, well, sound, natural.*
  gesunder Menschenverstand   *common sense.*
Gesundheit *f. health.*
  Gesundheit!   *God bless you!*
gesundheitlich *hygienic, sanitary.*
gesundheitshalber *for the sake of health.*
Getränk *n. drink, beverage.*
Getreide *n. grain.*
Getreidespeicher *m. granary.*
Getümmel *n. bustle, tumult.*
Gewächs *n. plant, growth, produce.*
gewachsen *equal to*
  Er ist der Arbeit gewachsen.   *He is equal to the task.*

  Er ist seinem Gegner gewachsen.   *He is a match for his opponent.*
Gewächshaus *n. conservatory (greenhouse).*
gewagt *risky.*
Gewähr *f. security, surety.*
gewähren *to grant.*
  jemanden gewähren lassen   *to let a person do as he pleases.*
GEWALT *f. power, authority, force, violence.*
  in der Gewalt haben   *to have command of, master.*
  mit aller Gewalt   *with all one's might.*
  sich in der Gewalt haben   *to have self-control.*
Gewaltherrschaft *f. despotism.*
gewaltsam *violent.*
gewalttätig *brutal, violent.*
gewandt *agile, skillful, clever.*
gewärtig *expecting, expectant.*
Gewebe *n. weaving, web, tissue, fabric.*
Gewehr *n. rifle, weapon.*
Gewerbe *n. trade, business, profession.*
Gewerbeschein *m. trade license.*
Gewerbeschule *f. trade, technical school.*
gewerbsmäßig *professional.*
Gewicht *n. weight.*
  ins Gewicht fallen   *to weigh with.*
gewichtig *weighty, important.*
Gewinn *m. winning.*
Gewinnanteil *m. dividend.*
gewinnbringend *profitable, lucrative.*
GEWINNEN *to gain, earn, win, produce, extract.*
Gewinner *m. winner.*
gewinnsüchtig *greedy (for victory).*
Gewirr *n. confusion, mess.*
GEWISS *certain, sure, fixed; certainly, indeed, of course, no doubt.*
  Gewiss!   *Surely!*
  In gewissem Sinne hat er recht.   *In a sense he is right.*
gewissenlos *unscrupulous.*
gewissermaßen *to some extent, so to speak, as it were.*
Gewissheit *f. certainty.*
Gewitter *n. thunderstorm.*
gewittern *to thunder.*
Gewitterregen *m. deluge.*
GEWÖHNEN *to accustom.*
  sich an etwas gewöhnen   *to get used to something.*
Gewohnheit *f. habit.*
gewöhnlich *usual, ordinary, common.*
gewöhnt *accustomed.*
Gewölbe *n. vault.*
Gewühl *n. turmoil, crowd.*
Gewürz *n. spice, seasoning, condiment.*
gewürzig *spiced.*
geziert *affected.*

gießen *to pour, water, spill.*

Gift *n. poison.*

giftig *poisonous, venomous.*

Gipfel *m. summit, peak, top.*

Gipfelpunkt *m. limit.*

Giraffe *f. giraffe.*

Gitter *n. railing, fence, grating.*

Glanz *m. brightness, glamour.*

glänzen *to shine, glitter, gleam.*

glänzend *shining, lustrous.*

Glanzleistung *f. (top) record, achievement.*

glanzvoll *brilliant, splendid, glorious.*

GLAS *n. glass, jar, pitcher.*

gläsern *of glass, vitreous.*

GLATT *even, smooth, slippery, flat; smoothly, slippery.*

Glatteis *n. slippery ice.*

Glaube *m. faith, confidence, trust, belief.*

GLAUBEN *to believe, trust, think, suppose.*

    Sie können ihm aufs Wort glauben. *You can take his word for it.*

glaubhaft *credible, likely, probable.*

gläubig *believing, faithful.*

gläublich *credible, likely.*

glaubwürdig *credible, reliable, authentic.*

Glaubwürdigkeit *f. credibility, authenticity.*

GLEICH *same, similar, alike, even, level, direct, equal, like, equivalent; equally, just, at once, immediately.*

    es einem gleich tun *to rival a person.*

    Es ist mir gleich. *It is all the same to me.*

    gleich darauf *immediately afterwards.*

    Gleich und Gleich gesellt sich gern. *Birds of a feather flock together.*

gleichberechtigt *entitled to the same rights.*

GLEICHEN *to be equal, resemble.*

gleichfalls *likewise.*

gleichförmig *uniform.*

gleichgesinnt *congenial.*

Gleichgewicht *n. equilibrium, balance, poise.*

gleichgültig *indifferent, unconcerned.*

Gleichgültigkeit *f. indifference.*

Gleichheit *f. equality, identity, similarity.*

gleichmäßig *proportional.*

Gleichstrom *m. direct current.*

gleichviel *no matter, just the same.*

gleichwertig *equivalent.*

gleichzeitig *simultaneous.*

Gletscher *m. glacier.*

Glied *n. limb, member, link.*

gliedern *to articulate, arrange, classify.*

glitzern *to glitter, glisten, twinkle.*

Globus *m. globe.*

Glocke *f. bell, clock.*

Glockenspiel *n. chime, carillon.*

Glockenturm *m. bell tower, belfry.*

GLÜCK *n. fortune, good luck, prosperity.*

    etwas auf gut Glück tun *to take a chance on something.*

    Glück haben *to be lucky.*

    Glück im Spiel, Unglück in der Liebe. *Lucky at cards, unlucky in love.*

    Glück wünschen *to congratulate.*

    Viel Glück! *Good luck! Many happy returns!*

    zu meinem Glück *fortunately.*

glücken *to succeed, be lucky.*

GLÜCKLICH *fortunate.*

    Glückliche Reise! *Have a pleasant trip!*

glücklicherweise *fortunately.*

Glücksfall *m. chance.*

Glücksspiel *n. game of chance.*

Glückwunsch *m. congratulations, good wishes.*

Glühbirne *f. electric bulb.*

glühen *to glow.*

glühend *glowing, fervent.*

Glühwurm *m. glowworm.*

Glut *f. glow, heat.*

Gnade *f. favor, mercy.*

Gnadengesuch *n. petition for clemency.*

GNÄDIG *merciful, gracious.*

    gnädige Frau *Madam.*

GOLD *n. gold.*

golden *gold, of gold, golden.*

Goldgrube *f. gold mine.*

goldig *shining like gold, adorable.*

    jedes Wort auf die Goldwaage legen *to weigh one's words carefully.*

Golf *m. golf.*

gönnen *to wish well, allow, permit; not to begrudge.*

Gotik *f. Gothic.*

GOTT *m. God.*

    Gott sei Dank! *Thank God!*

    Um Gottes willen! *For Heaven's sake!*

    Gott behüte! *God forbid!*

    in Gottes Namen! *in the name of God*

Götterdämmerung *f. twilight of the Gods.*

Gottesdienst *m. public worship, service (church).*

göttlich *divine, godlike.*

Grab *n. tomb, grave.*

Grabstein *m. tombstone.*

Grad *m. degree.*

Graf *m. count.*

Gräfin *f. countess.*

Gram *m. sorrow, grief.*

grämen *to grieve, worry.*

Gramm *n. gram. (1,000 grams equal 1 kilogram.)*

Grammatik *f. grammar.*

GRAS *n. grass.*

grässlich *terrible, horrible.*

Gräte *f. fish bone.*

Gratulant *m. congratulator, well-wisher.*

gratulieren *to congratulate.*

GRAU *gray.*

grauen *to be afraid, shudder, dread.*
　Es graut mir vor . . . *I am afraid of . . .*
grauenhaft *horrible, ghastly.*
grauenvoll *awful, dreadful.*
Grauhaar *n. gray hair.*
grausam *cruel.*
Grausamkeit *f. cruelty.*
grausig *gruesome, ghastly.*
Grazie *f. grace, charm.*
graziös *gracious.*
greifbar *tangible, palpable.*
greifen *to grip, grasp, catch, touch, strike.*
　ineinander greifen *to interlock.*
Greis *m. old man.*
Greisenalter *n. old age.*
Greisin *f. old woman.*
Grenze *f. boundary, limit, border.*
grenzenlos *boundless, infinite.*
Grenzverkehr *m. border traffic, border*
　　　trading.
Griff *m. grip, grasp, hold, catch.*
Grimm *m. anger, rage.*
grimmig *furious, grim.*
Grippe *f. influenza (flu).*
grob *thick, rough, coarse, clumsy.*
Grobheit *f. coarseness, rudeness.*
Groll *m. resentment, anger.*
grollen *to be resentful, angry.*
GROß *big, tall, large, great, huge, grand.*
　die großen Ferien *the summer vacation.*
　groß tun *to boast.*
　groß ziehen *to bring up.*
　große Kinder *grown-up children.*
　großer Buchstabe *capital letter.*
　im Großen und Ganzen *on the whole, for*
　　　the most part.
　das große Publikum *the general public.*
　eine große Zahl von *a great many (of).*
　groß auftreten *to assume airs.*
großartig *great, grand.*
GRÖßE *f. size, dimension, largeness, tallness,*
　　　celebrity, star.
Großeltern *pl. grandparents.*
Großhandel *m. wholesale trade.*
großjährig *of age.*
Großmacht *f. great power.*
großmütig *generous, magnanimous.*
Großmutter *f. grandmother.*
großspurig *arrogant.*
Großstadt *f. city.*
Großstädter *m. city dweller.*
größtenteils *for the most part, largely.*
Großvater *m. grandfather.*
großzügig *generous, on a large scale.*
Grün *n. green, verdure.*
GRÜN *green (adj.).*
　im Grünen *in country surroundings.*
　vom grünen Tisch aus *only in theory.*
GRUND *m. ground, bottom, cause, reason.*

　im Grunde *after all.*
　auf den Grund gehen *to investigate.*
　Aus welchem Grund? *For what reason?*
Grundbesitz *m. real estate.*
gründen *to found, establish, promote.*
Grundgedanke *m. fundamental idea.*
Grundlage *f. foundation.*
grundlegend *fundamental.*
gründlich *thorough, solid, profound.*
Gründlichkeit *f. thoroughness, solidity.*
Grundsatz *m. principle.*
grundsätzlich *fundamental.*
Grundstück *n. piece of land, lot.*
Gründung *f. foundation, establishment.*
grünen *to grow green, sprout.*
Gruppe *f. group.*
GRUß *m. greeting; salute (military).*
GRÜßEN *to greet, salute.*
　grüßen lassen *to send one's regards.*
gültig *valid, available, good, current.*
Gültigkeit *f. validity; currency (monetary).*
Gummi *m. rubber, eraser.*
Gummiabsatz *m. rubber heel.*
Gummiband *n. rubber band.*
Gummischuh *m. galosh.*
Gummiwaren *pl. rubber goods.*
Gunst *f. kindness, favor.*
　zu Gunsten von *in favor of.*
günstig *kind, favorable.*
Gurke *f. cucumber.*
Gürtel *m. belt, girdle.*
Guss *m. torrent, downpour.*
Gut *n. property, good, estate, farm.*
GUT *good, pleasant, kind, full; well,*
　　　pleasantly, kindly.
　es gut haben *to be well off.*
　Gute Besserung! *I hope you get well soon!*
　Guten Morgen! *Good morning!*
　kurz und gut *in short.*
　Schon gut! *All right!*
Gutachten *n. expert opinion, estimate.*
Gutachter *m. assessor, surveyor, consultant.*
gutartig *good-natured.*
Güte *f. kindness.*
Güterzug *m. freight train.*
gut gelaunt *in a good mood, in good spirits.*
gutgläubig *credulous.*
Guthaben *n. balance, credit.*
gut heißen *to approve, sanction.*
gutherzig *kindhearted; warmhearted.*
gütig *kind, good.*
gut machen *to make amends for.*
gutmütig *good-natured.*
Gutmütigkeit *f. good nature.*
Gutsbesitzer *m. landowner, gentleman farmer.*
Gutschein *m. token, voucher.*
gutwillig *willing, voluntary.*
Gymnasialbildung *f. classical education.*
Gymnasiast *m. (-in f.) high-school boy/girl.*

Gymnasium *n. high school.*
Gymnastik *f. gymnastics.*

H

HAAR *n.* (**Haare** *pl.*) *hair.*
  sich die Haare machen   *to do one's hair.*
  sich die Haare schneiden lassen   *to get a haircut.*
  Haare auf den Zähnen haben   *to stand up (to opponents).*
  um ein Haar   *nearly, narrowly; by a hair.*
  kein gutes Haar an einem lassen   *to pull a person to pieces.*
  sich in die Haare geraten   *to come to blows.*
  Lassen Sie sich darüber keine grauen Haare wachsen!   *Don't let that give you gray hair!*
Haarnadel *f. hairpin.*
Haarspalterei *f. hairsplitting.*
Haarwasser *n. hair tonic.*
Habe *f. property, belongings.*
  Hab und Gut   *goods and properties.*
  habhaft werden   *to obtain possession.*
HABEN *to have, own, possess, get.*
  Den Wievielten haben wir heute?   *What is the date today?*
  nichts auf sich haben   *to be of no consequence.*
  Recht haben   *to be right.*
  unter sich haben   *to be in charge of.*
  Was hast du?   *What is the matter with you?*
  zu haben sein   *to be obtainable.*
Habgier *f. greed, avarice.*
habgierig *greedy, avaricious.*
hacken *to chop, mince.*
Hafen *m. port, harbor.*
Hafenstadt *f. seaport.*
Haft *f. custody, arrest, detention.*
haftbar *responsible, liable.*
haften *to stick to, cling to.*
  haften für   *to answer for (bear the responsibility).*
Häftling *m. prisoner.*
haftpflichtig *liable, responsible.*
  mit beschränkter Haftung   *with limited liability.*
Haftung *f. liability, responsibility.*
Hagel *m. hail.*
Hagelschlag *m. hailstorm.*
HAHN *m. rooster, cock.*
Hai *m. shark.*
Haken *m. hook, mark.*
Halb *half.*
  auf halbem Wege   *midway, halfway.*
  ein halbes Pfund   *half a pound.*
  halb durchgebraten   *medium done (meat).*

  halb so viel   *half as much.*
  halb zwei   *half past one.*
  halb geschenkt   *practically given away.*
halbieren *to halve, bisect.*
Halbinsel *f. peninsula.*
Halbmond *m. crescent moon, half-moon.*
Hälfte *f. half.*
  Kinder zahlen die Hälfte.   *Children pay half price.*
Halle *f. hall, hangar.*
HALS *m. neck, throat.*
  Es hängt mir schon zum Hals heraus.   *I am sick and tired of it already.*
  Hals über Kopf   *headlong.*
  um den Hals fallen   *to embrace.*
  Es geht um den Hals.   *It's a matter of life and death.*
Halsband *n. necklace.*
halsbrecherisch *dangerous.*
Halsschmerzen *pl. sore throat.*
Halstuch *n. scarf.*
Halt *m. stop, halt, hold, footing.*
  Halt!   *Stop!*
haltbar *tenable, lasting, durable.*
Haltbarkeit *f. durability, defensibility.*
HALTEN *to hold, support, observe, keep, celebrate, last, stop, endure, continue, follow.*
  an sich halten   *to restrain oneself.*
  Et hält sich für sehr klug.   *He thinks he is very clever.*
  halt machen   *to stop.*
  halten für   *to consider, to think.*
  es halten mit   *to side with.*
  Halten Sie sich rechts!   *Keep to the right!*
  halten von   *to think of.*
  Was halten Sie von ihr?   *What do you think of her?*
  für schwer halten   *to be difficult.*
  sein Wort halten   *to keep one's word.*
  viel halten auf   *to think highly of.*
Haltestelle *f. stop, station.*
haltlos *without support, unsteady, unprincipled.*
Haltung *f. behavior, attitude, self-control.*
Hammer *m. hammer.*
HAND *f. hand, palm.*
  an der Hand führen   *to lead someone.*
  ihn auf den Händen tragen   *to treat him with every consideration.*
  aus zweiter Hand kaufen   *to buy something secondhand.*
  die Hände voll zu tun haben   *to be very busy.*
  Eine Hand wäscht die andere.   *One hand washes the other.*
  bei der Hand sein   *to be ready.*
  die Hand im Spiel haben   *to have a finger in the pie.*

einem die Hand geben *to shake hands with someone.*

Hand und Fuß haben *to be to the purpose.*

mit Händen und Füßen *with might and main (tooth and nail).*

unter der Hand *secretly.*

von der Hand gehen *to work well.*

von der Hand weisen *to decline.*

Handarbeit *f. manual work, labor.*

HANDEL *m. trade, business, affair.*

Handel treiben *to trade.*

handelseinig werden *to come to terms.*

handeln *to act, do.*

handeln mit *to trade with.*

handeln von *to deal with.*

sich handeln um *to be about, be a matter of.*

Handelskammer *f. chamber of commerce.*

Handfertigkeit *f. manual skill.*

Handgelenk *n. wrist.*

Handgepäck *n. hand luggage.*

handgreiflich *obvious, manifest.*

handgreiflich werden *to use one's fists.*

handhaben *to handle, manage.*

Handkoffer *m. suitcase.*

Händler *m. trader, dealer.*

handlich *handy.*

Handlung *f. act, action, deed, business.*

Handlungsweise *f. way of acting, method of dealing.*

Handschrift *f. handwriting.*

Handschuh *m. glove.*

Handstreich *m. surprise attack.*

Handtasche *f. handbag.*

Handtuch *n. towel.*

Handwerk *n. handicraft, trade.*

einem das Handwerk legen *to stop a person's illegal activities.*

hängen *to hang, suspend, fix, attach.*

hängen bleiben *to be caught.*

hänseln *to tease.*

Harm *m. grief, sorrow, insult, injury.*

harmlos *harmless.*

Harmlosigkeit *f. harmlessness, innocence.*

Harmonie *f. harmony.*

harmonieren *to harmonize, agree.*

HART *hard, firm, solid.*

hartherzig *hard-hearted.*

harthörig *hard of hearing.*

Härte *f. hardness, roughness, cruelty, severity.*

hartnäckig *obstinate, stubborn.*

Hase *m. hare.*

Hasenbraten *m. roast hare.*

Hass *m. hate, hatred.*

hassen *to hate.*

hässlich *ugly, nasty.*

Hässlichkeit *f. ugliness.*

Hast *f. hurry, haste.*

hastig *hurried, hasty.*

Haube *f. hood, cap.*

unter die Haube bringen *to marry off.*

Hauch *m. breath, slight breeze.*

hauchen *to breathe.*

Haufen *m. heap, pile.*

häufen *to heap, pile, accumulate.*

häufig *frequent, abundant.*

HAUPT *n. chief, head; principal.*

Hauptbahnhof *m. main station.*

Hauptmann *m. captain.*

Hauptperson *f. principal person, leading character (theater).*

Hauptpostamt *n. general post office.*

Hauptquartier *n. headquarters.*

Hauptsache *f. main thing.*

hauptsächlich *principal.*

Hauptstadt *f. capital.*

Hauptverkehrszeit *f. rush hour.*

Hauptwort *n. substantive, noun.*

HAUS *n. house, home, building.*

bei uns zu Hause *where I come from.*

das Haus hüten *to be confined to the house.*

nach Hause gehen *to go home.*

von Haus aus *originally.*

zu Hause *at home.*

Hausangestellte *m. & f. servant.*

Hausarbeit *f. housework.*

Hausaufgabe *f. homework.*

Häuschen *n. small house.*

Hausflur *m. hall, corridor.*

Hausfrau *f. housewife.*

Haushalt *m. household.*

haushalten *to keep house, to economize.*

Haushälterin *f. housekeeper.*

Hausherr *m. master.*

Hauslehrer *m. private tutor.*

häuslich *domestic.*

Häuslichkeit *f. family life, domesticity.*

Hausmeister *m. janitor.*

Hausschuh *m. slipper.*

Haussuchung *f. police raid.*

Haustier *n. domestic animal.*

Haustür *f. front door.*

Hauswirt *m. landlord.*

HAUT *f. skin, hide, coat.*

aus der Haut fahren *to lose one's patience.*

sich seiner Haut wehren *to defend oneself.*

Hautfarbe *f. complexion.*

heben *to lift, raise.*

Heer *n. army.*

Hefe *f. yeast.*

Heft *n. notebook, pamphlet.*

heften *to pin, fasten, stitch, fix.*

heftig *violent, strong.*

Heftigkeit *f. violence, vehemence, intensity.*

heikel *delicate, difficult.*

HEIL *unhurt, intact, safe, cured.*

heilbar *curable.*

heilen *to cure.*

heilig *holy, godly, sacred.*
   Heiligabend   *Christmas Eve.*
   heilighalten   *to hold sacred.*

heilkräftig *curative.*

Heilmittel *n. remedy.*

heilsam *curative.*

Heilsarmee *f. Salvation Army.*

Heilung *f. healing, cure.*

Heilverfahren *n. medical treatment.*

HEIM *n. home.*

heim *homeward.*

Heimat *f. native country, homeland.*

heimatlos *homeless.*

Heimatstadt *f. hometown.*

Heimkehr(-kunft) *f. homecoming.*

heimlich *secret, private, comfortable; secretly, privately.*

Heimsuchung *f. trial, misfortune.*

Heimtücke *f. malice.*

heimtückisch *malicious, insidious.*

Heimweg *m. way home, return.*

Heimweh *n. homesickness.*
   Heimweh haben   *to be homesick.*

HEIRAT *f. marriage.*

heiraten *to marry, get married.*

Heiratsantrag *m. proposal.*

heiser *hoarse.*
   heiser sein   *to be hoarse, have a sore throat.*

Heiserkeit *f. hoarseness, sore throat.*

HEIß *hot.*

HEIßEN *to call, name, be called.*
   das heißt   *that is.*
   es heißt   *they say.*
   Ich heiße Anna.   *My name is Ann.*
   Wie heißt das auf Englisch?   *What is that called in English?*
   jemand willkommen heißen   *to bid someone welcome.*

heiter *gay, cheerful.*

Heiterkeit *f. brightness, clearness, serenity, cheerfulness.*

heizbar *with heating.*

heizen *to heat.*

Heizkissen *n. heating pad.*

Heizung *f. heating, firing, radiator.*

Held *m. hero.*

HELFEN *to support, help, assist.*
   Ich kann mir nicht helfen.   *I can't help it.*

Helfer *m. helper, assistant.*

Helfershelfer *m. accomplice ("helper's helper").*

HELL *bright, shining, clear, light, fair, pale, sheer.*

Helle *f. clearness, brightness.*

hellhörig *keen of hearing.*

Helm *m. helmet.*

HEMD *n. shirt.*

hemmen *to check, stop, hinder, restrain.*

Hemmung *f. inhibition, check, stoppage, restraint.*

hemmungslos *free, unrestrained.*

HER 1. *adv. here, from, since, ago.*
   von Alters her   *of old, long ago.*
   2. *separable prefix (implies the idea of a movement toward the speaker).*
   Kommen Sie her!   *Come here!*

herab *down, downward.*

herablassen *to lower, let down, to stoop.*

Herablassung *f. condescension.*

herabsehen *to look down upon.*

herabsetzen *to lower, degrade, reduce (price).*

Herabsetzung *f. lowering, degradation; reduction (price).*

heran *on, up, near, along.*

heranbilden *to train, educate.*

herankommen *to come near.*
   die Dinge an sich herankommen lassen   *to bide one's time.*

heranwachsen *to grow up.*

HERAUF *up, upward.*

heraufgehen *to go up.*
   Kommen Sie herauf!   *Come up!*

HERAUS *out, from within.*
   Sie kommen heraus.   *They are coming out.*

herausbekommen *to get back (money); find out.*

herausnehmen *to take out, extract.*

herausstellen *to turn out, appear.*

herbei *here, near, hither.*

herbeischaffen *to bring near, procure, produce.*

HERBST *m. autumn.*

herbstlich *autumnal.*

Herd *m. hearth, fireplace.*

Herdplatte *f. hot plate.*

HEREIN *in.*
   Kommen Sie herein (Herein!)   *Come in!*
   Hier herein, bitte!   *This way, please!*

hereinfallen *to be taken in.*

herkommen *to come near, approach, originate.*

Herkunft *f. origin, descent.*

HERR *m. master, gentleman, lord, sir, Mr.*
   Meine Damen und Herren   *ladies and gentlemen.*
   Ist der Herr Doktor zu sprechen?   *Can I see the doctor?*
   eigener Herr sein   *to be one's own man.*
   Herr werden   *to master, overcome.*
   Herr im Hause sein   *to be the master of the house.*

herrichten *to arrange.*

herrisch *imperious, dictatorial.*

Herrschaft *f. power, rule, command, master and mistress (of an estate).*

herrschen *to rule, govern, prevail, exist.*

Herrscher *m. ruler, tyrant, dictator.*

herrschsüchtig *fond of power, tyrannical.*

herüber *across, to this side.*

herüberkommen *to come over.*

HERUM *around, round, near, about.*

  rundherum *all around.*

herumdrehen *to turn round.*

herumführen *to lead.*

herumreichen *to hand around.*

(sich) herumtreiben *to run around.*

HERUNTER *down, off.*

herunterkommen *to come down.*

  Komm gleich herunter! *Come down right away!*

heruntersetzen *to lower.*

hervor *out, forth.*

hervorbringen *to produce, yield.*

hervorheben *to make prominent.*

hervorragen *to stand out, project.*

hervorragend *prominent, excellent.*

(sich) hervortun *to distinguish oneself.*

Herz *n. heart, feeling, mind, courage.*

  ans Herz legen *to recommend to someone's care.*

  ins Herz schließen *to become fond of.*

  sich ein Herz fassen *to take courage.*

  sich zu Herzen nehmen *to take to heart.*

  von Herzen gern *with the greatest pleasure.*

  Was haben Sie auf dem Herzen? *What's on your mind?*

herzleidend *suffering from heart trouble.*

herzlich *hearty, cordial.*

  mit herzlichen Grüßen *with kindest regards.*

herzlos *heartless.*

Herzschlag *m. heart beat, heart failure.*

Heu *n. hay.*

Heufieber *n. hay fever.*

Heuchelei *f. hypocrisy.*

heucheln *to feign, pretend.*

Heuchler *m. hypocrite.*

HEUTE *today.*

  heute Abend *tonight.*

  heute früh; heute Morgen *this morning.*

  heute vor acht Tagen *a week ago.*

  heutzutage *nowadays.*

Hexe *f. witch.*

HIER *here.*

  hier und da *here and there.*

hierauf *hereupon.*

hierdurch *through this, this way, thereby.*

hierher *here, hither.*

hierherum *hereabout.*

hiermit *herewith, with this.*

hiernach *after this, thereupon.*

hierüber *over here, about this.*

hiervon *hereof, from this.*

hierzu *to this, moreover.*

HILFE *f. help, assistance, support, relief.*

  Hilfe leisten *to help, assist.*

  erste Hilfe *first aid.*

hilflos *helpless.*

hilfreich *helpful, charitable.*

hilfsbedürftig *indigent, needing help.*

HIMMEL *m. sky, heaven.*

  aus allen Himmeln fallen *to be bitterly disappointed.*

  Himmel und Menschen *a throng; many people.*

Himmelsrichtung *f. direction, point of compass.*

himmlisch *heavenly, celestial.*

HIN 1. *adv. there, thither.*

  hin und her *to and fro.*

  hin und her überlegen *to turn over in one's mind.*

  hin und wieder *now and then.*

  2. *separable prefix (implies the idea of a movement away from the speaker).*

  Gehen Sie hinaus! *Go out.*

hinab *down, downward.*

HINAUF *up, upward.*

  hinaufarbeiten *to work one's way up.*

  Er geht die Treppe hinauf. *He goes up the stairs.*

HINAUS *out, outside, past.*

  darüber hinaus *beyond that.*

  Ich schicke die Kinder hinaus. *I am sending the children outside.*

hinausgehen *to go out.*

hinauskommen *to come out.*

  auf eins hinauskommen *to come to the same thing.*

hinausschieben *to defer, postpone, put off.*

hinauswerfen *to throw out, expel.*

  hoch hinauswollen *to aim high.*

hinausziehen *to draw out, put off.*

Hinblick *m. look at or toward.*

  im Hinblick auf *with regard to.*

hinbringen *to take, bring, carry.*

hinderlich *in the way, hindering, obstructive.*

hindern *to prevent, hinder, hamper.*

hindurch *through, throughout, across.*

HINEIN *in, into.*

  Ich gehe in das Zimmer hinein. *I go into the room.*

hineingehen *to go into.*

hinfahren *to carry, drive to.*

Hinfahrt *f. to go there.*

hinfallen *to fall down.*

hinfällig *frail, weak.*

  hinfällig werden *to fail, come to nothing.*

hinfort *henceforth, in the future.*

Hingabe *f. surrender, devotion.*

hinhalten *to put off, to let someone wait.*

hinlänglich *sufficient, adequate.*

hinnehmen *to take, accept.*

hinsehen *to look at.*

(sich) hinsetzen *to set down, sit down.*

hinsichtlich *with regard to.*

hinstellen *to place, put down.*

hinten *behind, in the rear, at the back.*

HINTER 1. *prep. (dat. when answering the question* Wo? *acc. when answering the question* Wohin? *and depending on the idiom) behind, back, after.*

Hinter dem Haus ist eine Garage. *There is a garage behind the house.*

Sie hat schon viel hinter sich. *She has been through a lot.*

hinter sich bringen *to get over, cover.*

Hinterbliebene *m. & f. survivor.*

hintereinander *one after the other.*

zwei Tage hintereinander *two days running.*

Hintergedanke *m. underlying thought, unacknowledged motive.*

Hintergrund *m. background.*

Hinterhalt *m. ambush.*

hinterhältig *malicious, devious.*

hinterher *behind, afterward.*

hinterlassen *to leave, leave behind.*

Hat er keine Nachricht für mich hinterlassen? *Hasn't he left a message for me?*

hinterlistig *artful, cunning.*

Hinterrad *n. rear wheel.*

hinters (hinter das) *behind.*

HINÜBER *over, across, over there, to the other side.*

HINUNTER *down, downward, downstairs.*

Sie geht die Treppe hinunter. *She walks down the stairs.*

Hinweg *m. way there.*

hinweg *away, off.*

hinwegkommen (über) *to get over.*

hinwegsetzen (über) *to disregard.*

Hinweis *m. indication, hint, reference, direction.*

hinweisen *to show, indicate, refer.*

hinwerfen *to throw down.*

hinzu *to, near, there.*

hinzufügen *to add.*

hinzuziehen *to include, consult.*

Hirn *n. brain.*

Hitze *f. heat.*

hitzig *hot, hotheaded.*

HOCH *high, tall, lofty, great, noble.*

Es geht hoch her. *Things are getting pretty lively.*

Hände hoch! *Hands up!*

hoch anrechnen *to value greatly.*

Hoch leben . . . ! *Long live . . . !*

hochleben lassen *to toast.*

hochachten *to esteem, respect.*

Hochachtung *f. esteem, respect.*

hochachtungsvoll *yours respectfully.*

Hochbetrieb *m. intense activity.*

Hochdeutsch *n. high German, standard German.*

hochhalten *to cherish, raise.*

Hochhaus *n. skyscraper.*

hochherzig *high-minded, magnanimous.*

Hochmut *m. pride, arrogance.*

hochmütig *arrogant, proud.*

Hochschule *f. university, college.*

Hochsommer *m. midsummer.*

Hochspannung *f. high tension.*

Vorsicht! Hochspannung! *Caution! High tension wires!*

HÖCHST *highest, utmost, extreme, maximum; very, extremely.*

Hochstapelei *f. swindling.*

Hochstapler *m. swindler.*

höchstens *at best, at most.*

Höchstgeschwindigkeit *f. top speed, speed limit.*

Höchstgrenze *f. limit.*

Höchstleistung *f. maximum output, record performance.*

höchstwahrscheinlich *most likely.*

hochtrabend *high-sounding, pretentious.*

Hochverrat *m. high treason.*

Hochzeit *f. wedding, marriage.*

Hochzeitsreise *f. honeymoon trip.*

HOF *m. yard, court, farm.*

den Hof machen *to pay court to.*

HOFFEN *to hope.*

hoffen auf *to hope for.*

hoffentlich *hopefully.*

Hoffnung *f. hope.*

sich falsche Hoffnungen machen *to have false hopes.*

hoffnungslos *hopeless.*

hoffnungsvoll *hopeful.*

HÖHE *f. height, altitude, latitude, top, summit, amount.*

auf der Höhe sein *to be up-to-date, to be in top form.*

auf gleicher Höhe mit *on the same level with.*

sich nicht auf der Höhe fühlen *not to feel up to par.*

auf der Höhe von *at the altitude of.*

aus der Höhe *from on high.*

Das ist die Höhe. *That is the limit.*

in (der) Höhe von *in the amount of.*

Höhenstrahlen *pl. cosmic rays.*

höher *higher, superior.*

HOHL *hollow, concave, dull.*

Höhle *f. hole, cave.*

Hohlraum *m. empty space, cavity.*

Hohn *m. scorn, sneer, mockery, insult.*

höhnen *to mock, defy.*

höhnisch *scornful, sneering.*

HOLEN *to get, take, fetch.*
  sich Rat holen *to consult.*
  sich eine Erkältung holen *to catch a cold.*
  Atem holen *to catch one's breath.*
HÖLLE *f. hell.*
höllisch *hellish, infernal.*
HOLZ *n. wood, timber, lumber.*
hölzern *wooden.*
Honig *m. honey.*
horchen *to listen, lend an ear, listen in, spy.*
  Es horcht jemand. *Somebody is listening in.*
HÖREN *to hear, listen, attend, obey, understand.*
  schwer hören *to be hard-of-hearing.*
Horizont *m. horizon.*
Horn *n. horn, bugle.*
Horoskop *n. horoscope.*
  ein Horoskop stellen *to cast a horoscope.*
Hörspiel *n. radio play.*
Hose *f. trousers, pants.*
  Sie hat die Hosen an. *She wears the pants.*
Hosenträger *pl. suspenders.*
Hotel *n. hotel, inn.*
hübsch *pretty, charming, nice.*
Huf *m. hoof.*
Hügel *m. hill.*
HUHN *n. hen.*
  gebratenes Hühnchen *roast chicken.*
  junges Huhn *young chicken.*
Huld *f. grace, favor, charm.*
huldigen *to pay homage.*
Humor *m. sense of humor.*
humoristisch *humorous.*
HUND *m. dog.*
Hundert *n. hundred.*
  zu Hunderten *by the hundreds.*
HUNDERT *one hundred (adj.)*
HUNGER *m. hunger.*
  Hunger haben *to be hungry.*
hungern *to be hungry, starve.*
Hungersnot *f. famine.*
hungrig *hungry.*
husten *to cough.*
  Hustensirup *m. cough syrup.*
HUT *m. hat.*
  unter einen Hut bringen *to reconcile.*
hüten *to guard, keep, beware.*
  das Zimmer hüten *to be confined to one's room.*
Hütte *f. hut.*

I

ICH *I, self, ego.*
Ideal *n. ideal.*
Idealist *m. idealist.*

Idee *f. idea, notion.*
identifizieren *to identify.*
identisch *identical.*
IHM *dat. of er, es. (pers. pron., masc. and neut.) to him, to it.*
IHN *acc. of er (pers. pron. masc.) him, it.*
IHNEN (ihnen) *dat. of sie (pers. pron. pl) to them.*
IHNEN (Ihnen) *dat. of Sie (pers. pron. sing. polite form) to you.*
IHR *dat. of sie (pers. pron. fem.) to her, to it.*
IHR (Ihr) *poss. adj. (fem. and pl.) her, its, their.*
IHR (Ihr) *poss. adj. (sing. polite form) your.*
IHR (-ER, -E, -ES) *poss. pron. (fem. and pl.) hers, its, theirs.*
  poss. pron. (sing. polite form) your.
ihretwegen *on her (its, their) account, for her sake.*
Ihretwegen *on your account, for your sake.*
illustrieren *to illustrate.*
imitieren *to imitate.*
IMMER *always, ever.*
  auf immer *forever.*
  immer mehr *more and more.*
  immer wieder *again and again.*
  immerfort *continually, constantly.*
  wer auch immer *whoever.*
immerhin *for all that, still, nevertheless.*
immerzu *all the time, continually.*
imponieren *to impress.*
Import *m. imports, importation.*
Impuls *m. impulse.*
impulsiv *impulsive.*
IN *prep. (dat. answers the question Wo? acc. answers the question Wohin?) in, into, to, at.*
  Die Besucher gehen in die Oper. *The spectators go to the opera.*
  Der Lehrer sitzt in dem Zimmer. *The teacher is sitting in the room.*
  Der Lehrer tritt in das Zimmer ein. *The teacher goes into the room.*
  Der Sänger singt in der Oper. *The singer sings in the opera.*
  Goethe wurde in Frankfurt geboren. *Goethe was born in Frankfurt.*
  im Februar *in February.*
  im Kreise *in a circle.*
Inbegriff *m. embodiment, essence.*
inbegriffen *including, inclusive, included.*
INDEM *while, by, on, since.*
indirekt *indirect.*
indiskret *indiscreet, tactless.*
Indiskretion *f. indiscretion.*
Industrie *f. industry.*
Industrieller *m. manufacturer, producer.*
Infektionskrankheit *f. infectious disease.*

infolge *in consequence of, as a result of.*
  infolgedessen *because of that, consequently, hence.*
Ingenieur *m.* (-in *f.*) *engineer.*
Inhaber *m. proprietor.*
Inhalt *m. contents, area, extent, volume, capacity.*
inhaltlich *with regard to the contents.*
Inhaltsangabe *f. summary, table of contents.*
inhaltsleer *empty, meaningless.*
inhaltsreich *full of meaning, significant.*
Inhaltsverzeichnis *n. contents, table of contents, index.*
inmitten *in the midst of.*
innen *within, inside, in.*
INNER *interior, internal, inner.*
innerhalb *within, inside.*
innerlich *inward, internal, interior.*
innig *hearty, intimate.*
Innigkeit *f. intimacy, cordiality.*
ins (**in das**) *into that, into it.*
insbesondere *particularly.*
Inschrift *f. inscription, legend.*
Insekt *n. insect.*
INSEL *f. island.*
Inserat *n. advertisement.*
inserieren *to advertise.*
insgesamt *all together, collectively.*
insofern *in so far, as far as that goes.*
insoweit *in so far.*
Instandhaltung *f. upkeep.*
inständig *instant, urgent.*
Instinkt *m. instinct.*
instruieren *to instruct, brief.*
Instrument *n. instrument.*
intelligent *intelligent.*
Intelligenz *f. intelligence, understanding, intellect.*
interessant *interesting.*
Interesse *n. interest, advantage.*
interessieren *to interest.*
  sich interessieren (für) *to be interested in.*
international *international.*
interviewen *to interview.*
Inventar *n. inventory, stock.*
investieren *to invest.*
inzwischen *in between, in the meantime.*
IRGEND *any, some.*
  wenn irgend möglich *if at all possible.*
irgendetwas *something.*
irgendjemand *somebody, anybody.*
irgendwann *sometime.*
irgendwie *somehow.*
irgendwo *somewhere.*
irgendwoher *from some place or other.*
irgendwohin *to somewhere or other.*
ironisch *ironical.*
irre *astray, wrong, confused, insane.*
  irre werden an *to lose confidence in.*

IRRE *f. wandering, mistaken course.*
  in die Irre gehen *to lose one's way, go astray.*
  Irre machen *to confuse.*
irren *to err, wander, lose one's way, be mistaken, be wrong.*
  sich irren *to be mistaken.*
  irren ist menschlich *to err is human.*
Irrenanstalt *f. lunatic asylum.*
irrereden *to talk incoherently, to rave.*
irritieren *to irritate.*
Irrsinn *m. madness, insanity.*
irrsinnig *mad, insane.*
Irrtum *m. error, mistake.*
  Sie sind im Irrtum. *You are mistaken.*
irrtümlich *erroneous, wrong.*
Israeli *m. Israeli (person).*
israelisch *Israeli.*
Italiener *m. Italian (person).*
Italienisch *n. Italian (language).*
italienisch *Italian.*

J

JA *yes, really, indeed, certainly.*
  Da sind Sie ja! *So there you are!*
  Sie wissen ja, dass ich nicht gehen kann. *But you know that I can't go.*
  ja sogar *even.*
Jacke *f. jacket.*
Jackenkleid *n. lady's suit.*
JAGD *f. hunt, pursuit, hunting, shooting.*
  auf die Jagd gehen *to go hunting.*
Jagdschein *m. hunting license.*
jagen *to chase, pursue.*
Jäger *m. hunter, huntsman, sportsman.*
jäh *sudden, quick, steep.*
JAHR *n. year.*
  ein halbes Jahr *six months.*
Jahrestag *m. anniversary.*
Jahreswende *f. New Year, turn of the year.*
JAHRESZEIT *f. season.*
Jahrhundert *n. century.*
jährlich *yearly, annual.*
Jahrmarkt *m. fair.*
Jahrtausend *n. thousand years, millennium.*
Jahrzehnt *n. decade.*
Jähzorn *m. sudden anger, violent temper.*
jähzornig *hot-tempered, irascible.*
Jammer *m. misery, wailing.*
  Was für ein Jammer! *What a pity!*
jammern *to lament, wail, moan.*
JANUAR *m. January.*
Japaner *m. Japanese (person).*
japanisch *Japanese (language).*
jauchzen *to exult, shout, rejoice.*
JAWOHL *of course, indeed.*

JE *each, ever, at all times.*
  je zwei *two at a time.*
  Sie erhielten je ein Pfund. *They received a*
    pound each.
  je nach *according to.*
  je nachdem *according as.*
  Je eher umso (desto) besser. *The sooner,*
    the better.
jedenfalls *at all events, in any case.*
JEDER (jede, jedes) *every, each, either,*
  any.
jedermann *everyone, everybody.*
jederzeit *at any time, always.*
jedesmal *every time.*
  jedesmal wenn *whenever, as often as.*
jedoch *however, nevertheless.*
jeher (von jeher) *at all times, from times*
  immemorial.
jemals *at any time.*
jemand *somebody, someone.*
JENER (jene, jenes) *that, that one, the*
  former, the other.
  jenseitig *opposite, on the opposite side.*
JENSEITS 1. *adv. beyond, on the other side,*
  yonder.
  2. *prep. (gen.) that side, on the other side.*
  Er wohnt jenseits des Flusses. *He lives on*
    the other side of the river.
jetzig *present, actual.*
JETZT *now, at present.*
Joch *n. yoke.*
Jod *n. iodine.*
Journalist *m. (-in f.) journalist.*
Jubel *m. rejoicing, jubilation.*
Jude *m. Jew.*
Jüdin *f. Jew, Jewish woman.*
jüdisch *Jewish.*
JUGEND *f. youth, young people.*
Jugendfreund *m. friend of youth.*
jugendlich *youthful.*
Jugendliche *m. & f. young boy or girl.*
Jugendliebe *f. first love.*
Jugendzeit *f. youth, young days.*
JULI *m. July.*
JUNG *young, youthful.*
Junge *m. boy, lad.*
jungenhaft *boyish.*
jünger *younger.*
Jungfrau *f. virgin, maid, maiden.*
  alte Jungfer *old maid.*
Junggeselle *m. bachelor.*
Jüngling *m. young man.*
JUNI *m. June.*
Jura *pl. law.*
  Jura studieren *to study law.*
Jurist *m. (-in f.) law student, lawyer.*
Justiz *f. administration of the law.*
Juwel *n. jewel.*
Juwelier *m. jeweler.*

K

Kabarett *n. cabaret.*
Kabine *f. cabin.*
Kachel *f. glazed tile.*
KAFFEE *m. coffee.*
Kaffeekanne *f. coffeepot.*
Käfig *m. cage.*
kahl *bald, bare, naked.*
kahlköpfig *bald.*
Kai *m. wharf.*
Kaiser *m. emperor.*
Kalb *n. calf.*
Kalbfleisch *n. veal.*
  Kalbsbraten *m. roast veal.*
Kalender *m. calendar.*
kalkulieren *to calculate.*
KALT *cold, indifferent.*
kaltblütig *cold-blooded.*
Kälte *f. coldness, indifference.*
Kamel *n. camel.*
Kamera *f. camera.*
Kamerad *m. friend, comrade, fellow.*
Kameradschaft *f. fellowship, comradeship.*
Kamin *m. chimney, fireplace.*
Kamm *m. comb.*
kämmen *to comb.*
Kammer *f. small room, chamber*
  (government).
Kammermusik *f. chamber music.*
KAMPF *m. fight, combat, conflict, struggle.*
  Kampf ums Dasein *struggle for a living.*
KÄMPFEN *to fight.*
Kanadier *m. Canadian (person).*
kanadisch *Canadian.*
Kanal *m. canal, sewer.*
Kanarienvogel *m. canary.*
Kandidat *m. candidate.*
kandidieren *to be a candidate.*
Kaninchen *n. rabbit.*
Kanne *f. jug, pot, pitcher.*
Kanone *f. cannon.*
Kante *f. edge, corner.*
kantig *edged, angular.*
Kantine *f. canteen, mess.*
Kanzel *f. pulpit.*
Kapelle *f. chapel, band or orchestra.*
Kapital *n. capital.*
Kapitalanlage *f. investment.*
Kapitalismus *m. capitalism.*
Kapitalist *m. capitalist.*
kapitalkräftig *wealthy.*
Kapitän *m. captain.*
Kapitel *n. chapter.*
kapitulieren *to capitulate.*
kaputt *broken, ruined, out of order.*
Karfreitag *m. Good Friday.*
Karikatur *f. caricature.*

Karneval m. carnival.

Karotte f. carrot.

Karriere f. career, gallop.

KARTE f. card, ticket, map, menu.
　Karten legen　to tell one's fortune.

Kartenspiel n. card game, pack of cards.

KARTOFFEL f. potato
　Kartoffelpüree n.　mashed potatoes.
　Bratkartoffeln pl.　fried potatoes.
　Kartoffelsalat m.　potato salad.

Karton m. cardboard, box.

Karwoche f. Passion Week.

KÄSE m. cheese.

Kaserne f. barracks.

Kasse f. cash register.
　Zahlen Sie, bitte, an der Kasse!　Please
　　pay at the cash register.

Kassenschein m. receipt.

kassieren to receive money.

Kassierer m. cashier.

Kastanie f. chestnut.

Kasten m. box, chest, mailbox.

Katalog m. catalog.

Katastrophe f. catastrophe.

katastrophal catastrophic.

Katholik m. Roman Catholic.

katholisch Roman Catholic (adj.).

Katze f. cat.

kauen to masticate, chew.
　Kaugummi　n. chewing gum.

KAUF m. buy, purchase.
　mit in Kauf nehmen　to put up with.

KAUFEN to buy, purchase.
　sich etwas kaufen　to buy oneself
　　something.

Käufer m. buyer.

Kaufhaus n. department store, store,
　warehouse.

Kaufladen m. store, shop.

Kaufmann m. shopkeeper, merchant.

KAUM hardly, scarcely, barely.

Kavalier m. cavalier, gentleman.

keck bold, daring, impudent.

Keckheit f. boldness.

Kegel m. ninepin.
　mit Kind und Kegel　with bag and
　　baggage.

kegeln to bowl.

Kehle f. throat.

Kehlkopf m. larynx.

KEHREN turn, to sweep.
　ihm den Rücken kehren　to turn one's back
　　to him.
　kehrtmachen　to face about, turn back.

KEIN adj. no, not one, not any.

KEIN (-ER, -E, -ES) pron. none, neither.
　keiner von beiden　neither of them.

keinerlei of no sort.

KEINESWEGS on no account, not at all.

Kelch m. cup, goblet, chalice.

Keller m. cellar.

KELLNER m (-in, f.) waiter, (waitress).

KENNEN to know, be acquainted with.
　kennenlernen　to meet, become acquainted
　　with.

Kenner m. connoisseur.

Kennkarte f. identity card.

kenntlich recognizable, distinguishable.

KENNTNIS f. knowledge, information.
　in Kenntnis setzen　to inform.
　zur Kenntnis nehmen　to take note of.

Kennzeichen n. identity, mark.

Kern m. kernel, corn, seed, pit (fruit).

Kerze f. candle, spark plug.

Kessel m. boiler, kettle.

Kette f. chain, necklace.

Kettenhund m. watch dog.

keuchen to pant, puff.

Keuchhusten m. whopping cough.

Keule f. club, leg (of lamb, etc.).

keusch pure, chaste.

Keuschheit f. purity, chastity.

Kiefer m. jaw.

Kilogramm n. kilogram (2.204 pounds).

Kilometer m. kilometer (.621 miles).

Kilometerzähler m. odometer.

KIND n. child.
　kleines Kind　baby (infant).
　von Kind auf　from childhood on.

Kinderernährung baby feeding.

Kindergarten m. kindergarten, nursery
　school.

kinderlos childless.

Kindermädchen n. nursemaid.

Kinderstube f. nursery.

Kinderwagen m. baby carriage.

Kindheit f. childhood.

kindisch childish.

kindlich childlike.

Kinn n. chin.

Kino n. cinema, movies.

Kirche f. church, service.

Kirchhof m. cemetery.

Kirchtum m. church steeple.

Kirsche f. cherry.

Kissen n. cushion, pillow.

Kissenbezug m. cover, pillowcase.

Kiste f. box, chest, case.

kitzeln to tickle.

kitzlig ticklish.

Klage f. lament, complaint.

klagen to lament, complain, sue.

Kläger m. plaintiff.

kläglich lamentable, deplorable.

klamm numb, stiff, tight.

klammern to fasten, clasp, cling to.

Klang m. sound, tone, ringing of bell.

Klangfarbe f. timbre.

klanglos *soundless.*

klangvoll *sonorous.*

Klappstuhl *m. folding chair.*

Klapptisch *m. folding table.*

Klaps *m. slap.*

KLAR *clear, limpid, pure, plain, evident.*

  klar und deutlich *distinctly, plainly.*

  klar zum Gefecht *ready for action.*

  klar legen (stellen) *to clear up, explain.*

  sich klar darüber sein *to realize.*

Klarinette *f. clarinet.*

Klarinettist *m. clarinettist.*

KLASSE *f. class, form, order.*

Klassenlehrer *m. classroom teacher.*

Klassenzimmer *n. classroom.*

Klassik *f. classical art, classical period.*

Klatsch *m. smack, crack, slap, gossip.*

klatschen *to clap, lash, applaud, gossip.*

  Beifall klatschen *to applaud.*

Klavier *n. piano.*

Klavierspieler *m. pianist.*

kleben *to stick, glue.*

Klee *m. clover, shamrock.*

KLEID *n. dress, frock, gown.*

  die Kleider *pl. garments.*

kleiden *to dress, clothe, suit, become.*

  Er ist immer gut gekleidet. *He is always well-dressed.*

Kleiderbügel *m. coathanger.*

Kleiderbürste *f. clothes brush.*

Kleiderschrank *m. wardrobe.*

Kleidung *f. dress, clothes, clothing.*

KLEIN *little, small, tiny, minor.*

  klein schneiden *to cut in pieces.*

  klein schreiben *to write with small letters.*

  von klein auf *from infancy on.*

klein denken *to have narrow views.*

KLEINGELD *n. change (monetary).*

kleingläubig *of little faith.*

Kleinholz *n. sticks, firewood.*

Kleinkram *m. trifle.*

Kleinstadt *f. small provincial town.*

kleinstädtisch *provincial.*

klettern *to climb.*

Klima *n. climate.*

klimatisch *climatic.*

Klingel *f. bell.*

klingeln *to ring.*

Klinke *f. doorknob; handle.*

klipp *snapping sound, snap of the fingers.*

  klipp und klar *quite clear.*

klirren *to clink, jingle.*

klopfen *to beat, knock, tap.*

Kloster *n. monastery, convent.*

Klub *m. club.*

Klubsessel *m. lounge chair, easy chair.*

KLUG *intelligent, sensible, clever.*

  Ich werde nicht klug daraus. *I can't figure it out.*

Klugheit *f. intelligence.*

Klumpen *m. lump.*

KNABE *m. boy, lad.*

Knall *m. bang, detonation, crack.*

knapp *narrow, tight, close, poor.*

  knapp werden *to run short of.*

Knappheit *f. scarcity, shortage.*

Knecht *m. servant, farmhand, slave.*

Knechtschaft *f. servitude, slavery.*

kneifen *to pinch, nip.*

Kneipe *f. tavern, bar.*

Knie *n. knee.*

Kniehosen *pl. breeches, shorts.*

knistern *to rustle, crackle.*

KNOCHEN *m. bone.*

knöchern *of bone, bony.*

Knopf *m. button, knob, head.*

knöpfen *to button.*

Knopfloch *n. buttonhole.*

Knospe *f. bud.*

Knoten *m. knot.*

knurren *to growl, rumble.*

knusprig *crisp.*

Koch *m. cook.*

Kochbuch *n. cookbook.*

KOCHEN *to cook, boil.*

Kochgeschirr *n. pots and pans.*

Köchin *f. cook.*

Kochlöffel *m. ladle.*

Kochtopf *m. saucepan, pot, casserole.*

Koffer *m. trunk, bag, suitcase.*

Kognak *m. cognac, brandy.*

Kohl *m. cabbage.*

Kohle *f. coal, carbon.*

  auf Kohlen sitzen *to be on tenterhooks.*

Koje *f. cabin, berth.*

Kollege *m.* **(Kollegin** *f.)* *colleague.*

Kolonialwaren *pl. groceries.*

Kolonialwarenhandlung *f. grocery store.*

Komiker *m. comedian.*

komisch *comical, strange, odd.*

Komma *n. comma.*

kommandieren *to command, order.*

KOMMEN *to come, arrive, get, result, happen, occur.*

  Das kommt davon. *That's the result.*

  Das kommt nicht in Frage. *This is out of the question.*

  Es kommt darauf an. *It depends.*

  kommen lassen *to send for.*

  kommen sehen *to foresee.*

  nicht dazu kommen *to have no time to.*

  Wann komme ich an die Reihe? *When will it be my turn?*

  Wie kommet es, dass *how is it that.*

  zu sich kommen *to recover.*

kommend *next.*

  kommende Woche *next week.*

Kommentar *m. commentary.*

Kommode f. chest of drawers.

Komödiant m. comedian, hypocrite.

Komödie f. comedy.

Kompass m. compass.

komplett complete; completely.

Kompliment n. compliment.

komponieren to compose.

Komponist m. composer.

Konditor m. pastry cook.

Konditorei f. pastry shop, cafe.

Konfekt n. candy, chocolates, sweets.

Konfektion f. ready-made clothes.

Konferenz f. conference.

Konfession f. confession.

Konfitüre f. preserves, jam.

Konflikt m. conflict.

KÖNIG m. king.

königlich royal.

Konkurrent m. rival.

Konkurrenz f. competition.

konkurrieren to be in competition with, compete.

Konkurs m. bankruptcy.
   Konkurs anmelden   to declare bankruptcy.

KÖNNEN to be able to, be possible, understand.
   Das kann sein.   It may be.
   Das kann nicht sein.   It is impossible.
   Ich kann nicht mehr.   I am exhausted.
   Er kann nichts dafür.   It is not his fault.

konsequent consistent.

Konsequenz f. consistency, consequence.

konservativ conservative.

Konservatorium n. academy of music.

Konserve f. canned goods.

konstruieren to construct.

Konstrukteur m. construction worker.

Konsul m. consul.

Konsulat n. consulat.

Kontinent m. continent.

Konto n. account (financial).

Kontoauszug m. statement (account).

Kontrakt m. contract.

Kontrast m. contrast.

Kontrolle f. control.

Kontrolleur m. controller.

kontrollieren to control.

Kontroverse f. controversy.

Konversationslexikon n. encyclopedia.

Konzert n. concert.

KOPF m. head, brains, intellect, heading.
   auf den Kopf stellen   to turn upside down.
   aus dem Kopf   by heart.
   einem den Kopf waschen   to give a person a dressing-down.
   Es ist mir über den Kopf gewachsen.   It went right over my head.
   im Kopf behalten   to remember.
   Kopf oder Zahl   heads or tails.

   nicht auf den Kopf gefallen sein   to be no fool.
   sich den Kopf zerbrechen   to rack one's brains.
   sich etwas aus dem Kopf schlagen   to dismiss something from one's mind.
   sich in den Kopf setzen   to take into one's head.
   vor den Kopf stoßen   to hurt, offend.
   den Kopf verlieren   to lose one's head.
   ihm über den Kopf wachsen   to be in over his head.

Kopfarbeit f. brain work; white-collar work.

Kopfkissen n. pillow.

Kopfsalat m. head of lettuce.

kopfscheu timid.

Kopfschmerzen pl. headache.
   Ich habe Kopfschmerzen.   I have a headache.

Kopfweh n. headache.

Korb m. basket.

Kork m. cork, stopper.

Korkenzieher m. corkscrew.

Korn n. grain.
   aufs Korn nehmen   to aim at.

KÖRPER m. body.

körperlich bodily, physical.

Körperpflege f. physical culture, care of the body.

Körperwärme f. body heat.

korrekt correct.

Korrespondenz f. correspondence.

Korridor m. corridor.

korrigieren to correct.

Kosmetik f. cosmetics.

Kost f. food, board.

kostbar precious, costly; valuable.

Kostbarkeit f. preciousness, object of valor.

Kosten f. costs, expenses.
   auf seine Kosten kommen   to recover expenses, be satisfied with the deal.

KOSTEN to cost, require, taste.

kostenlos free (of charge).

kostenpflichtig liable for the cost.

Kostenpunkt f. expenses.

Kostenvoranschlag m. estimate.

köstlich precious, valuable, delicious.

kostspielig expensive.

Kostüm n. costume, tailored suit.

Kostümfest n. fancy dress ball.

Kotelett n. cutlet, chop.

Krabbe f. shrimp, crab.

Krach m. crash; noise, quarrel.
   mit Ach und Krach   with difficulty, just barely.

KRAFT f. strength, energy, power.
   außer Kraft setzen   to annul, abolish.
   Das geht über meine Kräfte.   That's too much for me.

in Kraft treten   *to come into force, effect.*

nach bestern Kräften   *to the best of one's ability.*

zu Kräften kommen   *to regain one's strength.*

kräftig *robust, strong.*

kraftlos *weak, feeble.*

Kragen *m. collar.*

KRANK *ill, sick.*

sich krank lachen   *to split one's sides (with laughter).*

krank werden   *to be taken ill.*

Kranke *m. patient.*

Krankenhaus *n. hospital.*

Krankenschwester *f. nurse.*

Krankenwagen *m. ambulance.*

Krankheit *f. illness, disease.*

Kranz *m. wreath, garland.*

kraus *crisp, curly.*

die Stirne krausziehen   *to knit one's brow.*

Kraut *n. cabbage.*

Krawatte *f. necktie.*

Krebs *m. crab, cancer.*

Kredit *f. credit.*

KREIS *m. circle, social group.*

einen Kreis ziehen   *to describe a circle.*

sich im Kreise drehen   *to turn around, rotate.*

in allen Kreisen des Lebens   *in every walk of life.*

kreisen *to circle, revolve, circulate.*

Kreislauf *m. circulation, course, revolution.*

KREUZ *n. cross; clubs (cards).*

das Kreuz schlagen   *to cross oneself.*

das Rote Kreuz   *the Red Cross.*

kreuz und quer   *in all directions.*

Kreuzung *f. crossing, intersection.*

Eisenbahnkreuzung   *railroad crossing.*

Kreuzverhör *n. cross-examination.*

Kreuzworträtsel *n. crossword puzzle.*

kriechen *to creep, crawl.*

KRIEG *m. war.*

im Krieg   *in wartime.*

Krieg führen   *to make war.*

Kriegsgefangener *m. prisoner of war.*

Kriegsschauplatz *m. theater of war.*

Kriminalpolizei *f. criminal investigation department.*

Kriminalroman *m. detective story.*

Kritik *f. criticism.*

Kritiker *m. critic.*

kritiklos *uncritical, undiscriminating.*

kritisch *critical.*

kritisieren *to criticize.*

Krone *f. crown.*

Kronleuchter *m. chandelier.*

Krug *m. pitcher, jar.*

Krümel *n. crumb.*

krümeln *to crumble.*

krumm *crooked, curved, bent.*

krümmen *to bend.*

Krümmung *f. curve.*

Krüppel *m. cripple.*

Kristall *n. crystal.*

KÜCHE *f. kitchen, cooking.*

Kuchen *m. cake, pastry.*

Küchenherd *m. stove.*

Kugel *f. bullet, ball, globe, sphere.*

Kuh *f. cow.*

Er ist bekannt wie eine bunte Kuh.   *He is well-known everywhere ("as well as a colorful cow").*

KÜHL *cool, fresh, chilly.*

Kühlanlage *cold storage plant.*

Kühle *f. coolness, freshness.*

kühlen *to cool.*

Kühler *m. radiator (car).*

Kühlschrank *m. refrigerator.*

Kühlung *f. cooling, freshness.*

kühn *bold, daring, audacious.*

Kühnheit *f. boldness, audacity.*

Kulisse *f. wing (of a stage).*

hinter den Kulissen   *backstage; behind the scenes (secretly).*

kultivieren *to cultivate.*

Kultur *f. culture.*

Kummer *m. grief, sorrow.*

kummervoll *sad, sorrowful.*

Kunde *f. customer, client, news.*

Kundgebung *f. announcement.*

kundig *well-informed, experienced.*

kündigen *to give notice (to quit).*

Kundschaft *f. customers.*

künftig *in the future.*

KUNST *f. art.*

Kunstausstellung *f. art exhibition.*

Kunstgalerie *f. art gallery.*

Kunsthandel *m. fine art trade.*

Kunsthändler *m. art dealer.*

Künstler *m. (-in f.) artist.*

künstlich *artificial, false.*

Kunstseide *f. artificial silk.*

Kunststoff *m. plastics, synthetic material.*

Kunststück *n. feat, trick.*

KUR *f. treatment, cure.*

Kurgast *m. visitor, patient.*

Kurhaus *n. casino.*

kurios *odd, strange, curious.*

Kurort *m. health resort.*

Kurs *m. course, rate of exchange.*

Kurve *f. curve, bend, turn.*

Gefährliche Kurve!   *Dangerous curve!*

KURZ *short, brief, abrupt; in short, briefly.*

den Kürzeren ziehen   *to be the loser.*

in Kürze   *soon, shortly.*

kurz darauf   *shortly after.*

auf kurz oder lang   *sooner or later.*

kurz und bündig   *concisely, briefly.*

   kurz und gut *in short.*

   vor kurzem *recently.*

   kurz abfertigen *to dismiss abruptly.*

Kürze *f. shortness, brevity.*

kürzen *to shorten, abridge.*

kurzgefasst *concise; in short.*

Kurzgeschichte *f. short story.*

kürzlich *lately, recently.*

Kurzschrift *f. shorthand.*

kurzsichtig *shortsighted.*

Kürzung *f. shortening, abbreviation.*

Kuss *m. kiss.*

   mit Grüssen und Küssen *with love and kisses.*

küssen *to kiss.*

Küste *f. coast, shore.*

Kuvert *n. envelope, cover, wrapping.*

L

Laborant *m. laboratory assistant.*

Laboratorium *n. laboratory.*

lächeln *to smile.*

   höhnisch lächeln *to sneer.*

Lachen *n. laugh, laughter.*

LACHEN *to laugh.*

lächerlich *laughable, ridiculous.*

   lächerlich machen *to ridicule.*

Laden *m. shop, store, shutter.*

Ladeninhaber *m. shopkeeper.*

Ladenschluss *m. closing time.*

Ladentisch *m. counter.*

Ladeplatz *m. loading point, goods platform.*

Lage *f. situation, position, site, condition, storage.*

Lager *n. bed, couch, layer, support.*

Lageraufnahme *f. inventory.*

Lagergeld *n. storage fee.*

Lagerhaus *n. warehouse.*

lagern *to lie down, camp; to be stored.*

lahm *lame, paralyzed.*

Laie *m. layman.*

Laken *n. sheet.*

LAMPE *f. lamp, light.*

Lampenfieber *n. stagefright.*

Lampenschirm *m. lamp shade.*

LAND *n. land, mainland, ground.*

   an Land gehen *to land, go ashore.*

   aufs Land gehen *to go to the country.*

   außer Landes gehen *to go abroad.*

landen *to land, put ashore.*

   aus aller Herren Ländern *from all parts of the globe, from all over the world.*

Landesbrauch *m. national custom.*

Landesfarben *pl. national colors.*

Landessprache *f. national language.*

Landestracht *f. national costume.*

Landesverrat *m. high treason.*

Landesverweisung *f. expulsion, banishment, exile.*

Landhaus *n. country house.*

Landkarte *f. map.*

Landschaft *f. landscape, scenery.*

landschaftlich *provincial.*

Landstraße *f. highway.*

Landung *f. landing, disembarkation.*

Landwirtschaft *f. farming, agriculture.*

landwirtschaftlich *agricultural.*

LANG *long, tall.*

   auf lange Sicht *long-term.*

   auf die lange Bank schieben *to put off.*

   den lieben langen Tag *the livelong day.*

   einen Tag lang *for a day.*

   Es dauert lange. *It takes long.*

   es ist schon lange her, dass . . . *It's been a long time since/that . . .*

   über kurz oder lang *sooner or later.*

langatmig *long-winded, lengthy.*

Länge *f. length, duration.*

   der Länge nach *lengthwise.*

   in die Länge ziehen *to drag on, spin out.*

langen *to suffice, last, be enough.*

Längengrad *degree of longitude.*

länger *longer.*

   je länger, je lieber *the longer, the better.*

   schon länger *for some time.*

Langeweile *f. boredom.*

langfristig *long-term, in the long-run*

LÄNGS *prep. (gen.) along.*

   Der Weg läuft längs des Stromes. *The road runs along the river.*

langsam *slow, tardy.*

   Langsam fahren! *Slow down!*

Langsamkeit *f. slowness.*

längst *long ago, long since.*

   schon längst *for a very long time.*

   am längsten *the longest.*

   längstens *at the latest, at the most.*

langweilen *to bore.*

   sich zu Tode langweilen *to be bored to death.*

langweilig *boring.*

Lärm *m. noise, din, row.*

LASSEN *to let, allow, permit, suffer, omit, abandon.*

   aus dem Spiel lassen *to leave out of it.*

   Das muss man ihm lassen. *One must credit him with that.*

   es beim Alten lassen *to let things remain as they are.*

   Lassen Sie von sich hören! *Let us hear from you.*

   holen lassen *to send for.*

   Lass das! *Don't!*

   Lass nur! *Never mind!*

Ich habe den Wagen waschen lassen.   *I had the car washed.*

machen (waschen, reinigen, richten, usw.) lassen   *to have made (washed, cleaned, fixed, etc.).*

mit sich reden lassen   *to be reasonable.*

sein Leben lassen   *to lose one's life.*

sich sagen lassen   *to be told, take advice.*

sich Zeit lassen   *to take time.*

warten lassen   *to keep someone waiting.*

lässig *lazy, idle, indolent.*

Last *f. load, weight, burden, charge.*

lästig *troublesome, annoying, irksome.*

Lastwagen *m. cart, truck, van.*

Laterne *f. lantern, lamp.*

Laub *f. foliage, leaves.*

Laubwerk *m. foliage.*

Lauer *f. ambush.*

lauern *to wait for in hiding.*

Lauf *m. race, course, run, current.*

in vollem Lauf   *at full gallop.*

freien Lauf lassen   *to give vent to.*

Laufbahn *f. career.*

LAUFEN *to run, flow, go on.*

laufen lassen   *to let things go.*

auf dem Laufenden sein   *to be up-to-date, abreast.*

Gefahr laufen   *to run the risk.*

laufend *running*

Laufjunge *m. errand boy.*

Laufwerk *n. drive (computer).*

Laune *f. mood, whim.*

guter Laune sein   *to be in a good mood.*

launisch *moody.*

Laut *m. sound, tone.*

laut 1. *adj. loud, noisy, audible.*

laut werden   *to become known, get about.*

2. *prep. (gen.) according to, in accordance with.*

laut Befehls   *by order.*

laut Rechnung   *as per account.*

lauten *to sound.*

läuten *to ring, toll.*

lautlos *silent.*

Lautlosigkeit *f. silence.*

Lautsprecher *m. loudspeaker.*

lauwarm *lukewarm.*

LEBEN *n. life, lifetime, living.*

am Leben bleiben   *to survive.*

am Leben sein   *to be alive.*

auf Leben und Tod   *a matter of life and death.*

einem Kind das Leben schenken   *to give birth to a child.*

ins Leben rufen   *to originate, start.*

Lebenshaltungskosten   *cost of living.*

LEBEN *to live, be alive, dwell, stay.*

lebendig *living, lively.*

Lebendigkeit *f. liveliness, animation.*

Lebensgefahr *f. danger, risk of one's life.*

lebensgefährlich *highly dangerous.*

Lebenslage *f. position.*

lebenslänglich *for life, perpetual.*

Lebenslauf *n. curriculum vitae, background.*

Lebensmittel *n. food, provisions.*

Lebensmittelgeschäft *food shop.*

lebensmüde *tired of life.*

Lebensraum *m. living space.*

Lebensunterhalt *m. livelihood, living.*

Lebensweise *f. mode of life.*

Leber *f. liver.*

lebhaft *lively, vivacious.*

Leck *n. leak.*

lecken *to lick.*

LEDER *n. leather.*

LEER *empty, vacant, blank, idle.*

mit leeren Händen   *with empty hands.*

Leere *f. emptiness, void, vacuum.*

Leerlauf *m. neutral (gear).*

leeren *to empty.*

LEGEN *to put, lay, place.*

sich legen   *to lie down, calm down, subside.*

Lehne *f. back of chair.*

lehnen *to lean against, rest on.*

sich lehnen   *to lean back.*

Lehnstuhl *m. armchair.*

Lehramt *n. teacher's post.*

Lehrberuf *m. teaching profession.*

Lehrbuch *n. textbook.*

Lehre *f. instruction, precept, advice, lesson.*

LEHREN *to teach, instruct.*

LEHRER *m. (-in f.) teacher.*

Lehrfach *n. subject.*

lehrhaft *didactic.*

Lehrjahre *pl. years of apprenticeship.*

lehrreich *instructive.*

Leib *m. body, belly, womb.*

Leibschmerzen *m. pl. stomachache, colic.*

Leiche *f. corpse.*

LEICHT *easy, light, slight, mild, careless, frivolous; easily.*

etwas leicht nehmen   *to take it easy.*

leicht möglich   *very probable.*

leichtfertig *thoughtless, frivolous.*

Leichtfertigkeit *f. thoughtlessness, frivolity.*

leichtgläubig *credulous, gullible.*

Leichtsinn *m. carelessness, thoughtlessness.*

leichtsinnig *careless, thoughtless.*

LEID *n. grief, sorrow, pain, harm.*

Er tut mir Leid.   *I am sorry for him.*

Es tut mir Leid.   *I am sorry about it.*

zu meinem Leid   *to my regret.*

leiden *to suffer, bear, endure, stand.*

leiden können, leiden mögen   *to know sb. is to like sb.*

Sie leidet schwer darunter.   *It's making her very miserable.*

Leidenschaft *f. passion.*
leidenschaftlich *passionately.*
leidenschaftslos *dispassionate.*
leider *unfortunately.*
  leider nicht *unfortunately not.*
Leihbibliothek *f. lending library.*
leihen *to lend.*
Leine *f. leash.*
Leinwand *f. linen, screen.*
leise *soft, gentle, dim.*
  mit leiser Stimme *in a low voice.*
Leiste *f. strip; ledge.*
leisten *to perform, carry out, accomplish.*
  es sich leisten können *to be able to afford
    something.*
leistungsfähig *capable, fit, efficient.*
Leistungsfähigkeit *f. capacity for work,
    efficiency, power.*
leiten *to lead, conduct, manage, direct.*
Leiter *m. leader, manager, principal, head.*
Leitung *f. direction, management, guidance,
    line, pipe.*
Leitungswasser *n. tap water.*
Lektion *f. lesson (in a book).*
lenkbar *manageable, steerable.*
lenken *to direct, conduct, drive, steer.*
lernbegierig *anxious to learn.*
LERNEN *to learn, study.*
Lesebuch *n. reader (book).*
LESEN *to read, lecture.*
lesenswert *worth reading.*
Leser *m. reader (person).*
leserlich *legible.*
LETZT (-ER, -E, -ES) *last, latest, final,
    extreme.*
  in letzter Zeit *lately, recently.*
  letzte Neuheit *latest novelty.*
  letzten Endes *after all.*
  letzten Sonntag *last Sunday.*
  Letztes hergeben *to do one's utmost.*
letztens *lately, of late.*
Leuchte *f. lamp, light.*
leuchten *to light, shine, beam, glow.*
Leuchter *m. candlestick.*
Leuchtturm *m. lighthouse.*
Leuchtuhr *f. luminous clock or watch.*
Leuchtzifferblatt *m. luminous dial.*
leugnen *to deny, disavow.*
LEUTE *pl. people, persons, folk.*
Leutnant *m. second lieutenant.*
leutselig *affable.*
Lexikon *n. dictionary.*
LICHT *n. light, candle, illumination.*
  Bitte, machen Sie das Licht an. *Please
    turn on the light.*
  Licht anzünden *to turn on the light.*
  Licht ausmachen *to turn off the light.*
  in ein falsches Licht setzen *to
    misrepresent.*

  Mir ging ein Licht auf. *It dawned on me.*
licht
  am lichten Tage *in broad daylight.*
  lichte Augenblicke *sane moments.*
lichtempfindlich *sensitive to light.*
lichten *to thin out, clear (forest).*
Lichterglanz *m. brightness.*
Lichtreklame *f. neon sign, illuminated
    advertisement.*
LIEB *dear, nice, beloved, agreeable.*
  Es ist mir lieb. *I am glad.*
  es wäre mir lieb *I should like.*
Liebchen *n. darling, love, sweetheart.*
LIEBE *f. love, affection, charity.*
  aus Liebe *for love.*
  mir zu Liebe *for my sake.*
LIEBEN *to love, like, be in love.*
liebenswürdig *amiable, kind.*
Liebenswürdigkeit *f. amiability, kindness.*
lieber *dearer, rather.*
Liebeserklärung *f. declaration of love.*
Liebesgedicht *n. love poem.*
Liebesgeschichte *f. love story.*
Liebespaar *n. lovers, couple.*
lieb gewinnen *to grow fond of.*
lieb haben *to love.*
Liebhaber *m. (-in f.) lover; amateur.*
Liebhaberei *f. fancy, liking, hobby.*
liebkosen *to caress, fondle.*
Liebkosung *f. caress, petting.*
lieblich *lovely, charming.*
Liebling *m. darling, favorite.*
Lieblingsgericht *n. favorite dish.*
Liebreiz *m. charm, attraction.*
Liebschaft *f. love affair.*
Liebste *m. & f. dearest, beloved, lover,
    sweetheart.*
LIED *n. song, air.*
Liederbuch *n. songbook, hymnbook.*
liederlich *slovenly, immoral, dissolute.*
lieferbar *available.*
Lieferfrist *f. term of delivery.*
liefern *to deliver, yield, produce.*
Lieferung *f. delivery, supply.*
LIEGEN *to lie, rest, be situated, stand.*
  Das liegt an mir. *It is my fault.*
  Mir liegt daran. *I am interested in the
    matter.*
  Mir liegt nichts daran. *I don't care for it.*
liegen lassen *to leave behind; to neglect.*
Likör *m. liqueur, cordial.*
Limonade *f. lemonade.*
lindern *to soften, ease, soothe.*
Linderung *f. relief.*
Linie *f. line, descent, branch (of a family).*
  in erster Linie *first of all.*
linkisch *awkward, clumsy.*
LINKS *to the left, on the left.*
  Gehen Sie nach links! *Go to the left!*

Sie ließ ihn ganz links liegen. *She gave him the cold shoulder.*
linkshändig *left-handed.*
Linnen *n. linen.*
Linse *f. lentil.*
Lippe *f. lip.*
Lippenstift *m. lipstick.*
List *f. cunning, craft.*
Liste *f. list, roll, catalogue.*
listig *cunning, crafty, sly, astute.*
Liter *n. liter (1.056 quarts).*
literarisch *literary.*
Literatur *f. literature, letters.*
Litfasssäule *f. billboard.*
Lizenz *f. license, permit.*
Lob *n. praise.*
loben *to praise.*
lobenswert *praiseworthy.*
lobpreisen *to praise.*
Loch *n. hole, gap.*
Locke *f. lock, curl.*
locken *to entice, allure.*
Löffel *m. spoon.*
Esslöffel. *m. tablespoon.*
Loge *f. box (theater).*
Logik *f. logic.*
logisch *logical.*
Lohn *m. compensation, reward, wages.*
Lohnempfänger *m. wage earner.*
Lohnerhöhung *f. wage increase.*
lohnen *to reward.*
Es lohnt sich. *It is worthwhile.*
Löhnung *f. pay.*
lokal *local, suburban.*
Lokomotive *f. engine (of a train).*
Los *n. lot, chance.*
LOS 1. *adv. loose, slack, free.*
Hier ist viel los. *There's plenty going on here.*
Mit ihm ist nicht viel los. *He is not up to much.*
Was ist los? *What's up?*
2. *separable prefix (implies the idea of separation or quick movement).*
Du kannst die Hunde losmachen. *You can untie the dogs.*
Eins, zwei, drei, los! *One, two, three, go!*
losbinden *to untie, loosen.*
löschen *to put out, extinguish.*
losgehen *to set out, become loose, go off.*
loskommen *to get away.*
loswerden *to get rid of.*
Löwe *m. lion.*
LUFT *f. air, breath, breeze.*
aus der Luft greifen *to invent.*
frische Luft schöpfen *to take the air.*
in die Luft sprengen *to blow up.*
keine Luft bekommen *not to be able to breathe.*

luftdicht *airtight.*
in die Luft fliegen *to be blown up.*
Es liegt etwas in der Luft. *Something is in the air.*
lüften *to air.*
luftig *airy, breezy.*
Luftkrankheit *f. airsickness.*
luftkrank sein *to be airsick.*
Luftkurort *m. health resort.*
luftleer *airless.*
luftleerer Raum   *vacuum.*
Luftpost *f. air mail.*
Luftraum *m. atmosphere.*
Lüge *f. lie, untruth, falsehood.*
lügen *to lie (falsify).*
Lunge *f. lung.*
Lungenentzündung *f. pneumonia.*
Lupe *f. magnifying glass.*
Lust *f. pleasure, joy, delight, inclination, lust.*
Lust haben   *to be inclined to.*
mit Lust und Liebe   *with heart and soul.*
lustig *gay, funny, jolly.*
sich lustig machen über   *to make fun of.*
Lustspiel *n. comedy.*
Luxus *m. luxury.*
Lyrik *f. lyrics.*

M

Machart *f. style, description, kind, sort.*
MACHEN *to make, to do, manufacture, cause, amount to.*
Das lässt sich machen. *This is feasible.*
Das macht nichts. *That does not matter.*
Was macht Ihre Erkältung? *How is your cold?*
Spaß machen   *to joke.*
Anspruch machen auf   *to claim.*
MACHT *f. strength, might, power, authority.*
mächtig *strong, mighty, powerful.*
machtlos *powerless.*
MÄDCHEN *n. girl, servant.*
Mädchen für alles   *general servant.*
mädchenhaft *girlish, maidenly.*
Mädchenname *m. maiden name.*
Magen *m. stomach.*
Ich habe einen verdorbenen Magen. *I have an upset stomach.*
Magenverstimmung *f. stomach upset.*
mager *thin, scanty.*
Magerkeit *f. leanness, skimpiness.*
mähen *to mow, cut, reap.*
MAHL *n. meal.*
mahlen *to grind, mill.*
Mahnbrief *m. request for payment; demand notice.*
mahnen *to remind, admonish, exort.*

Mahnung f. reminder, warning.
MAI m. May.
Maiglöckchen n. lily of the valley.
Mais m. corn, maize.
Major m. major.
MAL n. 1. landmark, monument, mark. 2. time, turn.
　dieses Mal　for once.
　ein für alle Mal　once and for all.
　mit einem Mal　suddenly.
　zum ersten Mal　for the first time.
mal times, once, just.
　Danke vielmals　thank you very much.
　Vier mal drei ist zwölf　Four times three is twelve.
malen to paint, portray, represent.
　sich malen lassen　to have one's portrait painted.
Maler m. (**-in** f.) painter.
malerisch pictorial, picturesque.
MAN one, they, people, you.
　man hat mir gesagt, dass . . .　I was told that . . .
　Man spricht hier Deutsch.　They (We) speak German here.
　Man sagt so.　So they say.
MANCHE many, some.
manch(-er, -e, -es) many a.
mancherlei various, diverse.
manchmal sometimes.
Mangel m. need, want, absence, lack.
　aus Mangel an　for want of.
mangelhaft faulty, defective.
mangeln to want, be wanting.
　es mangelt mir an　I am short of.
Manier f. manner, style.
manierlich polite, civil, mannerly.
MANN m. man; husband.
　mit zweitausend Mann　with 2,000 men (soldiers).
　ein Mann ein Wort　A man is as good as his word.
　wenn Not am Mann ist　if worse comes to worst.
Mannesalter n. manhood.
mannhaft manly.
männlich male, manly.
Manschette f. cuff.
Manschettenknopf m. cuff link.
MANTEL m. coat.
Mappe f. document case, writing case.
Märchen n. fairy tale.
märchenhaft fabulous, legendary.
Marine f. navy.
markant characteristic, striking.
Marke f. mark, sign, postage stamp, token.
MARKT m. market, marketplace.
Markthalle f. covered market.
Marktplatz m. marketplace.

Marmelade f. jam.
Marmor m. marble.
Marmorplatte f. marble slab.
Marsch m. march.
marschieren to march.
MÄRZ m. March.
Marzipan m. & n. marzipan.
MASCHINE f. machine, engine, typewriter.
　auf der Maschine schreiben　to typewrite.
Maske f. mask, disguise.
Maskenball m. fancy dress ball.
Maskerade f. masquerade.
MAß n. measure, dimension, size, degree, proportion, moderation.
　in hohem Maße　in a high degree.
　Maß nehmen　to measure.
　Maße und Gewichte pl.　weights and measurements.
　nach Maß gemacht　made to measure.
Maßarbeit f. made to measure (to order).
MASSE f. crowd, mass, quantity.
massenhaft in large quantities, wholesale.
maßgebend standard.
maßgeblich standard.
Maß halten to observe moderation, keep within limits.
mäßig reasonable, moderate, poor, mediocre.
mäßigen to observe moderation, restrain.
Mäßigkeit f. moderation, frugality.
maßlos boundless, without limit.
Maßregel f. measure, step.
Maßstab m. yard, measure, scale.
Material n. material, substance.
materialisieren to materialize.
materialistisch materialistic.
Mathematik f. mathematics.
Matratze f. mattress.
Matrose m. sailor.
matt weak, soft, dull; mate (chess).
　matt setzen　to mate (chess).
Matte f. mat.
Mauer f. wall.
mauern to build with stones.
Maultier n. mule.
Maurer m. mason, bricklayer.
Maus f. mouse (also computer).
Mechanik f. mechanics.
Mechaniker m. mechanic.
mechanisch mechanical.
Medikament n. medicament.
Medizin f. medicine, remedy.
Mediziner m. (**-in** f.) medical student.
MEER n. sea, seashore.
Meerenge f. channel, straights, narrows.
Meeresspiegel m. sea level.
Mehl n. flour.
MEHR more.
　desto mehr　all the more.

immer mehr   *more and more.*
je mehr . . . desto   *the more . . . the more.*
mehr als   *more than.*
nicht mehr   *no more, any more, any longer.*
nie mehr   *never again.*
nur mehr   *only, nothing but.*
um so mehr als . . .   *all the more as.*
Mehrbetrag *m. surplus.*
mehrere *several.*
mehreres *several things.*
mehrfach *manifold, numerous.*
Mehrheit *f. majority.*
mehrmals *several times, again and again.*
Mehrzahl *f. majority, plural.*
Meile *f. mile (1.609 kilometers).*
MEIN *poss. adj. my.*
MEIN(-ER, -E, -ES) *poss. pron. mine.*
MEINEN *to mean, think, believe, suppose.*
  Was meinen Sie damit?   *What do you*
    mean by that?
  So war es nicht gemeint.   *It wasn't meant*
    that way.
  Wie meinen Sie das?   *How do you mean*
    that?
meinerseits *for my part, as far as I am*
  concerned.
meinesgleichen *my equals, my peers.*
meinethalben *for my sake, for all I care.*
meinetwegen *for my sake, for me, on my*
  account, as far as I am concerned.
meinetwillen (um-) *for my sake.*
MEINUNG *f. meaning, opinion, view.*
  einem die Meinung sagen   *to give someone*
    a piece of one's mind.
  meiner Meinung nach   *in my opinion.*
meist *most, mostly.*
  die meisten   *most people.*
MEISTENS *mostly.*
MEISTER *m. master.*
  Übung macht den Meister.   *Practice makes*
    perfect.
Meisterschaft *f. championship.*
Meistersinger *m. mastersinger.*
Meisterstück *n. masterpiece.*
Meisterwerk *n. masterpiece.*
Meldeamt *n. registration office.*
melden *to report, announce, inform, apply.*
Meldezettel *m. registration form.*
Meldung *f. news, announcement, advice,*
  notification.
melken *to milk.*
Melodie *f. melody, tune.*
Menge *f. quantity, amount, lots, multitude.*
  in Mengen   *in abundance, plenty of.*
mengen *to mix, meddle, interfere.*
MENSCH *m. man, human being, person.*
  Es kam kein Mensch.   *Not a soul came.*
  seit Menschengedenken   *within the*
    memory of man; immemorial.

  Was für ein Mensch ist er?   *What sort of a*
    person is he?
Menschenalter *n. generation.*
menschenmöglich *humanly possible.*
Menschheit *f. human race.*
menschlich *human.*
Menschlichkeit *f. human nature.*
merkbar *noticeable.*
merken *to perceive, notice, observe, note.*
  sich merken   *to keep in mind.*
  sich nichts anmerken lassen   *to appear to*
    know nothing.
merklich *noticeable.*
Merkmal *n. characteristic, sign, mark.*
merkwürdig *characteristic, strange, peculiar,*
  remarkable.
merkwürdigerweise *strangely enough,*
  strange to say.
Merkwürdigkeit *f. strangeness, peculiarity.*
Messe *f. Mass; fair; mess (officers').*
MESSEN *to measure, survey, take the*
  temperature (of a patient).
  messen mit   *to compete with.*
  nicht messen können mit   *to be no match.*
MESSER *n. knife.*
Messergriff *m. knife handle.*
Messerstich *m. stab (with a knife).*
Messing *brass.*
Metall *n. metal.*
Meter *n. meter (39.37 inches).*
Metermaß *n. tape measure.*
Methode *f. method.*
Metzger *m. butcher.*
Metzgerei *n. butcher's shop.*
MICH *acc. of ich (pers. pron.) me, myself.*
Miene *f. expression (facial), air, countenance.*
  gute Miene zum bösen Spiel machen
    to put up a brave show.
MIETE *f. rent, lease.*
  Die Miete ist fällig.   *The rent is due.*
  zur Miete wohnen   *to be a tenant, to rent.*
mieten *to rent.*
Mieter *m. tenant.*
mietfrei *rent free.*
Mietshaus *n. apartment house.*
Mietvertrag *m. lease.*
Mikrofon *n. microphone.*
Mikroskop *n. microscope.*
mikroskopisch *microscopic.*
MILCH *f. milk.*
Milchgeschäft *n. dairy.*
Milchgesicht *n. baby face.*
Milchglas *n. opalescent glass, milk glass.*
Milchladen *m. dairy.*
Milchstraße *f. Milky Way.*
Milchzahn *m. milk tooth.*
MILD *mild, soft, gentle, mellow, kind.*
MILDE *f. gentleness, kindness.*
mildern *to soften, extenuate.*

mildernde Umstände   *extenuating circumstances.*
mildtätig *kind, generous.*
Militär *n. army, service.*
Militärdienst *m. active service.*
militärisch *military.*
Militarismus *m. militarism.*
MILLIARDE *f. billion.*
MILLION *f. million.*
Millionär *m.* (**-in** *f.*) *millionaire.*
MINDER *less, minor, inferior.*
minderbemittelt *of moderate means.*
Minderheit *f. minority.*
minderjährig *minor (age).*
   minderjährig sein   *to be a minor.*
Minderjährigkeit *f. minority (age).*
minderwertig *inferior.*
Minderwertigkeitsgefühl *n. inferiority complex.*
MINDEST *least.*
   nicht im Mindesten   *not in the least, by no means.*
mindestens *at least.*
Mindestlohn *m. minimum wage.*
Mine *f. mine.*
Mineral *n. mineral.*
Minister *m. minister.*
Ministerium *n. ministry.*
Ministerpräsident *m. prime minister.*
MINUTE *f. minute.*
   minutenlang   *for several minutes.*
MIR *dat. of ich (pers. pron.) to me, me, myself.*
mischen *to blend, mix, meddle, shuffle (cards).*
   sich einmischen   *to interfere.*
Mischung *f. blend, mix.*
missachten *to disregard, disdain.*
Missachtung *f. disregard, disdain.*
missbilligen *to disapprove.*
Missbilligung *f. disapproval.*
missbrauchen *to misuse, abuse.*
missen *to do without, to miss.*
Misserfolg *m. failure.*
Missetat *f. misdeed, crime.*
Missetäter *m. criminal.*
missfallen *to displease.*
Missgeschick *n. bad luck, misfortune.*
missglücken *to fail.*
missgönnen *to grudge.*
missgünstig *envious, jealous.*
Misstrauen *n. distrust, mistrust.*
misstrauen *to distrust, mistrust.*
misstrauisch *suspicious.*
missvergnügt *displeased.*
missverstehen *to misunderstand.*
MIT 1. *prep. (dat.) with, at, by.*
   Der Patient hat mit gutem Appetit gegessen. *The patient has eaten with a good appetite.*

mit anderen Worten   *in other words.*
mit der Post   *by mail.*
mit der Zeit   *gradually.*
Die Kosten sind mitberechnet.   *The costs are included.*
Mit fünf Jahren spielte er schon Klavier. *At the age of five, he already played the piano.*
Wir sind mit der Eisenbahn gereist. *We traveled by train.*
2. *separable prefix (implies accompaniment or participation).*
Kommen Sie mit?   *Are you coming along?*
mitarbeiten *to collaborate, cooperate, contribute.*
Mitarbeiter *m. collaborator.*
Mitbesitzer *m. joint proprietor.*
mitbringen *to bring along.*
Mitbürger *m. fellow citizen.*
miteinander *with each other, together, jointly.*
mitempfinden *to sympathize with.*
Mitgefühl *n. sympathy.*
Mitgift *f. dowry.*
Mitglied *n. member.*
mitkommen *to accompany, come along, keep up.*
Mitleid *n. sympathy, pity, mercy.*
Mitleidenschaft *f. compassion.*
   in Mitleidenschaft ziehen   *to affect.*
mitleidig *compassionate.*
mitleidlos *pitiless.*
mitmachen *to take part in, go through.*
   Sie hat sehr viel mitgemacht.   *She went through a lot.*
mitnehmen *to take along, affect.*
   Ihr Tod hat ihn sehr mitgenommen. *Her death affected him deeply.*
mitschuldig *implicated (in a crime).*
Mitschuldige *m. & f. accomplice.*
mitspielen *to join in a game; to accompany (music).*
MITTAG *m. noon, midday; south.*
   zu Mittag essen   *to have lunch.*
Mittagessen *n. lunch.*
mittags *at noon.*
Mittagspause *f. lunch hour.*
MITTE *f. middle, center, mean, medium.*
   Er ist Mitte dreißig.   *He is in his middle thirties.*
   goldene Mitte   *golden mean.*
mitteilen *to impart, communicate.*
Mitteilung *f. information, communication, intelligence.*
Mittel *n. means; remedy, cure, medicine.*
   Er ist ohne irgendwelche Mittel.   *He is penniless.*
   als Mittel zum Zweck   *as a means to an end.*
Mittelalter *n. Middle Ages.*

Mitteleuropa n. Central Europe.
mittellos without means.
mittelmäßig average, mediocre.
Mittelmeer n. Mediterranean.
Mittelstand m. middle class.
MITTEN midway, in the middle of.
　mitten auf (in)　in the midst of.
　mittendrin　right in the middle of.
　mittendurch　right across, right through.
　mitten auf der Straße　in/on the open
　　street.
　mitten in der Nacht　in the middle of the
　　night.
MITTERNACHT f. midnight.
mitternachts at midnight.
mittlerweile meanwhile, in the meantime.
MITTWOCH m. Wednesday.
mitunter sometimes, now and then.
Mitwelt f. our age, our generation.
Mitwisser m. confident, one in on the secret.
MÖBEL n. piece of furniture.
Möbel pl. furniture.
Möbelhändler m. furniture dealer.
Möbelstück n. piece of furniture.
möblieren to furnish.
Mode f. fashion.
Modell n. model, pattern, mold.
modern modern.
Modenschau f. fashion show.
modisch fashionable.
MÖGEN to want, wish, be able, be allowed;
　to like, care for.
　Das mag ich nicht.　I don't like that.
　Das mag sein　that may be so.
　Er ist faul, er mag nicht lernen.　He is lazy;
　　he does not want to learn.
　Ich möchte nicht.　I don't want to.
　Ich möchte wissen.　I'd like to know.
　wie das auch sein mag　be that as it may.
　lieber mögen　to prefer.
　Ich möchte lieber auf dem Land leben.
　　I'd rather live in the country.
möglich possible, practicable, feasible, likely.
　alles Mögliche　all sorts of things,
　　everything possible.
　möglichst wenig　as little as possible.
　möglichst schnell　as quickly as possible.
　Nicht möglich!　It can't be!
　sein Möglichstes tun　to do one's utmost.
möglicherweise possibly, perhaps.
Möglichkeit f. possibility, chance.
Moment m. moment.
　Einen Moment!　One moment!
Momentaufnahme f. snapshot.
Monarchie f. monarchy.
MONAT m. month.
monatelang for months.
monatlich monthly.
Mönch m. monk.

MOND m. moon.
Mondschein m. moonlight.
Monolog m. monologue.
MONTAG m. Monday.
Moor n. swamp.
Moos n. moss.
Mop m. mop.
moppen to mop.
Moral f. morality, morals, moral.
moralisch moral.
moralisieren to moralize.
Mord m. murder.
　Selbstmord　m. suicide.
Mordanschlag m. murderous attack.
Mörder m. (-in f.) murderer.
MORGEN m. morning, dawn, daybreak; the
　following day.
　früh morgens　early in the morning.
　Guten Morgen.　Good morning.
　heute Morgen　this morning.
　morgens　in the morning.
morgen tomorrow.
　morgen früh　tomorrow morning.
　morgen in acht Tagen　a week from
　　tomorrow.
　Morgen ist auch ein Tag.　Tomorrow is
　　another day.
Morgengrauen n. dawn, break of day.
morgenländisch eastern, oriental.
Morgenrock m. robe.
Motor m. motor, engine.
Motorboot n. motorboat.
Motorpanne f. engine trouble.
Motorrad n. motorcycle.
Matte f. moth.
Mücke f. mosquito (gnat).
Mückenstich m. mosquito bite.
MÜDE tired, weary.
　müde werden　to get tired.
Müdigkeit f. weariness, fatigue.
MÜHE f. labor, toil, effort.
　sich Mühe geben　to take pains.
　der Mühe wert　worthwhile.
　mit Müh und Not　only just, barely.
　Mühe machen　to give troubles.
　machen Sie sich keine Mühe!　Don't
　　bother.
mühelos easy, effortless.
mühevoll laborious, difficult.
Mühle f. mill.
Müller m. miller.
MUND m. mouth.
　den Mund halten　to keep one's mouth shut.
　den Mund vollnehmen　to brag.
　Er ist nicht auf den Mund gefallen.　He has
　　a ready tongue.
　nach dem Mund reden　to flatter.
　Sie leben von der Hand in den Mund.
　　They live from hand to mouth.

Mundwinkel *m. corner of the mouth.*

Munition *f. ammunition.*

munter *alive, wide-awake, gay.*

Münze *f. coin, medal.*

Sie nimmt alles für bare Münze.   *She takes everything at face value.*

mürrisch *morose, sullen.*

Museum *n. museum.*

Musik *f. music.*

musikalisch *musical.*

Muskel *m. muscle.*

Muskelkater *m. stiffness and soreness.*

MÜSSEN *to have to, be obliged to, must, ought to.*

Alle Menschen müssen sterben.   *All humans must die.*

Man müsste es ihr eigentlich sagen.   *Somebody really ought to tell her.*

Sie müssen nicht, wenn Sie nicht wollen.   *You don't have to if you don't want to.*

Muster *n. sample, model, design, pattern.*

musterhaft *exemplary, standard.*

mustern *to examine.*

Musterung *f. examination.*

MUT *m. courage, fortitude, state of mind.*

jemandem den Mut nehmen   *to discourage someone.*

Mut fassen   *to summon up courage.*

Mut machen   *to encourage.*

den Mut verlieren   *to lose one's courage.*

mutig *brave.*

mutlos *despondent, disheartened.*

MUTTER *f. mother.*

Muttermal *n. birthmark.*

Muttersprache *f. mother tongue.*

Mütze *f. cap.*

N

NACH 1. *prep. (with dat.) after, toward, according to, like, past, by, in.*

dem Namen nach kennen   *to know by name.*

der Sage nach   *according to the legend.*

Der Vater schickt die Kinder nach Hause.   *The father sends the children home.*

einer nach dem anderen   *one after another, one at a time.*

Es ist zehn nach fünf.   *It is ten after five.*

Es sieht nach Schnee aus.   *It looks like snow.*

Gehen Sie nach links!   *Turn left.*

meiner Meinung nach   *in my opinion.*

Nach dem Essen ruht er sich aus.   *He rests after meals.*

nach und nach   *little by little*

2. *adv. after, toward, according to.*

3. *separable prefix (implies coming after, following, imitation).*

Der Polizist lief dem Dieb nach.   *The policeman ran after the thief.*

Kannst du diese Arbeit nachmachen?   *Can you copy this work?*

nachahmen *to imitate.*

nachahmenswert *worthy of imitation.*

Nachahmung *f. imitation.*

Nachbar *m. (-in f.) neighbor.*

Nachbarschaft *f. neighborhood.*

nachdem *conj. after.*

Nachdem er sie verlassen hatte, weinte sie.   *After he had left, she cried.*

nachdenken *to reflect, think.*

nachdenken über   *to think over.*

nachdenklich *thoughtful.*

Nachdruck *m. stress, emphasis, reprint, reproduction.*

Nachdruck verboten   *reproduction forbidden.*

nachdrücklich *strong, emphatic.*

nacheifern *to emulate.*

nachforschen *to inquire into, investigate.*

Nachfrage *f. inquiry, demand.*

nachgeben *to yield, give way.*

nachgehen *to follow, investigate, inquire.*

Nachgeschmack *m. aftertaste.*

nachher *afterward, later.*

Nachhilfe *f. aid, help, coaching.*

nachkommen *to come later, follow.*

Nachkriegszeit *f. postwar period.*

nachlässig *negligent, careless.*

Nachlässigkeit *f. negligence, carelessness.*

nachlaufen *to run after.*

nachlesen *to look up (in a book).*

nachmachen *to imitate, copy, counterfeit, duplicate.*

NACHMITTAG *m. afternoon.*

nachmittags *afternoons, in the afternoon.*

Nachnahme *f. cash on delivery.*

Nachname *m. surname.*

nachprüfen *to test, check, verify.*

Nachricht *f. news, information, account, report, message.*

Ist eine Nachricht für mich da?   *Is there a message for me?*

nachsagen *to repeat after.*

nachsehen *to revise, check, examine.*

nachsenden *to send after.*

Nachsicht *f. indulgence.*

nachsichtig (-sichtsvoll) *indulgent, lenient.*

nächst *nearest, next, closest, following. prep. (dat.) next to, next after.*

Nächstenliebe *f. love for one's fellow men; charity.*

NACHT *f. night.*

bei Nacht, des Nachts   *at night.*

bis in die Nacht arbeiten   *to burn the midnight oil.*

über Nacht   *overnight.*

über Nacht bleiben   *to stay overnight.*

Nachteil *m. disadvantage.*

im Nachteil sein   *to be at a disadvantage.*

Nachthemd *n. nightgown.*

Nachtigall *f. nightingale.*

Nachtisch *m. dessert.*

Nachtrag *m. supplement.*

nachtragen *to add.*

nachträglich *additional, afterward.*

Nachweis *m. proof, evidence.*

nachweisen *to prove.*

Nachwirkung *f. aftereffect.*

Nachwuchs *m. aftercrop, next generation.*

Nacken *m. nape of the neck.*

nackt *naked, nude, bare, plain.*

Nadel *f. needle, pin.*

NAGEL *m. nail.*

Es brennt mir auf den Nägeln.   *The matter is urgent.*

den Nagel auf den Kopf treffen   *to hit the nail on the head.*

Nagelfeile *f. nail file.*

Nähe *f. nearness, proximity, vicinity.*

in der Nähe   *near to, close at hand.*

NAHE *near, close to, imminent, approaching.*

nahe daran sein   *to be about.*

zu nahe treten   *to hurt one's feelings, offend.*

nahen *to draw near, approach.*

nähen *to sew, stitch.*

näher *nearer, closer, more intimate, further.*

Nähere *n. details, particulars.*

Näherin *f. seamstress.*

(sich) nähern *to bring near, place near.*

nahe stehen *to be closely connected, be friends with.*

Nähgarn *n. sewing thread.*

Nähmaschine *f. sewing machine.*

Nähnadel *f. sewing needle.*

Nährboden *m. fertile soil.*

nähren *to feed, nurse, nourish.*

sich nähren von   *to live on.*

Nahrung *f. nourishment, food.*

Nahrungsmittel *pl. food, foodstuffs.*

NAME *m. name, appellation, character.*

dem Namen nach   *by name.*

im Namen *(with gen.)*   *on behalf of.*

namenlos *nameless.*

Namenstag *m. saint's day, name day.*

nämlich *namely, same, very.*

Narbe *f. scar.*

Narkose *f. anesthetic.*

Narr *m. fool, jester.*

zum Narren halten   *to make a fool of.*

narren *to fool.*

NASE *f. nose.*

Der Zug fuhr mir vor der Nase weg.   *I missed the train by a hair (nose).*

Sie schlug ihm die Tür vor der Nase zu.   *She slammed the door in his face.*

NASS *wet, damp.*

Die Straße ist nass.   *The street is wet.*

bei Nässe glatt.   *slippery when wet.*

nass werden   *to get wet.*

Nation *f. nation.*

national *national.*

Nationalhymne *f. national anthem.*

NATUR *f. nature, disposition, constitution.*

Naturalismus *m. naturalism.*

naturalistisch *naturalistic.*

Naturgeschichte *f. natural science.*

natürlich *natural, unaffected.*

Natürlich!   *Of course!*

Natürlichkeit *f. naturalness, simplicity.*

Naturschutzgebiet *n. national park.*

naturtreu *lifelike.*

Nebel *m. fog, mist, haze.*

nebelhaft *nebulous.*

nebelig (neblig) *misty, foggy.*

Nebelregen *m. drizzle.*

Nebelwetter *n. foggy weather.*

NEBEN 1. *prep. (dat. when answering the question Wo? acc. when answering the question Wohin?). next, next to, beside, among, besides.*

2. *adv. next to, beside, among.*

Setzen Sie sich neben mich!   *Sit down next to me!*

Er saß neben dem Mädchen.   *He was seated next to the girl.*

neben anderen Dingen   *among other things.*

nebenan *next door.*

Nebenanschluss *m. extension (telephone).*

Nebenbegriff *m. subordinate idea.*

nebenbei *on the side, by the way, adjoining.*

nebenbei bemerkt (gesagt)   *by the way, incidentally.*

Nebenberuf *m. additional occupation, sideline.*

nebeneinander *next to each other, side by side.*

Nebeneingang *m. side entrance.*

Nebeneinnahme *f. additional income.*

Nebenerzeugnis *n. by-product.*

Nebenfluss *m. tributary.*

Nebengebäude *n. additional building, annex.*

Nebengedanke *m. subordinate idea, mental reservation.*

nebenher (nebenhin) *by the side of.*

Nebenkosten *f. incidentals, extra.*

Nebenlinie *f. branch, secondary railroad line.*

Nebenmensch *m. fellow creature.*

Nebenperson *f. supporting character (theater).*

Nebenrolle f. supporting part (theater).

Nebensache f. matter of secondary importance.

nebensächlich unimportant, immaterial.

Nebensatz m. subordinate clause (grammar).

Nebenstraße f. side street.

Nebenzimmer n. next room.

necken to tease.

Neffe m. nephew.

negieren to deny, to negate.

NEHMEN to take, accept, receive.

  Abschied nehmen   to say good-bye.

  Anstoß nehmen   to object.

  es sich nicht nehmen lassen   to insist on something.

  es genau nehmen   to be pedantic.

  etwas zu sich nehmen   to eat something.

  genau genommen   strictly speaking.

  Nehmen Sie Platz!   Sit down!

  sich in Acht nehmen   to be careful.

  ihm beim Worte nehmen   to take him at his word.

  streng genommen   strictly speaking.

  eine Stellung nehmen   to express one's view about.

Neid m. envy, jealousy.

neidisch jealous, envious.

Neige f. slope, decline.

  zur Neige gehen   to be on the decline, come to an end.

neigen to incline, bow.

  geneigt sein   to be inclined.

Neigung f. slope, declivity, inclination, taste.

NEIN no.

Nektar m. nectar.

Nelke f. carnation.

NENNEN to name, call, mention.

  ein Ding beim rechten Namen nennen   to call a spade a spade.

nennenswert worth mentioning.

Nennwort n. noun.

Nerv m. nerve.

  auf die Nerven fallen   to get on one's nerves.

Nervenheilanstalt f. mental hospital.

nervenkrank neurotic, neurasthenic.

Nervenschwäche f. nervous debility, neurasthenia.

nervös nervous.

Nervosität f. nervousness.

Nerz m. mink.

Nest n. nest.

NETT nice, neat, pretty.

Netz n. net, network.

NEU new, fresh, recent, modern, latest.

  Was gibt's Neues?   What's new?

Neubau m. new building, reconstruction.

neuerdings recently, lately.

Neuerung f. innovation, change.

Neugier f. curiosity.

neugierig curious.

Neuheit f. novelty.

Neuhochdeutsch n. modern high German.

Neuigkeit f. news.

NEUJAHR n. New Year.

  Glückliches Neujahr!   Happy New Year!

neulich recently, the other day.

NEUN nine.

NEUNTE ninth.

NEUNZEHN nineteen.

NEUNZEHNTE nineteenth.

NEUNZIG ninety.

NEUNZIGSTE ninetieth.

neutral neutral.

Neuzeit f. modern times.

neuzeitlich modern.

NICHT not.

  auch nicht   neither, also not.

  ganz und gar nicht   not in the least.

  gar nicht   not at all.

  nicht einmal   not even.

  nicht mehr   no longer, no more.

  Nicht wahr?   Isn't it?

  noch nicht   not yet.

Nichtachtung f. disregard.

Nichte f. niece.

NICHTS nothing, not anything.

  gar nichts   nothing at all.

  Es macht nichts.   It doesn't matter.

  Ich will nichts mehr davon hören.   I don't want to hear another word about that.

  mir nichts, dir nichts   quite coolly.

  nichts als   nothing but.

  nichts anderes   nothing else.

  durchaus nichts   not at all.

nichtsdestoweniger nevertheless.

nichts sagend meaningless, insignificant.

Nichtstuer m. idler.

Nichtstun n. idling.

nie (mals) never.

  fast nie   hardly ever.

NIEDER down, low, mean.

  auf und nieder   up and down.

niedergeschlagen downhearted, depressed.

Niedergeschlagenheit f. depression.

Niederlage f. defeat.

niedertreten to trample.

niedrig low, inferior, humble.

NIEMAND nobody.

Niere f. kidney.

nimmer never.

nimmermehr nevermore, by no means.

nirgends nowhere.

nirgendwo nowhere.

NOCH still, yet, besides.

  noch dazu   in addition.

  noch ein   another.

noch einmal *once more.*
noch einmal so *twice as.*
noch etwas *something else.*
noch immer *still.*
noch nicht *not yet.*
noch nie *never before.*
weder . . . noch *neither . . . nor.*
nochmals *once again.*
Norden *m. north.*
  nach Norden *in the direction of the north.*
nordisch *nordic, northern.*
nördlich *northern.*
nordöstlich *northeastern.*
Nordpol *m. North Pole.*
Nordsee *f. North Sea.*
Norm *f. standard, rule.*
normal *normal.*
NOT *f. distress, want.*
  aus Not *from necessity.*
  Not bricht Eisen. *Necessity is the mother of invention.*
  ohne Not *without real cause.*
  seine liebe Not haben mit *to have a hard time with.*
  zur Not *if need be.*
Notar *m. notary public.*
notariell *attested by a notary.*
Notausgang *m. emergency exit.*
Notbehelf *m. expedient.*
Notbremse *f. emergency brake.*
Note *f. note (music, bank, dipl.); mark (school); (-n, pl., music).*
Notfall *m. emergency.*
notgedrungen *compulsory, forced.*
nötig *necessary, needful.*
  nötig haben *to need.*
nötigenfalls *if need be.*
notleidend *poor, distressed.*
Notlüge *f. white lie.*
notwendig *necessary.*
Notwendigkeit *f. necessity.*
Novelle *f. short story, short novel.*
NOVEMBER *m. November.*
nüchtern *empty, sober, insipid.*
Nüchternheit *f. emptiness, sobriety, insipidity.*
null *null.*
  null und nichtig *null and void.*
Null *f. zero.*
NUMMER *f. number, part, ticket, size, issue.*
  Seine Nummer ist besetzt. *His line is busy.*
  Welche Nummer tragen Sie? *What size do you wear?*
  die letzte Nummer *the last issue (magazine).*
nummerieren *to number*
  nummerierter Platz *m.* *reserved seat.*
NUN *now, well, then.*
  von nun an *henceforth, from now on.*
NUR *only, sole, merely, just, possibly.*

nur mehr *still more.*
Nur zu! *Go on!*
wenn nur *if only.*
wer nur immer *whoever.*
Lass mich nur machen! *Let me do it!*
nicht nur . . . sondern auch *not only . . . but also.*
Nuss *f. nut.*
Nussbaum *m. walnut tree.*
Nussknacker *m. nutcracker.*
nutzbar *useful, necessary.*
nutzbringend *profitable.*
Nutzen *m. profit, benefit.*
nützen *to be of use, be profitable, serve.*
  Es nützt nichts! *It's no use!*
nützlich *useful.*
Nützlichkeit *f. usefulness, utility.*
nutzlos *useless.*
Nutzlosigkeit *f. uselessness, futility.*
Nylon *n. nylon.*

O

OB *whether, if.*
  Wir möchten wissen, ob sie kommen. *We want to know whether they are coming.*
  als ob *as if, as though.*
OBEN *above, up, upstairs, on top.*
  auf . . . oben *at the top of.*
  dort oben *up there.*
  nach oben *upward.*
  oben auf *on top of.*
  von oben bis unten *from top to bottom.*
  von oben herab behandeln *to treat in a condescending manner.*
obendrein *into the bargain, in addition.*
ober *upper, supreme, above.*
  das obere Bett *the upper berth.*
Ober *m. waiter.*
  Herr Ober! *Waiter!*
Oberbefehlshaber *m. commander-in-chief.*
Oberfläche *f. surface, area.*
oberflächlich *superficial, superficially.*
oberhalb *above.*
Oberhemd *n. shirt.*
Oberkellner *m. headwaiter.*
Oberkörper *m. upper part of the body.*
Oberlippe *f. upper lip.*
Oberschule *f. high school.*
Oberst *m. colonel.*
oberst *highest, uppermost.*
Oberstleutnant *m. lieutenant colonel.*
obgleich *although.*
Oboe *f. oboe.*
Obrigkeit *f. authority.*
obschon *although.*
Obst *n. fruit.*

Obstgarten *m. orchard.*

Ochs *m. ox.*

ochsen *to grind, cram, work hard (slang).*

öde *dull, empty.*

ODER *or.*

 oder aber *instead, or else.*

 entweder . . . oder *either . . . or.*

Ofen *m. stove, furnace.*

offen *open, free, vacant, frank, sincere.*

 auf offener Strecke *on the road.*

 offen gestanden *frankly.*

 offene Rechnung *current account, unpaid bill.*

 offen für etwas sein *to be receptive to something.*

offenbar *obvious, evident.*

Offenbarung *f. disclosure, revelation.*

Offenheit *f. frankness, sincerity.*

offenherzig *frank, sincere.*

offensichtlich *obvious, apparent.*

öffentlich *public.*

Öffentlichkeit *f. publicity.*

offiziell *official.*

Offizier *m. officer.*

öffnen *to open, dissect.*

Öffnung *f. opening, gap, dissection.*

OFT *often, frequently.*

öfter *more often.*

 je öfter . . . desto *the more . . . the more.*

 des öfteren *frequently.*

öfters *quite often.*

oftmals *often, frequently.*

OHNE *prep. (acc.) without, but, for, except.*

 Er ging ohne ein Wort zu sagen. *He left without saying a word.*

 ohne Arbeit *out of work.*

 ohne dass *without (conj.).*

 ohne mit mir gesprochen haben *without having spoken to me.*

 ohne weiteres *right off.*

 ohne zu *without (before verb).*

 ohne zu antworten *without answering.*

 ohnehin *besides, apart.*

Ohnmacht *f. faintness, unconsciousness, faint.*

ohnmächtig *powerless, unconscious, helpless.*

 ohnmächtig werden *to faint.*

OHR *n. ear, hearing.*

 die Ohren steif halten *to keep one's courage.*

 ganz Ohr sein *to be all ears.*

Ohrring *m. earring.*

OKTOBER *m. October.*

ÖL *n. oil.*

Ölbaum *m. olive tree.*

Ölbild *n. oil painting.*

ölen *to oil, lubricate.*

Ölfarbe *f. paint.*

ölig *oily.*

Olive *f. olive.*

Omelett(e) *n. omelet.*

ONKEL *m. uncle.*

OPER *f. opera, opera house.*

Operation *f. operation.*

Operette *f. operetta.*

Opfer *n. sacrifice, martyr, victim.*

opfern *to sacrifice.*

Opferung *f. sacrifice.*

Optiker *m. optician.*

Optimismus *m. optimism.*

optimistisch *optimistic.*

Orange *f. orange.*

Orchester *n. orchestra.*

Orden *m. order, decoration.*

ordentlich *in order, neat, tidy.*

ordnen *to put in order, arrange.*

ORDNUNG *f. order, arrangement.*

 Das finde ich ganz in Ordnung. *I think it is quite all right.*

 in Ordnung bringen *to settle, straighten out.*

 Ist alles in Ordnung? *Is everything all right?*

 nicht in Ordnung *out of order.*

 zur Ordnung rufen *to call to order.*

Organ *n. organ (body).*

organisieren *to organize.*

organisch *organic.*

Organist *m. organist.*

Orgel *f. organ (music).*

original *original.*

ORT *m. place, spot, locality.*

 Wir fanden alles wieder an Ort und Stelle. *We found everything back in place.*

örtlich *local.*

Osten *m. east, orient.*

 nach Osten *in the direction of the east.*

Osterfest *n. Easter.*

Ostern *n. east.*

Österreicher *m. Austrian.*

österreichisch *Austrian.*

östlich *eastern.*

Ostsee *f. Baltic Sea.*

ostwärts *eastward.*

Ozean *m. ocean.*

P

Paar *n. pair, couple.*

 mit ein Paar Worten *in a few words.*

 ein Paar Strümpfe *a pair of socks.*

paar *few, some, even, matching.*

 ein paar *a few, several.*

 ein paarmal *several times.*

paaren *to pair, couple.*

Pächter *m. farmer, tenant, householder.*

Päckchen *n. small parcel.*

packen *to seize, grasp, pack.*
packend *thrilling, absorbing.*
Packung *f. package, packet.*
Paddelboot *n. canoe.*
paddeln *to paddle.*
Paket *n. parcel.*
Paketannahme *f. parcel-pickup office.*
Pakt *m. pact, agreement.*
Palast *m. palace.*
Palme *f. palm.*
panieren *to coat with breadcrumbs.*
Panik *f. panic.*
Panne *f. breakdown, trouble (motor).*
Pantoffel *m. slipper, mule.*
Pantoffelheld *m. henpecked husband.*
Panzer *m. armor, tank.*
panzern *to armor, plate.*
Pagagei *m. parrot.*
PAPIER *n. paper, identification paper,*
    document.
  zu Papier bringen   *to write down, put on*
    paper.
Papierbogen *m. sheet of paper.*
Papiergeld *n. paper money.*
Papierhandlung *f. stationery store.*
Papierkorb *m. wastepaper basket.*
Pappe *f. cardboard.*
Papst *m. Pope.*
Parade *f. parade, review.*
Paradies *n. paradise.*
paradiesisch *paradisiacal.*
parallel *parallel.*
Parfum or **Parfüm** *n. perfume.*
PARK *n. park, grounds.*
parken *to park.*
  Parkverbot!   *No parking!*
Parkplatz *m. parking place.*
Parlament *n. parliament.*
Parodie *f. parody.*
Partei *f. party, faction, tenant, side.*
  Partei nehmen für   *to take the side of.*
Parterre *n. ground floor (Brit.); first floor*
    (Am.).
Partie *f. part, section.*
  eine Partie Schach   *a game of chess.*
Partner *m. partner.*
Partnerschaft *f. partnership.*
Pass *m. pass, passage, passport.*
Passagier *m. passenger.*
Passamt *n. passport office.*
Passant *m. passer-by.*
PASSEN *to fit, suit, be convenient, be*
    suitable.
  zueinander passen   *to match, harmonize.*
PASSEND *suitable, convenient.*
passieren *to happen, go through, pass, cross.*
  Was ist passiert?   *What happened? (What's*
    the trouble?)
passiv *passive.*

Passkontrolle *f. passport control.*
Pastete *f. pie, pastry.*
Pastor *m. pastor, minister, clergyman.*
Pate *m. godfather.*
Patenkind *n. godchild.*
Patent *n. (letters) patent.*
Patentamt *n. patent office.*
pathetisch *pathetic.*
Patient *m. patient.*
Patin *f. godmother.*
Patriot *m. patriot.*
patriotisch *patriotic.*
Pauke *f. kettledrum.*
Pause *f. pause, interval, break, rest (music).*
pausieren *to pause.*
Pech *n. bad luck, pitch, tar*
pechschwarz *pitch-black.*
Pechvogel *m. unlucky person.*
Pedal *n. pedal.*
Pedant *m. pedant.*
pedantisch *pedantic.*
Pein *f. pain, agony, torture.*
peinigen *to torment, harass.*
Peiniger *m. tormentor.*
Peinigung *f. torment, torture.*
peinlich *painful, embarrassing.*
Peinlichkeit *f. painfulness; carefulness,*
    embarrassment.
Peitsche *f. whip, lash.*
Pellkartoffeln *pl. potatoes in their skins.*
PELZ *m. fur, pelt, skin, hide, fur coat.*
Pelzhändler *m. furrier.*
Pelzmantel *m. fur coat.*
Pension *f. pension; boardinghouse.*
  Er erhält eine Pension.   *He receives a*
    pension.
  in Pension sein   *to board.*
Pensionat *n. boarding school.*
pensionieren *to pension off.*
per *per.*
  per Post   *by mail.*
  per Adresse   *(in) care of.*
Periode *f. period.*
Perle *f. pearl, bead.*
perlen *to sparkle, glisten.*
Perlenkette *f. pearl necklace, string of pearls.*
PERSON *f. person, personage, character*
    (theater).
  in Person   *in person.*
Personal *n. staff, employees, personnel.*
Personalien *pl. particulars about a person,*
    data.
Personbeschreibung *f. personal description of*
    a person.
Personenaufzug *m. passenger elevator.*
Personenkraftwagen *m. automobile, car.*
Personenzug *m. passenger train.*
persönlich *personal; personally.*
Persönlichkeit *f. personality.*

Perücke f. wig.
pessimistisch pessimistic.
Pest f. plague, pestilence, epidemic.
Petersilie f. parsley.
Pfad m. path.
Pfadfinder m. (-in f.) boy (girl) scout.
Pfahl m. pole, stake, pile, post.
Pfand n. pledge, security, forfeit.
pfänden to seize, take in pledge.
Pfandhaus n. pawnshop.
Pfandleiher m. pawnbroker.
Pfandschein m. pawn ticket.
Pfanne f. pan.
Pfannkuchen m. pancake.
Pfarrer m. priest, pastor, minister.
Pfarrgemeinde f. parish.
Pfau m. peacock.
PFEFFER m. pepper.
Pfefferkuchen m. spiced cakes, gingerbread.
Pfefferminz n. & f. peppermint.
pfeffern to season with pepper.
Pfeife f. pipe, whistle.
pfeifen to whistle, pipe.
Pfeil m. arrow.
Pfeiler m. pillar, post.
PFERD n. horse.
Pfiff m. whistle, whistling, trick.
Pfingsten m. & f. Pentecost, Whitsuntide.
Pfirsich m. peach.
PFLANZE f. plant.
pflanzen to plant.
Pflanzenkunde f. botany.
Pflaster n. plaster, pavement.
Pflasterstein m. paving stone.
PFLAUME f. plum.
   gedörrte Pflaume f. prune.
Pflaumenmus n. plum jam.
PFLEGE f. care, attention, nursing.
Pflegeeltern pl. foster parents.
Pflegekind n. foster child.
pflegen to care for, cherish, nurse, cultivate.
PFLICHT f. duty, obligation.
Pflichteifer m. zeal.
Pflichtgefühl n. sense of duty.
pflichtgemäß obligatory.
pflücken to pick, gather, pluck.
Pflug m. plough.
pflügen to plough.
Pförtner m. gatekeeper.
Pfote f. paw.
Pfui! shame!; yuck.
Pfund n. pound.
Pfütze f. puddle.
Phänomen n. phenomenon.
Phantasie f. imagination, fancy.
phantasieren to daydream, imagine.
Phantast m. dreamer, visionary.
phantastisch fantastic, fanciful.
Philosoph m. philosopher.

Philosophie f. philosophy.
philosophieren to philosophize.
Photoapparat m. camera.
Photograph m. photographer.
Photographie f. photography.
photographieren to photograph.
Physik f. physics.
Pianist m. (-in f.) pianist.
Piano n. piano.
Picknick n. picnic.
Pietät f. reverence, piety.
pietätlos irreverent.
Pikkoloflöte f. piccolo.
Pilger m. pilgrim.
pilgern to go on a pilgrimage.
Pille f. pill.
Pilot m. pilot.
Pilz m. mushroom.
   Giftpilz m.   poisonous mushroom.
Pinsel m. brush, paintbrush.
pinseln to paint (art).
Pirat m. pirate.
Pistole f. pistol.
Plage f. plague.
plagen to plague, torment.
   sich plagen   to struggle, overwork
           oneself.
Plakat placard, poster.
   Keine Plakate.   Post no bills.
Plakatsäule f. signpost, billboard.
Plan m. plan, map, design; intention.
planen to plan, scheme.
Planet m. planet.
planlos without any fixed plan.
planmäßig according to plan; methodical.
Planung f. planning, plan.
Planwirtschaft f. economic planning.
Plastik f. plastic art, sculpture.
plastisch plastic.
Platin n. platinum.
plätschern to splash.
PLATT flat, level, insipid, dull.
Plattdeutsch n. Low German.
Platte f. plate, tray; record (phonograph).
   kalte Platte   cold meats.
PLATZ m. place, spot, room, seat; square
     (street).
   Platz machen   to make room.
   Bitte, nehmen Sie Platz.   Please have a
     seat.
   am Platz sein   to be opportune.
Platzanweiser m. (-in f.) usher.
Plätzchen n. little place; cookie.
platzen to burst, explode, crack.
Platzmangel m. lack of space.
Plauderei f. chat, small talk, conversation.
PLAUDERN to chat, talk, gossip.
PLÖTZLICH sudden; suddenly.
plump heavy, shapeless, tactless, clumsy.

Plumpheit *f. shapelessness, heaviness, clumsiness.*
plumpsen *to plump down.*
plündern *to plunder, pillage.*
Plünderung *f. plundering, sack.*
Plural *m. plural.*
Pöbel *m. mob, populace.*
pöbelhaft *vulgar, low.*
pochen *to knock, beat, throb.*
Podium *n. platform, rostrum.*
Poesie *f. poetry.*
Poet *m. poet.*
poetisch *poetical.*
Pol *m. pole.*
polar *polar, arctic.*
Polarforscher *m. polar explorer.*
Pole *m. Pole (native of Poland).*
polieren *n. polish.*
Poliermittel *n. polish.*
Politik *f. politics, policy.*
Politiker *m. politician.*
politisch *political.*
politisieren *to talk politics.*
Politur *f. polish, gloss, refinement.*
POLIZEI *f. police.*
　　Rufen Sie die Polizei!　*Call the police!*
　　Polizeibehörde　*police authorities.*
Polizeiamt *n. police station.*
Polizeiaufsicht *f. police control.*
polizeilich *of the police.*
Polizeistreife *f. police raid.*
Polizeistunde *f. curfew.*
Polizist *m. (-in f.) policeman/woman constable.*
polnisch *Polish.*
Polster *n. cushion, pillow, bolster, pad.*
Polstermöbel *pl. upholstered furniture.*
Polstersessel *m. easy chair.*
Polsterung *f. upholstery, padding, stuffing.*
Pomade *f. pomade, hair gel.*
Pomp *m. pomp.*
pomphaft *pompous, magnificent.*
pompös *pompous, magnificent.*
populär *popular.*
Pore *f. pore.*
porös *porous.*
Portemonnaie *n. purse.*
Portion *f. portion, helping, ration, order.*
Porto *n. postage.*
portofrei *postpaid, prepaid.*
portopflichtig *liable to postage fee.*
Porträt *n. portrait, likeness.*
porträtieren *to portray, paint a portrait.*
Porträtmaler *m. portrait painter.*
Porzellan *porcelain, china.*
Porzellanservice *n. set of china.*
positiv *positive.*
POST *f. post, mail, post office.*
Postfach *n. post office box (PO Box).*

Postamt *m. post office.*
Postanweisung *f. money order.*
Postbeamter *m. post-office clerk.*
Postbote *m. mailman, letter carrier.*
Posten *m. post, situation.*
　　auf dem Posten sein　*to feel well.*
Postkarte *f. postcard.*
postlagernd *general delivery (USA).*
postlich *postal.*
Postschließfach *n. PO Box.*
postwendend *by return mail.*
Pracht *f. splendor.*
Prachtausgabe *f. deluxe edition.*
prächtig *magnificent, splendid, lovely.*
prachtvoll *splendid, gorgeous, magnificent.*
prahlen *to brag, boast.*
Prahlerei *f. boasting, bragging.*
prahlerisch *boastful, ostentatious.*
praktisch *clever, handy, useful.*
　　praktischer Arzt　*general practitioner.*
praktizieren *to practice (a profession).*
prall *blazing, tight, tense.*
　　in der prallen Sonne　*in the full glare of the sun.*
Prämie *f. premium.*
prämieren *to award a prize to.*
Präposition *f. preposition.*
präsentieren *to present.*
Präsident *m. president.*
Präsidium *n. chair, presidency.*
prassen *to feast, revel.*
präzis *precise, exact, punctual.*
Präzision *f. precision.*
predigen *to preach.*
Prediger *m. preacher, minister.*
Predigt *f. sermon, lecture.*
PREIS *m. price, cost, rate, praise.*
　　um jeden Preis　*at any cost.*
　　um keinen Preis　*not at any price.*
　　zu festem Preis　*at fixed price.*
　　den Preis davontragen　*to take the prize.*
Preisangabe *f. quotation of prices.*
Preisausschreiben *n. prize competition.*
Preisbewerber *m. competitor.*
Preiselbeere *f. cranberry.*
preisen *to praise, extol, glorify.*
Preiserhöhung *f. rise in prices.*
Preisgabe *f. surrender, abandonment.*
preisgeben *to surrender, give up, abandon, sacrifice.*
Preislage *f. price range.*
Preisrichter *m. arbiter, judge.*
Preissturz *m. fall in prices.*
Preisträger *m. prizewinner.*
Preistreiberei *f. forcing up of prices.*
preiswert *reasonable, cheap.*
Premiere *f. first night.*
Presse *f. press.*
Pressestimme *f. press comment, review.*

Priester *m. priest.*
Prima *f. highest class of secondary school.*
prima *prime, first-rate, great.*
primitiv *primitive.*
Prinz *m. (-essin f.) prince(ss).*
Prinzip *n. principle.*
  aus Prinzip *as a matter of principle.*
prinzipiell *on principle.*
PRIVAT *private, privately.*
Privatrecht *n. civil law.*
Probe *f. trial, experiment, test, probation; rehearsal (theater).*
  auf die Probe stellen *to put to the test.*
  Probe ablegen *to give proof of.*
  die Probe bestehen *to pass the test.*
Probeabzug *m. proof.*
proben *to rehearse.*
probeweise *on approval, on trial.*
Probezeit *f. time of probation.*
probieren *to try, taste.*
  Darf ich das anprobieren? *May I try this on?*
  Er probiert die Suppe. *He tastes the soup.*
Problem *n. problem.*
problematisch *problematic.*
Produkt *n. product.*
Produktion *f. production.*
Produzent *m. producer, manufacturer.*
produzieren *to produce, show off, exhibit.*
Professor *m. (-in f.) professor.*
Prognose *f. forecast, prognosis.*
Programm *n. program.*
Projekt *n. project.*
Projektionsapparat *m. projector.*
Proklamation *f. proclamation.*
Prokura *f. procuration, power of attorney.*
prolongieren *to prolong.*
Promenade *f. promenade.*
Propaganda *f. propaganda.*
Prophet *m. prophet.*
prophetisch *prophetic.*
prophezeien *to prophesy.*
Prophezeiung *f. prophecy.*
Proportion *f. proportion.*
Prosa *f. prose.*
Prosit! *To your health!*
Prospekt *m. prospect.*
Protest *m. protest.*
  Protest erheben *to protest.*
Protestant *m. Protestant.*
protestantisch *protestant.*
Protestantismus *m. Protestantism.*
protestieren *to protest.*
Protokoll *n. protocol; proceedings.*
Proviant *m. provisions (mil.).*
Provinz *f. province.*
provinziell *provincial.*
Provision *f. brokerage.*
Prozent *n. percent.*

Prozentsatz *m. percentage.*
prozentual *expressed as percentage.*
PROZESS *m. lawsuit, process, proceedings, trial.*
  im Prozess liegen *to be involved in a lawsuit.*
  kurzen Prozess machen mit *to dispose of quickly.*
prozessieren *to be involved in a lawsuit.*
Prozession *f. procession.*
PRÜFEN *to test, investigate, inspect, examine.*
Prüfer *m. (-in f.) examiner.*
Prüfling *m. examinee.*
PRÜFUNG *f. investigation, examination.*
  eine Prüfung ablegen *to take an examination.*
Prunk *m. splendor, ostentation.*
prunkvoll *gorgeous, splendid.*
Psychiater *m. (-in f.) psychiatrist.*
Psychiatrie *f. psychiatry.*
psychisch *psychic.*
Psychologe *m. psychologist.*
Psychologie *f. psychology.*
psychologisch *psychological.*
Psychopath *m. (-in f.) psychopath.*
Publikum *n. public.*
Pudel *m. poodle.*
pudelnass *drenched, soaked.*
Puder *m. (toilet) powder.*
pudern *to powder.*
Puls *m. pulse.*
Pulsschlag *m. pulse beat.*
Pult *n. desk.*
Pulver *n. powder, gunpowder.*
Pulverfass *n. powder barrel.*
  auf dem Pulverfass sitzen *to sit on top of a volcano.*
PUNKT *m. point, dot, spot.*
  der springende Punkt *the salient point.*
  Punkt ein Uhr *at one o'clock sharp.*
  Ausgangspunkt *point of departure.*
pünktlich *on time, punctual, prompt.*
Pünktlichkeit *f. punctuality.*
Puppe *f. doll, puppet.*
Putz *m. trimming, ornament, dress.*
putzen *to clean, polish.*
Putzfrau *f. charwoman, cleaning lady.*
Putzlappen *m. duster, flannel, polishing cloth.*
Pyjama *n. & m. pajamas*

Quadrat *n. square.*
Quäker *m. Quaker.*
Qual *f. torment, torture, pain.*
quälen *to torment, worry, torture, bother.*

Quäler *m. tormentor.*
Quälerei *f. tormenting, torture.*
Quälgeist *m. nuisance (person).*
qualifizieren *to qualify.*
Qualität *f. quality.*
qualitativ *qualitative.*
Qualitätsware *f. quality goods pl.*
Qualm *m. dense smoke.*
qualmen *to smoke (chimney).*
qualmig *smoky.*
qualvoll *very painful, agonizing.*
Quarantäne *f. quarantine.*
   unter Quarantäne stellen   *to quarantine.*
Quecksilber *n. mercury.*
Quelle *f. spring, fountain.*
quellen *to gush, well, flow.*
Quellwasser *n. springwater.*
quer *cross, lateral, oblique; across, obliquely.*
   kreuz und quer   *all over.*
querfeldein *across country.*
Querschnitt *m. cross-section.*
Querstraße *f. crossroad.*
quetschen *to squeeze, smash.*
Quetschung *f. contusion.*
Quetschwunde *f. bruise.*
quietschen *to scream, squeal.*
quittieren *to give a receipt.*
Quittung *f. receipt.*
Quote *f. quota, share.*

R

Rabatt *m. discount.*
Rabbiner *m. rabbi.*
Rache *f. revenge.*
rächen *to revenge, avenge.*
   sich rächen   *take revenge, get revenge.*
   Deine Faulheit wird sich an dir rächen.   *You
     will have to suffer for your laziness.*
Rachsucht *f. thirst for revenge.*
rachsüchtig *revengeful.*
RAD *n. wheel, bicycle.*
Rad fahren *to cycle.*
Radfahrer *m. cyclist.*
Radfahrweg *m. cycle track.*
Radiergummi *m. eraser.*
Radierung *f. etching.*
Radio *n. radio.*
Radreifen *m. bicycle tire.*
raffiniert *refined, cunning.*
Rahm *m. cream.*
Rahmen *m. frame.*
Rakete *f. rocket.*
Rampe *f. ramp, platform; limelight.*
RAND *m. edge, brim, border, margin.*
   außer Rand und Band sein   *to be out of
     hand.*

   Schreiben Sie es an den Rand!   *Write it in
     the margin!*
Randbemerkung *f. marginal note.*
Rang *m. rank, order, quality, class.*
   den Rang ablaufen   *to get the better of.*
   ersten Ranges   *first class, first rate.*
   erster Rang   *first balcony, dress circle.*
   zweiter Rang   *second balcony, upper
     circle.*
Rangabzeichen *n. badge of rank.*
Rangordnung *f. order of precedence.*
Rangstufe *f. degree.*
rar *rare, scarce.*
Rarität *f. rarity, curiosity.*
rasch *quick, swift, speedy.*
raschein *to rustle.*
rasen *to rave, rage, speed (coll.).*
rasend *raving, raging, frantic.*
   rasend machen   *to make mad, enrage.*
Raserei *f. raving, fury; rage.*
Rasierapparat *m. safety razor.*
   elektrischer Rasierapparat   *electric razor.*
rasieren *to shave.*
   sich rasieren   *to shave (oneself).*
   sich rasieren lassen   *to get shaved.*
Rasierklinge *f. razor blade.*
Rasiermesser *n. razor.*
Rasierpinsel *m. shaving brush.*
Rasierzeug *n. shaving things.*
Rasse *f. race, breed.*
rassig *thoroughbred.*
rassisch *racial.*
Rast *f. resting, recreation, rest, repose.*
rasten *to rest.*
rastlos *restless, indefatigable.*
Rastlosigkeit *f. restlessness.*
RAT *m. counsel, advice, consultation, remedy.*
   Rat schaffen   *to devise means.*
   um Rat fragen   *to ask advice.*
   zu Rat ziehen   *to consult.*
   etwas zu Rate halten   *to economize.*
   mit Rat und Tat   *by word and deed.*
   ihm Rat erteilen   *to give him advice.*
Rate *f. installment.*
raten *to advise, guess, solve.*
ratenweise *by installments.*
Ratgeber *m. adviser.*
Ration *f. ration.*
rationell *rational; economical.*
ratlos *at a loss, helpless.*
Ratlosigkeit *f. helplessness, perplexity.*
Ratschläge *m. counsel, advice.*
Rätsel *n. riddle, enigma, puzzle.*
   Es ist mir ein Rätsel.   *It puzzles me.*
rätselhaft *mysterious, enigmatic.*
Ratte *f. rat.*
Raub *m. robbery, plundering.*
   auf Raub ausgehen   *to go prowling, to
     prowl about.*

rauben *to rob, plunder.*
Räuber *m. robber, thief.*
Raubmord *m. murder and robbery.*
Raubtier *n. beast of prey.*
Raubvogel *m. bird of prey.*
Rauch *m. smoke.*
RAUCHEN *to smoke.*
   Rauchen Verboten! *No Smoking!*
Raucher *m. (-in f.) smoker.*
räuchern *to smoke, cure, fumigate.*
Räucherwaren *pl. smoked meats and fish.*
Rauchtabak *m. tobacco.*
Rauchzimmer *n. smoking room.*
RAUH *uneven, rough, raw, hoarse, harsh.*
Rauheit *f. roughness, harshness.*
RAUM *m. place, room, space.*
   Raum geben *to give way, indulge.*
räumen *to clear away, remove, clean,*
   evacuate.
Rauminhalt *m. volume, capacity.*
räumlich *relating to space, spatial.*
Räumlichkeit *f. room, premises, space.*
Raummangel *m. lack of room.*
Räumung *f. removal, evacuation.*
Raupe *f. caterpillar.*
Raupenschlepper *m. caterpillar tractor.*
Rausch *m. intoxication, frenzy, drunkenness.*
rauschen *to rustle, rush, roar.*
Rauschgift *n. narcotic, drug.*
Reaktion *f. reaction.*
Rebe *f. grape, vine.*
Rebell *m. rebel.*
rebellieren *to rebel.*
Rechen *m. rake.*
Rechenmaschine *f. calculator.*
RECHNEN *to count, calculate.*
RECHNUNG *f. sum, account, bill,*
   calculation.
   auf eigene Rechnung *at one's own risk.*
   auf Rechnung setzen *to charge, put to*
     one's account.
   in Rechnung ziehen *to take into account.*
   laut Rechnung *as per invoice.*
   Die Rechnung, bitte. *Please bring me the*
     check.
   Sind Sie auf Ihre Rechnung gekommen?
     Did you get your money's worth? (Was
     it worthwhile?)
   die Rechnung führen *to keep accounts.*
Rechnungsprüfer *m. auditor.*
RECHT *n. right, privilege, title, claim, law.*
   alle Rechte vorbehalten *all rights*
     reserved.
   an den Rechten kommen *to meet one's*
     match.
   mit vollem Recht *for good reasons.*
   nach dem Rechten sehen *to see to things.*
   Recht behalten *to be right in the end.*
   Recht geben *to agree with.*

   Recht haben *to be right.*
   Recht sprechen *to administer justice.*
   von Rechts wegen *by rights, according to*
     the law.
   zu Recht bestehen *to be valid.*
RECHT *right, all right, right hand, correct,*
   proper, genuine, lawful.
   Das ist mir recht. *That's all right with me.*
   Das ist nur recht und billig. *That's only*
     fair.
   die rechte Hand *the right hand.*
   erst recht *all the more now, now more than*
     ever.
   Es geschieht ihm recht. *It serves him*
     right.
   es recht machen *to suit, please.*
   Man kann es nicht allen recht machen.
     You cannot please everybody.
   schlecht und recht *not bad.*
   zur rechten Zeit *in good time.*
   rechtzeitig *on time.*
   bürgerliches Recht *civil law.*
   wenn es Ihnen recht ist . . . *if it's*
     agreeable to you . . .
Rechteck *n. rectangle.*
rechteckig *rectangular.*
rechterhand *on the right hand.*
rechtfertigen *to justify, to exculpate.*
   sich rechtfertigen *to justify oneself.*
Rechtfertigung *f. justification.*
rechthaberisch *dogmatic, obstinate.*
rechtlich *just, lawful, legitimate.*
Rechtlichkeit *f. integrity, honesty.*
rechtmäßig *lawful, legitimate.*
RECHTS *to the right, on the right.*
   Biegen Sie rechts ab! *Turn to the right!*
   nach rechts *to the right.*
   Nehmen Sie die erste Strasse rechts. *Take*
     the first street on your right.
   Rechts halten! *Keep to the right!*
   Rechts um! *Right turn!*
Rechtsanspruch *m. legal claim.*
Rechtsanwalt *m. lawyer, counsel.*
rechtschaffen *honest, upright; very, extremely,*
   thoroughly.
Rechtschreibung *f. spelling.*
Rechtsfall *m. lawsuit.*
Rechtsgelehrter *m. jurist.*
rechtsgültig *legal, valid.*
Rechtsspruch *m. verdict.*
rechtsungültig *illegal, invalid.*
rechtsverbindlich *legally, binding.*
Rechtsweg *m. legal proceedings, law.*
rechtswidrig *illegal.*
Rechtswissenschaft *f. jurisprudence.*
rechtzeitig *in good time.*
recken *to stretch, extend.*
   die Glieder recken *to stretch one's limbs.*
Redakteur *m. editor.*

Redaktion f. editors, editorial staff; wording.
redaktionell editorial.
REDE f. talk, discourse, speech, conversation, rumor.
  Davon ist keine Rede! That's out of the question!
  Davon ist nicht dir Rede! That's not the point!
  eine Rede halten to make a speech.
  in die Rede fallen to interrupt.
  nicht der Rede wert not worth mentioning.
  Rede stehen to answer for.
  Wovon ist die Rede? What is it all about?
  zur Rede stellen to call to account, to take to task.
Redefreiheit f. freedom of speech.
redegewandt fluent, eloquent.
REDEN to talk, speak, converse, make a speech.
  begeistert reden to rave, enthuse.
  mit sich reden lassen to listen to reason.
  nicht zu reden von to say nothing of.
  von sich reden machen to cause a stir.
Redensart f. phrase, idiom, nonsense.
Redner m. orator, speaker.
reduzieren to reduce.
Reederei f. steamship company.
Referenz f. reference.
reformieren to reform.
Regal n. shelf.
rege active, brisk.
Regel f. rule, regulation, principle.
  in der Regel as a rule.
regelmäßig regular, proportional.
regeln to arrange, regulate.
  geregelt regular, well-ordered.
regelrecht regular, correct, proper.
REGEN m. rain, precipitation.
  Auf Regen folgt Sonnenschein. The calm follows the storm. ("After rain follows sunshine.")
Regenbogen m. rainbow.
regendicht waterproof.
Regenmantel m. raincoat.
Regenschirm m. umbrella.
Regenzeit f. rainy season.
Regie f. production (theater); administration, management.
regieren to rule, govern, reign.
Regierung f. government, reign, rule.
Regierungsbeamter n. government official.
Regiment n. regiment, government.
Regisseur m. stage manager.
Register n. register, index, table of contents.
registrieren to register.
REGNEN to rain
  Es regnet in Strömen. It's raining cats and dogs.
regnerisch rainy.

regsam active, agile, quick.
Regsamkeit f. agility, activity, quickness.
Regung f. movement.
Reh n. deer.
Rehbraten m. roast venison.
Reibeisen n. grater.
Reiben to rub, grate, grind.
  sich wundreiben to chafe oneself.
REICH rich, wealthy, well-off, plentiful, abundant.
Reich n. empire, kingdom.
  Deutsches Reich n. Germany.
  Österreich n. Austria.
reichen to give, present, hand.
reichhaltig full, rich, abundant.
Reichhaltigkeit f. fullness, richness.
reichlich plentiful, abundant, copious.
Reichtum m. wealth, abundance.
Reichweite f. range, reach.
Reif m. frost.
REIF ripe, mature, mellow.
Reifen m. tire.
reifen to ripen, mature.
Reifenpanne f. flat tire, blowout.
Reifenschaden m. flat tire, blowout.
Reifeprüfung f. final comprehensive examination.
Reifezeugnis n. final certificate, diploma.
reiflich maturely, carefully.
REIHE f. row, range, series, sequence.
  außer der Reihe out of one's mind.
  der Reihe nach successively, in rotation.
  Er ist an der Reihe. It is his turn.
Reihenfolge f. succession, sequence.
reihenweise in rows.
Reim m. rhyme.
reimen to rhyme.
REIN clean, plain, sheer, pure, genuine, tidy.
  aus reinem Trotz out of sheer obstinacy.
  reine Bahn machen to clear the way.
  reiner Gewinn net profit.
  reiner Zufall sheer luck, pure chance.
  aus reinem Mitleid out of sheer compassion.
Reingewinn m. net profit.
Reinheit f. purity, pureness.
REINIGEN to clean, cleanse, purify.
Reinigung f. cleaning, cleansing, cleaners.
reinlich clean, neat, tidy.
Reinlichkeit f. cleanliness, neatness, tidiness.
Reis m. rice.
REISE f. trip, journey, voyage.
  Glückliche Reise! Have a nice trip!
  eine Reise machen to take a trip.
  Reiseandenken n. souvenir (from a trip).
Reisebüro n. tourist office.
Reiseführer m. guidebook.
REISEN to travel.
REISENDE m. passenger, traveler.

Reisescheck m. traveler's check.
reißen to tear, pull, drag.
   an sich reißen   to seize, hold up, snatch
    , up.
   in Stücke reißen   to tear to pieces.
   sich reißen um   to fight for.
reißend ravenous, rapid, torrential.
   der reißende Strom m.   torrent.
Reißverschluss m. zipper.
reiten to ride a horse.
Reiter m. horseman, cavalryman.
Reithose f. riding pants.
Reitschule f. riding school.
REIZ m. charm, attraction; irritation;
   incentive.
reizbar sensitive, irritable, excitable.
reizen to irritate, excite, provoke, tempt.
reizend charming.
reizlos unattractive.
reizvoll charming, attractive.
REKLAME f. publicity, advertisement.
   Reklame machen   to advertise.
rekonstruieren to reconstruct.
Rekord m. record, competition.
Rektor m. university or school president.
relativ relative, relating to.
Religion f. religion.
religiös religious.
Rennbahn f. racecourse.
RENNEN to run, race.
Rennfahrer m. racing cyclist.
Rennstall m. racing stable.
renovieren to renovate, redecorate.
Rente f. pension, revenue.
Reparation f. reparation.
Reparatur f. repair.
   wegen Reparatur geschlossen   closed for
    repairs.
Reparaturwerkstätte f. repair shop.
Reportage f. commentary, eyewitness account.
repräsentieren to represent.
Republik f. republic.
Republikaner m. (-in f.) Republican.
republikanisch republican.
Reserve f. reserve.
Reserverad n. spare wheel.
reservieren to reserve.
Respekt m. respect.
respektabel respectable.
respektieren to respect.
respektios without respect, irreverent.
respektvoll respectful.
Rest m. rest, remains, remnant.
restaurieren to repair, restore (work of art).
Restbestand m. remainder, residue.
restlos complete, without anything left over.
Resultat n. result, answer.
retten to save, preserve, rescue, deliver.
Rettung f. rescue, saving, escape.

Rettungsboot n. lifeboat.
Rettungsgürtel m. lifebelt.
Reue f. repentance.
reuen to repent, regret.
   Es reut mich.   I regret.
reumütig repentant, penitent.
Revier n. hunting ground, district.
   Polizeirevier n.   district police station.
Revolte f. revolt, insurrection.
Revolution f. revolution.
revolutionär revolutionary.
Revolver m. revolver.
Rezept n. recipe, prescription.
rezitieren to recite.
Rheumatismus m. rheumatism.
rhythmisch rhythmical.
Richter m. (-in f.) judge.
RICHTIG right, correct, true, real, straight.
   Das ist nicht sein richtiger Name.   That's
    not his real name.
   Meine Uhr geht richtig.   My watch is right.
   Richtig!   Right!
Richtigstellung f. rectification.
Richtlinie f. guiding principle, rule.
Richtung f. direction, line, course, tendency.
riechen to smell.
Riemen m. strap.
Riese m. giant.
riesenhaft gigantic, colossal.
Rind n. ox, cow, cattle.
Rinde f. bark, rind of cheese, crust.
Rinderbraten m. roast beef.
Rindfleisch n. beef.
Ring m. ring, circle.
ringen to struggle, wrestle.
Ringkampf m. wrestling match.
Ringkämpfer m. wrestler.
Ringrichter m. umpire, referee.
rings round, around.
ringsum (-her) all around.
Rinne f. gutter, channel.
rinnen to flow, run.
Rinnstein m. gutter.
Rippe f. rib.
riskant risky.
riskieren to risk.
Riss m. tear, hole, gap, crack.
Ritter m. knight, cavalier.
Rittergut n. estate, manor.
ritterlich chivalrous, gallant.
Rivale m. rival.
Rock m. coat (man's); skirt.
rodeln to sled.
Rodelschlitten m. sled.
roden to root out, clear (forest, garden).
ROH raw, crude, coarse, rare (steak).
Rohmaterial n. raw material.
Rohr n. pipe, oven.
Röhre f. tube, valve.

Rolle f. roll, cylinder; part (theater).
 aus der Rolle fallen to misbehave.
 die Rollen verteilen to cast (a play).
 eine Rolle spielen to be important.
Rollenbesetzung f. cast.
Rollmops m. pickled herring.
Rollschuh m. rollerskate.
 Rollschuh laufen to rollerskate.
Rollstuhl m. wheelchair.
Rolltreppe f. escalator.
Roman m. novel.
Romanschriftsteller m. novelist.
Romantik f. Romanticism.
Romantiker m. romanticist.
romantisch romantic.
röntgen to x-ray.
Röntgenaufnahme f. X-ray (plate).
Röntgenbild n. X-ray picture.
Röntgenstrahlen pl. X-rays.
rosa pink, rose-colored.
Rose f. rose.
Rosenkohl m. brussels sprouts.
Rosine f. raisin.
Rost m. 1. rust.
 2. grate.
Rostbraten m. roast beef.
Röstbrot toast.
rösten to roast, grill, toast.
Rostfleck m. patch of rust.
rostfrei rustproof.
 rostfreier Stahl   stainless steel.
rostig rusty.
ROT red, ruddy.
 rot werden to blush.
rotblond auburn.
Röte f. red, redness, blush.
Rotkohl m. red cabbage.
Rotstift m. red pencil.
Rotwein m. red wine.
Rübe f. sugar beet.
 weiße Rübe turnip.
 gelbe Rübe carrot.
Rubin m. ruby.
Rückantwort f. reply.
Rückblick m. glance back, retrospect.
RÜCKEN m. back, rear.
 den Rücken kehren to turn one's back.
 in den Rücken fallen to attack in the rear;
  to stab in the back (fig.)
 Rücken gegen Rücken back to back.
 Es läuft mir kalt über den Rücken.
  A shiver runs down my spine.
rücken to move, push, move away.
Rückendeckung f. rear, cover, protection.
rückerstatten to refund, reimburse.
Rückfahrkarte f. return ticket.
Rückfahrt f. return trip.
Rückfall m. relapse.
rückfällig relapsing.

Rückflug m. return flight.
Rückfrage f. query, search back; further
  inquiry.
Rückgabe f. return.
Rückgang m. decline, falling off.
rückgängig retrogressive.
 rückgängig machen to cancel.
Rückgrat spine, backbone.
rückhaltlos unreserved, without reserve.
Rückkehr f. return.
Rücklehne f. back (of chair).
Rückmarsch m. retreat.
Rückporto n. return postage.
Rückreise f. return trip.
Rückschlag m. reverse, setback, reaction,
  recoil (of a gun).
Rückschritt m. step back, relapse.
Rückseite f. back, reverse side.
Rücksicht f. regard, consideration.
 Rücksicht nehmen auf to be considerate
  of.
rücksichtslos inconsiderate, reckless.
rücksichtsvoll considerate.
Rücksitz m. back seat.
Rücksprache f. discussion, consultation.
 Rücksprache nehmen to discuss, talk over.
Rückstand m. arrears, residue.
rückständig backward, old-fashioned.
Rücktritt m. retirement, resignation.
Rückwand f. back wall.
rückwärts backward; back.
Rückwärtsgang m. reverse gear.
Rückweg m. way back, return.
rückwirkend retroactive, retrospective.
Rückwirkung f. reaction, retroaction.
Rückzahlung f. repayment.
Rückzug m. withdrawal, retreat.
Ruder n. oar, rudder, helm.
 ans Ruder kommen to come into power.
Ruderboot n. rowboat.
rudern to row.
Ruf m. reputation, cry, call.
 in gutem Rufe stehen mit to have a good
  reputation with.
RUFEN to call, shout.
 Soll ich Sie rufen lassen? Shall I send for
  her?
 wie gerufen kommen to come at the right
  moment.
Rufname m. Christian (or given) name.
RUHE f. rest, repose, calm.
 Angenehme Ruhe! Sleep well!
 in aller Ruhe very calmly.
 Lassen Sie mich in Ruhe! Leave me
  alone!
 Nichts bringt ihn aus der Ruhe. Nothing
  upsets him.
 Ruhe! Silence! Quiet!
 sich zur Ruhe setzen to retire.

ruhelos   Saite

keine Ruhe haben *to have no peace.*
ruhelos *restless.*
RUHEN *to rest, sleep, stand still.*
ruhen auf *to rest on, be based on.*
Ruhestätte *f. resting place.*
Ruhestellung *f. at ease position (standing).*
Ruhestörer *m. brawler, rioter.*
RUHIG *still, quiet, silent, calm, composed.*
Bleiben Sie ruhig sitzen! *Don't get up!*
Seien Sie ruhig! *Be quiet!*
Ruhm *m. fame, glory.*
rühmen *to praise.*
sich rühmen *to boast, brag.*
rühmlich *glorious, praiseworthy.*
ruhmlos *inglorious, obscure.*
Rührei *n. scrambled egg.*
rühren *to move, stir.*
sich rühren *to touch, move.*
zu Tränen rühren *to move to tears.*
rührend *touching, moving, pathetic.*
rührig *active, quick.*
Rührung *f. emotion, feeling.*
Ruine *f. ruin.*
ruinieren *to ruin.*
RUND *round, circular, plump.*
rund heraus *flatly.*
rund (her)um *all around.*
Rundblick *m. panorama.*
RUNDE *f. circle, lap, beat.*
die Runde machen *to be passed around.*
runden *to make round, round.*
Rundfahrt *f. circular tour.*
Rundfrage *f. inquiry, questionnaire.*
RUNDFUNK *m. radio, broadcasting.*
im Rundfunk gehört *heard over the radio.*
Rundfunkhörer *m. listener (radio).*
Rundgang *m. stroll, round (military).*
rundlich *round, rounded.*
Rundschreiben *n. circular letter.*
Russe *m.* (**Russin** *f.*) *Russian (person).*
rußig *sooty.*
russisch *Russian.*
Russisch *n. Russian (language).*
rüsten *to arm, prepare for war.*
rüstig *strong, robust, vigorous.*
Rüstung *f. preparation, equipment, armor.*
Rutsch *m. slide, glide, landslide.*
rutschen *to slide, slip, skid.*
rutschig *slippery.*

Saal *m. large room, hall.*
Saat *f. seed.*
Säbel *m. saber.*
sabotieren *to sabotage.*
Sachbearbeiter *m. expert.*

sachdienlich *relevant, pertinent.*
SACHE *f. thing, subject, business, case, circumstances, cause, point, subject.*
bei der Sache sein *to pay attention.*
gemeinsame Sache machen *to make common cause with.*
zur Sache *to the point.*
Sachen *pl. things, clothes.*
seine sieben Sachen *all one's belongings.*
sachgemäß *appropriate, suitable.*
Sachkunde *f. expert knowledge.*
sachkundig *expert, competent.*
Sachlage *f. state of affairs.*
sachlich *factual, essential, objective.*
Sachlichkeit *f. reality, objectivity.*
Sachschaden *m. damage to property.*
sachte *soft, gentle.*
Sachverhalt *m. facts of the case.*
Sack *m. sack, bag, pocket, purse.*
Sackgasse *f. blind alley, dead end.*
säen *to sow.*
Saft *m. juice, liquid, sap.*
Apfelsinensaft *m.* *orange juice.*
saftig *juicy, succulent.*
saftlos *dry, sapless.*
Sage *f. legend, tale.*
Säge *f. saw.*
SAGEN *to say, tell, mean.*
Das hat nichts zu sagen. *That does not matter.*
Das ist leichter gesagt als getan. *That's easier said than done.*
Er hat es mir ins Ohr gesagt. *He whispered it in my ear.*
Gesagt, getan. *No sooner said than done.*
Man sagt *They say.*
sagen lassen *to send word.*
sage und schreibe *precisely.*
sich etwas gesagt sein lassen *to be warned.*
unter uns gesagt *between you and me.*
ihm gehörig die Meinung sagen *to give him a piece of one's mind.*
Er lässt sich nichts sagen. *he won't listen to reason.*
auf alles etwas zu sagen wissen *to have an answer for everything.*
ihr sagen lassen *to let her know.*
Dank sagen *to express thanks.*
Was sagen Sie dazu? *What do you say to that?*
Was wollen Sie damit sagen? *What do you mean by that?*
sagenhaft *legendary, fabulous, mythical.*
Sägewerk *n. sawmill.*
Sahne *f. cream.*
Saison *f. season.*
Saisonausverkauf *m. clearance sale.*
Saite *f. string, chord.*

Saiteninstrument *n. stringed instrument.*
Salat *m. salad.*
   grüner Salat   *green salad.*
Salbe *f. salve, ointment.*
salben *to anoint.*
Salon *m. drawing room, parlor.*
salutieren *to salute.*
SALZ *m. salt.*
salzen *to salt, season.*
Salzgurke *f. pickle.*
salzhaltig *containing salt.*
salzig *salted, salty.*
Same *m. seed.*
SAMMELN *to collect, gather, accumulate.*
Sammelplatz *m. assembly point, meeting*
      place.
Sammelstelle *f. assembly point, meeting*
      place.
Sammler *m. collector.*
Sammlung *f. collection.*
SAMSTAG *m. Saturday.*
Samt *m. velvet.*
samt *together with.*
   samt und sonders   *one and all.*
sämtlich *altogether, complete.*
Sanatorium *n. sanatorium.*
SAND *m. sand.*
Sandale *f. sandal.*
Sandboden *m. sandy soil.*
sandig *sandy.*
SANFT *soft, tender, delicate, gentle, smooth.*
Sanftheit *f. softness.*
sänftigen *to soften, appease.*
Sanftmut *f. gentleness.*
sanftmütig *gentle, meek.*
Sänger *m. (-in f.) singer.*
Sanitäter *m. medical aid (person).*
Sardelle *f. anchovy.*
Sardine *f. sardine.*
Sarg *m. coffin.*
sarkastisch *sarcastic.*
Satiriker *m. (-in f.) satirist.*
satirisch *satirical.*
SATT *full, satisfied, saturated.*
   Ich habe es satt.   *I've enough of it. I'm fed*
      up with it.
Sattel *m. saddle.*
   allen Sätteln gerecht sein   *to be good at*
      everything.
satteln *to saddle.*
sättigen *to satisfy.*
Satz *m. set, clause, sentence (grammar);*
      proposition (philo.); phrase (music);
      sediment.
Satzbau *m. sentence structure.*
Satzzeichen *n. punctuation mark.*
sauber *clean, neat, tidy.*
Sauberkeit *f. tidiness, cleanliness.*
säuberlich *cleanly, neatly.*

säubern *to clean, clear.*
Säuberung *f. cleaning.*
Sauce *f. sauce, gravy.*
SAUER *sour, acid, pickled.*
Sauerbraten *m. sauerbraten.*
Sauerkraut *n. sauerkraut.*
säuerlich *acid, acidulous.*
säuern *to make sour.*
Sauerstoff *m. oxygen.*
Sauerstoffgerät *n. oxygen apparatus.*
saugen *to suck, absorb.*
säugen *to suckle, nurse.*
Säugling *m. infant, baby.*
Säule *f. pillar, column.*
Saum *m. edge, border, hem.*
Säure *f. acid, sourness, tartness, acidity.*
säurehaltig *containing acid.*
Saxophon *n. saxophone.*
schäbig *shabby, worn out.*
Schäbigkeit *f. shabbiness.*
Schach *n. chess.*
   Schach bieten   *to defy.*
Schachbrett *n. chessboard.*
Schachfeld *n. square of a chessboard.*
schachmatt *checkmate.*
Schachpartie *f. chess game.*
Schachtel *f. box.*
SCHADE *too bad.*
   Es ist schade!   *It is a pity!*
   Wie schade!   *What a pity!*
   zu schade für   *too good to.*
Schaden *m. damage, harm, injury, bias.*
   Durch Schaden wird man klug.   *You learn*
      by your mistakes.
   Schaden anrichten   *to do damage.*
   zu Schaden kommen   *to come to harm.*
   Durch Schaden wird man klug.   *Once*
      bitten, twice shy.
SCHADEN *to hurt, damage, injure.*
   Es schadet nichts.   *It doesn't matter.*
Schadenersatz *m. compensation.*
Schadenfreude *f. malicious joy.*
schadenfroh *rejoicing over another's*
      misfortune.
schadhaft *damaged, defective, dilapidated.*
   sich schadlos halten   *to get even with.*
schädlich *harmful, bad.*
Schaf *n. sheep.*
Schäfchen *n. lamb.*
   sein Schäfchen ins Trockene bringen
      to feather one's nest.
Schäfer *m. shepherd.*
Schäferhund *m. sheepdog.*
schaffen *to create, produce, accomplish,*
      make, do.
   sich zu schaffen machen   *to be busy.*
   wie geschaffen für   *as though cut out for.*
schaffend *creative, working.*
Schaffner *m. conductor, (train) guard.*

Schal *m. shawl, scarf.*
Schale *f. skin, peel, rind, shell; bowl.*
schälen *to peel, shell, bark, skin.*
Schall *m. sound.*
schalldicht *soundproof.*
Schalleffekt *m. sound effect.*
schallen *to sound, resound.*
Schallplatte *f. record (phonograph).*
Schaltanlage *f. switch, gear.*
schalten *to deal with, use, direct, change gears.*
Schalter *m. switch, ticket window.*
Schaltjahr *n. leap year.*
Schaltung *f. gear change, connection.*
Scham *f. shame, modesty.*
(sich) schämen *to be ashamed.*
Schamgefühl *n. sense of shame.*
schamhaft *modest, bashful.*
schamlos *shameless, impudent.*
Schamlosigkeit *f. shamelessness, impudence.*
schamrot *blushing red.*
Schamröte *f. blush.*
schandbar *infamous.*
Schande *f. shame, disgrace.*
schänden *to spoil, disfigure, dishonor, rape.*
schändlich *shameful, disgraceful.*
Schändlichkeit *f. infamy.*
Schandtat *f. crime, misdeed.*
SCHARF *sharp, keen, harsh, pointed, piercing, acute, strong, quick.*
    Behalten Sie ihn scharf im Auge! *Keep a sharp eye on him!*
    Ich bin nicht so scharf darauf. *I am not so keen on that.*
Scharfblick *m. penetrating glance.*
Schärfe *f. sharpness, rigor, acuteness.*
schärfen *to sharpen.*
scharfkantig *sharp-edged.*
Scharfsicht *f. insight, perspicacity.*
scharfsichtig *insightful, penetrating.*
Scharlach *m. scarlet fever.*
SCHATTEN *m. shadow, shade, spirit, phantom.*
    in den Schatten stellen *to overshadow.*
    Sie folgt mir wie ein Schatten. *She follows me like a shadow.*
Schattenseite *f. shady side.*
schattieren *to shade.*
schattig *shady.*
Schatz *m. treasure.*
Schatzamt *n. treasury.*
Schatzanweisungen *f. treasury bonds.*
schätzen *to value, estimate, judge.*
schätzenswert *estimable.*
Schatzmeister *m. treasurer.*
Schätzung *f. estimate, taxation.*
schätzungsweise *approximately.*
SCHAU *f. sight, view, show, exhibition.*
    zur Schau stellen *to exhibit, display.*

Schauder *m. shudder, shivering, horror, terror, fright.*
schauen *to see, behold, gaze, view.*
Schauer *m. horror, terror, awe, thrill.*
schauerlich *awful.*
schauern *to shudder, shiver.*
    mich schaudert bei *I shudder at.*
Schauerroman *m. thriller.*
Schaufel *f. shovel, scoop.*
schaufeln *to shovel.*
Schaufenster *n. show window.*
Schaukasten *m. showcase.*
Schaukel *f. swing.*
schaukeln *to swing, rock.*
Schaukelstuhl *m. rocking chair.*
schaulustig *curious.*
SCHAUSPIEL *n. spectacle, scene, play, drama.*
Schauspieler *m. (-in f.) actor.*
Schauspielkunst *f. dramatic art.*
Schaustellung *f. exhibition.*
Schaustück *n. specimen; showpiece.*
Schaum *m. foam.*
    zu Schaum schlagen *to whisk (food).*
schäumen *to foam.*
schaumig *foamy, frothy.*
Scheck *m. check.*
Scheckbuch *n. checkbook.*
Scheckformular *n. blank check.*
Scheckinhaber *m. bearer.*
Scheibe *f. (window) pane, disk, slice, target.*
Scheibenwischer *m. window wiper.*
scheiden *to separate, divide, part, divorce.*
    sich scheiden lassen *to get a divorce.*
Scheidewand *f. partition.*
Scheidung *f. separation, divorce.*
Scheidungsklage *f. divorce suit.*
SCHEIN *m. appearance, air, look; shine; ticket, receipt.*
    Der Schein trügt. *Appearances are deceiving.*
scheinbar *apparent(ly).*
Scheinbild *n. phantom, illusion.*
SCHEINEN *to shine; seem; look.*
scheinheilig *hypocritical, sanctimonious.*
Scheintod *m. suspended animation, trance.*
Scheinwerfer *m. reflector, search light, headlight (car).*
Scheitel *m. top, crown, summit; parting of the hair.*
scheitern *to fail.*
Schelle *f. doorbell, little bell.*
Schema *n. order, arrangement, model.*
schematisch *systematic, mechanical.*
Schenkel *m. thigh.*
schenken *to give, present with, grant.*
    geschenkt bekommen *to get as a present.*
Schenker *m. donor.*
Schenkung *f. donation, gift.*

Schere *f. scissors.*
Scherz *m. joke, jest, pleasantry.*
scherzen *to joke.*
scherzhaft *joking.*
SCHEU *shy, timid.*
  scheu werden   *to become shy, to take fright.*
scheuen *to avoid, shun.*
  sich scheuen   *to shy away (from).*
scheuern *to scrub, rub, clean, chafe.*
Schicht *f. layer, bed, coat, shift, stratum.*
Schichtwechsel *m. change of shift.*
Schick *m. elegance, smartness, chic.*
SCHICKEN *to send, dispatch.*
  schicken nach   *to send for.*
  sich schicken in   *conform, adapt oneself to.*
  Waren ins Haus schicken   *to deliver goods to the door.*
  zuschicken   *to send by mail.*
schicklich *proper, decent.*
Schicksal *n. fate, destiny, lot.*
SCHIEBEN *to move, push, shove.*
  schieben auf   *to lay the blame on.*
  etwas auf die lange Bank schieben   *to postpone something.*
Schiebetür *f. sliding door.*
Schiebung *f. profiteering, graft.*
Schiedsrichter *m. umpire.*
schief *oblique, crooked, askance.*
Schiefer *m. slate, splinter.*
Schieferdach *n. slate roof.*
Schiene *f. rail, track, splint.*
schießen *to shoot, flash, fire.*
  einen Blick schießen auf   *to shoot a glance at.*
  ein Tor schießen   *to score a goal.*
SCHIFF *n. boat, ship, vessel.*
  zu Schiff   *on board, by boat.*
schiffbar *navigable.*
Schiffbruch *m. shipwreck.*
Schiffchen *n. small boat, shuttle.*
schiffen *to ship, sail.*
Schiffer *m. sailor.*
Schiffsbesatzung *f. crew.*
Schiffskörper *m. hull.*
Schiffsladung *f. cargo, freight.*
Schiffswerft *m. wharf, dock.*
Schild *m. shield, coat of arms, sign.*
  im Schilde führen   *to have something up one's sleeve.*
schildern *to relate, describe.*
Schilderung *f. description.*
Schimmel *m. mold, mildew.*
schimmelig *moldy.*
Schimmer *m. glitter.*
schimmern *to glitter, gleam.*
Schimpf *m. disgrace, insult.*
schimpfen *to kick, gripe, scold.*
  schimpfen mit   *to scold.*

schimpflich *disgraceful.*
Schimpfwort *n. rude name; term of abuse.*
SCHINKEN *m. ham.*
  Eier mit Schinken   *ham and eggs.*
Schirm *m. umbrella, shelter, lampshade.*
Schlacht *f. combat, battle.*
schlachten *to slaughter, kill, butcher.*
Schlächter *m. butcher.*
Schlachtfeld *n. battlefield.*
Schlachthaus *n. slaughterhouse.*
Schlachtschiff *n. battleship.*
SCHLAF *m. sleep.*
  im Schlaf liegen   *to be asleep.*
Schlafanzug *m. pajamas.*
Schläfchen *n. nap.*
SCHLAFEN *to sleep.*
  schlafen gehen   *to go to bed.*
Schlafenszeit *m. bedtime.*
schlaff *slack, loose, relaxed.*
Schlaffheit *f. laxity.*
Schlafkrankheit *f. sleeping sickness.*
schlaflos *sleepless.*
Schlaflosigkeit *f. insomnia.*
Schlafmittel *m. narcotic.*
schläfrig *sleepy.*
Schlafsaal *m. dormitory.*
Schlafwagen *m. sleeping car.*
Schlafwandler *m. sleepwalker.*
Schlafzimmer *n. bedroom.*
SCHLAG *m. blow, stroke, striking (clock).*
  zwei Fliegen mit einem Schlag treffen   *to kill two birds with one stone.*
Schlagader *f. artery.*
Schlaganfall *m. stroke, fit.*
SCHLAGEN *to beat, knock, hit, strike, throb.*
  sich schlagen   *to fight.*
  sich geschlagen geben   *to give up.*
  schlagen nach   *to take after.*
  eine geschlagene Stunde   *a whole hour.*
  etwas aus dem Kopfe schlagen   *to dismiss something from one's thoughts.*
  die Schanze schlagen   *to risk one's life.*
  einen Rekord schlagen   *to set a record.*
  Die Uhr schlägt zehn.   *The clock strikes ten.*
  seine Unkosten auf die Ware schlagen   *to add one's expenses to the price of the goods.*
schlagfertig *quick at repartee.*
Schlagfertigkeit *f. quickness at repartee.*
Schlagsahne *f. whipped cream.*
Schlagwort *n. slogan.*
Schlagzeile *f. headline.*
Schlagzeug *n. percussion instrument.*
Schlamm *m. mud, ooze.*
schlammig *muddy, oozy.*
Schlange *f. snake.*
  Schlange stehen   *to stand in line; to make a line.*

Schlangenbiss *m. snakebite.*
schlank *slim, slender.*
Schlankheit *f. slimness, slenderness.*
schlapp *weak, tired, limp, flabby.*
  schlapp machen   *to collapse.*
schlau *sly, cunning.*
Schlauberger *m. sly fox.*
Schlauch *m. hose, tube.*
Schlauheit *f. slyness, cunning.*
Schlaukopf *m. sly fox.*
SCHLECHT *bad, poor, inferior, ill, wicked.*
  mir ist schlecht   *I feel sick.*
  schlecht machen   *to run down.*
  schlecht und recht   *somehow.*
  schlecht werden   *to spoil (food).*
schlechtgelaunt *in a bad temper.*
Schlechtigkeit *f. badness, wickedness.*
schleichen *to creep, drag, sneak.*
  sich davonschleichen   *to steal away.*
  wie die Katze um den heißen Brei
    schleichen   *to beat around the bush*
    (*"to creep like the cat around the hot
    roast"*)
schlicht *simple, plain, even.*
schlichten *to make simple, smooth.*
Schlichtheit *f. simplicity.*
Schließe *f. clasp, fastening.*
SCHLIEßEN *to close, lock, shut, breakup.*
  in die Arme schließen   *to embrace.*
  geschlossen   *enclosed.*
  die Ehe schließen   *to get married.*
Schließfach *n. locker.*
schließlich *final, finally, after all.*
Schließung *f. closing.*
schlimm *bad, sore.*
  schlimmstenfalls   *if worse comes to
    worst.*
Schlips *m. necktie (coll.).*
Schlitten *m. sled, sleigh.*
Schlittenfahrt *f. sleigh ride.*
Schlittschuh *m. skate.*
  Schlittschuh laufen   *to skate.*
Schlittschuhläufer *m. skater.*
SCHLOSS *n. castle, lock.*
Schlosser *m. locksmith.*
Schluck *m. gulp, draught.*
Schluckauf *m. hiccup.*
schlucken *to gulp, swallow.*
Schlucker *m. hiccup.*
  armer Schlucker   *poor wretch.*
Schlummer *m. slumber.*
schlummern *to slumber.*
Schlüpfer *m. panties.*
SCHLUSS *m. closing, shutting, conclusion.*
Schlüssel *m. key, code.*
Schlüsselbund *m. bunch of keys.*
Schlüsselloch *m. keyhole.*
Schlusslicht *n. taillight.*
Schlusswort *n. summary, last word.*

Schmach *f. disgrace, dishonor, humiliation.*
schmachten *to languish.*
schmachvoll *disgraceful, humiliating.*
schmackhaft *tasty, savory.*
schmähen *to abuse.*
schmählich *disgraceful.*
SCHMAL *narrow, thin, slender, poor.*
schmälern *to diminish, lessen.*
Schmalz *n. drippings.*
SCHMECKEN *to taste, try.*
  Es schmeckt gut.   *It tastes good.*
  Es schmeckt mir nicht.   *I don't like it.*
  schmecken nach   *to taste of.*
  Wie schmeckt's?   *How do you like it?*
Schmeichelei *f. flattery.*
schmeichelhaft *flattering.*
Schmeichelkatze *f. wheedler, flatterer.*
schmeicheln *to flatter.*
Schmeichler *m. flatterer.*
schmeichlerisch *flattering.*
schmelzen *to melt.*
SCHMERZ *m. pain, ache, hurt, sorrow.*
SCHMERZEN *to hurt, pain, grieve.*
Schmerzensgeld *n. compensation.*
schmerzerfüllt *deeply affected.*
schmerzhaft *painful.*
schmerzlich *grievous, sad.*
schmerzlos *painless.*
schmerzstillend *soothing.*
Schmetterling *m. butterfly.*
Schmied *m. blacksmith.*
Schmiede *f. forge.*
schmieden *to forge, hammer.*
  Pläne schmieden   *to devise plans.*
schmiegen *to bend.*
schmiegsam *flexible, supple.*
Schmiegsamkeit *f. flexibility.*
schmieren *to spread, grease, smear.*
Schminke *f. rouge, paint, makeup.*
schminken *to make up, paint the face.*
Schmorbraten *m. stewed meat.*
SCHMUCK *m. jewelry, ornament,
    decoration.*
schmücken *to decorate, adorn.*
Schmuckstück *n. piece of jewelry.*
Schmuggel *m. smuggling.*
schmuggeln *to smuggle.*
schmunzeln *to grin, to smirk.*
Schmutz *m. dirt, mud.*
schmutzen *to dirty.*
Schmutzfleck *m. stain, spot.*
schmutzig *dirty.*
Schnabel *m. beak, bill.*
schnarchen *to snore.*
schnaufen *to breathe heavily, pant.*
Schnecke *f. snail.*
  wie eine Schnecke kriechen   *to go at a
    snail's pace.*
SCHNEE *m. snow.*

Schneeball *m. snowball.*
Schneedecke *f. blanket of snow.*
Schneefall *m. snowfall.*
Schneeflocke *f. snowflake.*
Schneekette *f. nonskid chain (automobile).*
Schneeschuh *m. snowshoe, ski.*
Schneetreiben *n. blizzard.*
schneeweiß *snow-white.*
SCHNEIDEN *to cut, carve.*
  sich schneiden *to cut oneself.*
schneidend *sharp, bitter.*
Schneider *m. tailor.*
schneien *to snow.*
SCHNELL *quick, fast, swift, prompt, speedy.*
Schnelligkeit *f. rapidity, velocity.*
Schnellzug *m. express train.*
(sich) schneuzen *to blow one's nose.*
Schnippchen *n. snap of the fingers.*
  ein Schnippchen schlagen *to play a trick.*
Schnitt *m. cut, cutting, incision.*
Schnittblumen *pl. cut flowers.*
Schnittmuster *n. cut pattern.*
Schnittwunde *f. cut.*
schnitzen *to carve, cut.*
Schnupfen *m. (head) cold.*
  sich einen Schnupfen holen *to get a (head) cold.*
schnupfen *to sniff.*
Schnur *f. string, cord.*
  über die Schnur hauen *to kick over the traces.*
Schnurrbart *m. moustache.*
schnurren *to hum; buzz, purr.*
Schnürsenkel *m. shoelaces.*
Schock *m. shock.*
Schokolade *f. chocolate.*
SCHON *already, all right, very, yet, even, indeed, certainly.*
  Schon gut! *All right!*
  Wenn schon! *So what!*
  Haben Sie es schon einmal gesehen? *Did you ever see it before?*
SCHÖN *beautiful, handsome, fine, nice, fair, noble.*
  Danke schön (Schönen Dank). *Thanks.*
  Das wäre noch schöner! *That's all we need!*
  die Schönen Künste *the fine arts.*
  schön tun *to flatter.*
  Schönen Gruß an Ihre Frau. *Best regards to your wife.*
  Schönsten Dank. *Many thanks.*
  sich schön machen *to smarten oneself up, beautify, do up.*
schonen *to spare, save, look after, preserve.*
schonend *careful, considerate.*
Schöngeist *m. wit; esthete.*
schöngeistig *esthetical.*
Schönheit *f. beauty.*

Schönheitsmittel *n. cosmetic.*
Schönheitspflege *f. beauty treatment.*
Schonung *f. indulgence.*
schonungslos *pitiless.*
schöpfen *to draw, create.*
Schöpferkraft *f. power, creative.*
Schöpflöffel *m. scoop, dipper.*
Schornstein *m. chimney.*
Schoß *m. lap.*
Schotte *m. Scotsman.*
schottisch *Scottish.*
schräg *diagonally.*
Schräge *f. slant, slope.*
Schramme *f. scratch, scar.*
schrammen *to scratch.*
Schrank *m. wardrobe.*
Schranke *f. fencing, enclosure, gate.*
  sich in Schranken halten *to keep within bounds.*
schrankenlos *boundless, without limits.*
Schrankkoffer *m. wardrobe trunk.*
Schraube *f. screw, propeller, bolt.*
schrauben *to screw, turn, wheel.*
Schraubenschlüssel *m. wrench.*
Schraubenzieher *m. screwdriver.*
SCHRECK(EN) *m. scare, fright, fear, dread, horror.*
  in Schrecken versetzen *to terrify.*
schrecken *to frighten.*
Schreckgespenst *n. terrible vision.*
schreckhaft *timid, easily frightened.*
schrecklich *terrible, awful.*
Schreckschuss *m. warning shot.*
Schrei *m. scream, cry.*
SCHREIBEN *to write, spell.*
  auf der Maschine schreiben *to type.*
  die Zeitung schreibt *the paper says.*
  Schreiben Sie sich das hinter die Ohren. *Make a special note of it; Take it to heart.*
Schreiberei *f. writing, correspondence.*
Schreibfehler *m. slip of the pen.*
Schreibmappe *f. portfolio, blotter.*
Schreibmaschine *f. typewriter.*
Schreibpapier *n. note paper.*
Schreibstube *f. office.*
Schreibwaren *pl. stationery.*
Schreibwarengeschäft *n. stationery store.*
Schreibwarenhändler *m. stationer.*
Schreibwarenhandlung *f. stationery store.*
SCHREIEN *to scream, shout, yell.*
schreiend *loud, gaudy.*
Schreier *m. shouter, bawler.*
Schreiner *m. carpenter, cabinetmaker.*
Schreinerei *f. cabinetmaker's shop.*
SCHRIFT *f. writing, handwriting, script.*
schriftlich *in writing, written.*
Schriftführer *m. secretary (association or politics).*

Schriftsteller *m. writer (author).*
SCHRITT *m. step, stride.*
  auf Schritt und Tritt *everywhere, all the time.*
  Schritt fahren! *Drive slowly!*
  Schritt für Schritt *step by step.*
  Schritt halten *to keep pace with.*
schroff *rugged, rough, uncouth.*
schrubben *to scrub.*
Schrubber *m. scrubber.*
schrumpfen *to shrink, contract.*
Schrumpfung *f. shrinking, contraction.*
Schublade *f. drawer.*
schüchtern *bashful, timid.*
Schüchternheit *f. bashfulness, timidity.*
Schuft *m. scoundrel.*
SCHUH *m. shoe.*
  einem etwas in die Schuhe schieben *to put the blame on someone.*
Schuhanzieher *m. shoehorn.*
Schuhkrem *f. shoe polish.*
Schuhmacher *m. shoemaker.*
Schuhriemen *m. shoelace.*
Schuhsohle *f. sole of a shoe.*
Schularbeit *f. lesson, homework.*
Schulbesuch *m. attendance at school.*
Schulbildung *f. schooling, education.*
SCHULD *f. obligation, debt, cause, blame.*
  in jemandes Schuld stehen *to have an obligation.*
  Schuld sein an *to be guilty of.*
  Schulden machen *to incur debts.*
  Schuld geben *to accuse.*
schuldbewusst *guilty, with a bad conscience.*
schulden *to owe.*
Schuldenmacher *m. contractor of debts.*
schuldig *owing, due, obliged, guilty.*
  schuldig sein *to be indebted.*
  Geld schuldig sein *to owe money.*
  keine Antwort schuldig bleiben *never to be at a loss for an answer.*
Schuldigkeit *f. duty, obligation.*
schuldlos *innocent.*
Schuldner *m. debtor.*
Schuldschein *m. bond, promissory note.*
SCHULE *f. school, academy, courses.*
  die Schule schwänzen *to cut classes.*
  Schule machen *to find followers.*
schulen *to school, train, teach.*
Schüler *m. student, pupil.*
Schulferien *pl. m. school vacations.*
schulfrei *having a vacation from school.*
Schulfreund *m. school friend.*
Schulgeld *n. school fees.*
Schulmappe *f. schoolbag, satchel.*
Schulmeister *m. schoolmaster, teacher.*
schulmeistern *to censure, to be pedantic.*
Schulstunde *f. school lesson.*
Schulter *f. shoulder.*

Schulung *f. school training.*
Schulzeugnis *n. school certificates, report card.*
Schuppe *f. scale (fish).*
Schürze *f. apron.*
Schuss *m. shot, report, round.*
schussbereit *ready to shoot.*
Schusswaffe *f. firearm.*
Schussweite *f. range.*
Schusswunde *f. bullet wound.*
schütteln *to shake.*
schütten *to pour in, to spill, to shed.*
SCHUTZ *m. shelter, protection, refuge.*
  im Schutz der Nacht *under cover of the night.*
  in Schutz nehmen *to defend.*
  Schutz suchen *to take shelter.*
Schutzbrille *f. safety goggles.*
schützen *to protect.*
  sich schützen *to protect oneself.*
Schutzengel *m. guardian angel.*
Schutzhaft *f. protective custody.*
Schutzimpfung *f. vaccination.*
schutzlos *defenseless, unprotected.*
Schutzmann *n. policeman.*
SCHWACH *weak, frail, faint, feeble.*
Schwäche *f. weakness, debility, frailty.*
schwächen *to weaken.*
Schwachheit *f. weakness, feebleness.*
schwächlich *weak, delicate.*
Schwächlichkeit *f. delicacy, infirmity.*
Schwachsinn *m. imbecility.*
schwachsinnig *imbecile.*
Schwager *m. brother-in-law.*
Schwägerin *f. sister-in-law.*
Schwalbe *f. swallow.*
Schwamm *m. sponge, mushroom.*
Schwan *m. swan.*
schwanger *pregnant.*
schwanken *to rock, toss, sway.*
Schwankung *f. variation.*
Schwanz *m. tail, end.*
Schwarm *m. crowd, multitude.*
schwärmen *to swarm, riot.*
Schwärmer *m. enthusiast, fanatic.*
Schwärmerei *f. enthusiasm.*
schwärmerisch *enthusiastic, fanatic.*
Schwarte *f. rind, skin.*
SCHWARZ *black, dark, dirty, gloomy.*
  ins Schwarze treffen *to hit the bull's eye.*
  schwarz auf weiß *in black and white.*
  Sie sieht immer alles schwarz *She always sees the dark side of things.*
Schwarzbrot *n. black bread.*
Schwarze *m. black (person).*
Schwarzhandel *m. black market.*
Schwarzwald *m. Black Forest.*
Schwatz *m. chat, talk.*
Schwatzbase *f. chatterbox.*

schwatzen, schwätzen *to chatter, gossip.*
Schwätzer *m* (**-in** *f.*) *gossip.*
schwatzhaft *talkative.*
Schwatzhaftigkeit *f. loquacity.*
Schwebe *f. state of suspense.*
  in der Schwebe sein   *to be undecided, to be pending.*
Schwebebahn *f. suspension railway.*
schweben *to be suspended, pending.*
  auf der Zunge schweben   *to have on the tip of the tongue.*
  in Gefahr schweben   *to be in danger.*
Schwede *m. Swede.*
schwedisch *Swedish.*
Schwefel *m. sulphur.*
schweigen *n. silence.*
schweigsam *silent, taciturn.*
Schweigsamkeit *f. taciturnity.*
Schwein *n. pig, hog.*
Schweinebraten *m. roast pork.*
Schweinefleisch *n. pork.*
Schweiß *m. sweat, perspiration.*
Schweißtropfen *m. bead of perspiration.*
Schweizer *m. Swiss.*
schweizerisch *Swiss.*
schweigen *to keep silent.*
Schwelle *f. threshold.*
schwellen *to swell, rise, grow.*
Schwellung *f. swelling, tumor, growth.*
SCHWER *heavy, hard, difficult, serious, strong; heavily, seriously, strongly.*
  etwas schwer nehmen   *to take something to heart.*
  schwer fallen (halten)   *to be difficult.*
  schweres Geld kosten   *to cost a lot of money.*
  schweren Herzens   *with a heavy heart.*
  schwer beleidigen   *to deeply offend.*
schwerblütig *melancholy.*
schwerfällig *phlegmatic.*
Schwerfälligkeit *f. heaviness, clumsiness.*
Schwergewicht *n. heavyweight.*
schwerhörig *hard of hearing.*
Schwerhörigkeit *f. deafness.*
Schwerkraft *f. force of gravity.*
Schwerkriegsbeschädigter *m. disabled soldier.*
schwerlich *hardly, scarcely, with difficulty.*
Schwermut *f. melancholy, sadness.*
schwermütig *melancholy, sad.*
Schwerpunkt *m. center of gravity.*
Schwert *n. sword.*
Schwerverbrecher *m. criminal, gangster.*
schwerwiegend *serious, grave.*
SCHWESTER *f. sister, hospital nurse.*
schwesterlich *sisterly.*
Schwiegereltern *pl. parents-in-law.*
Schwiegermutter *f. mother-in-law.*
Schwiegersohn *m. son-in-law.*
Schwiegertochter *f. daughter-in-law.*

Schwiegervater *m. father-in-law.*
schwierig *difficult.*
Schwierigkeit *f. difficulty.*
Schwimmbad *f. swimming pool.*
SCHWIMMEN *to swim, float, sail.*
Schwimmweste *f. life jacket.*
Schwindel *m. swindle; fraud; dizziness.*
Schwindelanfall *m. fit of dizziness.*
schwindeln *to swindle, cheat; be dizzy, to tell a lie.*
  Mir schwindelt.   *I feel dizzy.*
Schwindler *m. swindler.*
schwindlig *dizzy.*
schwingen *to swing, sway, oscillate, vibrate.*
Schwingung *f. oscillation.*
Schwips *m. Smack! Slap!*
  einen Schwips haben   *to be tipsy.*
schwören *to swear, take an oath.*
schwül *sultry, muggy.*
Schwung *f. swing (push), vault.*
  in Schwung bringen   *to set going.*
  im Schwung sein   *to be in full swing.*
schwungvoll *energetic.*
Schwur *m. oath.*
  Schwur leisten   *to take an oath.*
SECHS *six.*
SECHSTE *sixth.*
SECHZEHN *sixteen.*
SECHZEHNTE *sixteenth.*
SECHZIG *sixty.*
SECHZIGSTE *sixtieth.*
See *m. lake.*
SEE *f. sea, seaside.*
  an die See gehen   *to go to the seaside.*
  in See stechen *or* gehen   *to set sail; to put to sea.*
Seebad *n. seaside resort.*
seefest *seaworthy.*
  seefest sein   *to be a good sailor.*
Seehund *m. seal.*
seekrank *seasick.*
  seekrank sein   *to be seasick.*
Seekrankheit *f. seasickness.*
SEELE *f. soul, mind, spirit.*
  jemandem aus der Seele sprechen   *to express a person's thoughts.*
  Sie sind mit Leib und Seele dabei.   *They are in it with heart and soul.*
seelisch *spiritual, mental, emotional.*
Seemann *m. sailor.*
Seemeile *f. nautical mile (1.852 kilometers).*
Seenot *f. distress (at sea).*
Seewasser *n. seawater.*
Segel *n. sail, canvas.*
Segelboot *n. sailboat.*
Segelflugzeug *n. glider.*
segeln *to sail.*
Segelschiff *n. sailboat.*
Segen *m. blessing.*

segnen to bless.
SEHEN to see, look, behold, contemplate.
  darauf sehen   to watch carefully.
  gut sehen   to have good eyesight.
  Ich kenne sie nur vom Sehen.   I know her
    only by sight.
  schlecht sehen   to have poor eyesight.
  sehen nach   to look after.
  sich sehen lassen   to appear.
  Ich kann sie nicht sehen.   I can't stand the
    sight of her.
  ihm auf die Finger sehen   to watch him
    closely.
  nach der Uhr sehen   to look at the clock.
  sehen auf   to look at, to look over, to face,
    to see it.
sehenswert worth seeing, remarkable.
Sehenswürdigkeit f. point of interest.
Sehkraft f. eyesight.
Sehne f. sinew, ligament.
SEHNEN to long, yearn for.
  sich sehnen nach   to yearn for.
sehnlich ardent, longing.
Sehnsucht f. longing, yearning.
sehnsüchtig longing, yearning.
SEHR very; very much.
  Bitte sehr.   You are quite welcome.
seicht shallow.
SEIDE f. silk.
Seidenpapier n. tissue paper.
Seidenraupe f. silkworm.
seidig silky.
Seife f. soap.
Seifenflocken pl. soap flakes.
Seifenpulver n. soap powder.
Seil n. rope, line.
Seilbahn f. cable car, ski lift.
Sein n. being.
SEIN to be, exist.
  es sei denn, dass . . .   unless.
SEIN poss. adj. his, her, its.
SEIN (-ER, -E, -ES) poss. pron. his, hers.
  die Seinen   one's own people.
seinetwegen because of him, for his sake.
SEIT prep. (with dat.) since, for.
  Ich warte seit einer Stunde.   I have been
    waiting for an hour.
  seit kurzer Zeit   lately.
  seit meiner Ankunft   since my return.
  Seit wann?   since when?
Seitdem conj. since, since that time.
SEITE f. side, page, party, member.
  auf die Seite   aside, away.
  auf die Seite gehen   to step aside.
  Schwache Seite   weakness.
  Seite an Seite   side by side.
  zur Seite stehen   to stand by, help.
  auf dieser Seite   on this side.
  auf meiner Seite stehen   to be on my side.

  nach allen Seiten   in all directions.
Seitenflügel m. side, aisle, wing.
Seitenstraße f. side street.
Seitenzahl f. number of pages.
seither since then.
seitlich lateral, collateral.
seitwärts sideways, aside.
Sekt m. champagne.
Sekretär m. (-in f.) secretary.
SEKUNDE f. second (time, music, fencing).
Sekundenzeiger m. second hand (on clocks).
selbe (der, die, das) same.
selber self.
  ich selber   myself.
SELBST 1. adj. or pron. self.
  Ich habe es selbst getan.   I did it myself.
  Das versteht sich von selbst.   That goes
    without saying.
  2. adv. even.
  Ich habe alles zu Hause gelassen, selbst
    mein Geld.   I left everything at home,
    even my money.
selbständig independent.
Selbstbeherrschung f. self-control.
selbstbewusst self-assured.
Selbstbewusstsein n. self-assurance.
Selbsterhaltung f. self-preservation.
Selbsterkenntnis f. self-knowledge.
selbstgefällig self-satisfied, complacent, vain.
Selbstgefühl n. self-respect.
Selbstgespräch m. monologue, soliloquy.
selbstherrlich autocratic.
Selbstkostenpreis m. cost price.
selbstlos unselfish.
Selbstlosigkeit f. unselfishness.
Selbstmörder m. suicide.
selbstredend self-evident, obvious.
Selbstsucht f. selfishness, egoism.
selbstsüchtig selfish, egoistic.
SELBSTVERSTÄNDLICH evident, natural.
Selbstvertrauen n. self-confidence.
selbstzufrieden self-satisfied.
selig blessed.
Seligkeit f. happiness, bliss.
Sellerie f. celery.
SELTEN rare, unusual.
Seltenheit f. rarity, scarcity.
SELTSAM strange, unusual, odd.
Selterwasser n. soda (water).
Semester n. term, session.
Seminar n. teacher training college.
Senat m. senate.
senden to send, broadcast, transmit.
Sender m. transmitter.
Senderaum m. studio.
Sendung f. mission, transmission.
Senf m. mustard.
Senkel m. shoelace.
senken to lower, dip, sink.

sich senken *to settle.*
sensationell *sensational.*
Sensationslust *f. desire to cause a sensation.*
Sentimentalität *f. sentimentality.*
SEPTEMBER *m. September.*
Serie *f. series, issue.*
Service *n. service set, attendance.*
Servierbrett *n. tray.*
servieren *to serve, wait on a table.*
Serviette *f. table napkin.*
Sessel *m. armchair.*
sesshaft *settled, established.*
SETZEN *to put, set, place, fix, erect.*
  sich setzen *to sit down.*
  alles daran setzen *to risk everything.*
  gesetzt den Fall, dass *suppose that.*
  in Freiheit setzen *to set free.*
  Setzen Sie sich! *Sit down!*
  sich etwas in den Kopf setzen *to get an idea into one's head.*
  sich in Verbindung setzen mit *to get in touch with.*
  unter Druck setzen *to put pressure on.*
  außer Gebrauch setzen *to supersede, discard.*
  außer Kraft setzen *to invalidate.*
  in Bewegung setzen *to set into motion.*
  in die Zeitung setzen *to advertise in the newspapers.*
  übers Wasser setzen *to ferry across.*
  sich zur Ruhe setzen *to retire.*
Seuche *f. epidemic, pestilence.*
seufzen *to sigh.*
sezieren *to dissect.*
SICH *oneself, himself, herself, itself, yourself, yourselves, themselves, each other, one another.*
  sich selbst *itself, oneself, etc.*
SICHER *secure, safe, certain, positive, surely.*
  aus sicherer Hand *on good authority.*
  seiner Sache sicher sein *to be certain of a thing.*
  sicher gehen *to be on the safe side.*
  sicher rechnen auf *to have complete confidence in.*
  sicher stellen *to put in safe keeping.*
  sicher wissen *to know for certain.*
Sicherheit *f. safety, security.*
  in Sicherheit bringen *to secure.*
  Sicherheit leisten *to give security.*
sicherheitshalber *for safety's sake.*
Sicherheitsnadel *f. safety pin.*
Sicherheitsschloss *n. safety lock.*
sicherlich *surely, certainly.*
sichern *to protect.*
Sicherung *f. protection.*
SICHT *f. sight, visibility.*
  sichtbar *visible, apparent.*
sichten *to sight; to sift, sort.*

SIE (sie) *pers. pron. 3rd pers. sing. (fem. nom. & acc.); 3rd pers. pl. (m., f., n., nom. & acc.) she, her, it; they, them.*
SIE (Sie) *you (formal sing. & pl. nom. & acc.).*
Sieb *n. colander, strainer.*
sieben *to sift, strain.*
SIEBEN *seven.*
SIEBENTE *seventh.*
SIEBZEHNTE *seventeenth.*
SIEBZIG *seventy.*
SIEBZIGSTE *seventieth.*
siech *sickly, ailing, infirm.*
siedeln *to settle, colonize.*
SIEG *m. victory, triumph.*
Siegel *n. seal.*
Sieger *m. (-in f.) victor, winner.*
siegesgewiss *certain or confident of victory.*
siegreich *victorious.*
Signal *n. signal.*
Signalanlage *f. signaling system.*
Signalhupe *f. siren.*
signalisieren *to signal.*
Signatur *f. signature, mark, sign, characteristic, stamp.*
Silbe *f. syllable.*
Silber *n. silver.*
Silbergeschirr *n. silver plate, silverware.*
Silberpapier *n. silver paper, tinfoil.*
Silvesterabend *m. New Year's Eve.*
SINGEN *to sing.*
Singstimme *f. singing voice, vocal part.*
sinken *to sink, drop, fall.*
SINN *m. sense, faculty, mind, understanding, intellect.*
  anderen Sinnes werden *to change one's mind.*
  in gewissem Sinn *in a way, in a sense.*
  im Sinn haben *to intend.*
  sich etwas aus dem Sinn schlagen *to dismiss a thing from one's mind.*
Sinnbild *n. symbol, emblem, allegory.*
sinnbildlich *symbolic.*
sinnen *to think, reflect, meditate.*
  sinnen auf *to plot, devise.*
sinnlich *sensual, sensuous, material.*
sinnlos *senseless, absurd.*
Sinnlosigkeit *f. senselessness, foolishness.*
sinnreich *sensible, clever.*
Sirene *f. siren.*
Sitte *f. custom, habit.*
Sittengesetz *n. moral law, moral code.*
Sittenlehre *f. moral, philosophy, ethics.*
sittenlos *immoral, dissolute.*
sittlich *moral.*
sittsam *modest.*
Sittsamkeit *f. modesty, decency.*
SITZ *m. seat, residence.*
SITZEN *to sit, fit, adhere.*

etwas auf sich sitzen lassen *to put up with.*

sitzen bleiben *to remain seated; to be left back (school).*

sitzen lassen *to leave.*

im Gefängnis sitzen *to be in jail.*

Sitzgelegenheit *f. seating accommodation.*

Sitzplatz *m. seat.*

Skandal *m. scandal.*

Skelett *n. skeleton.*

skeptisch *skeptical.*

Ski *m. ski.*

skilaufen *to ski.*

Skiläufer *m. (-in f.) skier.*

Skispringen *n. ski-jumping.*

Skizze *f. sketch.*

skizzieren *to sketch.*

Sklave *m. slave.*

sklavisch *slavish, servile.*

Skrupel *m. scruple.*

SO *so, thus, in this way, like that, anyhow.*

Ach so! *Oh, I see!*

So? *Is that so? Indeed? Really?*

so . . . auch *however.*

so bald wie *as soon as.*

so . . . doch *yet, nevertheless.*

so ein *such a.*

so etwas *a thing like that.*

so gut wie *as if, practically.*

so oder so *this way or that way.*

so . . . so *though . . . yet.*

so wie *as, the way*

Socke *f. sock.*

sodann *then.*

sodass *so that.*

soeben *just, just now.*

sofern *so far as.*

sofort *immediately, at once.*

sogar *even.*

so genannt *so-called.*

sogleich *at once, immediately.*

Sohle *f. sole.*

sohlen *to resole.*

SOHN *m. son.*

solange *so, as long as.*

SOLCH *such, the same.*

solch ein *such a.*

Soldat *m. soldier.*

Solist *(-in f.) m. soloist.*

SOLLEN *ought, shall, to have to, must, be supposed to, be said to.*

Du sollst nicht töten. *Thou shalt not kill.*

Die Schüler sollen fleißig sein. *Students must be industrious.*

Er soll ein Millionär sein. *They say he is a millionaire.*

Sollte er nicht zu Hause sein? *Is it possible that he is not at home?*

Sollte er telefonieren? *Should he telephone?*

Was soll das heißen? *What is the meaning of that?*

Was soll es bedeuten? *What does that mean?*

Was sollte ich dagegen machen? *How could I help it?*

somit *consequently.*

SOMMER *m. summer.*

Sommernachtstraum *m. midsummer night's dream.*

Sommerfrische *f. health resort.*

Sommersprosse *f. freckle.*

Sommerzeit *f. summertime.*

Sonderausgabe *f. special edition.*

SONDERBAR *strange, peculiar.*

sonderbarerweise *strange to say.*

sondergleichen *unequaled, unique.*

Sonderling *m. strange character.*

Sondermeldung *f. special announcement.*

SONDERN *but (in a negative sentence).*

Ich wollte nichte ausgehen, sondern zu Hause bleiben. *I did not want to go out but to stay home.*

nicht nur . . . sondern auch *not only . . . but also.*

Sie war nicht nur schön, sondern auch gut. *She was not only beautiful but kind as well.*

SONNABEND *m. Saturday.*

SONNE *f. sun.*

(sich) sonnen *to sun oneself, bask.*

Sonnenaufgang *m. sunrise.*

Sonnenblume *f. sunflower.*

Sonnenbrand *m. sunburn.*

Sonnenbrille *f. sunglasses.*

Sonnenstrahl *m. sunbeam.*

Sonnenuntergang *m. sunset.*

sonnig *sunny.*

SONNTAG *m. Sunday.*

sonntags *on Sunday.*

SONST *else, moreover, besides, otherwise, formerly.*

Sonst noch etwas? *Anything else?*

sonst jemand *anybody else.*

Sonst nichts *nothing else.*

Sonst niemand? *No one else?*

sonst und jetzt *formerly and now.*

Was konnte ich sonst tun? *What else could I do?*

Wenn es sonst nichts wäre! *If that were all it was!*

wie sonst *as usual.*

sonst wie *in some other way.*

sonst wo *elsewhere.*

Sopran *m. soprano.*

Sopranistin *f. soprano singer.*

SORGE *f. grief, sorrow, anxiety, worry, trouble, care.*

einem Sorgen machen *to worry someone.*

sich Sorgen machen   *to worry.*

Sorge tragen   *to see about something.*

SORGEN *to care for, look after, take care of, provide.*

sich sorgen um   *to be concerned about; to see to, to take responsibility for.*

sorgen für   *to look after.*

Sorgenkind *n. problem child.*

sorgenvoll *worried.*

Sorgfalt *f. carefulness, care, accuracy.*

sorgfältig *careful, painstaking.*

sorglich *thoughtful.*

sorglos *carefree, careless.*

Sorglosigkeit *f. lightheartedness, thoughtlessness.*

SORTE *f. kind, sort, brand, grade.*

sortieren *to sort, arrange.*

SOVIEL *as much as, so far as.*

soweit *as far as.*

sowenig *as little as.*

sowie *as soon as.*

sowieso *anyway, anyhow.*

sozial *social.*

Sozialismus *m. socialism.*

Sozialist *m. socialist.*

sozialistisch *socialistic.*

Sozialwissenschaft *f. sociology.*

Sozius *m. partner.*

spähen *to be on the look out, patrol.*

Spalier bilden/stehen *to form an honor guard; to line.*

Spalt *m. crack, slot, gap.*

spalten *to split, divide.*

sich spalten   *to split.*

Spaltholz *n. firewood sticks.*

Spange *f. buckle, brooch.*

Spanier *m (-in f.) Spaniard*

spanisch *Spanish.*

Spanisch *n. Spanish (language).*

Spanne *f. short space of time, margin.*

SPANNEN *to put up, stretch, pull, tighten, grip, clamp.*

gespannt sein   *to be anxious, curious.*

Ich bin auf die Antwort gespannt.   *I am curious to know the answer.*

das Pferd hinter den Wagen spannen.   *to put the cart before the horse.*

spannend *fascinating, absorbing, thrilling.*

Spannung *f. tension, strain, suspense, voltage.*

Sparbüchse *f. money-box (piggy bank).*

Spareinlage *f. savings deposit.*

Spargel *m. asparagus.*

Sparkasse *f. savings bank.*

spärlich *scarce, frugal, thin, scanty.*

Spärlichkeit *f. scarcity.*

SPARSAM *economical, thrifty.*

Sparsamkeit *f. economy, thrift.*

Spass *m. joke, fun.*

zum Spass   *for fun.*

spassen *to joke.*

Spassmacher *m. joker.*

SPÄT *late, belated, backward.*

Besser spät als nie.   *Better late than never.*

zu spät kommen   *to be late.*

Wie spät ist es?   *What time is it?*

Spaten *m. spade.*

später *later, afterward.*

späterhin   *later on.*

spätestens *at the latest.*

Spatz *m. sparrow.*

SPAZIEREN *to walk about, stroll.*

spazierengehen   *to go for a walk.*

Spazierfahrt *f. drive, pleasure trip.*

Spaziergang *m. walk.*

Spaziergänger *m. walker, stroller.*

Speck *m. bacon.*

Speckschwarte *f. rind of bacon.*

Spediteur *m. mover, shipper, forwarding agent.*

Speicher *m. silo, granary, warehouse.*

speichern *to store, to save (computer).*

SPEISE *f. food, meal.*

Speiseeis *n. ice cream.*

Speisekarte *f. menu.*

Speisesaal *m. dining room.*

Speisewagen *m. dining car.*

Spekulant *m. speculator.*

spekulieren *to speculate.*

Spende *f. gift, present, donation.*

spenden *to dispense, bestow, administer.*

Spender *m. giver, donor, benefactor.*

spendieren *to give freely, lavishly.*

Sperre *f. gate, closing, barrier.*

sperrangelweit *wide open.*

sperren *to close, shut, block, barricade.*

ins Gefängnis sperren   *to put in prison.*

Sperrklinke *f. safety catch.*

Sperrholz *n. plywood.*

Spesen *f. pl. charges, expenses.*

Spezialarzt *n. specialist, doctor.*

spezialisieren *to specialize.*

speziell *special, particular.*

spezifisch *specific.*

spezifizieren *to specify.*

Spiegel *m. mirror.*

Spiegelbild *n. reflected image.*

spiegelglatt *smooth as a mirror.*

spiegeln *to shine, glitter.*

sich spiegeln   *to be reflected.*

SPIEL *n. game, deck of cards, playing, play, sport, touch (music).*

auf dem Spiel stehen   *to be at stake.*

aufs Spiel setzen   *to risk.*

Lassen Sie mich aus dem Spiel.   *Leave me out of this.*

leichtes Spiel haben   *to have no difficulties.*

seine Hand im Spiel haben   *to have a finger in the pie.*

sein Spiel treiben mit   *to make fun of.*
Ich bin am Spiel.   *It's my turn.*
ihm freies Spiel lassen   *to give him a (free) hand.*
Spielautomat *m. slot machine.*
Spielbank *f. casino.*
Spielergebnis *n. score (result of play).*
Spieldose *f. music box.*
SPIELEN *to play, act, perform, gamble, pretend.*
Was spielt man heute abend?   *What's playing tonight?*
Spielerei *f. trifle.*
Spielplan *m. program, repertory.*
Spielsachen *pl. toys.*
Spielverderber *m. killjoy.*
Spielzeug *n. toy.*
Spieß *m. lance, spear, pike.*
Spießbürger *m. bourgeois, narrowmindedness, commonplace.*
Spinat *m. spinach.*
Spinne *f. spider.*
spinnen *to spin.*
Spinngewebe *n. cobweb.*
Spinnrad *n. spinning wheel.*
Spion *m. spy.*
Spionage *f. spying, espionage.*
Spionageabwehr *f. counterespionage.*
spionieren *to spy.*
Spiritus *m. spirits, alcohol.*
Spital *n. hospital.*
SPITZ *pointed, sharp, acute, caustic.*
Spitze *f. point, tip (tongue), top, head, lace, sarcasm.*
etwas auf die Spitze treiben   *to carry to extremes.*
SPITZEN *to sharpen, point.*
seine Ohren spitzen   *to prick up one's ears.*
Spitzenleistung *f. record, maximum.*
Spitzenlohn *m. maximum pay.*
spitzfindig *pointed, sharp, sarcastic, subtle.*
Spitzfindigkeit *f. subtlety.*
spitzig *pointed, sharp, sarcastic.*
Spitzname *m. nickname.*
Splitter *m. splinter, chip, fragment.*
splittern *to splinter, split.*
spontan *spontaneous.*
Sporn *m. spur.*
Sport *m. sport.*
Sport treiben   *to go in for sports.*
Sportfunk *m. radio sports news.*
Sportler (-in *f.) m. sportsman (woman).*
sportlich *sporting, athletic.*
Sportname *m. nickname.*
Spott *m. mockery, ridicule.*
spotten *to mock, make fun of, defy.*
spöttisch *mocking, scoffing, sarcastic.*
SPRACHE *f. language, speech, talk.*
zur Sprache bringen   *to bring up a subject.*

zur Sprache kommen   *to be mentioned.*
gehobene Sprache   *elevated diction.*
Sprachfertigkeit *f. fluency (of speech).*
sprachgewandt *fluent.*
sprachkundig *proficient in languages.*
Sprachlehre *f. grammar.*
sprachlich *linguistic.*
sprachlos *speechless.*
Sprachschatz *m. vocabulary.*
Sprachschnitzer *m. grammatical blunder, mistake.*
Sprachstörung *f. speech defect.*
SPRECHEN *to speak, talk, say, converse, discuss.*
Der Herr Doktor ist nicht zu sprechen.   *The doctor is busy.*
gut zu sprechen sein auf   *to be kindly disposed to.*
Ich bin für niemanden zu sprechen.   *I am in to no one.*
sich herumsprechen   *to be whispered about town.*
Sie sprechen nicht miteinander.   *They are not on speaking terms.*
Sprechen Sie Deutsch?   *Do you speak German?*
Sprechen Sie langsam, bitte.   *Please speak slowly.*
das Urteil sprechen   *to pronounce judgment.*
zu sprechen kommen auf   *to come to speak of.*
Wen wünschen Sie zu sprechen?   *Whom do you want to see?*
Sprecher *m. speaker.*
Sprechstunde *f. office hours, office (doctor).*
Sprechstundenhilfe *f. doctor's receptionist.*
Sprechweise *f. diction.*
Sprechzimmer *n. consulting room.*
sprengen *to burst, blow up, blast, spray.*
Sprengung *f. blowing up, explosion.*
Sprichwort *n. proverb.*
Springbrunnen *m. fountain.*
SPRINGEN *to jump, skip, spring, play.*
Das ist der springende Punkt.   *That is the crucial point.*
in die Augen springen   *to be obvious.*
spritzen *to spray, splash, sprinkle.*
spröde *brittle, hard, inflexible.*
Sprosse *f. sprout, sprig, play.*
Sprössling *m. sprout, shoot, offshoot, son (heir).*
Spruch *m. aphorism, saying.*
spruchreif *ripe for decision.*
sprudeln *to bubble up.*
sprühen *to spark.*
Sprühregen *m. drizzle, drizzling rain.*
SPRUNG *m. leap, jump, crack.*

Es ist nur ein Sprung von meinem Haus. *It is only a stone's throw from my house.*

Ich war auf dem Sprung auszugeben. *I was just going to leave.*

Sprungschanze *f. ski jump.*

spucken *to spit.*

Spucken Verboten!` No spitting!`

spülen *to rinse.*

Spülwasser *n. dishwater.*

SPUR *f. trace, trail, track, footprint.*

einem auf die Spur kommen *to be on a person's tracks.*

Keine Spur! *Not in the least!*

keine Spur von *no trace of.*

spüren *to feel, perceive, experience.*

spüren nach *to track, follow.*

spurlos *trackless.*

Spürsinn haben *to have a flair.*

(sich) sputen *to hurry up.*

STAAT *m. state, government, pomp, parade, show.*

in vollem Staat *in full dress.*

Staat machen *to show off.*

staatlich *public, political.*

Staatsaktion *f. government undertaking.*

Staatsangehörige *m. & f. subject, national.*

Staatsangehörigkeit *f. nationality, citizenship.*

Staatsanwalt *m. prosecuting attorney.*

Staatsbeamte(r) *m. civil servant.*

Staatsbesitz *m. state/public property.*

Staatsgebäude *n. public building.*

Staatsdienst *m. civil service.*

Staatsmann *m. statesman, politician.*

staatsmännisch *statesmanlike.*

Stab *m. stick, rod, bat, condemn.*

den Stab brechen über *to condemn.*

stabil *stable.*

stabilisieren *to stabilize.*

Stachel *m. thorn, prickle, sting, spur.*

Stachelbeere *f. gooseberry.*

Stacheldraht *m. barbed wire.*

Stadion *n. stadium, arena.*

Stadium *n. phase, stage.*

STADT *f. town, city.*

Stadtbahn *f. city railway.*

stadtbekannt *known all over town.*

Städter (-in *f.)* *m. townsman (woman)*

Stadtgespräch *n. local call.*

städtisch *municipal, urban.*

Stadtteil *m. quarter (of a town).*

Stahl *m. steel.*

stählern *of steel.*

Stahlguss *m. steel.*

Stall *m. stable.*

Stamm *m. stem, root, trunk.*

Stammbaum *m. genealogical tree.*

stammeln *to stammer.*

stammen *to spring from, come from.*

Stammgast *m. regular customer.*

Stammhalter *m. eldest son and heir.*

stämmig *sturdy, strong, vigorous.*

stampfen *to stamp, mash, crush.*

Stand *m. standing position.*

einen schweren Stand haben *to have a tough job.*

einen guten Stand haben *to be well thought of.*

Stand der Dinge *State of affairs.*

Standbild *n. statute.*

Ständchen *n. serenade.*

Standesamt *n. registrar's office.*

Standesbeamter *m. registrar.*

Standesehe *f. marriage for position or rank.*

standesgemäß *in accordance with one's rank.*

Standesgericht *n. court-martial.*

Standesunterschied *m. difference of class.*

standhaft *steady, constant.*

standhalten *to hold firm.*

ständig *permanent.*

Standort *m. station, position.*

Standpunkt *m. point of view.*

Standuhr *f. grandfather's clock.*

Stange *f. pole, bar, perch.*

eine Stange Geld *a pile of money.*

von der Stange *ready-made.*

ein Anzug von der Stange *a suit off the rack.*

Stanze *f. stanza.*

stanzen *to stamp.*

STARK *strong, stout, considerable, hard.*

Das ist denn doch zu stark! *That is too much!*

stark auftragen *to exaggerate, boast.*

starke Erkältung *bad cold.*

starkes Gedächtnis *good memory.*

starker Regen *heavy rain.*

stark besetzt *well attended.*

stark übertrieben *grossly exaggerated.*

Stärke *f. strength, force, vigor, intensity, energy, violence.*

stärken *to strengthen, fortify, starch, confirm.*

Starkstrom *m. power, electric current.*

Starkstromleitung *f. electric circuit.*

starr *stiff, hard, paralyzed.*

starren vor Staunen *to be dumbfounded.*

starren *to stare, be numb.*

starrköpfig *stubborn.*

Starrsinn *m. obstinacy.*

Start *m. start.*

Startbahn *f. runway.*

starten *to start.*

Station *f. station, stop, ward.*

freie Station *free board and lodging.*

Stationsarzt *m. resident physician.*

Stationsvorsteher *m. stationmaster.*

Statistik *f. statistics.*

statistisch *statistical.*

STÄTTE *f. place, spot.*

STATT (anstatt) *prep. (gen.) instead of.*
stattfinden *to take place.*
stattgeben *to permit, allow.*
statthaft *admissible, legal.*
stattlich *stately, magnificent, imposing.*
Stattlichkeit *f. dignity, magnificence.*
Statue *f. statute.*
Staub *m. dust, powder.*
　in den Staub ziehen　*to depreciate.*
　Staub wischen　*to dust.*
staubig *dusty.*
Staublappen *m. duster.*
Staubsauger *m. vacuum cleaner.*
staunen *to be surprised.*
STECHEN *to stick, bite, sting.*
　sich stechen　*to prick oneself.*
　in die Augen stechen　*to take one's fancy.*
Stechfliege *f. horsefly.*
Steckdose *f. wall plug, socket.*
STECKEN *to stick, pin up, fasten, fix, plant, stuff.*
　Dahinter steckt etwas.　*There is something behind this.*
　in Brand stecken　*to set fire.*
stecken bleiben *to be stuck.*
Steckenpferd *n. hobby, pet project.*
Stecker *m. plug.*
Stecknadel *f. pin.*
STEHEN *to stand, stop, be, suit, become.*
　gut stehen　*to be becoming.* (Rot steht ihr. *Red is becoming to her.*)
　gut stehen mit　*to be on good terms with*
　geschrieben stehen　*to be written.*
　Das Thermometer steht auf Null.　*The thermometer reads zero.*
　Es steht bei ihr.　*It's up to her.*
　im Verdacht stehen　*to be under suspicion.*
　in einem Amte stehen　*to hold an office.*
stehen bleiben *to stop, remain standing.*
stehend *standing, stationary, permanent.*
　stehenden Fusses　*at once.*
stehen lassen *to leave (standing).*
Stehlampe *f. floor lamp.*
STEHLEN *to steal, rob, take away.*
steif *stiff.*
Steig *m. path.*
STEIGEN *to climb, go up, ascend, rise, increase.*
　zu Kopf steigen　*to go to one's head.*
steigend *growing, increasing.*
steigern *to raise, increase, intensify.*
　sich steigern in　*to intensify, work up.*
Steigerung *f. raising, increase, gradation, climax.*
steil *steep, precipitous.*
Steilhang *m. steep slope.*
STEIN *m. stone, rock, jewel.*
　Das hat den Stein ins Rollen gebracht.　*That started the ball rolling.*

　Das ist nur ein Tropfen auf den heißen Stein.　*That's only a drop in the bucket.*
　einen Stein im Brett haben bei　*to be in favor with.*
　Mit fällt ein Stein vom Herzen!　*I feel so relieved!*
　Stein des Anstoßes　*stumbling block.*
　Stein und Bein schwören　*to swear by all that is sacred.*
Steinbruch *m. quarry.*
steinern *of stone.*
steinhart *as hard as stone.*
steinig *stony, rocky.*
steinreich *very wealthy.*
Steinzeit *f. Stone Age.*
STELLE *f. spot, place, position, situation, passage.*
　auf der Stelle　*on the spot.*
　offene Stelle　*vacancy.*
　von der Stelle kommen　*to make progress.*
　zur Stelle sein　*to be present.*
　an Stelle von　*instead of.*
STELLEN *to put, place, set, arrange, regulate, provide, furnish.*
　auf den Kopf stellen　*to turn upside down.*
　auf sich selbst gestellt sein　*to be dependent on oneself.*
　eine Bedingung stellen　*to make a condition.*
　eine Frage stellen　*to ask a question.*
　Er ist sehr gut gestellt.　*He is very well off.*
　Antrag stellen auf　*to apply for.*
　in Dienst stellen　*to put into service.*
　auf die Probe stellen　*to put to the test.*
　etwas in Aussicht stellen　*to hold out the prospect of something.*
　sich stellen gegen　*to oppose.*
　sich stellen　*to stand.*
　kalt stellen　*to put in a cool place.*
　sich gut stellen mit　*to be on good terms with.*
　sich stellen zu　*to behave toward.*
　zur Verfügung stellen　*to place at one's disposal.*
Stellenangebot *n. job offer; vacancy.*
Stellengesuch *n. application for a position, situations wanted.*
stellenlos *unemployed.*
Stellennachweis *m. employment reference.*
Stellenvermittlung *f. employment agency.*
STELLUNG *f. position, situation, stand, job.*
　Stellung nehmen zu　*to express one's opinion.*
Stellungnahme *f. opinion, comment, point of view.*
Stellungsgesuch *n. application for a position.*
stellungslos *unemployed.*
Stellungswechsel *m. change of position.*

Stellvertreter m. representative.
Stempel m. stamp, postmark.
Stempelkissen n. ink pad.
stempeln to stamp, mark.
stenografieren to write in shorthand.
Stenogramm n. shorthand.
  Stenogramm aufnehmen to take down in shorthand.
Steppdecke f. quilt.
Sterbebett n. deathbed.
Sterben n. death.
  im Sterben liegen to be dying.
STERBEN to die.
sterblich mortal.
  sterblich verliebt madly in love.
Sterblichkeit f. death rate.
steril sterile.
sterilisieren to sterilize.
Stern m. star.
Sternbild n. constellation.
Sterndeuter m. astrologer.
Sternhimmel m. starry sky.
stets always, forever.
Steuer n. rudder, helm, steering wheel.
Steuer f. tax.
Steueraufschlag m. supplementary tax.
steuerfrei tax free.
steuern to steer, pilot, drive.
steuerpflichtig subject to taxation.
Steuerrad n. steering wheel.
Steuerzahler m. taxpayer.
Stich m. sting, prick, stitch.
  im Stich lassen to forsake.
  einen Stich haben to have a screw loose (coll.).
Stichtag m. fixed day.
Stichwort n. catchword, cue.
Stiefbruder m. stepbrother.
Stiefmutter f. stepmother.
Stiefmütterchen n. pansy.
Stiefschwester f. stepsister.
Stiefsohn m. stepson.
Stieftochter f. stepdaughter.
Stiefvater m. stepfather.
Stier m. bull.
Stierkämpfer m. bullfighter.
Stift m. pencil, crayon; charitable institution.
stiften to donate; to found, establish.
Stifter m. founder; donor.
Stiftung f. foundation.
Stil m. style, manner.
Stilgefühl n. stylish sense.
STILL still, quiet, silent, secret.
  Seien Sie still! Be quiet!
  stille Jahreszeit off-season, slow season.
  stille Liebe secret love.
  bei stiller Nacht in the dead of the night.
  sich still verhalten to keep still/quiet.
STILLE f. silence, calm, quietude, peace.

  im Stillen secretly.
  in aller Stille privately, secretly.
stillen to quiet, appease, satisfy, quench, nurse.
still halten to keep still.
Stillleben n. still life (art).
still legen to shut down, close, discontinue.
still schweigen to be silent.
stillschweigend silent.
Stillstand m. standstill, stop.
still stehen to stand still, stop.
  Still gestanden! Attention!
stilvoll in good style, taste.
Stimmabgabe f. vote, voting.
stimmberechtigt entitled to vote.
STIMME f. voice, part, comment, vote.
  Stimme abgeben to vote.
STIMMEN to tune, vote, be correct, impress someone, influence someone's mood.
  Das stimmt! That is correct!
  Werden Sie für oder dagegen stimmen? Are you going to vote for or against?
Stimmrecht n. right to vote.
STIMMUNG f. tuning, pitch, key, mood, humor, impression, atmosphere.
  Stimmung machen für to create a mood for, to make propaganda for.
Stimmungsmensch m. moody person.
stimmungsvoll impressive, appealing, romantic.
Stimmzettel m. ballot.
Stirn f. forehead, front, imprudence.
  die Stirn runzeln to frown.
  einem die Stirne bieten to show a bold front.
Stock m. stick, rod, cane, floor (story).
  über Stock und Stein over hill and dale.
  Welcher Stock? What floor?
stockdumm utterly stupid.
stocken to stop, stand still.
  ins Stocken geraten to get tied up.
  im Reden stocken to break down, hesitate.
  stock dunkel pitch dark.
stockfinster pitch-dark.
Stockfisch m. dried cod.
Stockwerk n. story, floor.
Stoff m. matter, substance, fabric.
stöhnen to groan.
stolpern to stumble, trip over.
stolz proud.
  stolz sein auf to be proud of.
stopfen to darn, fill, stuff.
Stopfgarn n. darning thread.
Stopfnadel f. darning needle.
stoppen to stop.
Stoppuhr f. stopwatch.
Stöpsel m. stopper, cork.
stöpseln to cork.
Storch m. stork.

STÖREN *to disturb, trouble, inconvenience.*
  Nicht stören! *Do not disturb!*
  gestörte Leitung *faulty electrical line.*
störrisch *stubborn.*
Störung *f. disturbance, upset.*
  geistige Störung *mental disorder.*
Stoß *m. push, poke, pile, jerk, shock.*
stoßen *to push, shove, hit, kick, knock.*
  stoßen auf *to run into.*
Stoßstange *f. bumper (on a car).*
stottern *to stutter, stammer.*
Strafanstalt *f. penitentiary.*
strafbar *punishable.*
Strafe *f. punishment, penalty, fine.*
  bei Strafe von *on pain of.*
strafen *to punish.*
Straferlass *m. amnesty.*
straff *stretched, tense, tight, strict.*
straffällig *punishable.*
straffen *to tighten.*
straffrei *exempt from punishment, unpunished.*
Strafgefangener *m. convict.*
Strafgericht *n. criminal court.*
sträflich *criminal, punishable.*
Strafmaßnahme *f. sanction.*
Strafporto *n. extra postage, surcharge.*
Strafprozess *m. criminal case.*
strafswürdig *punishable.*
STRAHL *m. ray, beam, stream.*
strahlen *to radiate, beam, shine.*
stramm *tight, close.*
  stramm stehen *to stand at attention.*
STRAND *m. seashore, beach, strand.*
Strandbad *n. seaside, resort.*
stranden *to run around or ashore.*
Strandschuhe *pl. beach shoes.*
STRANG *m. rope, cord, line.*
  am gleichen Strang ziehen *to act in concert.*
  an einem Strang ziehen *to act together.*
  über die Stränge schlagen *to kick over the traces.*
  wenn alle Stränge reißen *if worse comes to worst.*
Strapaze *f. fatigue.*
strapazieren *to tire, exhaust.*
STRAßE *f. street, highway, road.*
  an der Straße *by the wayside.*
  auf der Straße *in the street.*
Straßenarbeiter *m. roadworker.*
Straßenbahn *f. tram, streetcar.*
Straßenfeger *m. street cleaner.*
Straßenübergang *m. pedestrian crossing.*
Straßenverstopfung *f. traffic congestion, traffic jam.*
sträuben *to ruffle up, bristle.*
Strauch *m. shrub, bush.*
streben *to endeavor, aspire, aim at.*
Streber *m. climber, careerist.*

Strecke *f. distance, way, route, tract.*
  auf freier Strecke *on the road.*
strecken *to stretch, extend, stretch out.*
  die Waffen strecken *to lay down arms.*
  sich strecken *to stretch.*
Streich *m. stroke, blow.*
  einem einen Streich spielen *to play a trick on a person.*
streichen *to spread, rub, strike, erase, cancel, paint, wander, stroll, migrate.*
  Frisch gestrichen! *Wet paint!*
Streichholz *n. match.*
Streichmusik *f. string music.*
Streichquartett *n. string quartet.*
Streifen *m. stripe, marking.*
streifen *to touch lightly, stripe, brush, wander.*
Streik *m. strike.*
  in den Streik treten *to go on strike.*
streiken *to strike.*
STREIT *m. fight, quarrel, dispute.*
streiten *to fight.*
  sich streiten *to quarrel.*
Streitfall *m. quarrel, controversy.*
Streitfrage *f. matter in dispute.*
  einem etwas streitig machen *to contest a person's right to a thing.*
STRENG *strict, stern, severe.*
  streng genommen *strictly speaking.*
Strenge *f. severity, strictness.*
strenggläubig *orthodox.*
streuen *to strew, scatter, spread.*
Strich *m. dash, stroke, line, compass point.*
  gegen den Strich *against the grain.*
  Machen wir einen Strich darunter! *Let's put an end to that.*
  nach Strich und Faden *thoroughly.*
Strichpunkt *m. semicolon.*
Strick *m. cord, rope.*
  wenn alle Stricke reissen *if everything else fails.*
stricken *to knit.*
Stroh *n. straw.*
Strohhalm *m. straw (for drinking).*
STROM *m. large river, stream, current.*
  Es regnet in Strömen. *It's pouring.*
Strom abwärts *downstream.*
Strom aufwärts *upstream.*
strömen *to stream, flow, pour.*
Strömung *f. current, stream.*
Stromzähler *electric meter.*
Strudel *m. whirlpool; type of pastry.*
Strumpf *m. stocking, sock.*
Strumpfband *n. garter.*
Strumpfhalter *m. garter (woman's).*
struppig *bristly, unkempt.*
STUBE *f. room, chamber, living room.*
Stubenhocker *m. stay-at-home.*
stubenrein *housebroken (of dogs).*
STÜCK *n. piece, play, extract, morsel.*

aus einem Stück *all of a piece.*

aus freien Stücken *of one's free will.*

ein starkes Stück *an unbelievable matter.*

ein Stück Arbeit *a stiff job.*

ein Stück mitnehmen *to give a lift.*

Er hält große Stücke auf ihn. *He thinks a lot of him.*

in allen Stücken *in every respect.*

zwanzig Stück Vieh *twenty head of cattle.*

stückweise *piece by piece, by the piece.*

Student *m.* (**-in** *f.*) *student.*

Studie *f. study, sketch (art).*

studieren *to study.*

Studium *n. study, university education.*

Stufe *f. step, stair, level.*

auf gleicher Stufe mit *on a level with.*

stufenweise *by degrees, gradually.*

STUHL *m. chair, seat.*

stumm *dumb, silent, mute.*

Stummheit *f. dumbness.*

stumpf *blunt, obtuse, dull.*

mit Stumpf und Stiel *root and branch.*

Stumpfsinn *m. stupidity.*

stumpfsinning *stupid, dull.*

STUNDE *f. hour; lesson, period.*

stundenlang *for hours.*

Stundenplan *m. timetable.*

Stundenzeiger *m. hour hand.*

stündlich *hourly.*

STURM *m. storm, gale.*

stürmen *to take by storm.*

stürmisch *stormy, impetuous.*

Sturz *m. fall, crash, tumble, overthrow, collapse.*

zum Sturz bringen *to overthrow.*

stürzen *to overthrow, throw down, fall down, plunge into, crash.*

Nicht stürzen! *Handle with care!*

Stütze *f. stay, support, help.*

stutzen *to trim, cut short, stop short.*

stützen *to support, base, prop up.*

Stutzer *m. dandy, fop.*

Stützpfeiler *m. pillar, support.*

Stützpunkt *m. base, strong point.*

Subjekt *m. subject.*

Substantiv *n. substantive, noun.*

Substanz *f. substance.*

substrahieren *to subtract.*

Suche *f. search, quest.*

auf die Suche gehen *to go in search of.*

auf der Suche sein nach *to be in search of.*

SUCHEN *to look for, try, seek.*

das Weite suchen *to run away.*

nach Worten suchen *to be at a loss for words.*

Sie hat hier nichts zu suchen. *She has no business here.*

Sucht *f. addiction.*

Süden *m. south.*

Südfrüchte *pl. tropical fruits.*

südlich *southern, (to the) south.*

Südpol *m. south pole.*

Sühne *f. expiation, atonement.*

sühnen *to expiate, atone.*

Summe *f. sum, amount.*

summieren *to add up.*

Sumpf *m. swamp, marsh.*

Sünde *f. sin.*

Sünder *m* (**-in** *f.*) *sinner.*

sündhaft *sinful.*

sündigen *to sin.*

Suppe *f. soup, broth.*

Suppeneinlage *f. things (that are) added to the soup.*

suspendieren *to suspend.*

SÜß *sweet, fresh, lovely.*

Süße *f. sweetness.*

Süßigkeit *f. sweetness, sweets.*

süßlich *sweetish, mawkish.*

Symbol *n. symbol.*

symbolisch *symbolic.*

Sympathie *f. sympathy.*

sympathisch *nice, likable, congenial.*

Symphonie *f. symphony.*

Symptom *n. symptom.*

Synagoge *f. synagogue.*

System *n. system.*

Szene *f. scene.*

Szenerie *f. scenery, settings.*

T

Tabak *m. tobacco.*

Tabelle *f. table, index, schedule.*

Tablett *n. tray.*

Tablette *f. tablet.*

Tadel *m. reprimand, blame.*

tadellos *excellent, perfect.*

tadeln *to blame, find fault.*

TAFEL *f. board, blackboard, bar, plate, table.*

sich von der Tafel erheben *to rise from the table.*

TAG *m. day, daylight, life (one's days).*

alle acht Tage *every week.*

alle Tage *every day.*

am Tag *during the day, in the daytime.*

an den Tag bringen *to bring to light.*

auf ein paar Tage *for a few days.*

auf seine alten Tage *in his old age.*

bei Tage *in the daytime.*

den ganzen Tag *all day long.*

dieser Tage *one of these days.*

eines Tages *some day.*

Er lebt in den Tag hinein. *He has no care in the world.*

Guten Tag! *Good morning!*

in acht Tagen *in a week.*
Tag aus, Tag ein *day in, day out.*
Tag für Tag *day by day.*
einen Tag um den andern *every other day.*
Man soll den Tag nicht von dem Abend
    loben. *Don't count your chickens
    before they hatch.*
vierzehn Tage *two weeks.*
vor acht Tagen *a week ago.*
Tagebuch *n. diary.*
tagelang *for days on end.*
Tagesbericht *m. daily report, bulletin.*
Tageseinnahme *f. day's earnings.*
Tagesgespräch *n. topic of the day.*
Tageszeit *f. time of day.*
Tageszeitung *f. daily paper.*
Tagewerk *n. day's work.*
taghell *as light as day.*
täglich *daily.*
tagsüber *during the day.*
Tagung *f. conference, meeting.*
Taille *f. waist.*
Takt *m. time measure (music).*
Taktgefühl *n. tact.*
Taktik *f. tactics.*
taktisch *tactical.*
taktlos *tactless.*
Taktlosigkeit *f. tactlessness, indiscretion.*
taktvoll *tactful, discreet.*
Tal *n. valley.*
Talent *n. talent, ability.*
talentiert *talented.*
Talk *m. talcum powder.*
Talsperre *f. dam.*
talwärts *downhill.*
Tank *m. tank (car).*
tanken *to fill up (car).*
Tanne *f. fir tree.*
Tannenadeln *pl. fir needles.*
Tannenbaum *m. fir tree.*
Tannenzapfen *m. pinecone.*
Tanté *f. aunt.*
Tanz *m. dance, ball.*
Darf ich um den nächsten Tanz bitten?
    May I have the next dance?
TANZEN *to dance.*
Tänzer *m. (-in f.) dance partner.*
Tapete *f. wallpaper.*
tapezieren *to paper.*
Tapezierer *m. paperhanger.*
tapfer *brave, gallant.*
Tapferkeit *f. bravery, gallantry.*
Tarif *m. rate, tariff.*
tarifmäßig *in accordance with the tariff.*
tarnen *to camouflage, disguise.*
Tarnung *f. camouflage.*
TASCHE *f. pocket, bag, purse.*
jemandem auf der Tasche liegen *to be a
    financial drain to a person.*

Taschenausgabe *f. pocketbook edition.*
Taschengeld *n. change.*
Taschenbuch *n. pocketbook.*
Taschendieb *m. pickpocket.*
Taschenlampe *f. flashlight.*
Taschenmesser *n. pocketknife.*
Taschentuch *n. handkerchief.*
Taschenuhr *f. pocket watch.*
TASSE *f. cup.*
eine Tasse Kaffee *a cup of coffee.*
Taste *f. key (music and typewriter).*
tasten *to touch, feel.*
TAT *f. deed, act, fact, achievement, feat.*
auf frischer Tat *in the very act.*
in der Tat *indeed, as a matter of fact.*
tatenlos *inactive, idle.*
Täter *m. perpetrator, doer.*
tätig *active.*
tätig sein *to be active, hard at work.*
Tätigkeit *f. activity, job.*
tatkräftig *energetic, active.*
Tatsache *f. fact.*
tatsächlich *real, actual.*
Tau *m. dew.*
Tau *n. rope.*
taub *deaf, empty, hollow.*
Taube *f. pigeon.*
Taubheit *f. deafness.*
taubstumm *deaf-mute.*
Taubstumme(r) *m. deaf-mute.*
tauchen *to dive, dip, plunge.*
Taucher *m. diver.*
tauen *to thaw.*
Taufe *f. baptism, christening.*
aus der Taufe heben *to be godfather (or
    godmother).*
taufen *to baptize.*
Taufnahme *m. Christian name.*
taugen *to be of use.*
Taugenichts *m. good-for-nothing.*
Tauglichkeit *f. fitness, suitability.*
Tausch *m. exchange.*
tauschen *to exchange, swap.*
täuschen *to delude, deceive, disappoint.*
Mich können Sie nicht täuschen. *You can't
    fool me.*
sich täuschen lassen *to let oneself be
    fooled.*
Täuschung *f. deception.*
TAUSEND *thousand.*
tausendmal *a thousand times.*
Tauwetter *n. thaw.*
Taxe *f. tax, rate, duty.*
Taxi *n. taxi.*
ein Taxi holen *to call a cab.*
taxieren *to appraise, value.*
Technik *f. technology.*
Techniker *m. technician.*
technisch *technical.*

Tee *m. tea.*

Teelöffel *m. teaspoon.*

Teer *n. tar.*

Teich *m. pond.*

Teig *m. dough.*

TEIL *m. & n. part, share, portion.*

   ich für meinen Teil   *as for me.*

   sich seinen Teil denken   *to have one's own ideas.*

   zum Teil   *partly.*

   zum größten Teil   *for the most part.*

teilbar *divisible.*

Teilbeschäftigung *f. part-time work.*

Teilchen *n. particle.*

TEILEN *to divide, share, distribute, deal out.*

   geteilte Gefühle   *mixed feelings.*

   geteilter Meinung sein   *to be of a different opinion.*

   sich teilen lassen durch   *to be divisible by*

Teilhaber *m. partner, participant.*

Teilhaberschaft *f. partnership.*

Teilnahme *f. participation, condolences.*

   Meine aufrichtige Teilnahme   *my sincere condolences.*

teilnahmslos *indifferent.*

teilnahmsvoll *sympathetic.*

teilnehmen *to take part in.*

Teilnehmer *m. participant, subscriber.*

teilweise *partial.*

Teilzahlung *f. partial payment, installment.*

Telekopierer *m. fax*

telekopieren *to fax.*

Telefax *n. facsimile, fax.*

   ein Telefax übersenden   *to send a fax.*

   Ich möchte etwas faxen.   *I'd like to fax (something).*

TELEFON *n. telephone.*

Telefonanruf *m. telephone call.*

Telefonbuch *n. telephone directory.*

TELEFONIEREN *to telephone.*

telefonisch *by telephone.*

Telefonist *m. (-in f.) telephone operator.*

Telefonnummer *f. telephone number.*

Telefonzelle *f. telephone booth.*

Telefonzentrale *f. telephone exchange.*

Telegrafie *f. telegraphy.*

TELEGRAFIEREN *to telegraph.*

telegrafisch *by telegram.*

TELEGRAMM *n. telegram.*

Telegrammformular *n. telegraph form.*

Teller *m. plate.*

Temperament *n. temperament, character, disposition.*

temperamentvoll *high-spirited, impetuous.*

Temperatur *f. temperature.*

Temperaturanstieg *m. rise in temperature*

Temperaturschwankungen *pl. variations in temperature.*

Temperatursturz *m. fall/drop in temperature.*

Tempo *n. time, measure, speed.*

Tendenz *f. tendency, inclination.*

Tennis *n. tennis.*

Tennisplatz *m. tennis court.*

Tennisschläger *m. tennis racket.*

Tenor *m. tenor.*

Teppich *m. carpet.*

Termin *m. deadline.*

Terrasse *f. terrace.*

Territorium *n. territory.*

Testament *n. testament.*

TEUER *expensive, high, costly.*

Teuerung *f. dearness, scarcity, high cost-of-living.*

Teufel *m. devil.*

   den Teufel an die Wand malen.   *to be pessimistic, tempt fate.*

teuflisch *devilish, diabolical.*

Text *m. text, libretto.*

   aus dem Text kommen   *to lose the thread (of a story, plot).*

Textbuch *n. words, libretto.*

Textilien *pl. textiles.*

Textilwaren *pl. textiles.*

THEATER *n. theater, stage.*

Theaterbesuch *m. playgoing.*

Theaterbesucher *m. theatergoer.*

Theaterdirektor *m. manager of a theater.*

Theaterkasse *f. box office.*

theatralisch *theatrical.*

Theke *f. counter, bar.*

Thema *n. theme, subject.*

Theologe *m. theologian.*

Theoretiker *m. theoretician.*

Thermometer *n. thermometer.*

Thermometerstand *m. thermometer reading.*

Thron *m. throne.*

Thronbesteigung *f. accession to the throne.*

TIEF *deep, low, deeply, far.*

   Das lässt tief blicken.   *That gives food for thought.*

   in tiefer Nacht   *late at night.*

   aus tiefstem Herzen   *from the bottom of my heart.*

   tiefe Einsicht   *profound insight.*

   im tiefsten Winter   *in the dead of winter.*

Tiefe *f. depth, profundity.*

tiefgründig *deep, profound.*

tiefliegend *sunken.*

Tiefsee *f. deep sea.*

tiefsinnig *profound, pensive, melancholy.*

Tiefstand *m. lowness, low level.*

TIER *n. animal, beast.*

Tierarzt *m. veterinarian.*

Tiergarten *m. zoo.*

Tiger *m. tiger.*

Tinte *f. ink.*

   in der Tinte sitzen   *to be in a mess.*

Tintenfass *n. inkwell.*

Tintenfleck *m. blot, ink spot.*
TISCH *m. table.*
  bei Tisch   *during the meal.*
  Bitte, zu Tisch!   *Dinner is ready!*
  Er ist gerade zu Tisch gegangen.   *He has just gone out to lunch.*
  reinen Tisch machen   *to make a clean sweep.*
  unter den Tisch fallen   *to be ignored.*
Tischdecke *f. tablecloth.*
Tischler *m. cabinetmaker.*
Tischplatte *f. tabletop.*
Tischrede *f. dinner talk.*
Tischtennis *n. table tennis, ping-pong.*
Tischtuch *n. tablecloth.*
Tischzeit *f. dinnertime.*
Titel *m. title, claim.*
Titelbild *n. frontispiece.*
Titelblatt *n. title page.*
Titelhalter *m. titleholder.*
Toast *m. toast.*
toasten *to drink a toast.*
toben *to rage, rave.*
Tobsucht *f. raving madness.*
tobsüchtig *raving mad.*
TOCHTER *f. daughter.*
TOD *m. death, decease.*
  des Todes sein   *to be doomed.*
  sich den Tod holen   *to catch one's death of a cold.*
  Es geht um Leben und Tod.   *It's a matter of life and death.*
Todesanzeige *f. death notice.*
Todeskampf *m. death agony.*
Todesstrafe *f. capital punishment, death penalty.*
Todestag *m. death anniversary.*
todkrank *very ill.*
tödlich *fatal, deadly, mortal.*
todmüde *dead tired.*
Toilette *f. toilet, dress, dressing table, lavatory.*
  Toilette machen   *to dress, get dressed.*
tolerant *tolerant.*
toll *mad, insane, raving, awful.*
tölpisch *clumsy.*
Ton *m. sound, note, stress, accent.*
tönen *to sound, resound.*
Tonfall *m. musical intonation, cadence.*
tonlos *soundless, voiceless.*
Tonne *f. barrel, ton.*
Tönung *shading.*
Topf *m. pot.*
Tor *n. gate.*
Tor *m. fool.*
Torheit *f. foolishness, folly.*
töricht *foolish, silly.*
Torte *f. layer cake.*
tosen *to rage, roar.*

TOT *dead, dull.*
  tote Zeit   *dead season.*
  toter Punkt   *deadlock.*
(sich) totarbeiten *to kill oneself with work.*
Tote *m. & f. dead person, deceased.*
TÖTEN *to kill.*
  sich töten   *to commit suicide.*
  sich totlachen   *to die laughing.*
Totenbett *n. deathbed.*
totenbleich *deadly pale.*
totenstill *still as death.*
Tötung *f. killing, slaying.*
Tour *f. tour, excursion.*
  in einer Tour   *without stopping.*
Tournee *f. tour (theater).*
Trab *m. trot.*
  im Trab   *quickly.*
Tracht *f. dress, costume.*
trachten *to strive for, seek after.*
traditionell *traditional.*
TRAGEN *to carry, bear, wear, take, endure, suffer, produce.*
  die Schuld tragen an   *to carry the blame for.*
  Sie trägt Trauer.   *She is in mourning.*
TRÄGER *m. porter.*
Tragfähigkeit *f. capacity.*
Tragflügel *m. wing of aircraft.*
tragisch *tragic.*
Tragödie *f. tragedy.*
trainieren *to train.*
Träne *f. tear.*
Trank *m. drink.*
tränken *to water, soak.*
transpirieren *to perspire.*
Transport *m. transport.*
Traube *f. grape, bunch of grapes.*
Traubenlese *f. grape harvest.*
Traubenmost *m. grape juice.*
trauen *to marry, give in marriage, join, trust, rely.*
  Ich traue ihm alles zu.   *I believe him capable of anything.*
  sich trauen lassen   *to get married.*
Trauer *f. sorrow, grief, affliction.*
Traueranzeige *f. announcement of a death.*
Trauermarsch *m. funeral march.*
trauern *to mourn, grieve.*
Trauerspiel *n. tragedy.*
träufeln *to drop.*
traulich *intimate, cosy.*
TRAUM *m. dream, fancy, illusion.*
  Träume sind Schäume.   *All dreams are lies.*
träumen *to dream.*
Träumer *m. (-in f.) dreamer.*
träumerisch *dreamy.*
traumhaft *dreamlike.*
TRAURIG *sad, sorrowful, mournful.*

Traurigkeit *f. sadness.*
Trauschein *m. marriage certificate.*
Trauung *f. marriage ceremony.*
Trauzeuge *m. witness to a marriage.*
TREFFEN *to meet, hit, strike, affect, touch; fall upon.*
  Alle nötigen Vorbereitungen sind getroffen worden. *All the necessary arrangements have been made.*
  sich getroffen fühlen *to feel hurt.*
  sich gut treffen *to be lucky.*
  sich treffen *to meet.*
  Vorsichtsmaßregeln treffen *to take all the necessary precautions.*
  Wen trifft die Schuld? *Who is to blame?*
treffend *to the point.*
Treffer *m. target, luck, winning ticket, prize.*
trefflich *excellent, admirable.*
Trefflichkeit *f. excellence.*
treiben *to drive, set in motion, float, drift.*
  Wintersport treiben *to practice winter sports.*
Treibhaus *n. conservatory, hothouse.*
trennbar *separable, divisible.*
TRENNEN *to separate, divide, dissolve.*
  getrennt leben *to live separately.*
  sich trennen *to part.*
  sich trennen von *to part from.*
Trennung *f. separation.*
Treppe *f. stairway, stairs.*
Treppenabsatz *m. landing.*
Treppengeländer *n. banisters, railing.*
Tresor *m. treasury.*
TRETEN *to step, tread, walk, go.*
  in jemandes Fußstapfen treten *to follow in somebody's footsteps.*
  aus dem Dienste treten *to retire from active service.*
  in Erscheinung treten *to appear.*
  in Kraft treten *to go into effect.*
  mit Füßen treten *to trample under foot.*
  zu nahe treten *to hurt one's feelings.*
TREU *faithful, true, loyal.*
treubrüchig *faithless, perfidious.*
Treue *f. fidelity, faithfulness, loyalty.*
treuherzig *frank, naive.*
treulich *faithfully.*
treulos *unfaithful.*
Treulosigkeit *f. faithlessness.*
Tribüne *f. platform, rostrum.*
Tribüne *m. tribune.*
Trieb *m. sprout, shoot, driving force, motive power.*
trinkbar *drinkable.*
TRINKEN *to drink, absorb.*
Trinker *m. drunkard.*
Trinkgeld *n. tip.*
Trinkspruch *n. toast.*
Tritt *m. step, footstep.*

Triumph *m. triumph, victory.*
triumphieren *to triumph.*
trocken *dry, arid, dull.*
  trockener Empfang *cool reception.*
Trockenmilch *f. dry milk.*
trocknen *to dry up.*
Trommel *f. drum.*
trommeln *to beat the drum.*
Trompete *f. trumpet.*
Trompeter *m. trumpeter.*
Tropen *pl. tropics.*
tropfen *to drop, drip.*
tropfenweise *by drops, drop by drop.*
TROST *m. comfort.*
Trost bedürftig *in need of consolation.*
trösten *to comfort, console, cheer up.*
  sich trösten *to cheer up.*
tröstlich *consoling, comforting.*
trostlos *discouraged.*
Trostlosigkeit *f. despair, hopelessness.*
trostreich *comforting, consoling.*
Trottoir *m. pavement, sidewalk.*
TROTZ *prep. (gen.) in spite of.*
  Trotz der Kälte ging ich jeden Tag spazieren. *In spite of the cold, I took a walk every day.*
Trotz *m. obstinacy, stubbornness, defiance.*
  jemandem zum Trotz *in defiance of someone.*
  Trotz bieten *to defy.*
trotzdem *nevertheless, anyway, although.*
  Trotzdem es sehr kalt ist, werde ich spazieren gehen. *Although it is very cold, I shall take a walk.*
trotzen *to defy, be obstinate.*
trotzig *defiant.*
trüb(e) *dark, sad, gloomy.*
trüben *to dim, trouble, spoil.*
  Der Himmel trübt sich. *The sky is clouding over.*
Trübsal *f. affliction, misery; sorrow.*
trübselig *sad, gloomy, dreary, troubled.*
trübsinnig *melancholy, dejected.*
trügen *to deceive.*
trügerisch *deceitful.*
Truhe *f. chest, trunk.*
Trümmer *f. ruins, debris.*
  in Trümmer gehen *to be shattered.*
Trumpf *m. trump.*
trumpfen *to trump.*
Trunk *m. drink.*
Trunkenheit *f. drunkenness.*
Truppe *f. troop, company.*
Truthahn *m. turkey.*
Tube *f. tube.*
Tuberkulose *f. tuberculosis.*
TUCH *n. cloth, fabric, shawl.*
tüchtig *good, able, fit, qualified, competent, efficient.*

Tüchtigkeit f. *fitness, ability, efficiency.*

Tücke f. *malice, spite.*

tückisch *malicious, spiteful.*

TUGEND f. *virtue.*

tugendhaft *virtuous.*

Tulpe f. *tulip.*

Tumult m. *tumult, commotion.*

TUN *to do, make, act, perform, execute.*

Das tut nichts.   *That does not matter.*

des Guten zu viel tun   *to overdo something.*

Er tut nur so.   *He is only pretending.*

Es tut mir Leid.   *I am sorry.*

es zu tun bekommen mit   *to have trouble with.*

Haben Sie sich weh getan?   *Did you hurt yourself?*

tun als ob   *to pretend.*

Tun Sie als ob Sie zu Hause wären!   *Make yourself at home.*

Wir haben viel zu tun.   *We are very busy.*

Das lässt sich tun.   *That can be done.*

Tue ihm nichts!   *Don't do anything to him (Don't hurt him)!*

tunlich *feasible, practicable.*

Tunnel m. *tunnel.*

tupfen *to dot, touch lightly, dab.*

TÜR f. *door, doorway.*

ihn vor die Tür setzen   *to show him to the door; to throw him out of the house.*

Er wohnt zwei Türen von hier.   *He lives next door (one or two houses).*

Türgriff m. *doorknob.*

Türklinke f. *door latch (handle).*

Turm m. *tower, steeple.*

Turmuhr f. *tower clock.*

Turnen n. *gymnastics.*

turnen *to do gymnastics.*

Turnhalle f. *gymnasium.*

Turnier n. *tournament.*

Tusche f. *watercolor.*

Tüte f. *paper bag.*

typisch *typical.*

Tyrann m. *tyrant.*

tyrannisieren *to tyrannize.*

U

Übel n. *evil, ailment, misfortune, inconvenience.*

ÜBEL *evil, wrong, bad, ill.*

Das ist nicht übel.   *That is not bad.*

Mir ist übel.   *I feel sick.*

übel dran sein   *to be in a bad way.*

auf ihn übel zu sprechen sein   *to have nothing good to say about him.*

übel zumute   *ill at ease, uncomfortable.*

übel gelaunt *cross, grumpy.*

übel gesinnt *evil-minded.*

Übelkeit f. *nausea.*

übel nehmen *to take offense.*

übelnehmerisch *touchy, susceptible.*

Übeltäter m. *evildoer, criminal.*

üben *to exercise, practise.* -

ÜBER 1. *prep. (dat. when answering the question, Wo? acc. when answering the question Wohin? and depending on the idiom) higher, while, concerning, via.*

den Winter über   *the whole winter long.*

Er schwamm über den See.   *He swam across the lake.*

Er zog sich die Decke über den Kopf. *He pulled the blanket over his head.*

Ich wundere mich über ihre Einstellung. *I am surprised at her attitude.*

Sie sprach über ihre Sorgen.   *She spoke about her sorrows.*

über Bord   *overboard.*

Über der Erde ziehen Wolken.   *Clouds are floating above the earth.*

über kurz oder lang   *sooner or later.*

über und über   *over and over.*

Seine Liebe geht ihr über alles.   *She places his love above everything.*

überall   *all over.*

von Berlin über Straßburg nach Paris   *from Berlin to Paris via Strassburg.*

über dem Essen   *during the meal.*

über den Sommer   *during the summer.*

2. *adv. wholly, completely, in excess.*

3. *prefix a) separable (when meaning above).*

Das Flugzeug fliegt über dem Ozean. *The airplane flies above the ocean.*

b) *inseparable (in all uses where it does not mean above).*

Er übersetzt ein Gedicht von Schiller. *He translates a poem by Schiller.*

überaltert *outdated.*

überanstrengen *to overwork, overstrain.*

überarbeiten *to review, go over.*

sich überarbeiten   *to overwork oneself.*

überbelichten *to overexpose (photo).*

überbieten *to excel, surpass.*

Überblick m. *perspective, summary, survey, overview.*

überblicken *to survey, sum up.*

überdauern *to outlast.*

überdies *besides, moreover.*

Überdruss m. *boredom, satiety, disgust.*

überdrüssig *tired of, sick of, bored with.*

Übereifer m. *excess zeal.*

übereignen *to transfer, assign, convey.*

übereilen *to rush, hurry, precipitate.*

sich übereilen   *to be in a great hurry.*

Übereilen Sie sich nicht!   *Don't rush!*

Übereilung f. hastiness, rush.

überein kommen to agree.

Übereinkunft f. agreement, arrangement.

übereinstimmen to agree, concur.

Übereinstimmung f. agreement, conformity.

überessen to overeat.

überfahren to drive through (a signal), run over.

Überfahrt f. crossing.

Überfall m. holdup, attack.

überfallen to hold up, attack.

überfällig overdue.

überfliegen to fly over, skim through.

überfließen to overflow, run over.

Überfluss m. abundance, profusion.

   im Überfluss   abundantly.

   zum Überfluss   unnecessarily.

überflüssig superfluous, unnecessary.

überfordern to overcharge.

Überfracht f. excess freight, overweight.

überführen to convey, transport.

Überführung f. conveying, transfer.

überfüllen to overload, crowd.

Überfüllung f. overloading.

Übergabe f. delivery, surrender.

Übergang m. passage, crossing.

übergeben to hand over, deliver.

übergehen (separable prefix) to merge into sth, change into sth.

übergehen (separable prefix) to transfer.

   Das Geschäft ist in andere Hände übergegangen.   This store has changed hands.

übergehen (inseparable) to pass over, to omit.

   Er übergeht diese Frage im Kapital.   He passes over this question in the chapter (but will get back to it).

Übergewicht n. overweight, excess weight.

   das Übergewicht bekommen   to lose one's balance.

übergießen to spill.

Überhandnahme f. increase, prevalence.

überhandnehmen to increase, get out of control.

Überhang m. curtain, hangings.

überhängen to hang over.

ÜBERHAUPT in general, altogether.

   überhaupt nicht   not at all.

überheben to save, spare, exempt.

überheblich presumptuous.

Überheblichkeit f. presumption, arrogance.

überholen to pass (car), surpass, overhaul.

überholt outdated.

überhören to miss, ignore.

Überkleid n. overdress, overalls.

überkochen to boil over.

überladen to overload.

überlassen to leave, give up, relinquish.

überlasten to overload.

überlaufen to run over, boil over, desert.

Überläufer m. deserter.

überleben to survive, outlive.

   sich überlebt haben   to be outdated.

   Er hat sie überlebt.   He outlived her.

Überlebende m. survivor.

überlegen to reflect, consider.

   sich überlegen   to think over, consider.

   Ich habe es mir anders überlegt.   I've changed my mind.

überlegen adj. superior.

   überlegen sein   to feel superior to.

Überlegenheit f. superiority.

Überlegung f. consideration, thought, deliberation.

überliefern to deliver, transmit.

Überlieferung f. delivery, tradition, surrender.

ÜBERMACHT f. superiority, predominance.

Übermaß n. excess.

   im Übermaß   to excess, excessive.

übermäßig excessive, immoderate.

Übermensch m. superman.

übermenschlich superhuman.

übermitteln to transmit, convey.

Übermittlung f. transmission, conveyance.

ÜBERMORGEN the day after tomorrow.

übermüden to overtire.

Übermüdung f. overfatigue.

Übermut m. high spirits, bravado.

übermütig to be in high spirits.

übernachten to stay overnight, spend the night.

Übernahme f. taking over, takeover.

übernatürlich supernatural.

übernehmen to take over, seize.

   sich übernehmen   to overstrain oneself.

überraschen to surprise.

Überraschung f. surprise.

überreden to persuade.

überreichen to hand over, present.

überreif overripe.

Überrest m. remainder.

überschätzen to overrate, overestimate.

überschauen to look over, survey.

überschneiden to intersect, overlap.

überschreiten to cross, exceed, overstep.

Überschreitung f. crossing, excess, transgression.

Überschrift f. heading, title.

Überschuh m. overshoe.

Überschuss m. surplus, excess.

überschüssig in excess.

überschwemmen to inundate.

Überschwemmung f. inundation, flood.

Übersee f. overseas.

übersehen to survey, look over.

übersenden to send, transmit, forward.

   einen Telefax übersenden   to send a fax.

Übersendung f. transmission.

übersetzen to pass across.

ÜBERSETZEN *to translate.*
Übersetzer *m. translator.*
Übersetzung *f. translation.*
Übersicht *f. view, review, summary.*
übersichtlich *clear, visible.*
Übersichtlichkeit *f. clearness, lucidity.*
übersinnlich *transcendental.*
überspannen *to stretch over, span.*
überspannt *eccentric.*
überspringen *to jump across.*
überstehen *to endure, come through.*
überströmen *to overflow.*
Überstunden *pl. overtime.*
    Überstunden machen   *to work overtime.*
ÜBERSTÜRZEN *to rush, hurry, act hastily.*
    Überstürzen Sie sich nicht!   *Don't rush yourself!*
übertragbar *transferable.*
übertragen *to transfer, give up, entrust with, transmit, broadcast.*
Übertragung *f. transfer, transcription, transmission.*
übertreffen *to excel, surpass.*
übertreiben *to exaggerate.*
Übertreibung *f. exaggeration.*
übertreten *to go over (to), change over (to), violate.*
Übertretung *f. violation, transgression.*
übervölkert *overpopulated.*
überwachen *to watch over, supervise.*
Überwachung *f. observation, surprise.*
überwältigen *to overwhelm.*
Überwältigung *f. overwhelming.*
überweisen *to transfer, remit.*
    telegraphisch überweisen   *to send a cable.*
Überweisung *f. transfer, remittance.*
überwiegen *to outweigh.*
überwiegend *preponderant, predominant.*
überwinden *to overcome.*
Überwindung *f. overcoming, conquest.*
Überzahl *f. numerical superiority, majority.*
überzählig *surplus.*
überzeugen *to convince.*
Überzeugung *f. conviction, belief.*
    der Überzeugung sein   *to be convinced.*
überziehen *to cover, recover; to overdraw (bank account).*
    das Bett überziehen   *to change the sheets.*
üblich *usual, customary.*
U-Boot *n. submarine.*
ÜBRIG *left over, remaining, other.*
    das Übrige   *the rest.*
    ein übriges tun   *to do more than necessary.*
    Haben Sie ein paar Minuten für uns übrig?   *Can you spare us a few minutes?*
    im Übrigen   *otherwise.*
    nichts übrig haben für   *to care little for.*
    übrig bleiben   *to be left over.*
    übrig lassen   *to leave (over).*

    zu wünschen übrig lassen   *to leave much to be desired.*
ÜBRIGENS *besides, by the way.*
ÜBUNG *f. exercise, practice, drill.*
UFER *n. shore, bank (river).*
UHR *f. hour, clock, watch.*
    nach der Uhr sehen   *to look at the time.*
    um fünf Uhr   *at five o'clock.*
    Um wie viel Uhr?   *At what time?*
    Wie viel Uhr ist es?   *What time is it?*
Uhrmacher *m. watchmaker.*
Uhrzeiger *m. clock hand.*
UM 1. *prep. (acc.), at, about, around, because of, for the sake of, for, up.*
    Der Zug verlässt Düsseldorf um drei Uhr.   *The train leaves Düsseldorf at three o'clock.*
    Ihre Zeit ist um.   *Your time is up.*
    Tag um Tag   *every day, day after day.*
    Wir ängstigen uns um sie.   *We worry about her.*
    Wir sitzen um den Tisch.   *We sit around the table.*
    Um Himmels willen!   *For God's sake!*
    um jeden Preis   *at any cost.*
    um keinen Preis   *not at any price.*
    um so besser   *all the better.*
    um zwei Jahre älter   *two years older.*
    2. *Adv. around.*
    um herum   *all around.*
    3. *Conj. (um . . . zu), in order to.*
    Um den Frieden zu erhalten, dankt der Prinz ab.   *The prince abdicates in order to preserve peace.*
    4. *Prefix. a) inseparable (implies the meaning of around).*
    Gärten umgeben das Schloss.   *The castle is surrounded by gardens.*
    b) *separable (implies the meaning of to upset, to transform).*
    Er warf den Stuhl um.   *He overturned the chair.*
umändern *to change, alter.*
Umänderung *f. change, alteration.*
umarbeiten *to remodel.*
Umarbeitung *f. remodeling.*
umarmen *to embrace, hug.*
Umarmung *f. embrace, hug.*
Umbau *m. rebuilding, reconstruction.*
umbinden *to tie around, put on.*
umblättern *to turn over.*
umblicken *to look about.*
umdrehen *to turn, turn round.*
Umdrehung *f. turning round.*
umfahren *to drive around, make a detour.*
Umfahrt *f. circular tour.*
umfallen *to topple over.*
Umfang *m. circumference, extent, size.*
umfangreich *comprehensive, extensive.*

umfassen *to clasp, embrace, enclose.*

umfassend *comprehensive, extensive, complete, full.*

umformen *to transform, remodel.*

Umfrage *f. inquiry.*

Umgang *m. association, relations.*

umgänglich *sociable.*

Umgangssprache *f. colloquial speech.*

umgeben *to surround.*

Umgebung *f. surroundings, environs.*

Umgegend *f. neighborhood, vicinity.*

UMGEHEN *to go around, circulate, haunt, evade.*

   umgehend antworten *to answer (respond) immediately.*

umgekehrt *opposite, reverse, contrary.*

umgestalten *to alter, transform, reform.*

umgraben *to dig, break up (earth).*

UMHER *around, about, here and there.*

umherblicken *to glance around, look around.*

umhin *about.*

   Ich kann nicht umhin. *I can't help (refrain from).*

umhüllen *to wrap, cover, veil, envelope.*

Umkehr *f. return, change.*

UMKEHREN *to turn back, turn around, turn upside down, invert, reverse.*

Umkehrung *f. inversion, reversal.*

umkleiden *to change clothes.*

umkommen *to perish, die*

Umkreis *m. circle, circuit, periphery.*

umkreisen *to revolve, circle around.*

Umkreisung *f. encirclement.*

Umlauf *m. rotation, revolution, circulation.*

   in Umlauf setzen *to circulate.*

umleiten *to divert (traffic).*

Umleitung *f. detour.*

   Strassenbau! Umleitung! *Road under repair! Detour!*

umliegend *surrounding, neighboring.*

umpflanzen *to transplant.*

umreissen *to knock down, to pull, to blow down (trees).*

Umriss *m. sketch, outline, contour.*

Umsatz *m. sale, turnover.*

umschalten *to switch over.*

Umschalter *m. switch, commutator.*

UMSCHLAG *m. envelope, cover, wrapper, hem, compress, change.*

umschlagen *to fell, knock down, put on, change, sell.*

umschließen *to enclose.*

umschwärmen *to swarm around.*

Umschwung *m. change, revolution.*

umsehen *to look back, round.*

   Sie sehen sich nach einer neuen Wohnung um. *They are looking for a new apartment.*

Umsicht *f. circumspection, prudence, caution.*

umsichtig *cautious, prudent.*

umsonst *gratis, for nothing; in vain.*

UMSTAND *m. circumstances, fact.*

   ohne Umstände *without ceremony.*

   mildernde Umstände *extenuating circumstances.*

   sich Umstände machen *to put oneself out.*

   Sie ist in anderen Umständen. *She is expecting a baby.*

   Umstände machen *to make a fuss.*

   unter allen Umständen *in any case, by all means.*

   unter keinen Umständen *on no account.*

   unter gewissen Umständen *in certain circumstances.*

   in anderen Umständen sein *to be pregnant, expecting a child.*

umständlich *laborious.*

Umsteigefahrschein *m. transfer ticket.*

   einen Umsteigefahrschein verlangen *to ask for a transfer (ticket).*

umsteigen *to change trains.*

umstritten *disputed, controversial.*

Umsturz *m. downfall, revolution.*

umstürzen *to throw down, overturn.*

Umtausch *m. exchange, conversion of money.*

umtauschen *to change for.*

umtun *to drape around.*

umwechseln *to exchange, change (money).*

Umweg *m. detour.*

Umwelt *f. surroundings, environment.*

umwenden *to turn, turn over.*

umwickeln *to wrap up.*

umziehen *to change clothes.*

Umzug *m. procession, change of residence, move.*

unabhängig *independent.*

Unabhängigkeit *f. independence.*

unabkömmlich *indispensable, essential.*

unablässig *incessant.*

unabsehbar *incalculable.*

unabsichtlich *unintentional.*

unabwendbar *inevitable.*

unachtsam *careless, negligent.*

unangebracht *out of place.*

unangemessen *inadequate, improper.*

unangenehm *unpleasant, disagreeable.*

unannehmbar *unacceptable.*

Unannehmlichkeit *f. inconvenience, trouble.*

Unansehnlichkeit *f. annoyance.*

unanständig *improper, indecent.*

unappetitlich *unappetizing, uninviting.*

Unart *f. bad behavior, rudeness.*

unartig *naughty, uncivil.*

unauffindbar *undiscoverable.*

unaufgefordert *unasked.*

unaufhaltsam *inevitable, impetuous.*

unaufhörlich *incessant, incessantly.*

unaufmerksam *inattentive.*

unaufrichtig *insincere.*
unausbleiblich *unfailing, certain.*
unausführbar *impracticable, not feasible.*
unaussprechlich *inexpressible.*
unausstehlich *intolerable, unbearable.*
unbarmherzig *unmerciful, pitiless, brutally.*
Unbarmherzigkeit *f. harshness,*
    mercilessness.
unbeabsichtigt *unintentional, inadvertent.*
unbeachtet *unnoticed.*
unbeanstandet *not objected to, unopposed.*
unbeantwortet *unanswered.*
unbedachtsam *inconsiderate, thoughtless.*
unbedenklich *harmless.*
unbedeutend *insignificant, trifling.*
unbedingt *unconditional, absolute.*
  Sie müssen unbedingt dabei sein. *You*
    must be there whatever may happen.
unbeeinflusst *unprejudiced.*
unbefangen *impartial, unprejudiced.*
Unbefangenheit *f. impartiality; facility.*
unbefriedigend *unsatisfactory,*
    unsatisfactorily.
unbefriedigt *unsatisfied.*
unbefugt *unauthorized, incompetent.*
unbegabt *not gifted, not clever.*
unbegreiflich *inconceivable.*
unbegrenzt *unbounded, unlimited.*
unbegründet *unfounded, groundless.*
Unbehagen *n. discomfort.*
unbehaglich *uncomfortable.*
unbehilflich *helpless.*
unbehindert *unrestrained.*
unbeholfen *clumsy.*
UNBEKANNT *unknown.*
  Er ist hier unbekannt. *He is a stranger*
    here.
unbekümmert *unconcerned.*
unbeliebt *unpopular.*
unbemerkt *unnoticed.*
UNBEQUEM *uncomfortable, inconvenient.*
Unbequemlichkeit *f. discomfort.*
unberechenbar *incalculable.*
unberechtigt *unauthorized, unjustified.*
unberührt *untouched, intact, innocent.*
unbeschädigt *undamaged, uninjured.*
unbescheiden *immodest, insolent.*
unbeschreiblich *indescribable.*
unbeschwert *unburdened.*
unbesehen *without inspection, hesitation.*
unbesiegbar *invincible.*
Unbesonnenheit *f. indiscretion, imprudence.*
unbesorgt *unconcerned.*
  Seien Sie unbesorgt! *Don't worry.*
unbeständig *unstable, unsteady.*
unbestechlich *incorruptible.*
unbestimmt *undetermined, undefined,*
    indefinite.
unbestreitbar *indisputable.*

unbeträchtlich *trivial.*
unbeugsam *inflexible, stubborn.*
unbeweglich *immovable, fixed.*
unbewohnt *uninhabited.*
unbewusst *unconscious.*
unbezahlbar *priceless, invaluable.*
unbezwingbar *invincible.*
unbrauchbar *useless, of no use.*
UND *and*
  und so weiter *and so forth.*
Undank *m. ingratitude.*
undankbar *ungrateful.*
Undankbarkeit *f. ingratitude.*
undenkbar *inconceivable.*
undeutlich *indistinct, vague.*
Unding *n. absurdity, monstrosity.*
unduldsam *intolerant.*
undurchdringlich *impenetrable.*
uneben *uneven, rough.*
unecht *not genuine, false, improper, artificial.*
unehelich *illegitimate.*
unehrbar *indecent, immodest.*
unehrenhaft *dishonorable, discreditable.*
unehrlich *dishonest.*
uneigennützig *unselfish.*
uneinig *disunited.*
Uneinigkeit *f. discord, disagreement.*
unempfindlich *insensible, robust.*
UNENDLICH *infinite, endless, infinitely.*
  unendlich klein *infinitesimal.*
unentbehrlich *indispensable.*
unentgeltlich *free of charge.*
unentschieden *undecided.*
unentschlossen *irresolute.*
unentschuldbar *inexcusable.*
unentwickelt *undeveloped.*
unerbittlich *inexorable.*
unerfahren *inexperienced.*
unerforschlich *impenetrable.*
unerfreulich *unpleasant, unsatisfactory.*
unerfüllbar *unrealizable.*
unerhört *unheard of, insolent.*
unerklärlich *inexplicable.*
unerlaubt *illicit, unlawful.*
unermesslich *boundless, infinite.*
unermüdlich *untiring.*
unerreichbar *inaccessible.*
unerreicht *unequaled.*
unerschrocken *fearless.*
unerschütterlich *imperturbable.*
unersetzlich *irreplaceable.*
unerträglich *unbearable, intolerable.*
unerwartet *unexpected.*
unerwünscht *undesired, unwelcome.*
unerzogen *uneducated, ill-bred.*
UNFÄHIG *incapable, unable.*
Unfähigkeit *f. inefficiency.*
Unfall *m. accident.*
Unfallversicherung *f. accident insurance.*

unfehlbar *certainly, unfailing.*
unfreiwillig *involuntary.*
unfreundlich *unfriendly, unpleasant.*
unfruchtbar *unproductive, sterile.*
Unfug *m. wrong, mischief, nonsense.*
ungeachtet *not esteemed; notwithstanding.*
ungebildet *uneducated.*
ungebührlich *excessive, undue.*
ungebunden *unbound, unrestrained.*
ungedeckt *uncovered (also for a check).*
ungeduldig *impatient, impatiently.*
ungeeignet *unsuitable, unfit.*
UNGEFÄHR *approximately, about, nearly.*
   von ungefähr *from about.*
ungefährlich *harmless.*
ungehalten *angry.*
Ungeheuer *monster.*
ungeheuer *huge, enormous, vast, monstrous.*
ungehorsam *disobedient.*
ungelegen *inconvenient.*
ungelernt *unskilled.*
ungemein *unusual, extremely.*
ungemütlich *uncomfortable.*
ungenießbar *inedible, unpalatable.*
ungenügend *insufficient.*
ungepflegt *neglected, untidy.*
UNGERECHT *unjust.*
ungerechtfertigt *unjustified.*
Ungerechtigkeit *f. injustice.*
UNGERN *unwillingly, reluctant.*
ungeschehen *undone, remedied.*
Ungeschick *n. misfortune.*
Ungeschicklichkeit *f. awkwardness.*
ungeschickt *awkward, clumsy.*
ungesetzlich *illegal.*
ungestört *undisturbed.*
ungestüm *impetuous, vehement.*
ungesund *unhealthy.*
ungetreu *faithless.*
ungewiss *uncertain.*
Ungewissheit *f. uncertainty.*
ungewöhnlich *unusual, strange.*
ungewohnt *unaccustomed, unfamiliar.*
ungezogen *ill-bred, naughty.*
Unglaube *m. disbelief.*
ungläubig *incredulous, skeptical.*
unglaublich *incredible.*
ungleich *unequal, unlike.*
UNGLÜCK *n. misfortune, bad luck, accident.*
unglücklich *unfortunate, unlucky.*
unglücklickerweise *unfortunately.*
Unglücksvogel *m. unlucky person.*
Ungnade *f. disgrace, displeasure.*
   in Ungnade fallen bei *to displease*
      someone, to fall into disgrace.
ungültig *void, invalid.*
   für ungültig erkären *to annul.*
ungut *bad.*
   Nichts für ungut. *no harm meant.*

Unheil *n. mischief, harm, disaster, calamity.*
unheilbar *incurable, irreparable.*
unheilvoll *disastrous.*
unheimlich *sinister.*
unhöflich *impolite, rude.*
Uniform *f. uniform.*
UNIVERSITÄT *f. university, college.*
unkenntlich *unrecognizable.*
Unkenntnis *f. ignorance, unawareness.*
unklar *not clear, unclear.*
unklug *imprudent, unwise.*
Unkosten *pl. expenses.*
Unkraut *n. weeds.*
unleserlich *illegible.*
unliebenswürdig *unamiable, unkind.*
unlogisch *illogical.*
unmäßig *immoderate, inordinate.*
unmenschlich *inhuman.*
Unmenschlichkeit *f. inhumanity, cruelty.*
unmerklich *imperceptible.*
unmittelbar *immediate, direct.*
UNMÖBLIERT *unfurnished.*
unmodern *old-fashioned, antiquated.*
UNMÖGLICH *impossible.*
Unmöglichkeit *f. impossibility.*
unmoralisch *immoral.*
unmündig *underage, minor.*
   unmündig sein *to be a minor.*
unnachgiebig *unyielding, inflexible.*
unnachsichtig *strict, severe.*
unnahbar *unapproachable, inaccessible.*
unnatürlich *unnatural, affected.*
UNNÖTIG *unnecessary, needless.*
unordentlich *disorderly, untidy.*
UNORDNUNG *f. disorder.*
   in Unordnung bringen *to mess up.*
unparteiisch *impartial.*
unpassend *inappropriate.*
unpersönlich *impersonal.*
unpraktisch *impractical.*
unpünktlich *unpunctual.*
Unrecht *n. injustice.*
   im Unrecht *in the wrong.*
   Unrecht haben *to be wrong.*
UNRECHT *wrong, unjust, unfair.*
unredlich *dishonest.*
unregelmäßig *irregular.*
unreif *unripe.*
unrein *unclean.*
   ins Unreine schreiben *to make a rough*
      copy.
Unruhe *f. uneasiness.*
Unruhen *pl. riots.*
unruhig *restless, uneasy.*
Unruhstifter *m. agitator (pol.), troublemaker*
UNS *acc. and dat. of the pers. pron. wir;*
     reflexive and reciprocal pron.: us, to
     us, ourselves, each other.
unsachlich *subjective, personal.*

unsagbar *unspeakable.*
unsauber *dirty, filthy.*
Unsauberkeit *f. dirt, filth.*
unschädlich *harmless.*
  unschädlich machen   *to render harmless, neutralize, disarm.*
unschätzbar *invaluable.*
unscheinbar *insignificant, plain, homely.*
unschlüssig *wavering, irresolute.*
UNSCHULDIG *innocent.*
unselbständig *helpless, dependent.*
UNSER *Poss. adj. our.*
UNSER (-ER, -E -ES) *Poss. pron. ours.*
unsereins *people like us.*
unsererseits *as for us, for our part.*
unseresgleichen *people like us.*
unserethalben *for our sakes, on our behalf.*
unseretwegen *for our sake.*
unseretwillen *for our sake.*
UNSICHER *unsafe, uncertain, unsteady.*
Unsicherheit *f. insecurity, uncertainty.*
Unsinn *m. nonsense.*
Unsitte *f. bad habit, abuse.*
unsterblich *immortal.*
unstet *unsteady, variable.*
unsympathisch *unpleasant.*
untätig *inactive.*
UNTEN *below, beneath, underneath.*
  von oben bis unten   *from top to bottom, from head to foot.*
  nach unten   *downward.*
  von unten auf   *right from the bottom.*
UNTER 1. *Prep. (dat. when answering the question, Wo? acc. when answering the question, Wohin? and depending on the idiom): under, underneath, below, beneath, among, during, by.*
  Ich habe meine Schuhe unter das Bett gestellt.   *I put my shoes under the bed.*
  Ich saß unter den Zuschauern.   *I sat among the spectators.*
  Unter Anderem hat sie mir gesagt . . .   *Among other things, she told me . . .*
  unter freiem Himmel   *in the open air.*
  unter uns gesagt   *between us.*
  unter vier Augen   *privately ("under four eyes").*
  unter Vorbehalt aller Rechte   *all rights reserved.*
  jemandem etwas unter die Nase reiben   *to rub one's nose in something.*
  unter diesen Umständen   *under these circumstances.*
  2. *Prefix.* a) *separable (when meaning under).*
  Die Sonne geht im Westen unter.   *The sun sets in the west.*
  b) *inseparable when not meaning under.*

  Wir unterhielten uns über die Ferien.   *We talked about the holidays.*
unterbauen *to lay a foundation.*
unterbelichten *to underexpose (photo).*
Unterbewusstsein *n. subconsciousness.*
unterbieten *to undersell.*
UNTERBRECHEN *to interrupt, disconnect, cut off.*
  Fräulein, wir sind unterbrochen worden.   *Operator, we have been cut off.*
Unterbrechung *f. interruption.*
unterbringen *to put up, accommodate, place.*
unterdessen *meanwhile, in the meantime.*
unterdrücken *to oppress, suppress.*
Unterdrückung *f. repression, oppression.*
untereinander *among ourselves, reciprocally.*
Unterernährung *f. malnutrition.*
Unterführung *f. underpass.*
Untergang *m. setting, going down, destruction, fall; decline.*
  der Sonnenuntergang   *the sunset.*
UNTERGEHEN *to go down, set, sink.*
Untergrundbahn *f. subway.*
unterhalb *below.*
Unterhalt *m. maintenance, living.*
UNTERHALTEN *to support, maintain, keep up.*
  sich gut unterhalten   *to have a good time.*
  sich unterhalten   *to converse, talk.*
unterhandeln *to negotiate, to confer.*
Unterhemd *n. undershirt, vest.*
Unterhosen *pl. shorts, drawers (underwear).*
unterirdisch *underground.*
Unterkleidung *f. underwear.*
unterkommen *to find accommodation, find employment.*
Unterkunft *f. accommodation.*
Unterlage *f. foundation, support, base (plate), evidence, pad.*
Unterlass *m. stopping.*
  ohne Unterlass   *incessantly.*
unterlassen *to discontinue, neglect, fail to.*
unterlegen *to lay under, put under.*
unterliegen *to be defeated, to be subject to.*
Unterlippe *f. lower lip.*
Untermieter *m. subtenant.*
UNTERNEHMEN *to undertake, attempt.*
unternehmend *enterprising.*
Unternehmer *m. contractor.*
Unternehmung *f. enterprise, undertaking.*
unterordnen *to subordinate, submit.*
Unterordnung *f. subordination.*
unterreden *to converse, confer with.*
Unterredung *f. talk, conference (press).*
UNTERRICHT *m. instruction, teaching, education, lesson.*
unterrichten *to teach, instruct.*
Unterrock *m. slip, petticoat.*
unterschätzen *to underestimate, underrate.*

unterscheiden *to distinguish, differentiate, discriminate.*
  sich unterscheiden *to differ.*
Unterscheidung *f. distinction, discrimination.*
UNTERSCHIED *m. difference.*
  ohne Unterschied *alike.*
unterschiedlich *different, distinct.*
unterschiedslos *indiscriminately.*
unterschlagen *to embezzle, to suppress.*
Unterschlagung *f. embezzlement, suppression.*
unterschreiben *to sign.*
Unterschrift *f. signature.*
Unterseeboot *n. submarine.*
unterstehen *to stand under, be subordinate.*
  sich unterstehen *to dare.*
unterstützen *to support, aid, assist.*
Unterstützung *f. support, aid, relief.*
untersuchen *to examine, investigate.*
Untersuchung *f. examination, investigation.*
Untertasse *f. saucer.*
Untertitel *m. subtitle (movie).*
Unterwäsche *f. underwear.*
unterwegs *on the way.*
Unterweisung *f. instruction.*
Unterwelt *f. underworld.*
unterwerfen *to subjugate.*
unterwürfig *submissive.*
unterzeichnen *to sign, ratify.*
Unterzeichner *m. signatory.*
Unterzeichnung *f. signature, ratification.*
untragbar *not negotiable; unbearable.*
untrennbar *inseparable.*
UNTREU *untrue, unfaithful.*
untröstlich *disconsolate.*
unübersehbar *immense, vast.*
unübertrefflich *unequaled.*
ununterbrochen *continuously.*
unverantwortlich *irresponsible.*
unverbesserlich *incorrigible.*
unverbindlich *not obligatory, without obligation.*
unverdient *undeserved.*
unverdorben *unspoiled, pure.*
unvergänglich *imperishable, immortal.*
unvergleichlich *incomparable.*
unverheiratet *unmarried.*
unverhofft *unexpected.*
unverkennbar *unmistakable.*
unverletzt *unhurt, uninjured.*
unvermeidlich *inevitable.*
Unvermögen *n. inability, incapacity, powerlessness.*
unvermutet *unexpected.*
unvernünftig *unreasonable.*
unverrichtet *unperformed, unaccomplished.*
  unverrichteter Sache *unsuccessfully.*
unverschämt *impudent, fresh.*
unversehens *unexpectedly.*
unversehrt *intact, safe, undamaged.*

unverständlich *unintelligible, incomprehensible.*
unverwüstlich *indestructible, inexhaustible.*
unverzeihlich *unpardonable.*
unverzollt *duty unpaid.*
unverzüglich *immediate, instant, prompt.*
unvollkommen *imperfect.*
unvollständig *incomplete, defective.*
unvorhergesehen *unforeseen.*
UNVORSICHTIG *careless.*
unvorteilhaft *unprofitable, unbecoming.*
unweiblich *unwomanly.*
unweit *not far off, near.*
Unwesen *n. mischief, abuse.*
  sein Unwesen treiben *to be up to mischief.*
unwesentlich *unessential, immaterial.*
  Das ist ganz unwesentlich. *That does not matter.*
Unwetter *n. violent, stormy weather; storm.*
unwiderruflich *irrevocable.*
unwiderstehlich *irresistible.*
Unwille *m. indignation.*
unwillkommen *unwelcome.*
unwillkürlich *instinctively, involuntarily.*
unwirksam *ineffective, inefficient.*
unwirtlich *inhospitable, dreary.*
unwirtschaftlich *uneconomic.*
unwissend *ignorant, unaware.*
UNWOHL *not well, indisposed.*
Unwohlsein *n. indisposition.*
unwürdig *unworthy.*
Unzahl *f. endless number.*
unzählig *countless.*
unzeitgemäß *old-fashioned.*
unzerbrechlich *unbreakable.*
unzivilisiert *uncivilized, barbarian.*
unzufrieden *dissatisfied.*
unzulänglich *unimportant.*
unzulässig *inadmissible.*
unzureichend *insufficient.*
unzuverlässig *unreliable.*
unzweideutig *unequivocal, explicit.*
unzweifelhaft *undoubted, indubitable.*
üppig *luxuriant, abundant, voluptuous.*
Üppigkeit *f. luxury, abundance.*
uralt *very old, ancient, primeval.*
Uraufführung *f. first performance, opening night.*
Ureinwohner *m. original inhabitant.*
Urgroßeltern *pl. great-grandparents.*
Urkunde *f. deed, document, record.*
Urkundenfälscher *m. forger of documents.*
urkundlich *documentary, authentic.*
Urlaub *m. leave, furlough, vacation.*
  der bezahlte Urlaub *the paid vacation.*
Urquell *m. primary source.*
URSACHE *f. cause, reason.*
  Keine Ursache! *Don't mention it!*
Ursprung *m. source, origin, beginning.*

ursprünglich *original.*
URTEIL *n. judgment, decision, sentence, opinion.*
  ein Urteil fällen über *to sentence.*
urteilen *to judge, pass a sentence, give an opinion.*
urteilsfähig *competent to judge.*
urteilslos *without judgment.*
Urteilsspruch *m. sentence, verdict.*

V

Vagabund *m. vagabond.*
Vanille *f. vanilla.*
Variante *f. variant.*
Variation *f. variation.*
variieren *to vary.*
Vase *f. vase.*
VATER *m. father.*
Vaterhaus *n. home (of one's childhood).*
Vaterland *n. native land, fatherland.*
vaterländisch *national, patriotic.*
väterlicherseits *on the father's side.*
vaterlos *fatherless.*
Vaterstadt *f. native town.*
vegetarisch *vegetarian.*
Veilchen *n. violet.*
Vene *f. vein.*
Ventil *n. valve, air valve, vent.*
verabreden *to agree upon, make an agreement.*
  verabredet sein *to have a date or appointment.*
Verabredung *f. agreement, engagement; appointment.*
verabscheuen *to detest.*
verabschieden *to dismiss, discharge.*
  sich verabschieden *to say good-bye.*
verachten *to despise, scorn, disdain.*
verächtlich *contemptuous, disdainful.*
Verachtung *f. contempt, scorn, disdain.*
verallgemeinern *to generalize.*
veraltet *old, obsolete.*
veränderlich *variable, unstable.*
VERÄNDERN *to change, alter, vary.*
Veränderung *f. change, alteration, variation.*
verängstigt *intimidated.*
Veranlagung *f. talent.*
veranlassen *to cause.*
Veranlassung *f. reason, suggestion.*
veranschlagen *to estimate.*
  zu hoch veranschlagen *to overrate.*
veranstalten *to arrange, organize, set up.*
Veranstaltung *f. arrangement, performance, event.*
verantworten *to answer for, account for.*
verantwortlich *responsible.*

VERANTWORTUNG *f. responsibility.*
  auf seine Verantwortung *at his own risk.*
  zur Verantwortung ziehen *to call to account.*
verantwortungslos *irresponsible.*
verarbeiten *to process, work up, manufacture, to treat.*
Verarbeitung *f. workmanship, manufacturing.*
Verband *m. bandage, association.*
verbannen *to banish, exile.*
Verbannung *f. banishment, exile.*
verbergen *to hide.*
VERBESSERN *to improve, correct.*
Verbesserung *f. improvement, correction.*
verbeugen *to bow.*
Verbeugung *f. bow, reverence.*
verbiegen *to bend, twist.*
verbieten *to forbid.*
  Rauchen verboten! *No smoking!*
  Strengstens verboten! *Strictly forbidden!*
verbinden *to tie, bind, bandage, connect, combine, join.*
  Sie haben mich falsch verbunden! *You connected me to the wrong number!*
  sich verbinden *to unite.*
  sich zu Dank verbunden fühlen *to feel indebted to.*
verbindlich *obligatory, courteous.*
Verbindlichkeit *f. obligation.*
VERBINDUNG *f. union, combination.*
  sich in Verbindung setzen mit *to get in touch with.*
Verbindungsstraße *f. connecting road, access road.*
verblüffen *to disconcert, perplex.*
verblüffend *amazing.*
Verblüffung *f. stupefaction, amazement.*
verbluten *to bleed to death.*
verborgen *hidden, concealed, secret.*
Verborgenheit *f. concealment, retirement, seclusion.*
Verbot *n. prohibition, ban.*
verboten *prohibited, forbidden.*
Verbrauch *m. consumption.*
verbrauchen *to consume, use.*
Verbraucher *m. consumer.*
Verbrechen *n. crime.*
Verbrecher *m. criminal.*
verbrecherisch *criminal.*
verbreiten *to spread, diffuse.*
verbrennen *to burn, cremate.*
  sich verbrennen *to burn oneself.*
Verbrennung *f. burning, combustion.*
verbringen *to spend, pass time.*
verbunden *connected.*
verbürgen *to guarantee, vouch for.*
Verdacht *m. suspicion.*
verdächtig *suspicious.*

verdächtigen *to distrust.*
verdammen *to condemn.*
verdammenswert *damnable.*
Verdammnis *f. damnation, perdition.*
Verdammung *f. condemnation.*
verdanken *to owe something.*
Verdauung *f. digestion.*
Verdeck *n. covering, awning.*
Verderben *n. ruin, destruction.*
  jemanden ins Verderben stürzen   *to ruin a person.*
VERDERBEN *to spoil, ruin.*
  Ich möchte es mir nicht mit ihm verderben.
  I don't want to displease him.
  sich den Magen verderben   *to upset one's stomach.*
Verderber *m. corrupter.*
verderblich *perishable, pernicious.*
verdienen *to earn, gain, deserve, merit.*
Verdienst *m. gain, profit, earnings.*
Verdienst *n. merit.*
verdienstvoll *deserving.*
verdient *deserving, worthy.*
  sich verdient machen um   *to be worthy of.*
Verdikt *n. verdict.*
verdolmetschen *to interpret, translate.*
verdoppeln *to double.*
verdorben *spoiled.*
verdrängen *to displace, push aside.*
verdrehen *to twist, sprain.*
  einem den Kopf verdrehen   *to turn one's head, to throw someone crazy.*
verdrießen *to annoy, displease.*
verdummen *to grow stupid.*
verdünnen *to thin, dilute.*
Verdünnung *f. attenuation, rarefaction, dilution.*
verdunsten *to evaporate.*
Verdunstung *f. evaporation.*
verdursten *to die of thirst.*
veredeln *to ennoble, improve, refine, finish.*
verehren *to respect, worship, adore.*
Verehrer *m.* (**-in** *f.*) *worshipper.*
Verehrung *f. respect, veneration.*
vereidigen *to swear in.*
Vereidigung *f. swearing in, taking of an oath.*
Verein *m. union, association.*
vereinbar *compatible, consistent.*
Vereinbarung *f. agreement, arrangement.*
vereinfachen *to simplify.*
vereinigen *to join, unite, reconcile.*
  die Vereinigten Staaten von Amerika.
  The United States of America.
vereisen *to turn to ice.*
vereiteln *to frustrate, thwart.*
verelenden *to sink into poverty.*
vererben *to bequeath, transmit, hand down.*
verewigen *to perpetuate, immortalize.*
verfahren *to act, behave.*

Verfall *m. decay, ruin.*
  im Verfall geraten   *to go to ruin, decay.*
verfallen *to decline, go to ruin, grow weaker, expire.*
  verfallen lassen   *to let go to waste.*
  verfallene Züge   *sunken features.*
verfassen *to compose, write.*
Verfasser *m.* (**-in** *f.*) *author, writer.*
Verfassung *f. state, condition, constitution.*
verfaulen *to decay.*
verfliegen *to fly away, disappear, vanish.*
verfolgen *to follow, pursue, prosecute.*
  heimlich verfolgen   *to shadow.*
  gerichtlich verfolgen   *to prosecute.*
Verfolgung *f. pursuit, prosecution.*
verfügbar *available.*
verfügen *to arrange, decree, obtain.*
  verfügen über   *to dispose of, have at one's disposal.*
  zur Verfügung stellen   *to place at one's disposal.*
verführen *prevail upon, seduce, to lead astray.*
Verführer *m. tempter, seducer.*
verführerisch *tempting, seductive.*
Verführung *f. temptation.*
Vergangenheit *f. past; past tense (grammar).*
vergänglich *transitory, perishable.*
Vergaser *m. carburetor.*
vergeben *to give away, dispose of, confer, forgive.*
vergebens *in vain, vainly.*
Vergebung *f. pardon, forgiveness, bestowal.*
vergelten *to pay back, repay, retaliate.*
Vergeltung *f. recompense, reprisal.*
VERGESSEN *to forget, neglect.*
vergesslich *forgetful.*
Vergesslichkeit *f. forgetfulness.*
vergiften *to poison.*
Vergiftung *f. poisoning.*
Vergleich *m. comparison, agreement, arrangement.*
VERGLEICHEN *to compare, check, settle.*
VERGNÜGEN *n. pleasure, joy, fun.*
vergnügen (sich) *to amuse, enjoy oneself.*
VERGNÜGT *pleased, glad.*
  Ich komme mit Vergnügen.   *I'll be delighted to come.*
  Viel Vergnügen!   *Have a good time!*
  Vergnügungsreise *f.   pleasure trip.*
vergnügungssüchtig *pleasure-seeking.*
vergraben *to bury, hide in the ground.*
vergriffen *out of print.*
vergrößern *to enlarge, magnify.*
Vergrößerung *f. enlargement.*
Vergünstigung *f. privilege, favor.*
Verhältnis *n. relation, ratio, love affair.*
verhältnismäßig *relative, proportional.*
verhasst *hated, hateful, odious.*

verheimlichen *to conceal, keep secret.*
verheiraten *to marry off.*
  sich verheiraten *to get married.*
verherrlichen *to glorify.*
Verherrlichung *f. glorification.*
verhindern *to hinder, prevent.*
Verhinderung *f. hindrance, drawback.*
Verhör *n. examination, trial.*
verhören *to examine, interrogate.*
verhungern *to die of hunger.*
verirren *to lose one's way, go astray.*
VERKAUF *m. sale.*
VERKAUFEN *to sell.*
  billiger verkaufen *to undersell.*
  zu verkaufen *for sale.*
VERKÄUFER *m. (-in f.) salesperson, vendor.*
verkäuflich *saleable.*
VERKEHR *m. traffic, circulation, communication, trade.*
Verkehrsschild *n. traffic sign, road sign.*
Verkehrsmittel *n. means of communication or transport, passenger vehicle.*
Verkehrsordnung *f. traffic regulations*
Verkehrsstauung *f. traffic jam, congestion.*
Verkehrszeichen *n. traffic sign, road sign.*
verkehren *to associate, transform, to reverse. convert, change, run (buses).*
  verkehren mit *to associate with, see a great deal of.*
Verkehrsampel *f. traffic light.*
Verkehrsschutzmann *m. traffic policeman.*
Verkehrsunfall *m. traffic accident.*
verkehrt *wrong, backward, upside down, absurd.*
  verkehrt gehen *to go the wrong way.*
verkennen *to fail to recognize, mistake, misunderstand, undervalue.*
verkleiden *to disguise, camouflage.*
Verkleidung *f. disguise, camouflage.*
verkommen *to be ruined, become bad, degenerate.*
Verkommenheit *f. depravity, degeneracy.*
verkörpern *to personify, incarnate, embody.*
Verlag *m. publication (Austria), publishing firm.*
verlangen *to demand, desire, require.*
  auf Verlangen *by request, on demand.*
  verlangen nach *to long for, to desire.*
verlängern *to extend, prolong.*
Verlängerung *f. extension, prolonging.*
Verlass *m. trustworthiness.*
  Auf ihn ist kein Verlass. *He cannot be relied on.*
VERLASSEN *to leave, abandon, desert.*
Verlauf *m. lapse, development (time).*
verlaufen *to elapse, to take its course*
  sich verlaufen *to get lost.*
verlegen *embarrassed, self-conscious, confused.*

  um etwas verlegen sein *to be at a loss for.*
  um Geld verlegen sein *to be short of money.*
Verlegenheit *f. embarrassment, difficulty.*
Verleger *m. publisher.*
verleihen *to lend, confer, bestow, grant.*
verletzbar *vulnerable, susceptible.*
verletzen *to hurt, injure, offend.*
Verletzung *f. injury, offense, violation.*
verleugnen *to deny, injure, offend.*
Verleugnung *f. denial, denunciation.*
verleumden *to malign, slander.*
Verleumder *m. slanderer.*
verleumderisch *slanderous.*
Verleumdung *f. slander, defamation, libel.*
(sich) VERLIEBEN *to fall in love.*
verliebt *in love.*
  Sie ist verliebt bis über die Ohren. *She is head over heels in love.*
VERLIEREN *to lose, waste, disappear.*
  An ihm ist nicht viel verloren. *He's no great loss.*
  Ich habe keinen einzigen Augenblick zu verlieren. *I don't have a single moment to lose.*
(sich) verloben *to get engaged.*
Verlobte *m. & f. fiancé(e).*
Verlobung *f. engagement.*
Verlust *m. loss, waste, escape.*
vermehren *to increase.*
Vermehrung *f. increase.*
vermieten *to rent, let, hire out.*
Vermieter *m. landlord.*
vermissen *to miss.*
vermuten *to suppose, presume, suspect.*
vermutlich *presumable, probable.*
vernachlässigen *to neglect.*
Vernachlässigung *f. neglect.*
verneigen *to bow.*
Verneigung *f. bow.*
vernichten *to annihilate, destroy.*
Vernichtung *f. annihilation, destruction.*
VERNUNFT *f. reason, understanding, intelligence, good sense, judgment.*
  Vernunft annehmen *to listen to reason.*
  zur Vernunft bringen *to bring to one's senses.*
vernünftig *reasonable, sensible.*
veröffentlichen *to publish.*
Veröffentlichung *f. publication.*
verordnen *to order, decree.*
Verordnung *f. order, decree, prescription.*
verpacken *to pack up, wrap up.*
Verpackung *f. packing up, wrapping up.*
verpfänden *to pawn, mortgage.*
verpflegen *to board, to provide for.*
Verpflegung *f. feeding, board, food.*
  Zimmer mit Verpflegung. *room and board.*
verpflichten *to oblige, bind, engage.*

sich verpflichten *to commit (bind) oneself.*
verpflichtet sein *to be under obligation.*
Verpflichtung *f. obligation, duty, engagement.*
Verrat *m. treason, betrayal.*
verraten *to betray, disclose, reveal.*
Verräter *m. traitor.*
verräterisch *treacherous.*
verrechnen *to reckon, charge, account; miscalculate.*
Verrechnung *f. settling of an account, reckoning.*
verreisen *to go away.*
verreist sein *to be away.*
verrichten *to execute, perform, accomplish.*
die Hausbeit verrichten *to do the housework.*
Verrichtung *f. execution, performance, function, work.*
VERRÜCKT *crazy, mad.*
Vers *m. verse, stanza.*
versagen *to deny, refuse; fail, miss.*
VERSAMMELN *to assemble, bring together, gather.*
sich versammeln *to gather.*
Versammlung *f. gathering, assembly, meeting.*
versäumen *to neglect, omit, miss.*
verschaffen *to get, obtain, secure, procure.*
verschenken *to give away.*
verschicken *to send away, dispatch, evacuate.*
Verschickung *f. dispatch, transportation, evacuation.*
VERSCHIEDEN *different from, distinct, various.*
verschlafen *to oversleep, sleepy.*
verschlimmern *to aggravate, to make worse.*
Verschlimmerung *f. deterioration.*
verschlucken *to swallow the wrong way.*
Verschluss *m. lock, fastener, clasp, seal, plug, zipper.*
verschmachten *to languish.*
verschonen *to spare, exempt from.*
verschönern *to beautify, embellish, adorn.*
Verschönerung *f. embellishment.*
verschreiben *to prescribe, order in writing, write for.*
sich verschreiben *to make a mistake in writing.*
verschwenden *to waste, lavish.*
Verschwender *m. spendthrift, extravagant person.*
verschwenderisch *wasteful, extravagant.*
verschwieger *discreet, close.*
Verschwiegenheit *f. secrecy, discretion.*
verschwistert *like brothers and sisters, closely united.*
Versehen *n. mistake, oversight.*
VERSEHEN *to provide, furnish, supply with; to overlook.*
aus Versehen *by mistake.*

ehe man sich's versieht *unexpectedly, suddenly.*
den Dienst eines andern versehen *to stand in for someone*
sich versehen *to make a mistake.*
VERSETZEN *to displace, transfer, pledge, pawn.*
den Verstand verlieren *to go out of one's mind. "Just put yourself in my place."*
Versetzung *f. transfer, moving up.*
VERSICHERN *to insure, affirm.*
Versicherung *f. insurance.*
versinnbildlichen *to symbolize, represent.*
versöhnen *to reconcile, conciliate.*
Versöhnung *f. reconciliation.*
versorgen *to provide, supply.*
Versorger *m. support, breadwinner.*
Versorgung *f. maintenance, providing (for).*
verspätet *late.*
Verspätung *f. delay, lateness.*
Verspätung haben *to be late.*
verspielen *to lose, gamble away.*
VERSPRECHEN *to promise.*
Ich habe mich nur versprochen. *It was only a slip of the tongue.*
sich etwas versprechen von *to expect much of.*
Versprechen *m. promise.*
VERSTAND *m. mind, sense, brain, intellect.*
den Verstand verlieren *to go out of one's mind.*
zu Verstand kommen *to arrive at the age of discretion.*
verständig *intelligent, sensible, wise.*
verständigen *to inform, notify.*
sich verständigen *to come to an understanding with.*
Verständigung *f. communication.*
verständlich *understandable, clear, comprehensible.*
sich verständlich machen *to make oneself understood.*
Verständlichkeit *f. intelligibility, clearness.*
Verständnis *comprehension, understanding.*
Verständnis haben für *to appreciate.*
verständnislos *unappreciative, stupid.*
verständnisvoll *understanding, appreciative.*
Versteck *n. hiding place.*
verstecken *to hide, conceal.*
versteckt *hidden, concealed.*
versteckte Absichten *ulterior motives.*
VERSTEHEN *to understand, comprehend, know.*
falsch verstehen *to misunderstand.*
Ich verstehe nicht! *I don't understand!*
sich verstehen *to understand each other.*
sich von selbst verstehen *to go without saying.*

Was verstehen Sie darunter? *What do you understand by that?*

zu verstehen geben   *to give to understand.*

versteifen *to stiffen.*

versteigern *to sell at auction.*

Versteigerung *f. auction.*

verstellbar *adjustable.*

verstellen *to change order or position, shift, block, disguise.*

Verstellung *f. dissimulation, disguise, hypocrisy.*

versteuern *to pay duty on. -*

verstimmen *to annoy, upset.*

Verstimmung *f. ill humor, bad temper.*

Versuch *m. experiment, trial, attempt.*

VERSUCHEN *to try, attempt, taste, endeavor.*

es versuchen mit   *to give a trial to, put to the test.*

Versuchung *f. temptation.*

vertagen *to adjourn.*

vertauschen *to exchange, substitute, mix up.*

verteidigen *to defend.*

Verteidiger *m. defender, advocate, attorney.*

Verteidigung *f. defense.*

verteilen *to distribute, dispense, assign.*

Verteiler *m. distributor, retailer.*

Verteilung *f. distribution.*

Vertrag *m. contract, treaty, agreement.*

VERTRAGEN *to carry away, bear, stand, endure, tolerate, digest.*

ich kann diese Speise nicht vertragen. *This food does not agree with me.*

sich vertragen   *to get along.*

sich wieder vertragen   *to settle one's differences, to be reconciled.*

einen Spass vertragen   *to take a joke.*

Vertrauen *n. confidence.*

vertrauen *to trust.*

vertrauensvoll *trusting.*

vertrauenwürdig *trustworthy.*

vertraulich *confidential.*

Vertraulichkeit *f. confidence.*

vertraut *familiar.*

im Vertrauen   *in confidence, confidentially.*

im Vertrauen auf   *relying on, trusting to.*

sich vertraut machen   *to become familiar.*

Vertraute(r) *m. & f. intimate friend.*

vertreiben *to drive away, expel, scatter.*

vertreten *to represent, substitute for; to sprain.*

Vertreter *m. representative, substitute.*

VERTRETUNG *f. representation, replacement.*

eine Vertretung übernehmen   *to take the place of, represent.*

vertrösten *to console, put off.*

verunglücken *to have an accident.*

verursachen *to cause.*

verurteilen *to sentence, condemn.*

Verurteilung *f. sentence, condemnation.*

vervielfältigen *to multiply, duplicate, reproduce.*

verwachsen *overgrown, deformed.*

verwahren *to keep, put away.*

verwaisen *to become an orphan.*

verwaist *orphaned, deserted.*

verwandeln *to transform.*

verwandt *related, similar, allied.*

Verwandte *m. f. relation, relative.*

Verwandtschaft *f. relationship, relations.*

verwechseln *to take for, mistake for.*

Verwechslung *f. mistake, confusion.*

verweigern *to deny, refuse.*

Verweigerung *f. denial, refusal.*

Verweis *m. reproof, reprimand, reference.*

Verweisung *f. exile, banishment.*

verwendbar *applicable.*

VERWENDEN *to use, utilize, employ, expend.*

sich verwenden für   *to put in a good word for.*

verwenden auf   *to put in (spend) a lot of time on.*

Zeit verwenden auf   *to devote time to.*

Verwendung *f. use, utilization, application.*

verwirklichen *to realize, materialize.*

Verwirklichung *f. realization, materialization.*

Verwöhnung *f. spoiling, pampering.*

verwundern *to surprise.*

Verwunderung *f. surprise, astonishment.*

verzagen *to lose heart, despair.*

VERZEIHEN *to pardon, forgive, excuse.*

Verzeihen Sie! *Excuse me!*

verzeihlich *excusable.*

VERZEIHUNG *f. pardon, excuse.*

Ich bitte Sie um Verzeihung! *Please excuse me!*

Verzicht *m. resignation, renunciation.*

verzichten *to renounce, resign, forgo.*

verzinsen *to pay interest on.*

verzögern *to delay.*

verzollen *to pay duty on.*

Haben Sie etwas zu verzollen? *Have you anything to declare?*

Verzollung *f. payment of duty, clearance.*

verzweifeln *to despair*

verzweifelt *desperate, despairing.*

Verzweiflung *f. despair, desperation.*

zur Verzweiflung bringen   *to drive one mad.*

Veto *n. veto.*

Veto einlegen   *to veto a thing.*

VETTER *m. cousin.*

Vieh *n. cattle.*

Viehhändler *m. cattle dealer.*

VIEL *much, a great deal, a lot of.*

ein bisschen viel   *a little too much.*

sehr viel   *a great many.*

in vielem *in many respects.*
noch einmal so viel *as much again.*
viele *many.*
zu viel *far too much.*
Viel Glück! *Lots of luck!*
Viel Vergnügen! *Have a good time!*
vielgerühmt *much praised.*
VIELLEICHT *perhaps.*
vielmalig *frequent, repeated.*
vielseitig *versatile; many-sided.*
vielumstritten *widely discussed/disputed.*
VIER *four.*
zu vieren, zu viert *four of us.*
Viereck *n. square.*
viereckig *square, quadrangular.*
VIERTE *fourth.*
VIERTEL *n. quarter, fourth.*
Es ist Viertel vor zwei. *It is a quarter to
    two.*
vierteljährlich *quarterly.*
Viertelstunde *f. a quarter of an hour.*
viertelstündlich *every quarter of an hour.*
VIERZEHN *fourteen*
vierzehn Tage *two weeks.*
VIERZEHNTE *fourteenth.*
VIERZIG *forty.*
VIERZIGSTE *fortieth.*
Violine *f. violin.*
virtuos *masterly.*
Virtuose *m. (-sin f.) virtuoso.*
Virtuosität *f. virtuosity.*
Vision *f. vision.*
Visite *f. visit.*
Visitenkarte *f. business card.*
Vitrine *f. showcase.*
VOGEL *m. bird.*
den Vogel abschießen *to carry off the
    prize, to steal the show.*
Vogelscheuche *f. scarecrow.*
Vokabel *f. word.*
Vokabelschatz *m. vocabulary (range).*
VOLK *n. people, nation, crowd.*
das arbeitende Volk *the working classes.*
der Mann aus dem Volk *the man in the
    street.*
Volksabstimmung *f. plebiscite.*
Volkslied *n. folk song.*
Volksschule *f. elementary or primary school.*
volkstümlich *national, popular, cultural.*
Volksversammlung *f. public-meeting.*
VOLL 1. *adj. & adv. full, filled, complete,
    whole, entire; fully, completely.*
aus vollem Herzen *from the bottom of the
    heart.*
aus voller Kehle *at the top of one's voice.*
den Mund voll nehmen *to boast.*
Die Rechnung ist voll bezahlt. *The bill is
    paid in full.*
in voller Fahrt *at full speed.*

Er nimmt den Mund zu voll. *One cannot
    take him too seriously.*
2. *Prefix.* a) *separable (meaning to fill)*
Sie gießt die Gläser voll. *She fills up the
    glasses.*
b) *inseparable (meaning to accomplish,
    finish).*
Er vollführte eine gute Leistung.
    He executed a good performance.
Vollbart *m. beard.*
vollblutig *full-blooded.*
vollbringen *to finish, accomplish, complete.*
Volldampf *m. full steam.*
vollenden *to complete, to bring to a close.*
Vollendung *f. completion, perfecting.*
volles Vertrauen *complete confidence.*
völlig *complete, entire, quite.*
volljährig *of age.*
Volljährigkeit *f. majority (of age).*
VOLLKOMMEN *perfect, complete.*
Vollkommenheit *f. perfection.*
Vollkraft *f. full vigor.*
Vollmacht *f. full power, power of attorney.*
Vollmilch *f. whole milk.*
Vollmond *m. full moon.*
vollständig *complete.*
vollzählig *complete, full, completely,
    absolutely.*
VON 1. *pret. (dat.) from, by, with, of, on,
    upon, about.*
Amerika wurde von Kolumbus entdeckt.
    America was discovered by Columbus.
Der Platz war voll von Menschen.
    The place was full of people.
ein Gedicht von Heine *a poem by Heine.*
eine Feder von Gold *a gold pen.*
von heute ab *from today on.*
Von meinem Fenster sehe ich auf den
    Garten. *From my window I see the
    garden.*
2. *adv.: apart, separate.*
von einander *apart.*
von klein auf *from childhood (on).*
von mir aus *as far as I am concerned.*
von selbst *by itself, automatically.*
von Nutzen sein *to be needful, necessary.*
VOR 1. *prep. (dat. when answering the
    question, Wo? acc. when answering the
    question, Wohin? and depending on the
    idiom), before, in front of, ahead of,
    for, with, against, from.*
Das Bild ist vor mir. *The picture is in front
    of me.*
Es ist ein Viertel vor elf. *It is a quarter to
    eleven.*
Ich werde sie vor ihm warnen. *I will warn
    her against him.*
nach wie vor *as usual.*
nicht vor *not until.*

vor acht Tagen   *a week ago.*

vor allem   *above all, first of all.*

vor der Klasse   *before class.*

vor Hunger sterben   *to die of hunger.*

Vor ihm müssen Sie sich in Acht nehmen.
    With him, you must be on your guard.

vorzeiten   *formerly*

vorab   *before.*

2. *separable prefix (implies movement
    forward, presentation, demonstration).*

Der Lehrer las ein Gedicht vor.   *The teacher
    read a poem aloud.*

Die Soldaten rückten vor.   *The soldiers
    moved forward.*

Wir bereiten uns auf die Prüfung vor.   *We
    prepare ourselves for the examination.*

Vorabend *m. evening before.*

vorahmen *to have a presentiment.*

Vorahnung *f. presentiment.*

voran *ahead.*

vorangehen *to precede.*

  mit gutem Beispiel vorangehen   *to set a
    good example.*

Voranschlag *m. estimate.*

Voranzeige *f. preliminary advertisement.*

Vorarbeit *f. preliminary work.*

Vorarbeiter *m. foreman.*

VORAUS *in front of, ahead of.*

  etwas voraus haben vor   *to have an
    advantage over a person.*

  im Voraus   *in advance.*

  weit voraus   *way ahead.*

  vorausgehen   *to lead the way, precede.*

Voraussage *f. prediction, prophecy.*

voraussetzen *to presuppose, assume.*

Voraussetzung *f. supposition, assumption.*

voraussichtlich *presumable, probable.*

Vorbehalt *m. reservation, proviso.*

  ohne Vorbehalt   *unconditionally.*

  unter Vorbehalt aller Rechte   *all rights
    reserved.*

vorbehalten *to keep in reserve, withhold.*

  sich vorbehalten   *to reserve to oneself.*

vorbehaltlos *unconditional.*

vorbei *by, along, past, over, gone.*

vorbereiten *to prepare, make ready.*

Vorbereitung *f. preparation.*

Vorbeugungsmaßregel *m. preventive
    measure.*

Vorbild *n. model, standard.*

vorbildlich *model, ideal.*

Vorbildung *f. preparatory training, education.*

vorder *fore, forward, anterior.*

Vordergrund *m. foreground.*

Vorderhaus *n. front part of the house.*

vordringlich *urgent.*

voreilig *hasty, rash.*

Voreiligkeit *f. precipitation, rashness.*

voreingenommen *prejudiced.*

Voreingenommenheit *f. prejudice.*

vorenthalten *to keep back, withhold.*

Vorfall *m. occurrence, event.*

vorfallen *to occur, happen, take place.*

Vorfreude *f. joy of anticipation.*

vorführen *to demonstrate, produce.*

Vorführung *f. demonstration.*

Vorgang *m. occurrence.*

Vorgänger *m. predecessor.*

VORGEHEN *to go on, go forward, go first,
    lead, take place, occur, act, be of
    special importance.*

  Gehen Sie vor!   *Go right ahead!*

Vorgeschichte *f. prehistory.*

Vorgeschmack *m. foretaste.*

Vorgesetzte *m. & f. chief, boss*

VORGESTERN *the day before yesterday.*

vorhaben *to intend, plan.*

  Haben Sie morgen etwas vor?   *Do you
    have any plans for tomorrow?*

vorhalten *to hold up, to hold out.*

Vorhang *m. curtain.*

vorher *before, beforehand, in advance,
    previously.*

vorherrschen *to predominate, prevail.*

vorherrschend *predominant, prevailing.*

Vorkenntnis *f. previous knowledge.*

vorkommen *to come forward, occur, happen.*

  Es kommt Ihnen nur so vor.   *You are just
    imagining that.*

Vorkommnis *n. occurrence, event.*

Vorlage *f. presentation of documents.*

vorlassen *to give precedence to.*

vorläufig *preliminary.*

Vorleger *m. mat, rug.*

vorlesen *to read aloud.*

Vorlesung *f. lecture.*

vorletzt *one before the last.*

Vorliebe *f. predilection, preference.*

vormachen *to put, place before, impose on
    someone, fool.*

vormerken *to make a note of, put down.*

Vormittag *m. morning ("before noon").*

Vormund *m. guardian.*

Vormundschaft *f. guardianship.*

VORN *in front, in front of.*

  nach vorn   *forward.*

  nach vorne heraus wohnen   *to live in the
    front part of a house.*

  von vorn   *from the front.*

  von vorn anfangen   *to start afresh.*

  vor vorn herein   *from the first.*

Vorname *m. Christian name, given name.*

vornehm *of high rank, noble, distinguished.*

Vornehmheit *f. distinction, high rank.*

vornehmlich *principally, chiefly, especially.*

Vorort *m. suburb.*

Vorplatz *m. court, hall, vestibule.*

Vorrang *m. precedence, priority.*

Vorrat m. store, stock, provision.
vorrätig in stock, on hand.
  nicht mehr vorrätig   out of stock.
Vorratskammer f. storeroom, pantry.
Vorrede f. words of introduction; opening speech.
vorsagen to dictate, say, prompt.
Vorsatz m. purpose.
Vorschlag m. proposal, proposition.
vorschlagen to propose, offer.
vorschreiben to set a copy of.
Vorschrift f. copy, direction.
vorschriftsmäßig according to instructions.
vorsehen to provide for, consider, take care.
Vorsehung f. providence.
VORSICHT f. foresight, caution, prudence.
  Vorsicht!   Take care! Beware!
  Vorsicht Stufe!   Mind the step!
vorsichtig cautious, prudent.
vorsichtshalber as a precaution.
Vorsichtsmaßregel f. precautionary measure.
Vorsitz m. presidency, chairperson.
  den Vorsitz führen   to preside in the chair.
Vorspeise f. hors d'oeuvre.
vorsprechen to pronounce, recite.
Vorsprung m. projection, projecting part.
Vorstadt f. suburb.
Vorstand m. board of directors.
vorstellen to place before, put in front of, demonstrate, introduce, represent, act.
  sich etwas vorstellen   to imagine something.
  sich vorstellen   to introduce oneself.
VORSTELLUNG f. introduction, presentation, performance, picture.
  Wann fängt die Vorstellung an?   When does the performance start?
Vorstellungsvermögen n. imagination.
Vorteil m. advantage, profit.
VORTEILHAFT advantageous, favorable.
  vorteilhaft aussehen   to look one's best.
Vortrag m. reciting, delivery, execution, lecture.
vortragen to carry forward, recite, declaim, execute, perform.
vortrefflich excellent, admirable, splendid.
Vortrefflichkeit f. excellence.
vorüber past, over, by, along.
vorübergehen to go by, pass.
Vorurteil n. prejudice.
vorurteilslos unprejudiced.
Vorverkauf m. booking in advance (theater); advance sale.
vorvorgestern three days ago.
Vorwahl f. primary election.
Vorwand m. pretext, pretense, excuse.
VORWÄRTS forward, onward, on.
  Vorwärts!   Go on! Go ahead!
vorwärtsgehen to go on, advance, progress.

vorwärtskommen to get on, advance, prosper.
vorwärtskommend predominant.
Vorwurf m. reproach.
  Vorwürfe machen   to blame.
vorwurfsvoll reproachful.
vorzeigen to show, produce, exhibit, display.
vorzeitig premature, precocious.
vorziehen to draw forward, prefer.
Vorzimmer n. antechamber.
Vorzug m. preference, superiority.
vorzüglich excellent, superior, first choice.
Vorzüglichkeit f. excellency, superiority.
Vorzugspreis m. special price.
Vorzugsrecht n. privilege.

W

WAAGE f. balance, scales.
  einem die Waage halten   to be a match for.
  sich die Waage halten   to counterbalance each other.
  wagerecht   horizontal level.
WACH awake, alive, brisk.
Wachdienst m. guard duty.
Wache f. guard, watch, sentry.
WACHEN to be awake, remain awake.
  wachen über   to watch over.
Wachs n. wax.
wachsam vigilant, watchful.
Wachsamkeit f. vigilance.
WACHSEN to grow, increase, extend.
  ans Herz wachsen   to grow fond of.
  einem gewachsen sein   to be a match for one.
  einer Sache gewachsen sein   to be equal to a task.
Wachstum n. growth, increase.
Wacht f. guard, watch.
Wächter m. watchman, guard.
wack(e)lig shaky, unsteady.
Waffe f. weapon, arm.
Waffel f. wafer, waffle.
Waffeleisen n. waffle iron.
Waffenschein m. gun license.
Waffenstillstand m. armistice.
WAGEN m. car, automobile, railroad car, cab, wagon.
wagen to venture, risk, dare.
  gewagt   daring, risky, perilous.
Wagnis n. risk.
WAHL f. choice, selection, election.
  seine Wahl treffen   to make one's choice.
  vor die Wahl stellen   to let one choose.
wahlberechtigt entitled to vote.
WÄHLEN to choose, select, pick out, elect, dial.
  Wählen abhalten   to hold elections.

Wähler *m.* (**-in** *f.*) *elector, voter.*
wählerisch *particular, fastidious.*
Wahlkampf *m. election, contest.*
wahllos *indiscriminately.*
Wahlstimme *f. vote.*
Wahn *m. delusion, illusion.*
Wahnsinn *m. insanity, madness, craziness.*
wahnsinnig *insane, mad.*
WAHR *true, sincere, genuine, real, proper, veritable.*
   etwas nicht wahr haben wollen   *not to want to admit something.*
   Nicht wahr?   *Isn't it? Don't you think so?*
   so wahr ich lebe   *as sure as I live.*
   wahr werden   *to come true.*
WÄHREND 1. *prep. (gen.): during, for, in the course of.*
   Während des Winters verbringen wir unsere Ferien in den Bergen.   *During the winter we spend our vacations in the mountains.*
   2. *conj. while.*
   Sie kam während Sie weg waren.   *She came while you were out.*
WAHRHEIT *f. truth.*
   Ich habe ihm gehörig die Wahrheit gesagt.   *I really gave him a piece of my mind.*
wahrheitsgetreu *truthful, true.*
wahrnehmbar *perceptible, noticeable.*
wahrsagen *to foretell, to predict.*
Wahrsagerin *f. fortune-teller.*
WAHRSCHEINLICH *probable, likely.*
Wahrscheinlichkeit *f. probability, likelihood.*
Währung *f. standard, currency.*
Waise *f. & m. orphan.*
Waisenhaus *m. orphanage.*
Wal *m. whale.*
WALD *m. forest, woodland.*
waldig *wooded.*
Waldung *f. woodland, wood.*
Wall *m. rampart, dike.*
Walnuss *f. walnut.*
walzen *to waltz.*
Walzer *m. waltz.*
WAND *f. wall, partition.*
Wandel *m. change, alteration.*
   Handel und Wandel   *trade, commerce.*
wandelbar *perishable, changeable, fickle.*
wandern *to wander, to hike.*
Wanderschaft *f. trip, tour, travels.*
Wanderung *f. traveling, migration.*
Wandgemälde *n. mural, fresco.*
Wandschrank *m. cupboard.*
Wandteppich *m. tapestry, wall hanging.*
Wankelmut *m. inconsistency, fickleness.*
WANN *when*
   wann immer   *whenever.*
   dann und wann   *now and then.*

Wanne *f. bathtub.*
WARE *f. article, goods, merchandise.*
Warenhaus *n. department store.*
WARM *warm.*
   Ist es Ihnen warm genug?   *Are you warm enough?*
   warm stellen   *to keep hot.*
Wärme *f. heat, warmth.*
WÄRMEN *to warm, heat.*
Wärmflasche *f. hot-water bottle*
warnen *to warn, caution.*
Warnung *f. warning.*
Warnungssignal *n. danger signal.*
WARTEN *to wait, attend to, nurse.*
   warten auf   *to wait for.*
   warten lassen   *to keep waiting.*
Wärter *m. attendant, caretaker.*
Wartesaal *m. waiting room.*
Wartezimmer *n. doctor's waiting room.*
WARUM *why, for what reason.*
WAS *what, whatever, that which, which, that.*
   Ach was!   *Nonsense!*
   Nein so was!   *Well, I never!*
   was . . . auch immer   *no matter what, whatever.*
   was für ein   *what sort of, what a.*
   was mich betrifft   *as for me.*
   Ich will dir was sagen.   *I'll tell you something.*
Waschbecken *n. wash basin.*
WÄSCHE *f. wash; linen, underclothing.*
   in die Wäsche geben   *to send to the laundry.*
   schmutzige Wäsche   *soiled linen, dirty clothes.*
Wäschegeschäft *n. haberdashery, lingerie store.*
Wäscheklammer *f. clothespin.*
Wäscheleine *f. clothesline.*
waschen *to wash.*
Wäscherei *f. laundry.*
Waschmaschine *f. washing machine.*
WASSER *n. water.*
   fließendes Wasser   *running water.*
   mit allen Wassern gewaschen sein   *to be cunning.*
   sich über Wasser halten   *to keep one's head above water.*
   zu Wasser und zu Lande   *by land and sea.*
Wasserabfluss *m. drain.*
Wasserball *m. water polo.*
Wasserbehälter *m. reservoir, tank.*
wasserdicht *waterproof.*
Wasserfall *m. waterfall.*
Wasserfarbe *f. watercolor.*
Wasserflugzeug *n. sea plane.*
Wasserglas *n. glass, tumbler.*
wasserhaltig *containing water.*
wässerig *watery.*

einem den Mund wässerig machen
    to make a person's mouth water.
Wasserkanne *f. watering can.*
Wasserleitung *f. water supply, water pipes,*
    faucet.
Wasserspiegel *m. water surface.*
Wasserstiefel *pl. rubber boots.*
Wasserstoffbombe *f. hydrogen bomb*
    (H-bomb).
Wasserstraße *f. waterway.*
Watte *f. wadding, raw cotton.*
weben *to weave.*
Weber *m. weaver.*
Wechsel *m. change, succession, turn.*
    gezogener Wechsel *draft.*
Wechselgeld *n. change (money).*
    Bitte, zählen Sie ihr Wechselgeld nach.
      Please count your change.
Wechselkurs *m. rate of exchange.*
WECHSELN *to change, exchange, alternate,*
    shift.
    seinen Wohnort wechseln *to move; to*
      change one's residence.
    den Besitzer wechseln *to change*
      ownership.
wechselseitig *reciprocal, mutual, alternate.*
WECKEN *to wake, awaken.*
Wecker *m. alarm clock.*
weder *neither.*
    weder . . . noch *neither . . . nor.*
WEG *m. way, path, road, street, walk.*
    am Weg *by the roadside.*
    auf halbem Weg *halfway.*
    aus dem Weg gehen *to make way for,*
      stand aside.
    in die Wege leiten *to prepare for.*
    seiner Wege gehen *to go one's way.*
    sich auf den Weg machen *to set out.*
    in den Weg kommen *to get into the way.*
    im Wege stehen *to stand in the way.*
    auf dem Wege *on the way.*
WEG 1. *adv. away, off, gone, lost,*
    disappeared.
    Hände weg! *Hands off!*
    Ich muss weg. *I must go.*
    2. *separable prefix (implies a motion away*
    from the speaker).
    Er warf das alte Buch weg. *He threw the*
      old book away.
    Geh weg! *Go away!*
wegbleiben *to stay away, be omitted.*
wegbringen *to take away, remove.*
WEGEN *prep. (gen.): because of, for the sake*
    of, owing to.
    Wegen des Krieges konnte ich nicht von
      Europa zürückkommen. *Because of*
      the war, I could not come back from
      Europe.
wegfahren *to drive off, away.*

weggehen *to go away, depart, leave.*
weglegen *to put away.*
wegnehmen *to take away, carry off,*
    confiscate, occupy.
Wegweiser *m. signpost, roadsign.*
wegwerfen *to throw away.*
wegwerfend *disparaging, contemptuous.*
WEH *sore, aching, painful.*
    weh tun *to ache, to hurt.*
wehleidig *plaintive.*
Wehmut *f. sadness, melancholy.*
wehmütig *sad, melancholy.*
Wehrdienst *m. military service.*
wehren *to hinder, forbid, arrest, defend.*
wehrfähig *able-bodied.*
wehrlos *unarmed, defenseless, weak.*
Wehrmacht *f. armed forces.*
Wehrpflicht *f. conscription.*
wehrpflichtig *liable to military service.*
Weib *n. woman.*
weiblich *female, feminine, womanly.*
Weiblichkeit *f. womanhood, feminine nature.*
WEICH *soft, pliable, mellow, tender, smooth.*
    weiches Ei *soft-boiled egg.*
weichen *to retreat, give in, yield; soften, soak.*
weichherzig *soft-hearted.*
weichlich *soft, flabby, weak.*
weigern *to refuse.*
Weigerung *f. refusal.*
Weihe *f. consecration, initiation,*
    inauguration.
weihen *to consecrate, dedicate, devote.*
WEIHNACHTEN *pl. Christmas.*
weihnachtlich *of Christmas.*
Weihnachtsabend *m. Christmas Eve.*
Weihnachtsbaum *m. Christmas tree.*
Weihnachtslied *n. Christmas carol.*
WEIL *because, since.*
WEILE *f. while, space of time.*
    Damit hat es gute Weile. *There is no hurry.*
    Eile mit Weile. *Haste makes waste.*
WEIN *m. wine, vine.*
Weinberg *m. vineyard.*
WEINEN *to weep, cry.*
Weinessig *m. wine vinegar.*
Weinfass *n. wine cask.*
Weinkarte *f. wine list.*
Weinlese *f. vintage.*
Weinprobe *f. wine-tasting.*
Weinrebe *f. vine.*
Weinstock *m. vine.*
Weinstube *f. tavern.*
Weintraube *f. grape.*
WEISE *f. manner, way, tune.*
    auf diese Weise *in this way.*
    in der Weise, dass *in such a way that, so*
      that.
WEISEN *to show, refer, direct, point out,*
    point at.

Weisheit f. wisdom, prudence.

weismachen to make one believe, hoax.

WEIß white, blank, clean.

  Weißer Sonntag Sunday after Easter.

weissagen to predict, prophesy.

Weissager m. (-in f.) prophet.

WEIT distant, far, vast, loose, wide, big.

  bei Weitem by far, by much.

  bei Weitem nicht by no means.

  es weit bringen to get on well, be successful.

  nicht weither sein not to be worth much.

  von Weitem from a distance.

  weit gefehlt quite wrong.

  weit und breit far and wide.

  weit voraus way ahead.

  weit weg far away.

  wenn alles so weit ist when everything is ready.

weitab far away.

weitaus by far.

Weite f. width, size, extent, distance, length.

WEITER further, farther, more, else, additional.

  bis auf Weiteres until further notice.

  des Weiteren furthermore.

  nichts weiter nothing more.

  niemand weiter no one else.

  Nur weiter! Go on!

  ohne Weiteres immediately.

  und so weiter and so on.

  was weiter what else.

  wenn's weiter nichts ist if that's all there is to it.

Weitere n. rest, remaining part.

weiterführen to continue, carry on.

weitergeben to pass on to.

weiterhin furthermore, moreover.

Weiterreise f. continuation of a trip.

weitgehend far-reaching, full, much.

weither from afar.

weitläufig distant, wide, extensive, roomy.

weitschweifig detailed, tedious.

weitsichtig farsighted.

Weizen m. wheat, corn.

WELCH (ein) what (a)

  Welch ein Zufall! What a coincidence!

WELCH(-ER, -E, -ES) 1. inter. pron. & adj. what, who, whom, which.

  2. rel. pron. what, which, that, who, whom.

Welle f. wave, surge.

  Wellen schlagen to rise in waves.

Wellenlinie f. wavy line.

Wellenreiter m. surfer.

WELT f. world, universe, people.

  alle Welt everybody, everyone in the world.

  auf der Welt on earth.

  auf die Welt kommen to come into the world, be born.

  aus der Welt schaffen to put out of the way.

  in der ganzen Welt on earth.

  in die Welt setzen (zur Welt bringen) to give birth to.

Weltall n. universe.

Weltanschauung f. world outlook.

weltbekannt world famous.

weltfremd secluded, solitary.

Weltmacht f. world power.

Weltmann m. man of the world.

Weltmeister m. world champion.

Weltraum m. space, universe.

Weltuntergang m. end of the world.

WEM dat. of wer. to whom.

WEN acc. of wer. whom.

Wende f. turn, turning point.

wenden to turn, turn around.

  Bitte wenden! Please turn over!

  sich wenden an to return to (someone).

Wendepunkt m. turning point.

WENIG little, few, a few.

  ein wenig a little, a bit.

WENIGER less, fewer, minus.

  immer weniger less and less.

  nichts weniger als anything but.

  vier weniger eins four minus one.

wenigst (-er, -e, -es) least.

wenigstens at least.

WENN if, in case of, when.

  auch wenn even if.

  immer wenn whenever.

  Rufen Sie mich an, wenn Sie kommen wollen! Call me when you want to come.

  selbst wenn even if, supposing that.

  wenn auch (wenngleich, wenn schon) although.

  Wenn das nur wahr wäre! If it were only true!

  wenn nur provided that.

  wenn schon! What of it!

  wenn Sie kommen könnten If you could come.

WER inter. pron. who, what.

  wer anders who else.

  wer auch immer whoever.

  Wer (ist) da? Who is it?

werben to recruit, win, advertise.

Werbung f. advertising.

WERDEN 1. to become, turn out, prove, happen.

  Was soll aus ihr werden? What's to become of her?

  2. aux, verb to form future and passive. shall, will, is, are.

werfen to throw, cast, toss.

WERK n. work, labor, production, doing, performance, deed.

ans Werk! *Go to it! Begin!*
ins Werk setzen *to set going.*
Das ist sein Werk. *That's his doing.*
Werkstatt *f. workshop.*
Werkstelle *f. place of work.*
Werktag *m. workday.*
werktags *on weekdays.*
werktätig *active*
die werktätige Bevölkerung *working classes.*
Werkzeug *m. utensil.*
WERT *worth, valuable, worthy, honored, esteemed.*
im Werte von *at a price of.*
nichts wert sein *to be no good.*
Wertangabe *f. declaration of value.*
Wertgegenstand *pl. valuables.*
wertlos *worthless.*
Wertpapier *n. security, bond.*
Wertsachen *pl. valuables.*
Wertung *f. evaluation, appraisal.*
wertvoll *valuable, precious.*
Wesen *n. creature, soul, personality.*
wesentlich *essential, substantial.*
WESSEN *gen. of wer. whose?*
Weste *f. waistcoat, vest.*
Westen *m. the West, Occident.*
nach Westen *west (direction).*
westlich *western, occidental.*
Wettbewerb *n. contest.*
Wette *f. bet, wager.*
eine Wette machen *to make a bet.*
um die Wette laufen *to race someone.*
wetteifern *to emulate; to vie.*
wetten *to bet, wager.*
WETTER *n. weather.*
Alle Wetter! *My word!*
Heute ist das Wetter wunderschön!
The weather is wonderful today!
Wetterbericht *m. meteorological report.*
Wetterlage *f. weather conditions.*
Wettkampf *m. match, contest, prizefighting.*
Wettrennen *n. race, racing.*
WICHTIG *important.*
sich wichtig machen *to act important.*
WIDER 1. *prep. (acc.) against, contrary to, versus.*
Wider meinen Willen *against my will.*
2. *inseparable prefix. (con-, re-, anti-, contra-).*
widerhallen *to echo, resound.*
widerlegen *to refute.*
Widerlegung *f. refutation.*
widerlich *repulsive, disgusting.*
Widerrede *f. contradiction.*
widerrufen *to revoke, withdraw, retract, cancel.*
widersetzen (sich) *to oppose, resist.*
widerspiegeln *to reflect, mirror.*

widersprechen *to contradict, to talk back to.*
Widerspruch *m. contradiction, disagreement.*
Widerstand *m. resistance, opposition.*
Widerwille *m. repugnance, disgust.*
widerwillig *reluctant, unwilling.*
widmen *to dedicate.*
Widmung *f. dedication.*
WIE *how, as, such, like.*
so ... wie *as ... as.*
wie auch immer *however.*
Wie bitte? *What did you say?*
wie dem auch sei *be that as it may.*
Wie geht es Ihnen? *How are you?*
wie gesagt *as has been said.*
WIEDER 1. *adv. again, anew, back, in return for.*
hin und wieder *now and then.*
immer wieder *again and again.*
2. *prefix.* a) *inseparable. In verb wiederholen (to repeat).* b) *separable (implies the idea of repetition or opposition).*
wiederbekommen *to get back, recover.*
wieder beleben *to revive, reanimate.*
Wiederbelebungsversuch *m. attempt at resuscitation.*
wieder erkennen *to recognize.*
wiedererlangen *to get back.*
wieder erobern *to reconquer.*
wieder finden *to find, recover.*
Wiedergabe *f. return; reproduction, recital (work of art).*
wiedergeben *to give back, return.*
wiedergewinnen *to recover, regain, reclaim.*
Wiedergutmachung *f. reparation.*
WIEDERHOLEN *to repeat, renew, reiterate, fetch, bring back.*
Wiederholung *f. repetition, reiteration.*
im Wiederholungsfalle *if it should happen again.*
wiederhören *to hear again.*
auf Wiederhören! *Good-bye! (phone)*
WIEDERSEHEN *to see again, meet again.*
auf Wiedersehen! *Good-bye! So long!*
Wiege *f. cradle.*
wiegen *to weigh, to rock, move to, shake, sway.*
Wiese *f. meadow.*
wieso *why.*
WIE VIEL *how much.*
Der Wievielte ist heute? *What date is today?*
wie viele *how many.*
WILD *wild, rough, angry, furious, savage, untidy.*
Wild *n. game (hunting).*
Wildbraten *m. venison.*
Wilddieb *m. poacher.*
Wildente *f. wild duck.*

Wildleder *n. deerskin, suede.*

Wildnis *f. wilderness, desert.*

WILLE *m. will, say, determination, purpose.*

  aus freiem Willen   *voluntarily.*

  guter Wille   *kind intention.*

  letzter Wille   *last will.*

willenlos *lacking willpower, irresolute.*

Willenlosigkeit *f. lack of willpower.*

Willenskraft *f. willpower.*

Willkommen *n. welcome, reception.*

Willkür *f. discretion, arbitrariness.*

willkürlich *arbitrary, despotic.*

WIND *m. wind, breeze.*

  bei Wind und Wetter   *in storm and rain (all types of bad weather).*

  guter Wind   *fair wind.*

  in den Wind reden   *to talk in vain.*

  in den Wind schlagen   *to disregard.*

  vor dem Wind segeln   *to run before the wind.*

Windel *f. baby's diaper.*

windeln *to swaddle.*

winden *to wind.*

windig *windy, breezy.*

Windstille *f. calm.*

Wink *m. sign, nod, wink.*

Winkel *m. corner, angle, secret spot.*

winken *to wave, nod, wink.*

WINTER *m. winter.*

  im Winter   *in winter.*

Winterschlaf *m. hibernation.*

Wintersport *m. winter sports.*

Wintersportplatz *m. winter resort.*

winzig *tiny, diminutive.*

Winzigkeit *f. tininess.*

Wirbel *m. whirlpool, eddy.*

Wirbelknochen *m. vertebra.*

wirbeln *to whirl.*

Wirbelsäule *f. spine.*

Wirbelsturm *m. tornado, hurricane.*

wirken *to act, do, work, produce.*

WIRKLICH *real, actual, true, genuine.*

Wirklichkeit *f. reality, actuality.*

wirksam *active, effective.*

Wirkung *f. action, working, operation.*

wirkungslos *ineffectual, inefficient.*

wirkungsvoll *effective, striking.*

Wirt *m. host, proprietor, landlord.*

wirtlich *hospitable.*

Wirtschaft *f. housekeeping, economy, tavern, public house.*

  die Wirtschaft führen   *to keep house, to manage things.*

wirtschaften *to manage, run the business.*

Wirtschaftsgeld *n. housekeeping money.*

Wirtschaftslage *f. economic situation.*

Wirtshaus *n. inn, public house.*

WISSEN *n. knowledge, learning.*

  meines Wissens   *as far as I know.*

wider besseres Wissen   *against one's better judgment.*

WISSEN *to know, be aware of, understand, be acquainted with.*

  Ich weiß nicht.   *I don't know.*

  nicht dass ich wüsste   *not that I am aware of.*

  Bescheid wissen über   *to be well-informed about.*

  wissen um   *to know of or about.*

  wissen von   *to be informed or aware of.*

  Sie wissen lassen   *to let you know.*

Wissenschaft *f. science.*

Wissenschaftler *m. (-in f.) scientist.*

wissenswert *worth knowing, interesting.*

Witwe *f. widow.*

Witwer *m. widower.*

Witz *m. wittiness, witticism, wit, joke, pun.*

witzig *witty.*

WO *where, in which; when.*

  wo auch immer   *wherever.*

woanders *elsewhere.*

wobei *in the course of which, whereby, in which, upon which.*

WOCHE *f. week.*

  diese Woche   *this week.*

  heute in einer Woche   *a week from today.*

Wochenende *n. weekend.*

wochenlang *for weeks.*

wochentags *on weekdays.*

Wochenschau *newsreel; weekly publication.*

wöchentlich *weekly.*

wodurch *by which, whereby, how.*

wofür *for which, for what.*

WOHER *from where, from what place?*

  Woher wissen Sie das?   *How do you know that?*

WOHIN *to where, to what place?*

WOHL *n. welfare, prosperity, good health.*

  sich wohl fühlen   *to feel well.*

WOHL *well, all right, probably, presumably, very likely, indeed.*

  Er wird wohl noch kommen.   *He may yet come.*

  Ich verstehe wohl.   *I can well understand.*

  Leben Sie wohl!   *Good-bye!*

  wohl oder übel   *willy-nilly.*

  Zum Wohl!   *To you! (a toast)*

Wohlbehagen *n. comfort, ease.*

wohl bekannt *well-known, familiar.*

Wohlfahrt *f. welfare.*

wohl gefällig *pleasant, agreeable.*

Wohlgefühl *f. pleasant feeling, sense of well-being.*

wohlhabend *well-to-do, wealthy.*

Wohlklang *m. harmony, melody.*

wohlschmeckend *tasty, palatable.*

Wohlstand *m. well-being, wealth, fortune.*

wohltuend *comforting, pleasant.*

wohl verdient *well-deserved, merited.*

WOHNEN *to live, dwell, reside, stay.*

  zur Miete wohnen *to live as a tenant, renter.*

wohnhaft *living, dwelling.*

wohnlich *comfortable, cozy.*

WOHNUNG *f. house, dwelling, residence, flat.*

Wohnviertel *n. residential district.*

Wohnzimmer *n. living room*

Wolf *m. wolf.*

Wolke *f. cloud.*

  aus allen Wolken fallen *to be thunderstruck.*

Wolkenbruch *m. cloudburst.*

Wolkenkratzer *m. skyscraper.*

WOLLE *f. wool.*

WOLLEN *to want, wish, will, desire, like, mean.*

  Das will etwas heißen. *That means something.*

  Das will was heißen. *That's really something.*

  Er mag wollen oder nicht. *Whether he likes it or not.*

  Wie Sie wollen. *As you like.*

WOMIT *with what, by which, with which.*

  Womit kann ich dienen? *What can I do for you?*

womöglich *if possible.*

WORAN *whereon, by what.*

  woran liegt es? *how is it that? what is the reason for it?*

WORAUF *on what, upon which.*

WORAUS *of what, out of which.*

WORIN *in which, in what.*

WORT *n. word, expression, saying, promise.*

  aufs Wort gehorchen *to obey implicitly.*

  das große Wort führen *to brag.*

  das Wort ergreifen *to begin to speak.*

  das Wort führen *to be spokesperson.*

  einen beim Wort nehmen *to take one at one's word.*

  Er hat sein Wort gebrochen. *He broke his promise.*

  Ich habe kein Wort davon gewusst. *I did not know a thing about it.*

  ins Wort fallen *to interrupt, cut short.*

  mit anderen Worten *in other words.*

  Sie macht viele Worte. *She talks too much.*

  ums Wort bitten *to ask for the floor.*

  zu Wort kommen lassen *to let one speak.*

  geflügelte Worte *familiar quotations.*

Wörterbuch *n. dictionary.*

Wortschatz *m. vocabulary.*

wortwörtlich *word for word.*

WORÜBER *of what, about which, whereof.*

WORUNTER *among what, which.*

WOVON *about what, which.*

WOVOR *of what, for what, before what, which.*

WOZU *to which end, of what, for what, which.*

wund *sore, wounded.*

Wunde *f. wound.*

Wunder *n. wonder, miracle.*

  sein blaues Wunder erleben *to be amazed.*

  Wunder verrichten *to perform miracles.*

WUNDERBAR *wonderful, marvelous.*

  Wunderbar! *Wonderful! Splendid!*

wunderbarerweise *strange to say.*

Wunderkind *n. child prodigy.*

wunderlich *strange, odd.*

WUNDERN *to astonish, surprise.*

  sich wundern *to be surprised, wonder.*

wunderschön *beautiful, lovely, exquisite.*

WUNSCH *m. wish, desire, request.*

  auf Wunsch *by request, if desired.*

  Hätten Sie noch einen Wunsch? *Is there anything else you'd like?*

  nach Wunsch *as one desires.*

WÜNSCHEN *to wish, desire, long for.*

  Glück wünschen *to congratulate (wish luck).*

  Was wünschen Sie? *May I help you?*

  Ich wünsche Ihnen alles Gute. *I wish you all the best.*

Würde *f. dignity, honor, title, rank.*

  in Amt und Würden *holding a high office.*

würdelos *undignified.*

würdevoll *dignified.*

würdig *worthy, deserving of, respectable.*

würdigen *to value, appreciate.*

  jemanden keines Blickes würdigen *to ignore someone completely.*

Würfel *m. die (sing. of dice), cube.*

  Der Würfel ist gefallen. *The die is cast.*

würfeln *to play dice.*

Würfelspiel *n. dice game.*

Würfelzucker *m. sugar cube*

würgen *to choke, strangle.*

Wurm *m. worm.*

Wurst *f. sausage.*

Würze *f. seasoning, spice, condiment.*

Wurzel *f. root.*

würzen *to season.*

würzig *spicy.*

wüst *waste, deserted, desolate, wild, dissolute.*

Wüste *f. desert.*

WUT *f. rage, fury.*

  in Wut geraten *to fly into a rage.*

  vor Wut kochen *to boil, fume with rage.*

wüten *to rage, be furious.*

wütend *enranged, furious.*

X

X-Achse f. (math) x-axis.
x-beliebig at random.
x-mal every so often, any number of times.

Y

Y-Achse f. (math) y-axis.
Yacht (or **Jacht**) f. yacht.
Yard n. yard.
Yen m. yen.

Z

zagen to be afraid, hesitate.
zäh tough, tenacious, stubborn, stingy.
ZAHL f. figure, number, numeral.
zahlbar payable, due.
zahlen to pay.
ZÄHLEN to count, number, calculate.
   gezählt numbered.
Zahlkarte f. money-order form.
zahllos countless, innumerable.
zahlreich numerous.
Zahltag m. payday.
Zahlung f. payment.
Zahlungsanweisung f. postal or money order.
zahlungsfähig solvent (financially).
zahm tame, domestic.
zähmen to tame, break in.
ZAHN m. tooth.
   ein schlechter Zahn a bad tooth.
   sich die Zähne putzen to brush one's
     teeth.
   einem auf den Zahn fühlen to sound out a
     person.
   falsche Zähne false teeth, denture.
Zahnarzt m. (-in f.) dentist.
Zahnbürste f. toothbrush.
Zahnfleisch n. gum(s).
Zahnfüllung f. filling.
zahnlos toothless.
Zahnpasta f. toothpaste.
Zahnschmerzen pl. toothache.
Zahnstein m. tartar.
Zahnstocher m. toothpick.
Zahnweh n. toothache.
Zange f. pincers, tongs, pliers.
Zank m. quarrel.
zanken to quarrel.
zanksüchtig quarrelsome.
ZART tender, soft, delicate, fragile, frail.
zartfühlend tactful, sensitive.

Zartgefühl n. delicacy of feeling.
Zartheit f. tenderness, delicacy.
Zauber m. magic, charm, spell.
Zauberei f. magic, witchcraft.
Zauberflöte f. magic flute.
zauberhaft magical, enchanting.
Zauberkünstler m. illusionist.
zaubern to practice magic, conjure.
zaudern to hesitate, delay.
Zaun m. hedge, fence.
   Streit von Zaune brechen to pick a
     quarrel.
Zebra n. zebra.
Zehe f. toe.
Zehenspitze f. point of the toe.
   auf Zehenspitzen gehen to tiptoe.
ZEHN ten.
zehnfach tenfold.
ZEHNTE tenth.
Zeichen n. sign, signal, token, brand.
   zum Zeichen dass as a proof that.
Zeichensetzung f. punctuation.
Zeichensprache f. sign language.
ZEICHNEN to draw, design, mark.
ZEICHNUNG f. drawing, sketch, design.
Zeigefinger m. forefinger, index.
ZEIGEN to show, point at, point out, exhibit,
   display.
Zeiger m. hand of the clock, pointer.
ZEIT f. time, duration, period, epoch,
   season.
   Damit hat es Zeit. There is no hurry.
   die freie Zeit leisure, spare time.
   Es ist an der Zeit. It is high time.
   höchste Zeit high time.
   in der letzten Zeit lately.
   in jüngster Zeit quite recently.
   Lassen Sie sich Zeit! Take your time!
   mit der Zeit gradually, in the course of
     time.
   Zeit seines Lebens during life.
   zu gleicher Zeit at the same time.
   zur rechten Zeit in the nick of time.
   zur Zeit at present.
Zeitablauf m. lapse of time.
Zeitalter n. age, generation.
zeitgemäß timely, seasonable.
Zeitgenosse m. contemporary (person).
zeitgenössisch contemporary.
ZEITIG early, timely, mature, ripe.
Zeitmangel m. lack of time.
Zeitrechnung f. chronology.
Zeitpunkt m. time, moment.
Zeitschrift f. journal, periodical, magazine.
ZEITUNG f. newspaper, paper.
Zeitungsausschnitt m. press clipping.
Zeitungskiosk m. newsstand.
Zeitungsnotiz f. notice, item, paragraph.
Zeitungsstand m. newsstand.

Zeitungsinserat *n. newspaper advertisement, notice.*

Zeitungsverkäufer *m. news vendor.*

Zeitverschwendung *f. waste of time.*

Zeitvertreib *m. pastime, amusement.*

Zeitwort *n. verb.*

Zelle *f. cell, booth.*

Zelt *n. tent, canopy.*

Zement *m. cement.*

Zentimeter *m. & n. centimeter (.3937 inch).*

Zentrale *f. central office, station, telephone exchange.*

Zentralheizung *f. central heating.*

ZENTRUM *n. center.*

zerbrechen *to break, smash.*

  sich den Kopf zerbrechen *to rack one's brains.*

zerbrechlich *fragile.*

Zerbrechlichkeit *f. fragility, brittleness.*

Zeremonie *f. ceremony.*

zerreißbar *tearable.*

zerreißen *to tear, rip up.*

zerren *to drag, pull.*

  eine Muskel zerren *to strain a muscle.*

zerschmettern *to crush, destroy.*

zerstören *to destroy, demolish, devastate, ruin.*

Zerstörer *m. destroyer, devastator.*

Zerstörung *f. devastation, demolition, destruction.*

zerstreuen *to disperse, scatter, dissipate, divert.*

zerstreut *absentminded.*

Zerstreuung *f. dispersion, distraction.*

Zerwürfnis *n. disagreement, quarrel, strife.*

Zettel *m. slip, note, label, ticket, poster, bill.*

Zeug *n. stuff, material, cloth, fabric, utensils, things.*

Zeuge *m. witness.*

zeugen *to testify, bear witness, give evidence.*

Zeugenaussage *f. evidence, deposition.*

Zeugenvernehmung *f. hearing of witnesses.*

Ziege *f. goat.*

Ziegel *m. brick, tile.*

Ziegelstein *m. brick.*

ZIEHEN *to pull, draw, haul, tug, tow, extract, move, migrate, weigh.*

  den Kürzeren ziehen *to get the worst of it.*

  nach sich ziehen *to have consequences.*

  Er zieht den Hut. *He tips his hat.*

  zur Rechenschaft ziehen *to call to account.*

  ein Gesicht ziehen *to make faces.*

  in Betracht ziehen *to take into consideration.*

Ziehung *f. drawing of lottery.*

Ziel *n. goal.*

  sich ein Ziel setzen *to set a goal.*

zielbewusst *systematic, methodical.*

zielen *to aim (at).*

ziellos *aimless.*

Zielscheibe *f. target.*

  Zielscheibe des Spottes sein *to be a laughingstock.*

ziemen *to become, be suitable.*

ZIEMLICH *rather, pretty, fairly, quite, considerable.*

  so ziemlich *about, pretty much.*

  ziemlich viele *quite a few.*

Zierde *f. ornament, decoration.*

zieren *to decorate, adorn, embellish.*

zierlich *elegant, graceful, delicate.*

Ziffer *f. figure, cipher.*

Zifferblatt *n. dial, face.*

ZIGARETTE *f. cigarette.*

Zigarettenetui *n. cigarette case.*

Zigarettenspitze *f. cigarette holder.*

Zigarre *f. cigar.*

Zigarrenkiste *f. cigar box.*

Zigeuner *m. gypsy.*

ZIMMER *n. room, apartment, chamber.*

Zimmerdecke *f. ceiling.*

Zimmermädchen *n. chambermaid.*

Zimmermann *m. carpenter.*

zimperlich *supersensitive, prudish, affected.*

Zimt *m. cinnamon.*

Zinn *n. tin, pewter.*

Zins *m. tax, duty, rent; interest.*

  auf Zinsen ausleihen *to lend money with interest.*

  mit Zins und Zinseszins *in full measure.*

Zinseszins *m. compound interest.*

Zinssatz *m. rate of interest.*

Zirkel *m. compasses.*

Zirkus *m. circus.*

Zitat *n. quotation.*

Zitrone *f. lemon.*

Zitronenlimonade *f. lemonade.*

Zitronensaft *m. lemon juice.*

zittern *to tremble, shake, quiver, shiver.*

zivil *civil, reasonable, moderate.*

  in Zivil *in plainclothes.*

Zivilbevölkerung *f. civilian population.*

Zivilisation *f. civilization.*

zivilisieren *to civilize.*

zögern *to hesitate, delay, linger.*

ZOLL *m. duty, toll, tariff, customs.*

Zoll *m. inch.*

Zollabfertigung *f. customs inspection, clearance.*

ZOLLAMT *n. customhouse.*

Zollbeamte *m. customhouse officer.*

zollfrei *duty free.*

Zollgebühr *f. duty.*

Zöllner *m. customs collector.*

zollpflichtig *subject to customs.*

Zollstock *m. yardstick.*

Zone *f. zone.*

Zopf *m. braid, pigtail.*

Zorn *m. anger, rage, wrath.*

zornig *angry.*

ZU 1. *prep. (dat.). to, at, by, near, beside, for, with, in front of, on.*

Die Deutschen essen gern Kartoffeln zum Fleisch. *Germans like to eat potatoes with meat.*

Er war nicht zu Hause. *He was not at home.*

Ich gehe zu meiner Tante. *I am going to my aunt's house.*

Setzen Sie sich zu mir! *Sit down by me.*

Wenn es friert, wird das Wasser zu Eis. *When it freezes, water turns to ice.*

Wir essen Eier zum Frühstück. *We eat eggs for breakfast.*

zu Fuß/zu Pferd *on foot, on horseback.*

zu meinem Erstaunen *to my surprise.*

zum König gekrönt werden *to become a king.*

zum Teil *partly.*

zum "Weißen Ross" *at the "White Horse" (inn).*

2. *adv. too (more than enough), toward.*

zu viel *too much.*

3. *before infinitive to.*

Sie wussten nicht was zu tun. *They did not know what to do.*

4. *Separable prefix (implies direction toward the speaker, increase, continuation, closing, confession).*

Sie liefen dem Walde zu. *They ran toward the forest.*

Der Verbrecher gab es zu. *The criminal confessed.*

Ich darf nicht mehr zunehmen. *I must not gain more weight.*

Mach die Tür zu! *Close the door!*

Zubehör *m. & n. accessories, trimmings, belongings.*

zubereiten *to prepare, cook, mix.*

Zubereitung *f. preparation.*

Zucht *f. breeding, training, education; breed, race, stock.*

züchten *to breed, grow, cultivate, train.*

züchtig *chaste, modest.*

züchtigen *to punish, correct, chastise.*

zucken *to jerk, twitch.*

mit den Achseln zucken *to shrug one's shoulders.*

ZUCKER *m. sugar.*

Zuckerguss *m. icing.*

zuckerhaltig *containing sugar.*

zuckerkrank *diabetic.*

zuckern *to sugar, sweeten.*

Zuckerwerk *n. confectionary, sweets.*

zudem *besides, moreover.*

zudrücken *to shut, close.*

ein Auge zudrücken *to turn a blind eye, to overlook.*

zuerst *at first, in the first place.*

Zufahrt *f. driveway, approach.*

Zufall *m. chance, accident, occurrence.*

durch Zufall *by accident.*

zufällig *casual, by accident, by chance.*

zufällig tun *to happen to do.*

zufälligerweise *by chance.*

Zuflucht *f. refuge, shelter.*

seine Zuflucht nehmen zu *to take refuge with.*

ZUFRIEDEN *satisfied, content.*

sich zufrieden geben *to rest content with.*

zufrieden lassen *to let alone, leave in peace.*

Zufriedenheit *f. contentment, satisfaction.*

zufriedenstellen *to content, satisfy.*

zufriedenstellend *satisfactory.*

ZUG *m. train; drawing, draft; procession, march, impulse; feature, characteristic.*

Er liegt in den letzten Zügen. *He is breathing his last.*

Zug um Zug *without delay, uninterruptedly.*

Wann kommt der Schnellzug aus Berlin an? *When does the express train from Berlin arrive?*

Das ist ein Zug seines Charakters. *This is a feature of his character.*

Zugabe *f. extra, addition, encore, confession.*

Zugang *m. entrance, door, access.*

zugänglich *accessible, open to.*

zugeben *to add, allow, permit, admit.*

Zügel *m. bridle, rein.*

zügellos *unbridled, unrestrained.*

Zugeständnis *n. concession, admission.*

Zugluft *f. draught, current of air.*

zugunsten *in favor of, for the benefit of.*

zugute (halten) *to allow for, take into consideration, give credit for.*

zugute kommen *to come in handy, be an advantage to.*

Zuhilfenahme *f. (unter Zuhilfenahme von) with the help of.*

zuhören *to listen to.*

Zuhörer *m. hearer, listener.*

Zuhörerschaft *f. audience.*

ZUKUNFT *f. future.*

zukünftig *future.*

zulächeln *to smile at.*

Zulage *f. addition, raise.*

zulangen *to hand, give.*

zulässig *admissible, permissible.*

Zulassung *f. admission, permission.*

zulegen *to add something to.*

ZULETZT *finally, ultimately,*

zuletzt kommen *to arrive last.*

zuliebe (tun) *to do for someone's sake.*

einen zuliebe tun   *to please someone.*
zumachen *to close, shut, fasten; to hurry.*
zumal *especially, particularly.*
zumindest *at least.*
zumuten *to expect of.*
  sich zu viel zumuten   *to attempt too much.*
Zumutung *f. unreasonable demand.*
zunächst *first, first of all, above all.*
zünden *to catch fire, inflame, arouse
  enthusiasm.*
zunehmen *to grow, increase, get fuller.*
zuneigen *to lean forward, incline.*
Zuneigung *f. liking, affection, sympathy,
  inclination.*
ZUNGE *f. tongue.*
  Das Wort liegt mir auf der Zunge.   *I have
    the word on the tip of my tongue.*
  eine belegte Zunge   *a coated tongue.*
  eine feine Zunge haben   *to be a gourmet.*
zurechnungsfähig *responsible, of sound mind.*
Zurechnungsfähigkeit *f. accountability,
  responsibility before the law.*
zurecht *right, in order, in time.*
zurechtfinden *to find one's way around.*
**zurechtsetzen (einem den Kopf
  zurechtsetzen)** *to bring one to reason.*
ZURÜCK *1. adv. back, backward, late,
  behind. 2. separable prefix (implies a
  return motion; back).*
  Wir kamen erst um elf Uhr zurück.
    We only came back at eleven.
zurückbehalten *to keep back, retain.*
zurückbekommen *to get back, recover.*
zurückbleiben *to stay behind.*
zurückbringen *to bring back.*
zurückfahren *to drive back, return.*
zurückfordern *to demand back.*
zurückgehen *to go back, return, retreat,
  decrease, decline.*
zurückgezogen *retired, secluded, lonely.*
Zurückgezogenheit *f. retirement, seclusion.*
zurückhalten *to hold back, delay, detain.*
zurückhaltend *reserved.*
zurückkehren *to return, go back, come back.*
zurückklassen *to leave behind.*
zurücknehmen *to take back.*
zurücksetzen *to put back, replace, reduce,
  neglect.*
Zurücksetzung *f. reduction.*
zurückstellen *to put back, replace, reserve,
  put aside.*
zurücktreten *to step back, withdraw, resign.*
zurückversetzen *to put back, restore.*
  sich in eine Zeit zurückversetzen   *to go
    back (in imagination) to a time.*
zurückweisen *to send away, to turn back,
  send back, repulse.*
zurückzahlen *to pay back, repay.*
Zurückzahlung *f. repayment.*

zurückziehen *to draw back, take back.*
Zuruf *m. acclamation, shout, call.*
zurufen *to call to, shout to.*
Zusage *f. acceptance, promise.*
ZUSAGEN *to promise, please, appeal.*
  einem etwas auf den Kopf zusagen   *to tell
    a person plainly.*
ZUSAMMEN *together, altogether.*
zusammenfassen *to sum up, summarize.*
zusammenfassend *comprehensive.*
zusammengehören *to belong together, match,
  be correlated.*
Zusammenhalt *m. holding together, cohesion,
  solidarity.*
Zusammenhang *m. connection, relationship.*
zusammenhangslos *disconnected.*
Zusammenkunft *f. meeting, reunion,
  assembly.*
Zusammenstoß *m. collision, clash, crash.*
zusammenstoßen *to smash, collide.*
zusammentreffen *to meet each other,
  coincide.*
zusammenzählen *to count up, add up.*
Zusatz *m. addition.*
zusätzlich *additional.*
ZUSCHAUER *m. (-in f.) spectator.*
Zuschauerraum *m. theater auditorium.*
Zuschlag *m. addition, increase in price.*
zuschlagpflichtig *liable to additional
  payment.*
zuschließen *to lock, lock up.*
Zuschrift *f. letter, communication.*
zuschulden *adv. guilty.*
  sich etwas zuschulden kommen lassen
    to be guilty of doing something.
zusehen *to look on, watch for, wait.*
zusichern *to assure of, promise.*
Zusicherung *f. insurance.*
zusprechen *to encourage.*
  Trost zusprechen   *to comfort, console.*
Zuspruch *m. consolation, exhortation,
  encouragement, pep talk.*
ZUSTAND *m. state, condition, position,
  situation.*
  zustande bringen   *to do, get done, achieve.*
zuständig *belonging to, responsible,
  authorized, competent.*
Zuständigkeit *f. competence, power,
  jurisdiction.*
zustimmen *to consent, agree.*
Zustimmung *f. consent.*
Zustrom *m. influx, crowd, multitude.*
zutrauen *to believe (one) capable of.*
zutraulich *confiding, trusting.*
zutreffend *correct, right, applicable.*
ZUTRITT *m. admission, entrance.*
  Zutritt verboten!   *No admittance!*
zuverlässig *reliable, trustworthy.*
Zuversicht *f. confidence, trust.*

zuversichtlich *confident.*
ZU VIEL *too much.*
zuvor *before, previously, formerly.*
zuvorkommen (**jmdm.**) *to beat someone to it.*
zuvorkommend *obliging.*
Zuvorkommenheit *f. politeness, kindness.*
ZUWEILEN *sometimes, now and then, occasionally.*
zuwider (**sein**) *to be repugnant.*
    Das ist mir zuwider. *I hate it.*
zuzahlen *to pay extra.*
zuziehen *to draw together, call, invite, consult.*
Zwang *m. compulsion, constraint, force, pressure.*
    Zwang antun *to do violence to*
    sich keinen Zwang antun *not to stand on ceremony.*
zwanglos *free and easy.*
Zwanglosigkeit *f. freedom, ease.*
Zwangslage *f. condition of constraint, quandary, "jam."*
    sich in einer Zwangslage befinden *to be under compulsion.*
zwangsläufig *necessarily, inevitably.*
ZWANZIG *twenty.*
Zwanziger *m. number 20, a 20-year-old.*
    in den Zwanzigern sein *to be in one's twenties.*
ZWANZIGSTE *twentieth.*
ZWAR *indeed, although.*
    und zwar *in fact, namely.*
ZWECK *m. purpose, design, aim, object, end, goal.*
    keinen Zweck haben *to be of no use.*
    Zu welchem Zweck? *Why? For what purpose?*
zwecklos *useless, purposeless.*
Zwecklosigkeit *f. uselessness, aimlessness.*
zweckmäßig *expedient.*
ZWEI *two.* **zwo** *two* (coll.)
    zu zweien *by pairs, two by two.*
zweideutig *ambiguous.*
zweifach *twofold, double.*
ZWEIFEL *m. doubt, suspicion.*
zweifelhaft *doubtful.*
zweifellos *indubitable.*
zweifeln *to doubt, question, suspect.*
Zweifelsfall *m.*
    im Zweifelsfall *in case of a doubt.*

Zweig *m. branch.*
Zweigstelle *f. branch (office).*
Zweikampf *m. duel.*
zweimal *twice.*
zweireihig *having two rows, columns; double-breasted.*
Zweisitzer *two-seater.*
ZWEITE *second, next.*
    zu zweit *two by two.*
zweitens *secondly, in the second place.*
Zwerg *m. dwarf.*
Zwieback *m. rusk, biscuit.*
Zwiebel *f. onion, bulb (plant).*
Zwielicht *n. twilight, dusk.*
Zwilling *m. twin.*
zwingen *to compel, force, get through, finish.*
zwingend *forcible.*
zwinkern *to blink, wink.*
Zwirn *m. thread.*
ZWISCHEN *prep. (dat. when answering the question Wo? acc. when answering the question Wohin? and depending on the idiom). among, between.*
    Zwischen den Städten Duisburg und Köln liegt Düsseldorf. *Between the cities of Duisburg and Cologne lies Düsseldorf.*
    zwischen drei und vier *between three and four.*
    Er läuft zwischen die Wagen. *He walks between the cars.*
Zwischenbemerkung *f. incidental remark, verbal aside.*
Zwischendeck *n. lower deck.*
zwischendurch *through, in the midst of.*
Zwischenfall *m. incident, episode.*
Zwischenlandung *f. intermediate landing or stop (flight).*
Zwischenpause *f. interval, break.*
Zwischenraum *m. space, gap, interval.*
Zwischenzeit *f. interval.*
    in der Zwischenzeit *in the meantime.*
zwitschern *to twitter, chirp.*
ZWÖLF *twelve.*
ZWÖLFTE *twelfth.*
Zyklus *m. cycle, course, series.*
Zylinder *m. cylinder.*
Zyniker *m. cynic.*
zynisch *cynical.*
Zynismus *m. cynicism.*

GLOSSARY OF
PROPER NAMES

Albrecht *Albert.*
Alfred *Alfred.*
Andress *Andrew.*
Anne *Ann.*
Anton *Anthony.*
August *August.*
Barbara *Barbara.*
Bernhard *Bernard.*
Bertha *Bertha.*
Eduard *Edward.*
Elisabeth (Else) *Elizabeth.*
Emilie *Emily.*
Emma *Emma.*
Erich *Eric.*
Ernst *Ernest.*
Eugen *Eugene.*
Franz *Frank.*
Franziska *Frances.*
Friederich *Frederick.*
Fritz *Fred.*
Genoveva *Genevieve.*
Georg *George.*
Gertrud (Trudchen) *Gertrude.*
Gretchen *Margaret.*
Gustav *Gustave.*
Heinrich *Henry.*
Helene *Helen.*
Ilse *Elsie.*
Jakob *James, Jacob.*
Johann *John.*
Johanna *Jane, Joan.*
Josef *Joseph.*
Karl *Charles.*
Katharina (Kätchen) (Käthe)
      Katherine (Kate).
Klaus *Nicholas.*
Lotte *Charlotte.*
Ludwig *Lewis.*
Luise *Louise.*
Maria *Mary.*
Mark *Mark.*
Martha *Martha.*
Michael *Michael.*
Minna *Wilhelmina.*
Moritz *Maurice.*
Otto *Otto.*
Paul *Paul.*
Paula *Paula.*
Peter *Peter.*
Richard *Richard.*
Robert *Robert.*
Rosa *Rose.*
Rüdiger *Roger.*
Rudolph *Ralph.*
Susanne *Susan.*

Theodor *Theodore.*
Therese *Theresa.*
Thomas *Thomas.*
Walter *Walter.*
Wilhelme *William.*

GLOSSARY OF
GEOGRAPHICAL NAMES

Aachen n. *Aix-la-Chapelle.*
Afrika n. *Africa.*
Ägypten n. *Egypt.*
die Alpen pl. *Alps.*
Amerika n. *America.*
   die Vereinigten Staaten pl. *the United
      States (of America).*
   Nord-Amerika n. *North America.*
   Süd-Amerika n. *South America.*
   Mittel-Amerika n. *Central America.*
Antwerpen n. *Antwerp.*
Asien n. *Asia.*
Atlantik m. *(der Atlantische Ozean)
      Atlantic (the Atlantic Ocean).*
Australien n. *Australia.*
Belgien n. *Belgium.*
Berlin n. *Berlin.*
Bonn n. *Bonn.*
Bosnien n. *Bosnia.*
Brasilien n. *Brazil.*
Brüssel n. *Brussels.*
Dänemark n. *Denmark.*
Deutschland n. *Germany.*
England n. *England.*
Europa n. *Europe.*
Frankfurt a.M. n. *Frankfurt on the Main.*
Frankreich n. *France.*
Griechenland n. *Greece.*
Haag (Den) *The Hague.*
Hamburg n. *Hamburg.*
Herzegowina n. *Herzegovina*
Holland n. *Holland.*
Indien n. *India.*
Irland n. *Ireland.*
Israel n. *Israel.*
Italien n. *Italy.*
Japan n. *Japan.*
Jugoslawien n. *Yugoslavia.*
Kanada n. *Canada.*
Köln n. *Cologne.*
Kroatien n. *Croatia*
London n. *London.*
Madrid n. *Madrid.*
Mexiko n. *Mexico.*
Moskau n. *Moscow.*
München n. *Munich.*
Norwegen n. *Norway.*
Nürnberg n. *Nuremberg.*

Österreich *n.*   *Austria.*
Pazifischer Ozean (der)   *Pacific Ocean.*
Paris *n.*   *Paris.*
Polen *n.*   *Poland.*
Portugal *n.*   *Portugal.*
Preußen *n.*   *Prussia.*
Rhein *m.*   *Rhine.*
Rheinland *n.*   *Rhineland.*
Rom *n.*   *Rome.*
Rumäulen *n.*   *Rumania.*
Russland *n.*   *Russia.*
Saar *f.*   *Saar.*

Sachsen *n.*   *Saxony.*
Schlesien *n.*   *Silesia.*
Schottland *n.*   *Scotland.*
Schweden *n.*   *Sweden.*
Schweiz *f.*   *Switzerland.*
Serbien *n.*   *Serbia.*
Slowakei *f.*   *Slovakia.*
Spanien *n.*   *Spain.*
Tschechische Republik *f.*   *Czech Republic.*
Türkei *f.*   *Turkey.*
Ungarn *n.*   *Hungary.*
Wien *n.*   *Vienna.*

English-German

A

a (an) *ein, eine.*
abandon (to) *verlassen.*
abbreviate (to) *abkürzen.*
abbreviation *Abkürzung, f.*
ability *Fähigkeit, f.*
able *fähig.*
able (to be) *können.*
abolish (to) *abschaffen.*
about *ungefähr, um* (acc.) (around).
above *über, oberhalb.*
abroad *im Ausland.*
absence *Abwesenheit, f.*
absent *abwesend.*
absolute *unbedingt, völlig.*
absorb (to) *aufsaugen.*
abstain (to) *sich enthalten.*
abstract *abstrakt.*
absurd *unvernünftig, sinnlos.*
abundant *reichlich.*
abuse *Missbrauch, m.*
academy *Akademie, f.*
accent *Akzent, m.*
accent (to) *betonen.*
accept (to) *annehmen.*
acceptance *Annahme, f.*
accident *Unfall, m.; Zufall, m.* (chance).
accidental *zufällig.*
accidentally *nebenbei.*
accommodate (to) *unterbringen, sich an
    passen.*
accommodation *Unterkunft, f.*
accompany (to) *begleiten.*
accomplish (to) *vollführen, erreichen.*
accord *Übereinstimmung, f.*
according to *zu* (dat.); *zufolge dem.*
account *Rechung, f.; Konto, n.* (balance).
    on no account   *auf keinen Fall.*
    to pay the account   *die Rechnung bezahlen.*
accuracy *Genauigkeit, f.*
accurate *genau, richtig, akkurat.*
accuse (to) *anklagen, beschuldigen.*
accustom (to) *(sich) gewöhnen.*
ace *Ass, n.*
ache *Schmerz, m.*
ache (to) *schmerzen.*
achieve (to) *vollbringen, leisten.*
achievement *Vollbringung, f.; Leistung*
    (result).
acid *sauer* (adj.). *Säure* (noun), *f.*
acknowledge (to) *anerkennen.*
acknowledgment *Anerkennung, f.*
acquaintance *Bekannte, m. & f.*
acquire (to) *erwerben.*
across *gegenüber.*
act *Handlung, f.; Akt, m.* (of a play); *Gesetz, n.*
    (law).

active *tätig.*
activity *Tätigkeit, f.*
actor *Schauspieler, m.*
actress *Schauspielerin, f.*
actual *wirklich.*
acute *akut.*
adapt (to) *anpassen.*
add (to) *zufügen.*
addition *Zusatz, m.; Addition, f.* (math).
    in addition to   *zusätzlich zu* (dat.).
address *Adresse, f.; Anschrift, f.; Ansprache,
    f.; Anrede, f.* (speech).
address (to) *adressieren; anreden,
    ansprechen, sich wenden an* (speech).
adequate *ausreichend, genügend.*
adjective *Eigenschaftswort, Adjektiv, n.*
adjoining *angrenzend, anstossend.*
administer (to) *verwalten.*
admiral *Admiral, m.*
admiration *Bewunderung, f.*
admire (to) *bewundern.*
admission *Eintritt, m.*
admit (to) *einlassen; zugeben* (concede).
admittance *Zutritt, m.*
    no admittance   *Zutritt verboten.*
adopt (to) *adoptieren* (child); *annehmen*
    (idea).
adult *Erwachsene(r)* (noun), *m. & f.;
    erwachsen* (adj.).
advance (to) *vorangehen* (lead); *steigen*
    (price).
    in advance   *im Voraus.*
advantage *Vorteil, m.*
adventure *Abenteuer, n.*
adverb *Adverb, n.*
advertise (to) *anzeigen; Reklame machen.*
advertisement *Anzeige, f.; Reklame, f.*
advice *Rat, m.*
advise (to) *raten.*
affair *Sache, f.* (thing); *Angelegenheit, f.;
    Veranstaltung* (party, meeting) *f.*
affect (to) *betreffen.*
affected *geziert, affektiert* (pretentious):
    gerührt (moved).
affection *Zuneigung, f.*
affectionate *herzlich, zärtlich, liebevoll.*
affirm (to) *bestätigen, bekräftigen.*
affirmation *Bestätigung, f.; Bekräftigung, f.*
afloat *schwimmend, auf dem Meere.*
afraid *ängstlich.*
after *nach* (dat.).
afternoon *Nachmittag, m.*
afterward *nachher.*
again *wieder.*
against *gegen* (acc.); *wider* (acc.).
age *Alter, n.* (also old age); *Epoche, f.*
    (history).
agency *Vertretung, f.*
agent *Agent, m.*

aggravate (to) *verschlimmern; ärgern*
(annoy), *reizen.*
ago *vor* (dat.).
three days ago   *vor drei Tagen.*
agree (to) *übereinstimmen.*
agreeable *angenehm.*
agreed *abgemacht.*
agreement *Übereinstimmung, f.; Vertrag, m.*
(contract).
to be in agreement with   *einverstanden sein*
agricultural *landwirtschaftlich.*
agriculture *Landwirtschaft, f.*
ahead *voran, voraus.*
aid *Hilfe, f.*
first aid   *Erste Hilfe.*
aid (to) *helfen.*
aim *Ziel, n.; Zweck, m.*
aim (to) *erreichen; zielen* (shooting).
to aim at   *richten gegen.*
air *Luft, f.*
air force *Luftwaffe, f.*
airfield *Flugplatz, m.*
airmail *Luftpost, f.*
airplane *Flugzeug, n.*
airport *Flughafen, m.*
aisle *Seitenschiff, n.* (church); *gang, m.* (hall).
alarm *Alarm, m.*
alarm clock *Wecker, m.*
alcohol *Alkohol, m.*
alike *gleich, ähnlich.*
all *ganz, alles.*
all right   *in Ordnung, bestimmt.*
not at all   *keineswegs überhaupt micht.*
alliance *Verbindung f.; Allianz, f.* (pact).
allow (to) *erlauben, gestatten.*
allowed *gestattet.*
ally *Verbündete, m.*
almost *fast, beinahe.*
alone *allein.*
along *entlang.*
already *schon, bereits.*
also *auch.*
altar *Altar, m.*
alter (to) *ändern, verwandeln.*
alternate *abwechselnd.*
alternate (to) *abwechseln.*
although *obwohl, obgleich.*
altitude *Höhe, f.*
altogether *zusammen; gänzlich* (wholly).
always *immer.*
amaze (to) *erstaunen.*
amazement *Verwunderung, f.*
ambassador *Botschafter, m.*
ambassadress *Botschafterin, f.*
ambitious *ehrgeizig.*
amend (to) *berichtigen, (ab)ändern,*
verbessern.
American *Amerikaner* (noun) *m.;*
amerikanisch (adj.); *Amerikanerin, f.*

among *mitten; unter* (dat. or acc.).
amount *Betrag, m.*
ample *geräumig, umfassend.*
amuse (to) *amüsieren.*
amusement *Unterhaltung, f.*
amusing *amüsant.*
analyze (to) *analysieren.*
ancestors *Vorfahren, pl.*
anchor *Anker, m.*
ancient, *uralt, alt, aus alten Zeiten.*
and *und.*
anecdote *Anekdote, f.*
angel *Engel, m.*
anger *Ärger, m.*
angry *ärgerlich, bös.*
animal *Tier, n.*
animate (to) *beleben.*
annex *Nebengebäude, n.*
annihilate (to) *vernichten.*
anniversary *Hochzeitstag, m.*
announce (to) *ansagen.*
announcement *Anzeige, f.*
annoy (to) *ärgern, belästigen.*
annual *jährlich.*
annul (to) *annulieren; ungültig machen.*
anonymous *anonym.*
another *ein anderer.*
answer *Antwort, f.*
answer (to) *antworten.*
answering machine *Anrufbeanworter, m.*
anterior *vorhergehend.*
anticipate (to) *vorhersehen* (foresee).
erwarten (expect).
antique *altertümlich, antik.*
anxiety *Unruhe, f.; Ängstlichkeit f.*
anxious *unruhig, ängstlich, bekümmert.*
any *etwas* (some); *irgend ein; irgend welche*
(whatever).
anybody *irgendjemand.*
anyhow *sowieso.*
anyway   *sowieso.*
anything *irgendetwas.*
anywhere *irgendwo.*
apart *abseits, getrennt.*
apartment *Wohnung, f.*
apiece *pro Stück.*
apologize (to) *sich entschuldigen.*
apparent *scheinbar, anscheinend.*
appeal (to) *gefallen.*
appear (to) *erscheinen.*
appearance *Erscheinung, f.*
appease (to) *besänftigen.*
appendix *Anhang, m.*
appetite *Appetit, m.*
applaud (to) *applaudieren; klatschen.*
applause *Applaus, m.*
apple *Apfel, m.*
application *Antrag, m.* (request);
Gewissenhaftigkeit, f. (diligence).

application form *Anmeldungs—*
    Antragsformular.
apply (to) *sich bewerben um* (for a job);
    auftragen (use).
appoint (to) *ernennen.*
appointment *Verbredung, f.*
appreciate (to) *schätzen.*
appreciation *Anerkennung, f.*
appropriate *angemessen.*
approve (to) *genehmigen.*
April *April, m.*
apron *Schürze, f.*
arbitrary *eigenwillig, beliebig.*
arcade *Arkade, f.*
architect *Architekt, m.; Baumeister, m.*
architecture *Architektur, f.*
ardent *feurig, glühend.*
area *Gebiet, n.*
argue (to) *verhandeln, diskutieren.*
argument *Wortwechsel, m.*
arise (to) *aufsteigen; auftauchen* (emerge);
    aufstehen (get up).
arm *Arm, m.*
    firearms *Waffen, pl.*
arm (to) *bewaffnen.*
arms control *Abrüstung, f.*
army *Heer, n.; Armee, f.*
around *herum, um* (acc.).
arouse (to) *erregen* (revolt); *erwecken*
    (suspicion); *aufwecken* (wake up).
arrange (to) *ordnen, arrangieren.*
arrangement *Ordnung, f.* (order); *Anordnung,*
    f. (preparation).
arrest *Verhaftung, f.*
arrest (to) *verhaften.*
arrival *Ankunft, f.*
arrive (to) *ankommen.*
art *Kunst, f.*
article *Artikel, m.*
artificial *künstlich.*
artificial intelligence *künstliche Intelligenz*
    (computer), *f.*
artist *Künstler, m.*
artistic *künstlerisch, kunstvoll.*
as *als* (when); *so* (as much); *da* (because).
    as . . . as so . . . *wie.*
    as long as *so lange wie.*
    as soon as *sobald.*
    as to *mit Bezug auf* (business);
        was . . . anbetrifft.
    as well *sowohl, auch.*
    as yet *bis jetzt.*
ascertain (to) *feststellen.*
ash *Asche, f.*
ashamed *beschämt, verschämt* (shy).
aside *beiseite, abseits.*
ask (to) *fragen, bitten* (um).
asleep *schlafend.*
aspire (to) *streben nach.*

aspirin *Aspirin, n.*
assault *Angriff, m.*
assemble (to) *sich versammeln.*
assembly *Versammlung, f.* (congress);
    Gesellschaft, f.
assign (to) *zuteilen, aufgeben.*
assist (to) *beistehen,* (aus) *helfen.*
assistant *Gehilfe, m., Gehilfin, f.; Assistent, m.*
    (-in) *f.*
associate (to) *anschließen, verbinden.*
assume (to) *annehmen.*
assurance *Versicherung, f.*
assure (to) *versichern.*
astonish (to) *erstaunen.*
astound (to) *verblüffen.*
astronaut *Astronaut, m.* (-in) *f.*
asylum *Asyl, n.*
at *in* (dat. or acc.); *beim, zu* (dat.).
    at home *zu Hause* (heim)
    at first *zuerst.*
    at last *endlich.*
    at once *sofort.*
    at times *zuweillen, manchmal*
        (sometimes).
athlete *Athlet, m.*
athletics *Gymnastik, f.*
atmosphere *Atmosphäre, f.*
attach (to) *anhängen.*
attain (to) *erreichen.*
attempt (to) *versuchen.*
attend (to) *beiwohnen, besuchen* (school).
attendant *Gehilfe, m.*
attention *Aufmerksamkeit, f.*
attic *Dachkammer, f.; Dachstube, f.*
attitude *Haltung, f.; Einstellung, f.* (mental).
attorney *Anwalt, m.*
attract (to) *anziehen.*
attraction *Anziehung, f.*
attractive *schön, anziehend, reizend.*
audience *Zuhörer, pl, Zuhörerschaft f.;*
    Audienz, f.; Publikum n.
August *August, m.*
aunt *Tante, f.*
author *Autor, m.*
authority *Autorität, f.*
authorize (to) *ermächtigen.*
automatic *automatisch.*
automobile *Auto, n.*
autumn *Herbst, m.*
available *vorhanden, verfügbar, erhältlich.*
average *Durchschnitt, m.*
avoid (to) *vermeiden.*
awake *wach.*
awake (to) *wecken; erwachen* (oneself).
award *Belohnung, f.*
award (to) *zuerkennen, zusprechen, verleihen.*
aware *gewahr, bewusst.*
    I'm fully aware that . . . *Es ist mir völlig*
        bewusst (klar), dass . . .

away *fort, weg.*
  to go away *weggehen.*
awful *furchtbar.*
awkward *ungeschickt.*

B

baby *Kind, n.*
back *Rücken (noun) m. (body); zurück (adv.).*
background *Hintergrund, m.*
backward *rückwärts.*
bacon *Speck, m.*
bad *schlecht.*
badge *Marke, f., Abzeichen, n. (Verdienst);*
    Medaille f. (military).
bag *Beutel, m., Tüte, f. (paper bag).*
baggage *Gepäck, n.*
baker *Bäcker, m.*
bakery *Bäckerei, f.*
balance *Gleichgewicht, n.*
balcony *Balkon, m.*
ball *Ball, m.*
balloon *Ballon, m.*
banana *Banane, f.*
band *Band, n.; Musikkapelle, f.*
bandage *Verband, m.*
banister *Treppengeländer, n.*
bank *Bank, f., Ufer, n. (of a river).*
banknote *Banknote, f.*
bankruptcy *Bankrott, m.; Konkurs, m.*
banquet *Bankett, n.; Festessen, n.*
bar *Bar, f. (for drinks).*
barber *Frisör, m.*
bare *bloss, bar, unbekleidet, nackt.*
barefoot *barfuß.*
barge *Barke, f. Lastschiff, n.*
barn *Scheune, f.*
barrel *Fass, n.*
barren *unfruchtbar.*
basin *Becken, n.*
basis *Grundlage, f.*
basket *Korb, n.*
bath *Bad, n.*
bathroom *Badezimmer, n.*
bathe (to) *baden.*
battle *Schlacht, f.; Kampf, m.*
bay *Bucht, f.*
be (to) *sein.*
  to be hungry *hungrig sein, Hunger haben.*
  to be right *Recht haben.*
  to be thirsty *Durst haben, durstig sein.*
  to be tired *müde sein.*
  to be wrong *Unrecht haben, im Unrecht*
    sein.
beach *Strand, m.*
bean *Bohne, f.*
bear (to) *aushalten, ertragen.*

beard *Bart, m.*
beat (to) *schlagen.*
beautiful *schön, wunderschön.*
beauty *Schönheit, f.*
beauty parlor *Schönheitssalon, m.*
because *weil, denn (for) da.*
become (to) *werden.*
becoming *passend, vorteilhaft.*
bed *Bett, n.*
beef *Rindfleisch, n.*
beer *Bier, n.*
beet *Rübe, f.*
before *vor (dat. or acc.); bevor (conj.).*
beg (to) *betteln.*
beggar *Bettler, m.*
begin (to) *beginnen, anfangen.*
beginning *Anfang, f.*
behave (to) *sich betragen, sich benehmen.*
behavior *Verhalten, n.; Benehmen, n.*
behind *hinter (dat. or acc.).*
belief *Glaube, m.*
believe (to) *glauben.*
bell *Glocke, f.*
belong (to) *gehören.*
below *unter (dat. or acc.).*
belt *Gürtel, m.*
bench *Bank, f.*
bend (to) *biegen.*
beneath *unten; unter (dat. or acc.).*
benefit *Vorteil, m.*
beside *neben (dat. or acc.).*
besides *ausserdem.*
best *beste (der, die, das) (adj.); am besten*
    (adv.).
bet *Wette, f.*
bet (to) *wetten.*
betray (to) *verraten.*
better *besser.*
between *zwischen (dat. or acc.).*
beware (to) *sich hüten.*
  Beware! *Achtung!*
beyond *jenseits (gen.).*
bicycle *Fahrrad, n.*
bid (to) *bieten; befehlen (order).*
big *gross.*
bill *Rechnung, f.*
billion *Milliarde (Am.), Billion.*
bind (to) *binden.*
bird *Vogel, m.*
birth *Geburt, f.*
birthday *Geburtstag, m.*
biscuit *Zwieback, m., Keks, m.*
bishop *Bischof, m.*
bit *Stück, n.*
bite *Biss, m.*
bite (to) *beißen.*
bitter *bitter.*
bitterness *Bitterkeit, f.*
black *schwarz, Schwarze (person) m. & f.*

blade *Klinge, f.* (razor); *Blatt, n.* (grass).
blame *Schuld, f.; Tadel, m.*
blame (to) *tadeln, rügen.*
blank *unbeschrieben* (page); *verwundert*
   (expression).
blanket *Decke, f.*
bleed (to) *bluten.*
bless (to) *segnen.*
blessing *Segnung, f.; Segen, m.*
blind *blind.*
block *Block, m.*
block (to) *versperren.*
blood *Blut, n.*
blotter *Löschpapier, n.*
blouse *Bluse, f.*
blow *Schlag, m.*
blow (to) *blasen; putzen* (nose).
blue *blau.*
blush (to) *erröten.*
board *Brett, n.* (plank); *Verpflegung, f.*
   (food).
boarding pass *Bordkarte, f., Einsteigarte, f.*
boardinghouse *Pension, f.*
boast (to) *prahlen.*
boat *Boot, n.*
body *Körper, m.*
boil (to) *kochen, sieden.*
boiler *Kessel, m., Heißwasserspeicher, m.*
bold *kühn.*
bomb *Bombe, f.*
   atom bomb. *Atombombe, f.*
bond *Aktie, f.* (stock).
bone *Knochen, m.*
book *Buch, n.*
bookseller *Buchhändler, m.*
bookstore *Buchhandlung, f.*
border *Grenze, f.*
boring *langweilig.*
born *geboren.*
borrow (to) *borgen, leihen.*
boss *Boss, m., Chef, m.*
both *beide.*
bother (to) *ärgern, plagen, bemühen.*
   Don't bother! *Bemühen Sie sich nicht!*
bottle *Flasche, f.*
bottle opener *Flaschenöffner, m.*
bottom *Boden, m.*
bounce (to) *aufspringen.*
bowl *Schale, f.*
box *Schachtel, f.*
boy *Junge, m.*
bracelet *Armband, n.*
braid *Borte, f.; Zopf, m.* (hair), *Haarflechte, f.*
brain *Gehirn, n.*
brake *Bremse, f.*
branch *Ast, m.* (tree); *Filiale, f.* (business).
brave *tapfer.*
brassiere *Büstenhalter, m.*
bread *Brot, n.*

break (to) *brechen; lösen* (engagement).
breakfast *Frühstück, n.*
   have breakfast *frühstücken.*
breath *Atem, m.*
breathe (to) *atmen.*
breeze *Wind, m.; Brise, f.*
bribe (to) *bestechen.*
brick *Backstein, m.*
bride *Braut, f.*
   bridegroom *Bräutigam, m.*
bridge *Brücke, f.*
brief *kurz.*
bright *hell, klar.*
brighten (to) *erheitern; sich aufklären*
   (weather).
brilliant *glänzend.*
bring (to) *bringen.*
bring up (to) *erziehen* (a person).
British *britisch.*
broad *weit, breit.*
broil (to) *braten.*
broken *zerbrochen.*
brook *Bach, m.*
broom *Besen, m.*
brother *Bruder, m.*
brother-in-law *Schwager, m.*
brown *braun.*
bruise (to) *quetschen, stossen.*
brush *Bürste, f.*
bubble *Blase, f.*
bucket *Eimer m.*
buckle *Schnalle, f.*
bud *Knospe, f.*
budget *Budget, n; Wirtschaft, f.* (house).
build (to) *bauen.*
building *Gebäude, n.*
bulletin *Bulletin, n., Bekanntmachung, f.;*
   Ansage, f.
bundle *Bündel, n.*
burn (to) *(ver)brennen.*
burst (to) *bersten; platzen.*
bus *Autobus, m. Omnibus, m.*
bush *Busch, m.*
business *Geschäft, n.*
businessman *Geschäftsmann, m.;*
   Kaufmann, m.; **businesswoman**
   Geschäftsfrau, f.
busy *beschäftigt.*
but *aber; sondern* (neg.).
butcher *Metzger, m.; Fleischer, m.*
butcher shop *Metzgerei, f.; Fleischerei, f.*
butter *Butter, f.*
button *Knopf, m.*
buy (to) *kaufen.*
buyer *Käufer, m.*
by *von* (dat.); *durch* (acc.); *neben*
   (dat. & acc.) (close to); *um* (acc.)
   (time).
byte *Byte, m.*

C

cab *Taxi, n.*
cabbage *Kohl, m.; Kraut, n.*
cable *Kabel, n.*
cage *Käfig, m.*
cake *Kuchen, m.*
calendar *Kalender, m.*
calf *Kalb, n.*
call *Ruf, m.; Anruf* (telephone) *m.*
call (to) *rufen; anrufen; telefonieren*
        (telephone); *heissen* (name).
calm *ruhig.*
camera *Kamera, f.; Fotoapparat m.*
camp *Lager, n.*
camp (to) *lagern, zelten.*
can *Büchse, f.; Dose, f.*
can (to be able) *können.*
can opener *Büchsenöffner, m.*
cancel (to) *rückgängig machen, absagen,*
        annulieren (annul), *durchstreichen.*
candidate *Kandidat, m.*
candle *Kerze, f.*
candy *Bonbons, pl.*
cap *Mütze, f.*
capital *Hauptstadt, f.* (city); *Kapital, n.*
        (finance).
capital punishment *Todesstrafe* (death
        penalty), *f.*
capricious *launisch; eigensinning*
        (temperamental).
captain *Hauptmann, n.* (army); *Kapitän, m.*
        (navy).
captive *Gefangene, m.*
capture (to) *fangen; einnehmen.*
car *Wagen, m., Auto, n.*
carbon paper *Durchschlagpapier, n.*
card *Karte, f.; Ausweis* (I.D.) *m.*
care *Sorge, f.* (anxiety); *Sorgfalt, f.* (caution).
        care of   *per Adresse.*
        take care of   *pflegen.*
care (to) *sich sorgen.*
        care about   *sich kümmern um.*
        care for (to like)   *gern haben.*
        I don't care.   *Das ist mir gleich.*
career *Laufbahn, f.; Karriere, f.*
careful *vorsichtig, sorgfältig.*
careless *nachlässig, sorglos.*
caress *Liebkosung, f.*
carpenter *Zimmermann, m.*
carpet *Teppich, m.*
carry (to) *tragen.*
carve (to) *schnitzen.*
case *Fall, m.; Aktentasche, f.*
        in case   *im Falle, falls.*
cash *Bargeld, n.*
        to pay cash   *bar zahlen.*
cash (to) *einlösen, kassieren.*

cashier *Kassierer, m.*
cassette *Kassette, f.*
        cassette tape deck   *Kassettendeck, n.*
castle *Schloss, n.*
cat *Katze, f.*
catch (to) *fangen.*
category *Kategorie, f.*
cathedral *Dom, m.*
Catholic *katholisch.*
cause *Grund, m.; Ursache, f.*
cause (to) *verursachen.*
cease (to) *aufhören.*
ceiling *Decke, f.*
celebrate (to) *feiern.*
cellar *Keller, m.*
cement *Zement, m.*
cemetery *Friedhof, m.*
censorship *Zensur, f.*
cent *Cent, m.*
center *Zentrum, n.; Mittelpunkt, m.*
central *zentral.*
central heating *Zentralheizung, f.*
century *Jahrhundert, n.*
cereal *Getreide, n.* (grain); *Mehlspeise, f.*
        (prepared).
ceremony *Zeremonie, f.*
certain *gewiss, sicher.*
certainty *Gewissheit, f.; Sicherheit, f.*
certificate *Zeugnis, n.; Zertifikat, n.*
chain *Kette, f.*
chair *Stuhl, m.*
chairman (-woman) *Vorsitzende, m. (f)*
        Präsident, m.
chalk *Kreide, f.*
challenge *Herausforderung, f.; Aufforderung, f.*
challenge (to) *herausfordern.*
champion *Meister, m.*
        world champion   *Weltmeister, m.*
chance *Zufall, m.*
change *Veränderung, f.; Kleingeld, n.* (money).
change (to) *ändern; wechseln* (money).
chapel *Kapelle, f.*
chapter *Kapitel, n.*
character *Charakter, m.*
characteristic *charakteristisch.*
charge (to) *beladen; berechnen* (price);
        anklagen (law).
charitable *wohltätig.*
charity *Wohltätigkeit, f. Nächstenliebe, f.*
charming *reizend.*
chase (to) *jagen.*
chat (to) *plaudern.*
cheap *billig.*
cheat (to) *betrügen.*
check *Scheck, m.; Rechnung, f.* (in a
        restaurant).
check (to) *kontrolliern; aufgeben, nachprüfen*
        (luggage).
cheek *Wange, f.*

cheer (to) *aufheitern.*

cheerful *heiter, freudig, fröhlich.*

cheese *Käse, m.*

chemical *chemisch.*

cherish (to) *schätzen.*

cherry *Kirsche, f.*

chest *Brust, f.; Kiste, f.* (box).
   chest of drawers   *Kommode, f.*

chestnut *Kastanie, f.*

chew (to) *kauen.*

chicken *Huhn, n.; Hühnchen, n.*

chief *Leiter, m., Vorgesetze(r), m.; chef, m.*

chief (adj.) *haupt-.*

chime *Glockenspiel, n.*

chimney *Schornstein, m.*

chin *Kinn, n.*

china *Porzellan, n.*

chip *Span, m.; Splitter, m.*

chocolate *Schokolade, f.*

choice *Wahl, f.*

choir *Chor, m.*

choke (to) *ersticken.*

choose (to) *auswählen.*

chop *Kotelett, n.* (cook.); *Schlag, m.* (blow).

Christian *Christ* (noun) *m.; christlich* (adj.).

Christmas *Weihnachten, f. pl.*

church *Kirche, f.*

cigar *Zigarre, f.*

cigarette *Zigarette, f.*

circle *Kreis, m.*

circular *rund.*

circulate (to) *kreisen, umlaufen.*

circumstances *Umstände, pl.*

citizen *Bürger, m.*

city *Stadt, f.*

city hall *Rathaus, m.*

civil *zivil, bürgerlich.*

civilization *Zivilisation, f.*

civilize (to) *zivilisieren.*

claim *Forderung, f.; Rechtsanspruch, m.*

claim (to) *fordern.*

clamor *Geschrei, n.*

clap (to) *klatschen.*

class *Klasse, f.; Kategorie, f.*

classify (to) *klassifizieren.*

clause *Klausel, f.; Satzglied, m.*

clean *rein, sauber.*

clean (to) *reinigen.*

cleaners *Reinigung, f.*

cleanliness *Reinlichkeit, f.; Sauberkeit, f.*

clear *klar.*

clerk *Angestellte, m.*

clever *klug, schlau.*

climate *Klima, n.*

climb (to) *steigen* (stairway); *besteigen*
         (mountain).

clip *Klammer, f.*

clip (to) *beschneiden* (cut); *scheren*
         zusammenfügen (attach); *festhalten.*

clock *Uhr, f.*

close *nahe.*

close (to) *zumachen, schließen.*

closed *geschlossen.*

closet *Schrank, m.*

cloth *Tuch, n.*

clothes *Kleider, pl.*

cloud *Wolke, f.*

cloudy *bewölkt.*

clover *Klee, m.*

club *Klub, m.; Kreuz* (cards).

coal *Kohle, f.*

coarse *roh.*

coast *Küste, f.*

coat *Mantel, m.* (overcoat); *Anzug, m.* (suit).

code *Gesetzbuch, n.* (law); *Kodex, m.*

coffee *Kaffee, m.*

coffin *Sarg, m.*

coin *Münze, f.*

cold *kalt.*

coldness *Kälte, f.*

collaborate (to) *zusammenarbeiten.*

collar *Kragen, m.; Halsband, n.* (dog).

collect (to) *sammeln.*

collection *Sammlung, f.*

collective *gesamt.*

college *Universität, f.*

colonial *kolonial.*

colony *Kolonie, f.*

color *Farbe, f.*

color (to) *färben.*

column *Spalte, f., Kollonne, f.* (military);
         Säule, f. (arch).

comb *Kamm, m.*

comb (to) *kämmen.*

combination *Verbindung, f.;*
         Zusammenstellung, f.; Verknüpfung, f.

combine (to) *verbinden, zusammenstellen.*

come (to) *kommen.*
   come back   *zurückkommen.*

comedy *Komödie, f.*

comet *Komet, m.*

comfort *Behaglichkeit, f.; Trost, m.* (moral).

comfort (to) *trösten.*

comfortable *bequem.*

comma *Komma, n.*

command *Befehl, m.*

command (to) *befehlen.*

commander *Befehlshaber, m.*

commercial *geschäftsmässig, handelsüblich;*
         Fernsehwerbung, f. (TV commercial).

commission *Kommission, f.*

commit (to) *begehen.*

common *gemein, gewöhnlich.*

communicate (to) *mitteilen.*

communication *Mitteilung, f.*

community *Gemeinde, f.*

compact disc (CD) *Compact Disc, f.;*

companion *Genosse, m.*

company *Gesellschaft, f.* (social); *Kompanie, f. (military).*
compare (to) *vergleichen.*
comparison *Vergleich, m.*
compel *zwingen, nötigen.*
compete (to) *konkurrieren.*
competition *Konkurrenz, f.; Tournier, n.* (sports), *Wettbewerb, n.* (sports).
complain (to) *sich beklagen.*
complaint *Klage, f.*
complete *vollenden.*
complex *Komplex,* (noun) *m.; verwickelt* (adj.); *kompliziert* (adj.).
complexion *Gesichtsfarbe, f.*
complicate (to) *verwickeln, komplizieren.*
complicated *verwickelt, kompliziert.*
compliment *Kompliment, n.*
compose (to) *komponieren.*
composer *Komponist, m.*
composition *Komposition, f.*
compromise *Kompromiss, m.; Vergleich, m.*
compromise (to) *einen Kompromiss machen, kompromittieren.*
computer *Computer, m.*
conceit *Einbildung, f.*
conceited *eingebildet.*
conceive (to) *ersinnen, ausdenken, schwanger werden* (med.).
concentrate (to) *konzentrieren.*
concern *Angelegenheit, f.* (matter); *Sorge, f.* (anxiety); *Geschäft, n.* (business).
concern (to) *betreffen.*
concert *Konzert, n.*
concrete *konkret.*
condemn (to) *verurteilen, verdammen.*
condense (to) *kondensieren.*
condition *Zustand, m.*
conduct *Benehmen, n.*
conduct (to) *führen; dirigieren* (music).
conductor *Führer, m.* (guide); *Schaffner, m.* (vehicle); *Dirigent, m.* (music).
confess (to) *gestehen; beichten* (church).
confession *Geständnis, n.; Beichte, f.* (church).
confidence *Vertrauen, n.*
confident *vertrauend, vertrauensvoll.*
confidential *vertraulich, geheim.*
confirm (to) *bestätigen.*
confirmation *Bestätigung, f.*
congratulate (to) *gratulieren.*
congratulations *Glückwunsch, m.*
connect (to) *verbinden.*
connection *Verbindung, f.*
conquer (to) *erobern, besiegen.*
conquest *Eroberung, f.; Sieg, m.*
conscience *Gewissen, n.*
conscientious *gewissenhaft.*
conscious *bewusst.*
consent *Einwilligung, f.; Genehmigung, f.*
conservative *konservativ.*

consider (to) *betrachten* (look); *bedenken* (think).
considerable *beträchtlich, bedeutend.*
consideration *Betrachtung, f.*
consist of (to) *bestehen aus* (dat.).
consistent *übereinstimmend, fest, dicht.*
constant *beständig.*
constitution *Verfassung, f.; Gesundheit, f.* (health).
constitutional *verfassungsmäßig.*
consul *Konsul, m.*
contagious *ansteckend.*
contain (to) *enthalten.*
container *Behälter, m.*
contemporary *Zeitgenosse* (noun) *m.; zeitgenössich* (adj.).
content *zufrieden.*
content (to) *befriedigen.*
contents *Inhalt, m.; Gehalt, m.*
continent *Kontinent, m.*
continual *fortwährend.*
continue (to) *fortfahren.*
contract *Vertrag, m.*
contractor *Unternehmer, m.*
contradict (to) *widersprechen.*
contradiction *Widerspruch, m.*
contradictory *widersprechend.*
contrary *Gegenteil* (noun) *n.; entgegengesetzt* (adj.).
   on the contrary   *im Gegenteil.*
contrast *Gegensatz, m.*
contrast (to) *vergleichen, gegenüberstellen.*
contribute (to) *beitragen.*
contribution *Beitrag, m.*
control *Kontrolle, f.*
control (to) *kontrollieren.*
controversy *Meinungsverschiedenheit, f.; Kontroverse, f.; Angemessenheit, f.*
convenience *Bequemlichkeit, f.*
convenient *passend; bequem* (practical).
convent *Kloster, n.*
convention *Versammlung, f.*
conversation *Gespräch, n.; Unterhaltung, f.*
converse (to) *sich unterhalten.*
convert (to) *umwandeln einlösen* (bonds).
convict (to) *verurteilen.*
conviction *Verurteilung, f.*
convince (to) *überzeugen.*
cook *Koch, m.; Köchin, f.*
cook (to) *kochen.*
cool *kühl.*
cool (to) *kühlen.*
copy *Kopie, f.*
cork *Kork(en) m.; Stöpsel, m.*
corkscrew *Korkenzieher, m.*
corn *Mais, m.*
corner *Ecke, f.*
corporation *Körperschaft, f., Gesellschaft, f.*
correct *richtig.*

correct (to) *berichtigen, korrigieren.*
correction *Verbesserung, f., Berichtigung, f.*
correspond (to) *korrespondieren.*
correspondence *Briefwechsel, m.*
correspondent *Korrespondent, m.*
corresponding *entsprechend.*
corrupt (to) *verderben.*
corruption *Verdorbenheit, f.*
cost *Kosten, f.*
costume *Kostüm, n.*
cottage *Häuschen, n.*
cotton *Baumwolle, f.; Watte, f.* (pharmacy).
couch *Sofa, n., Couch, f.*
cough *Husten, m.*
count *Graf, m.* (nobility); *Zählung, f.*
count (to) *zählen.*
counter *Ladentisch, m.*
countess *Gräfin, f.*
countless *zahllos.*
country *Land, n.; Vaterland, n.* (fatherland).
countryman *Landsmann, m.*
couple *Paar, n.*
coupon *Coupon, Kupon, m.*
courage *Mut, m.*
course *Lauf, m.* (direction); *Kursus, m.*
        (studies), *Verlauf, m.* (illness).
court *Gericht, n.*
courteous *zuvorkommend.*
courtesy *Höflichkeit, f.*
courtyard *Hof, m.; Spielplatz, m.*
cousin *Vetter, m.; Cousine, f.*
cover *Decke, f.*
cow *Kuh, f.*
crack *Riss, m.*
crack (to) *knacken.*
cradle *Wiege, f.*
crash *Zusammenbruch, m., Absturz, m.*
        (plane); *Zusammenstoss, m.* (auto).
crazy *verrückt.*
cream *Sahne, f., Rahm, m.*
create (to) *schaffen.*
creature *Geschöpf, n.; Wesen, n.*
credit *Kredit, m.*
creditor *Gläubiger, m.*
crime *Verbrechen, n.*
crisis *Krise, f.*
crisp *knusprig.*
critic *Kritiker, m.*
critical *kritisch.*
criticize (to) *kritisieren.*
crooked *krumm.*
crop *Ernte, f.*
cross *Kreuz, n.*
crossing *Übergang, m.*
crossroad *Straßenkreuzung, f., Kreuzweg, m.*
crouch (to) *hocken.*
crow *Krähe, f.*
crowd *Menge, f.; Gedränge, n.*
crowd (to) *überfüllen, zusammendrängen.*

crowded *überfüllt, wimmelnd.*
crown *Krone, f.*
crown (to) *krönen.*
cruel *grausam, unmenschlich.*
cruelty *Grausamkeit, f.*
crumb *Krume, f., Krümel, m.*
crumble (to) *zerbröckeln.*
crust *Kruste, f.*
crutch *Krücke, f.*
cry *Ruf, m.; Geschrei, n.*
cry (to) *weinen* (weep); *schreien* (shout).
cuff *Manschette, f.*
cunning *listig, verschmitzt, verschlagen.*
cup *Tasse, f.*
cure *Heilung, f.*
curiosity *Neugier, f.*
curious *neugierig.*
curl *Locke, f.*
current *Strom* (noun) *m.; laufend* (adj.), *jetzig*
        (adj.), *gegenwärtig.*
curtain *Vorhang, m., Gardine, f.*
curve *Kurve, f.*
cushion *Kissen, n.*
custom *Sitte, f.*
customary *gebräuchlich.*
customer *Kunde, m.; (-in) f.*
customshouse *Zollamt, n.*
customs official *Zollbeamte, m.*
cut *Schnitt, m.*
cut (to) *schneiden.*

D

dagger *Dolch, m.*
daily *täglich.*
dainty *zierlich.*
dairy *Milchgeschäft, n.*
dam *Damm, m., Deich, m.*
damage *Schaden, m.*
damage (to) *beschädigen.*
damp *feucht.*
dance *Tanz, m.*
dance (to) *tanzen.*
danger *Gefahr, f.*
dangerous *gefährlich.*
dark *dunkel.*
darkness *Dunkelheit, f.*
dash (to) *sich beeilen, bespritzen* (water),
        losstürzen (auf).
data processing *Datenverarbeitung f.*
date *Datum, n.; Verabredung, f.* (meeting).
daughter *Tochter, f.*
dawn *Morgendämmerung, f.*
day *Tag, m.*
    day after tomorrow   *übermorgen.*
    day before yesterday   *vorgestern.*
    yesterday   *gestern.*

dazzle (to) *blenden, verblüffen.*
dead *tot.*
deaf *taub.*
deal *Teil, m.; Geschäft, n.* (business).
  a great deal of   *sehr viel.*
  to strike up a deal with someone
     jemandem ein Geschäft machen.
  It's a deal (coll.)   *abgemacht!*
  no big deal!   *keine große Sache.*
deal (to) *ausgeben* (cards), *verteilen, zuteilen,*
    handeln (mit).
dealer *Händler, m.; Geber, m.* (cards).
dear *lieb; teuer* (also expensive).
death *Tod, m.*
debate *Debatte, f., Verhandlung, f.*
debt *Schuld, f.*
debtor *Schuldner, m.*
decanter *Karaffe, f.*
decay *Verfall, m.* (ruin) *Fäulnis, f.* (rot).
decay (to) *verfallen, verfaulen.*
deceased *verstorben.*
deceit *Falschheit, f.*
deceive (to) *betrügen.*
December *Dezember, m.*
decent *anständig.*
decide (to) *entscheiden.*
decided *entschieden.*
decision *Entscheidung, f.; Entschluss, m.*
decisive *entscheidend.*
deck *Deck, n.*
declare (to) *erklären.*
decline *Untergang, m.; Fall, m.*
decline (to) *verfallen, abweisen; deklinieren*
  (grammar); *untergehen.*
decrease *Abnahme, f.; Verminderung, f.*
decrease (to) *abnehmen, vermindern.*
decree *Verordnung, f.*
dedicate (to) *widmen.*
deed *Tat, f.*
deep *tief.*
deer *Hirsch, m.; Reh, n.*
defeat *Niederlage, f.*
defeat (to) *besiegen.*
defect *Fehler, m.*
defend (to) *verteidigen.*
defense *Verteidigung, f.*
defiance *Trotz, m.*
define (to) *definieren.*
definite *bestimmt.*
defy (to) *trotzen.*
degree *Grad, m.*
delay *Verzögerung, f.*
delay (to) *aufhalten.*
delegate *Delegierte(r), m.,*
    Bevollmächtigte(r), m.
delegate (to) *delegieren.*
deliberate (to) *erwägen.*
deliberately *absichtlich.*
delicacy *Delikatesse, f.; Leckerbissen, m.*

delicate *zart.*
delicious *köstlich.*
delight *Freude, f.; Vergnügen, n.*
delighted *erfreut.*
deliver (to) *liefern.*
deliverance *Befreiung, f.*
delivery *Ablieferung, f.; Abgabe, f.*
demand *Forderung, f.; Nachfrage, f.*
    (business); *Verlangen, n.*
demand (to) *fordern.*
democracy *Demokratie, f.*
demonstrate (to) *demonstrieren.*
demonstration *Darlegung, f.; Demonstration,*
    f. (political).
denial *Verleugnung, f.*
denounce (to) *denunzieren, öffentlich*
    anklagen.
dense *dicht.*
density *Dichte, f.*
dentist *Zahnarzt, m.*
deny (to) *ableugnen, verleugnen.*
departure *Abreise, f.*
department *Abteilung, f.*
depend (to) *abhängen.*
dependent *abhängig.*
deplore (to) *bedauern, beweinen.*
deposit *Anzahlung, f.*
depreciation *Wertminderung, f.*
depress (to) *niederdrücken.*
depression *Depression, f.*
deprive (to) *berauben, entziehen.*
depth *Tiefe, f.*
deride (to) *verlachen, verhöhnen.*
derive (to) *ableiten.*
descend (to) *abstammen.*
descendant *Nachkomme, m; Abkömmling, m.*
descent *Abstieg, m.; Abstammung, f.* (family).
describe (to) *beschreiben.*
description *Beschreibung, f.*
desert *Wüste, f.*
desert (to) *verlassen.*
deserve (to) *verdienen.*
design *Zeichnung, f.* (drawing); *Absicht, f.*
    (intention).
designer *Zeichner, m. (-in) f.*
desirable *wünschenswert.*
desire (to) *wünschen.*
desire *Wunsch, m.*
desirous *begierig.*
desk *Pult, n.*
desolate *trostlos.*
despair *Verzweiflung, f.*
despair (to) *verzweifeln.*
desperate *verzweifelt.*
despise (to) *verachten.*
despite *trotz* (gen.).
dessert *Nachtisch, m.*
destiny *Schicksal, n.*
destroy (to) *zerstören.*

destruction *Zerstörung, f.*
detach (to) *ablösen, freimachen*
detail *Einzelheit, f.*
detain (to) *aufhalten.*
detect (to) *entdecken, aufdecken* (crime).
detective *Detektiv, m.*
detective story *Kriminalgeschichte, f.;*
    Detektivroman, m.
determination *Entschlossenheit, f.*
determine (to) *bestimmen.*
detest (to) *verabscheuen.*
detour *Umweg, m.*
detract (to) *abziehen, entziehen, vermindern.*
detrimental *schädlich.*
develop (to) *entwickeln.*
development *Entwicklung, f.*
device *Kunstgriff, m; Gerät, n.*
devil *Teufel, m.*
devise (to) *ersinnen, ausdenken.*
devoid *ohne* (acc.), *bar* (gen.).
devote (to) *widmen.*
devour (to) *verschlingen, verzehren.*
dew *Tau, m.*
dial *Zifferblatt, n.* (clock); *Wählscheibe, m.*
    (phone).
dial (to) *wählen.*
dialect *Dialekt, m.*
dialogue *Dialog, m.*
diameter *Durchmesser, m.*
diamond *Diamant, m.*
diary *Tagebuch, n.*
dictate (to) *diktieren.*
dictation *Diktat, n.*
dictionary *Wörterbuch, n.; Lexikon, n.*
die (to) *sterben.*
diet *Diät, f.*
differ (to) *sich unterscheiden.*
difference *Unterschied, m.*
different *verschieden.*
difficult *schwierig.*
difficulty *Schwierigkeit, f.*
dig (to) *graben.*
digest (to) *verdauen.*
dignity *Würde, f.*
dim *trübe.*
dimension *Dimension, f.; Mass, n.; Ausmass, n.*
diminish (to) *vermindern.*
dining room *Speisesaal, m.*
dinner *Abendessen, n.*
dine (to) *essen, speisen.*
dip (to) *senken, (ein)tauchen.*
diplomacy *Diplomatie, f.*
diplomat *Diplomat, m.*
direct *direkt.*
direct (to) *den Weg zeigen* (show the way).
direction *Richtung, f.*
director *Direktor, m.*
directory *Adressbuch, n.; Telefonbuch*
    (phone), *n.*

dirt *Schmutz, m.*
dirty *schmutzig.*
disability *Unfähigkeit, f.;*
    Körperbehinderung, f.
disabled *unfähig, behindert.*
disadvantage *Nachteil, m.*
disagree (to) *uneinig sein, nicht zustimmen.*
disagreeable *unangenehm.*
disagreement *Meinungsverschiedenheit, f.*
disappear (to) *verschwinden.*
disappearance *Verschwinden, n.*
disappoint (to) *enttäuschen.*
disapprove (to) *missbilligen, ablehnen.*
disaster *Unglück, n.; Katastrophe, f.*
disastrous *unheilvoll, schrecklich.*
discharge *Entlassung, f.* (dismissal); *Abfeuern,*
    n. (gun).
discharge (to) *entlassen* (person); *abfeuern*
    (firearm), *abschiessen* (firearm).
discipline *Zucht, f., Disziplin, f.*
disclaim (to) *bestreiten.*
disclose (to) *enthüllen, offenbaren.*
disclosure *Enthüllung, f.; Mitteilung f.;*
    Offenbarung, f.
discomfort *Unbehaglichkeit, f.*
disconnect (to) *trennen, abschalten.*
discontent *unzufrieden.*
discontinue (to) *aufhören.*
discord *Zwietracht, f.*
discount *Diskonto, m.* (financial); *Rabatt, m.*
discourage (to) *entmutigen.*
discouragement *Entmutigung, f.*
discover (to) *entdecken.*
discovery *Entdeckung, f.*
discreet *diskret, vorsichtig.*
discretion *Besonnenheit, f.; Urteil, n.*
discuss (to) *besprechen, sich unterhalten*
    (über)
discussion *Besprechung, f.; Diskussion, f.*
disdain *Verachtung, f.*
disdain (to) *verschmähen, verachten.*
disease *Krankheit, f.*
disgrace *Schande, f.* (shame); *Ungnade, f.*
disguise *Verkleidung, f.*
disguise (to) *verkleiden.*
disgust *Ekel, m.; Abscheu, m.*
disgust (to) *(an)ekeln.*
disgusted *ekelhaft, angeekelt.*
dish *Speise, f.* (food); *Teller, m.* (plate).
dishonest *unehrlich.*
disk *Scheibe, f.*
diskette *Diskette, f.*
dislike *Widerwillen, m.; Abneigung, f.; der*
    Widerwille, m.
dislike (to) *nicht mögen, nicht lieben.*
dismiss (to) *entlassen.*
    dismissal *Entlassung, f.*
disobey (to) *nicht gehorchen.*
disorder *Unordnung, f.*

dispense (to) *verteilen.*
displace *verschieben, verrücken, verdrängen.*
display *Entfaltung f.* (unfold); *Schau, f.* (exposition).
displease (to) *missfallen, missachten.*
displeasure *Missfallen, n.*
disposal *Verfügung, f.*
dispose (to) *anordnen, verfügen.*
dispute *Streit, m.*
dispute (to) *streiten.*
dissolve (to) *auflösen.*
distance *Entfernung, f.*
distant *entfernt.*
distinct *deutlich.*
distinction *Auszeichnung, f.; Unterschied, m.* (difference).
distinguish (to) *unterscheiden.*
distort (to) *verdrehen.*
distract (to) *verwirren, ablenken.*
distress *Not, f.*
distress (to) *betrüben, beunruhigen.*
distribute (to) *verteilen.*
district *Distrikt, m.*
distrust *Misstrauen, n.*
distrust (to) *misstrauen.*
disturb (to) *stören.*
disturbance *Störung, f.*
ditch *Graben, m.*
dive (to) *tauchen.*
divide (to) *verteilen.*
divine *göttlich.*
division *Teilung, f.; Trennung, f.*
divorce (to) *scheiden.*
divorced *geschieden.*
dizziness *Schwindel, m.*
dizzy *schwindlig.*
do (to) *tun, machen.*
dock *Dock, n.; Anlegeplatz, m.*
doctor *Arzt, m.*
doctrine *Lehre, f.*
document *Urkunde, f.; Dokument, n.*
dog *Hund, m.*
doll *Puppe, f.*
dome *Kuppel, f.*
domestic *häuslich; einheimisch* (native).
domestic animal *Haustier, n.*
dominate (to) *beherrschen.*
door *Tür, f.*
dose *Dosis, f.*
dot *Punkt, m.*
double *doppelt.*
doubt *Zweifel, m.*
doubt (to) *zweifeln.*
doubtful *zweifelhaft.*
doubtless *ohne Zweifel.*
dough *Teig, m.*
down *unter* (dat. or acc.); *hinunter, herunter.*
dozen *Dutzend, n.*

draft *Wechsel, m.* (money); *Zeichnung, f.* (drawing); *draft; Zug, m.* (air); *ziehen, n.* (milit.); *Bier vom Fass* (beer), *n.*
drag (to) *schleppen.*
drain (to) *entwässern, abfließen lassen.*
drama *Drama, n.*
draw (to) *zeichen.*
draw back (to) *zurückziehen, zurückweichen.*
drawer *Schublade, f.*
drawing room *Gesellschaftszimmer, n.; Salon, m.*
dread *Furcht, f.*
dread (to) *fürchten.*
dreadful *furchtbar, schrecklich.*
dream *Traum, m.*
dream (to) *träumen.*
dreamer *Träumer, m.*
dress *Kleid, n.*
dress (to) *sich anziehen.*
dressmaker *Schneiderin, f.*
drink *Getränk, n.*
drink (to) *trinken.*
drip (to) *tropfen, tröpfeln.*
drive (to) *fahren.*
drive (computer) *Laufwerk, n.*
driver *Chauffeur, m.*
drop *Fall, m.; Tropfen, m.* (liquid).
drown (to) *ertrinken.*
drug *Droge, f.*
drug addiction *Rauschgiftsucht, f.*
drug dealer *Drogenhändler, m.; Pusher, m.* (coll.).
drugstore *Apotheke, f.; Drogerie, f.*
drum *Trommel, f.*
drunk *betrunken.*
dry *trocken.*
dry (to) *trocknen.*
dryness *Trockenheit, f.*
duchess *Herzogin, f.*
duck *Ente, f.*
due *Verfallszeit, f.; Fälligkeitstermin* (due date), *fällig sein* (to be due).
duke *Herzog, m.*
dull *trübe* (weather); *matt* (color); *dumpf* (sound), *fad(e)* (book).
dumb *stumm; dumm* (stupid).
   deaf and dumb *taubstumm.*
during *während* (gen.).
dust *Staub, m.*
dust (to) *abstauben; ausbürsten* (clothes).
dusty *staubig.*
Dutch *holländisch.*
duty *Pflicht, f.; Dienst, m.* (service); *Zoll, m.* (customs).
dwarf *Zwerg, m.*
dwell (to) *wohnen.*
dye *Farbe, f.*
dye (to) *färben.*

E

each *jeder.*
  each other   *einander.*
  each time   *jedesmal.*
eager *eifrig.*
eagle *Adler, m.*
ear *Ohr, n.*
early *früh.*
earn (to) *verdienen.*
earnest *ernst.*
earth *Erde, f.*
ease *Bequemlichkeit, f.* (comfort); *Ruhe, f.*
  (calm); *Linderung, f.* (relief);
  Leichtigkeit, f. (facility).
ease (to) *lindern, erleichtern.*
easily *leicht.*
east *Osten, m.*
Easter *Ostern, pl.*
eastern *östlich.*
easy *leicht.*
eat (to) *essen.*
echo *Echo, n.; Widerhall, m.*
echo (to) *widerhallen.*
economical *wirtschaftlich; sparsam.*
economize (to) *sparen.*
economy *Sparsamkeit, f.; Wirtschaft, f.* (of a
  country).
economy class *Touristenklasse, f.*
edge *Schneide, f.* (blade); *Rand, m.* (rim);
  Kante, f.; Vorteil (advantage), f.
edition *Ausgabe, f.; Auflage, f.*
editor *Redakteur, m. (-in) f.*
editorial *Leitartikel* (noun) *m.; redaktionell*
  (adj.).
education *Bildung, f.; Erziehung, f.*
effect *Wirkung, f.*
effective *wirkungsvoll.*
efficiency *Leistungsfähigkeit, f.*
effort *Anstrengung, f.; Bestreben, n.*
  (endeavor).
egg *Ei, n. (Eier, pl.).*
egoism *Egoismus, m.; Selbstsucht, f.*
eight *acht.*
eighteen *achtzehn.*
eighteenth *achtzehnt.*
eighth *achte, m. & f.*
eightieth *achtzigste, m. & f.*
eighty *achtzig.*
either *oder.*
  either . . . or   *entweder . . . oder.*
elastic *elastisch.*
elbow *Ellbogen, m.*
elder *älter.*
elderly *älterer, ältlich.*
eldest *Älteste, m. & f.*
elect (to) *erwählen.*
election *Wahl, f.*

elector *Wähler, m.*
electrical *elektrisch.*
electricity *Elektrizität, f.*
electronic mail (e-mail) *elektronische Post, f.*
electronic mail address *elektronischer*
  Briefkasten, m.
elegant *elegant.*
element *Element, n.*
elementary *elementar.*
elephant *Elefant, m.*
elevator *Aufzug, m.; Fahrstuhl, m.*
eleven *elf.*
eleventh *elfte.*
eliminate (to) *ausscheiden, beseitigen.*
eloquence *Beredsamkeit, f.; Redegabe, f.*
eloquent *beredt, redegewandt.*
else *ander, anders; sonst* (otherwise).
  anyone else   *irgend ein anderer.*
  elsewhere   *anderswo.*
  everybody else   *jeder andere.*
  nobody else   *sonst niemand.*
  someone else   *ein anderer.*
elude (to) *ausweichen, entgehen.*
embark (to) *(sich) einschiffen.*
embarrass (to) *in Verlegenheit bringen.*
embarrassing *unangenehm, beschämend.*
embarrassment *Verlegenheit, f.*
embassy *Botschaft, f.*
embody *verkörpern.*
embrace (to) *umarmen.*
embroidery *Stickerei, f.*
emerge (to) *herauskommen, hervortreten.*
emergency *Notfall, m.*
eminent *hervorragend.*
emotion *Erregung, f.; Rührung, f.*
emperor *Kaiser, m.*
emphasis *Betonung, f.*
emphasize (to) *betonen.*
emphatic *nachdrücklich.*
empire *Reich, n.*
employee *Angestellte, m. or f.*
employer *Arbeitgeber, m.*
employment *Arbeit, f.; Beschäftigung, f.;*
  Tätigkeit, f.
empty *leer.*
enable (to) *befähigen.*
enamel *Email, n.; Emaille, f.*
enclose (to) *einschließen.*
enclosure *Anlage, f.* (letter); *Einzäunung, f.*
  (fence).
encourage (to) *ermutigen.*
encouragement *Ermutigung, f.*
end *Ende, n.*
end (to) *enden, aufhören.*
endeavor *Bestreben, n.; Bemühung, f.*
endeavor (to) *sich bemühen.*
endorse (to) *unterzeichnen* (a check),
  gutheissen.
endure (to) *ertragen, aushalten.*

enemy *Feind, m. (-in) f.*
energy *Energie, f.*
energy crisis *Energiekrise, f.*
enforce (to) *durchsetzen.*
engage (to) *anstellen.*
engaged *beschäftigt (busy); verlobt.*
engagement *Verpflichtung, f. (appointment); Beschäftigung, f. (business); Verlobung, f. (marriage).*
engine *Maschine, f.; Lokomotive, f. (train).*
engineer *Ingenieur, m.*
English *englisch.*
engrave (to) *eingravieren.*
enjoy (to) *genießen, amüsieren.*
  enjoy oneself *sich amüsieren.*
enjoyment *Vergnügen, n.*
enlarge (to) *vergrößern.*
enlist (to) *sich freiwillig melden (military); anwerben (soldiers); Dienste in Anspruch nehmen (one's services).*
enormous *ungeheuer.*
enough *genug.*
enter (to) *hineingehen.*
  Enter! *Herein!*
entertain (to) *unterhalten.*
entertainment *Unterhaltung, f.; Schau, f. (show).*
enthusiasm *Begeisterung, f.*
enthusiastic *begeistert.*
entire *ganz.*
entitle (to) *berechtigen.*
entrance *Eingang, m.*
entrust (to) *anvertrauen.*
enumerate (to) *aufzählen.*
envelope *Umschlag, m.; Kuvert, n.*
envious *neidisch.*
envy *Neid, m.*
envy (to) *beneiden.*
episode *Episode, f.; Nebenhandlung, f.*
equal *gleich.*
equal (to) *gleichen.*
equality *Gleichheit, f.; Gleichberechtigung, f. (pol.).*
equator *Äquator, m.*
equilibrium *Gleichgewicht, n.*
equip (to) *ausrüsten.*
equipment *Ausrüstung, f.*
era *Zeitalter, n.*
erase (to) *ausstreichen, ausradieren.*
eraser *Gummi, m.*
erect (to) *errichten.*
err (to) *sich irren.*
errand *Auftrag, m.*
error *Irrtum, m.*
escalator *Rolltreppe, f.*
escape *Flucht, f.*
escape (to) *entlaufen.*
escort (to) *begleiten, eskortieren.*
especially *besonders.*

essay *Aufsatz, m.*
essence *Essenz, f. (extract); Wesen, n.*
essential *wesentlich.*
establish (to) *errichten, gründen.*
establishment *Gründung, f.*
estate *Vermögen, n. (wealth); Gut, n. (land).*
esteem *Achtung, f.*
esteem (to) *(hoch) schätzen, (hoch) achten.*
estimate *Kostenanschlag, m. (cost); Schätzung, f. (appraisal); Meinung (opinion).*
estimate (to) *veranschlagen, schätzen.*
eternal *ewig.*
eternity *Ewigkeit, f.*
euro *Euro, m.*
European *Europäer (noun) m.; europäisch (adj.).*
evade (to) *entfliehen.*
evasion *Ausflucht, f.*
eve *Vorabend, m.*
even *eben (adj.); sogar (adv.).*
evening *Abend, m.*
  Good evening! *Guten Abend!*
evening clothes *Gesellschaftsanzug, m.*
evening dress *Abendkleid, n. (woman's).*
event *Ereignis, n.*
ever *je, jemals.*
every *jeder.*
  everybody *jedermann.*
  everything *alles.*
  everywhere *überall.*
evidence *Beweis, m.; Zeugnis, n.*
evident *offenbar, klar.*
evil *Übel (noun) n.; schlecht (adj.).*
evoke (to) *hervorrufen.*
evolve (to) *herausarbeiten, sich entwickeln.*
exact *genau.*
exaggerate (to) *übertreiben.*
exaggeration *Übertreibung, f.*
exalt (to) *erheben, veredeln.*
examination *Prüfung, f.*
examine (to) *prüfen.*
example *Beispiel, n.*
exceed (to) *überschreiten.*
excel (to) *übertreffen.*
excellence *Vortrefflichkeit, f.*
excellent *vortrefflich, ausgezeichnet.*
except *ausgenommen; außer (dat.).*
except (to) *ausnehmen, ausschliessen.*
exception *Ausnahme, f.*
exceptional *außergewöhnlich.*
exceptionally *ausnahmsweise.*
excess *Übermaß, n.*
excessive *übermäßig.*
exchange *Tausch, m.*
exchange (to) *wechseln.*
excite (to) *aufregen.*
excitement *Aufregung, f.*
exclaim (to) *ausrufen.*

exclamation *Ausruf, m.*
exclude (to) *ausschließen.*
exclusive *auschliesslich.*
excursion *Ausflug, m.*
excuse *Verzeihung, f.; Entschuldigung, f.*
excuse (to) *verzeihen, entschuldigen.*
  Excuse me   *Verzeihung!*
    (Entschuldigung!)
execute (to) *ausführen* (carry out); *hinrichten*
  (put to death).
execution *Ausführung, f.* (of plan or idea);
  Hinrichtung, f. (of person).
exempt (to) *befreien.*
exercise *Übung, f.*
exercise (to) *üben.*
exert (to) *sich anstrengen.*
exertion *Anstrengung, f.*
exhaust (to) *erschöpfen.*
exhaustion *Erschöpfung, f.*
exhibit (to) *ausstellen.*
exhibition *Ausstellung, f.*
exile *Verbannung, f.*
exile (to) *verbannen.*
exist (to) *existieren.*
existence *Existenz, f.*
exit *Ausgang, m.*
expand (to) *(sich) ausdehnen.*
expansion *Ausdehnung, f.*
expensive *teuer.*
experience *Erfahrung, f.*
experience (to) *erfahren.*
experiment (to) *experimentieren.*
expert *Fachmann, m.*
expire (to) *verscheiden, ablaufen.*
explain (to) *erklären.*
explanation *Erklärung, f.*
explanatory *erklärend.*
explode (to) *explodieren.*
exploit *Heldentat, f.*
exploit (to) *ausnützen.*
explore (to) *erforschen.*
explosion *Explosion, f.*
export (to) *ausführen, exportieren.*
export *Ausfuhr, f.; Export, m.*
expose (to) *aussetzen.*
express *Schnellzug, m.* (train).
express (to) *ausdrücken.*
expression *Ausdruck, m.*
expressive *ausdrucksvoll.*
expulsion *Ausstoßung, f.; Vertreibung, f.*
exquisite *vorzüglich, köstlich.*
extend (to) *verlängern, ausdehnen.*
extensive *ausgedehnt.*
extent *Weite, f.* (distance); *Umfang, m.;*
  Verlängerung, f. (time).
exterior *Äußere* (noun) *n.; äußerlich* (adj.).
exterminate (to) *ausrotten.*
external *äußerlich, auswärtig.*
extinction *Erlöschen, n.*

extinguish (to) *erlöschen.*
extra *extra.*
extraordinary *außergewöhnlich.*
extravagant *verschwenderisch, überspannt.*
extreme *äußerst.*
eye *Auge, n.*
eyebrow *Augenbraue, f.*
eyeglasses *Brille, f.*
eyelash *Wimper, f.*
eyelid *Augenlid, n.*
eyesight *Sehkraft, f.*

F

fable *Fabel, f.*
face *Gesicht, n.*
face (to) *unter die Augen treten,*
  gegenüberstehen.
facilitate (to) *erleichtern.*
facility *Leichtigkeit, f.; Erleichterungen, f.*
facsimile *Faksimile, n.; Telefax, n.* (document,
  machine); *Telebrief, m.; Fax, n.*
fact *Tatsache, f.*
  in fact   *in der Tat.*
  as a matter of fact   *im übrigen.*
factory *Fabrik, f.*
factual *tatsächlich.*
faculty *Fähigkeit, f.* (ability); *Fakultät, f.*
  (school).
fade (to) *welken.*
faded *verschossen, verblichen* (color).
fail (to) *fehlen; unterlassen* (neglect);
  durchfallen (exam).
  without fail   *ganz gewiss, unfehlbar.*
failure *Misserfolg, m.*
faint (to) *ohnmächtig werden.*
fainting spell *Ohnmacht, f.*
fair *schön* (weather); *hell* (complexion);
  ehrlich (just), *gerecht, fair.*
  fair play   *ehrliches Spiel.*
faith *Glaube, m.* (religion); *Treue, f.*
faithful *treu.*
fall *Fall, m.; Sturz, m.; Herbst, m.* (autumn).
fall (to) *fallen, stürzen.*
false *falsch.*
fame *Ruhm, m.*
familiar *vertraut, bekannt.*
family *Familie, f.*
famine *Hungersnot, f.*
famous *berühmt.*
fan *Ventilator, m.* (ventilator); *Windfahre, f.* (of
  a windmill); *Lüfter, m.* (electric).
fancy *Neigung* (noun) *f.; fein* (adj.).
fantastic *fantastisch.*
far *weit, fern.*
farce *Posse, f.*
fare *Fahrpreis, m.*

farewell *Abschied, m.*
 Farewell! *Lebe wohl!*
farm *Bauernhof, m.*
farmer *Landwirt, m.*
farming *Landwirtschaft, f.*
farther *weiter, ferner.*
fashion *Mode, f.*
fashionable *elegant, modisch, modern.*
fast *schnell.*
fasten (to) *befestigen.*
fat *Fett* (noun) *n.; fett, dick* (adj.).
fatal *tödlich, fatal.*
fate *Schicksal, n.*
father *Vater, m.*
father-in-law *Schwiegervater, m.*
faucet *Wasserhahn, m.*
fault *Fehler, m.*
favor *Gunst, f.*
 Do me a favor. *Tun Sie mir einen*
  Gefallen!
favor (to) *vorziehen, bevortzugen,*
  begünstigen.
favorable *günstig, vorteilhaft.*
favorite *Günstling, m.; Liebling, m.;*
  Lieblings-, (adj.).
fax *Telefax, m.* (document, machine); *Fax, m.*
fax machine *Telefax, m.; Telefaxgerät, n.*
fear *Furcht, f.*
fear (to) *fürchten.*
fearless *furchtlos.*
feather *Feder, f.*
feature *(Gesichts)zug, m.;* (facial) *Merkmal,*
  n.; Film, m. (movie).
February *Februar, m.*
federal *Bundes-, föderativ* (adj.).
federation *Staatenbund, -e, m.; Bundesstaat,*
  -en, m.
fee *Gebühr, f.*
feeble *schwach.*
feed (to) *füttern.*
feel (to) *fühlen.*
feeling *Gefühl, n.*
fellow *Kamerad, m.*
fellowship *Kameradschaft, f.; Gemeinschaft, f.*
female *weiblich.*
feminine *fraulich.*
fence *Zaun, m.*
fencing *Fechten, n.*
fender *Kotflügel, m.*
ferocious *wild.*
ferry *Fähre, f.*
fertile *fruchtbar.*
fertilize (to) *befruchten.*
fertilizer *Düngemittel, n.; Dünger, m.*
fervent *inbrünstig, feurig.*
fervor *Inbrunst, f.*
festival *Fest, n.*
fetch (to) *holen.*
fever *Fieber, n.*

few *wenige.*
 a few *ein paar.*
fiction *Dichtung, f.*
field *Acker, m.; Feld, n.*
fierce *wild.*
fiery *feurig*
fifteen *fünfzehn.*
fifteenth *fünfzehnte.*
fifth *fünfte.*
fiftieth *fünfzigste.*
fifty *fünfzig.*
fig *Feige, f.*
fight *Kampf, m.*
fight (to) *kämpfen.*
figure *Figur, f.; Ziffer* (number).
file *Feile, f.* (tool); *Registratur, f.;*
  Briefordner, m.
fill (to) *füllen.*
filling (tooth) *Füllung, f.*
film *Film, m.*
filthy *schmutzig.*
final *endgültig.*
finance *Finanz, f.*
finance (to) *finanzieren.*
financial *finanziell.*
find (to) *finden.*
fine *Geldstrafe* (noun) *f.; fein* (adj.) (opp. of
  coarse); *schön* (adj.) (elegant).
finger *Finger, m.*
finish (to) *beenden.*
fire *Feuer, n.*
fireman *Feuerwehrmann, m.*
fireplace *Kamin, m.*
firm *Firma,* (noun) *f.; fest, stark* (adj.).
first *erster.*
 at first *zuerst.*
fish *Fisch, m.*
fish (to) *fischen.*
fisherman *Fischer, m.*
fishing *Fischen, n.; Angeln, n.*
fist *Faust, f.*
fit *Anfall,* (noun) *m.; passend* (adj.)
  (becoming); *tauglich* (adj.) (capable).
fitness *Angemessenheit, f.; Eignung, f.*
five *fünf.*
fix (to) *reparieren.*
flag *Fahne, f.*
flame *Flamme, f.*
flank *Seite, f.*
flash *Blitz, m.* (lightning); *Aufflammen, n.*
flashlight *Taschenlampe, f.; Blitzlicht, n.,*
  (camera flash).
flat *flach.*
flatter (to) *schmeicheln.*
flatterer *Schmeichler, m.*
flattery *Schmeichelei, f.*
flavor *Aroma, n.; Geschmack, m.*
fleet *Flotte, f.*
flesh *Fleisch, n.*

flexibility *Biegsamkeit, f.*
flexible *biegsam.*
flight *Flug, m.*
fling (to) *werfen, Schleudern.*
flint *Kieselstein, m.; Feuerstein, n.*
float (to) *treiben.*
flood *Überschwemmung, f.; Flut, f.*
flood (to) *überschwemmen.*
floor *Boden, m.; Stock, m. (story).*
floppy disk *Floppy-disk, f.; Diskette, f.*
flourish (to) *blühen.*
flourishing *blühend.*
flow (to) *fließen, strömen.*
flower *Blume, f.*
fluid *flüssig.*
fly *Fliege, f.*
fly (to) *fliegen.*
foam *Schaum, m.*
fog *Nebel, m.*
fold *Falte, f.*
fold (to) *falten.*
foliage *Laubwerk, n.*
follow (to) *folgen.*
following *folgend.*
fond *zärtlich, liebevoll, zugetan.*
fondness *Zärtlichkeit, f.*
food *Essen, n.*
fool *Narr, m.*
foolish *töricht, lächerlich.*
foot *Fuß, m.*
football *Fußball, m.; Fußballspiel, m.*
footstep *Schritt, m.*
for *für (acc.); zu (dat.); wegen (gen.) (on account of); denn (because).*
   as for me   *was mich betrifft.*
   for a year   *während eines Jahres.*
   for example   *zum Beispiel.*
   word for word   *Wort für Wort.*
forbid (to) *verbieten.*
force *Kraft, f.; Gewalt, f.*
force (to) *zwingen.*
foreground *Vordergrund, m.*
forehead *Stirn, f.*
foreign *fremd, ausländisch.*
foreigner *Fremder, m.; Ausländer, m.*
forest *Wald, m.*
forget (to) *vergessen.*
forgetfulness *Vergesslichkeit, f.*
forget-me-not *Vergissmeinnicht, n.*
forgive (to) *vergeben, verzeihen.*
forgiveness *Vergebung, f.*
fork *Gabel, f.*
form *Form, f.*
formal *offiziell, formell.*
formation *Bildung, f.*
former *früher; erster (as opposed to latter), vorherig, ehemalig.*
formerly *vormals.*
formula *Formel, f.*

forsake (to) *verlassen.*
fort *Festung, f.*
fortieth *vierzigste.*
fortunate *glücklich.*
fortunately *glücklicherweise.*
fortune *Vermögen, n.; Glück, n. (luck).*
forty *vierzig.*
forward *vorwärts.*
forward (to) *absenden, nachschicken.*
foster (to) *pflegen.*
foul *faul.*
found (to) *gründen.*
foundation *Gründung, f.; Grundlage, f.*
founder *Gründer, m.*
fountain *Brunnen, m.*
fountain pen *Füllfederhalter, m.*
four *vier.*
fourteen *vierzehn.*
fourteenth *vierzehnte.*
fourth *vierte.*
fowl *Geflügel, n.*
fox *Fuchs, m.*
fragile *zerbrechlich.*
fragment *Bruchstück, n.*
fragrance *Duft, m.*
fragrant *duftig.*
frail *zart, gebrechlich.*
frame *Rahmen, m.*
frame (to) *rahmen.*
frank *aufrichtig, freimütig.*
frankness *Offenheit, f.*
free *frei.*
freedom *Freiheit, f.*
freeze (to) *frieren.*
freight *Fracht, f.*
French *französisch.*
frequent *häufig.*
frequently *oft, öfters, häufig.*
fresh *frisch.*
friction *Reibung, f.; Friktion, f.*
Friday *Freitag, m.*
fried *gebraten.*
friend *Freund, m.*
friendly *freundlich.*
friendship *Freundschaft, f.*
frighten (to) *erschrecken.*
frightening *schrecklich, erschreckend.*
fringe *Rand, m.*
frivolity *Leichtsinn, f.*
frog *Frosch, m.*
from *von, aus (dat.); nach (dat.) (according to).*
   from morning till night   *von früh bis spät.*
   from time to time   *von Zeit zu Zeit.*
   from top to bottom   *von oben bis unten.*
front *Vorderseite, f.; Front, f. (military).*
frozen *gefroren.*
fruit *Frucht, sing. f.; Obst, coll., n.*
fry (to) *braten*

   fried eggs *Spiegeleier, pl.*
   fried potatoes *Bratkartoffeln, pl.*
frying pan *Bratpfanne, f.*
fuel *Brennstoff, m.; Treibstoff, m.*
fulfill (to) *erfüllen.*
full *voll.*
fully *voll.*
fun *Scherz, m.; Spaß, m.*
   to have fun *sich amüsieren.*
   to make fun *sich lustig machen.*
function *Funktion,* (math) *f.; Tätigkeit, f.; amtliche Pflicht, f.*
function (to) *funktionieren.*
fund *Fonds, m.; Kapital, m.*
fundamental *grundlegend; wesentlich.*
funeral *Begräbnis, n.*
funny *komisch.*
fur *Pelz, m.*
furious *wütend, rasend.*
furnace *Ofen, m.*
furnish (to) *möblieren.*
furniture *Möbel, f.*
furrow *Furche,* (agric.) *f.; Runzel* (on skin), *f.*
further *weiter.*
fury *Wut, f.*
future *Zukunft* (noun) *f.; zukünftig* (adj.).

G

gaiety *Fröhlichkeit, f.; Heiterkeit, f.*
gain *Gewinn, m.*
gain (to) *gewinnen; zunehmen* (weight).
gallant *tapfer, ritterlich.*
gallery *Galerie, f.*
gallop *Galopp, m.*
gamble (to) *spielen.*
game *Spiel, n.*
garage *Garage, f.*
garbage *Abfall, m.; Müll, m.*
garden *Garten, m.*
gardener *Gärtner, m.*
garlic *Knoblauch, n.*
gas *Gas, n.*
gasoline *Benzin, n.*
gate *Tor, n.; Sperre, f.* (railroad).
gather (to) *sammeln, sich versammeln*
gay *lustig.*
gear *Getriebe, n.; Gang, m.* (motor).
gem *Edelstein, m.*
general *General, m.* (military); *allgemein* (adj.).
generality *Allgemeinheit, f.*
generalize (to) *verallgemeinern.*
generation *Generation, f.*
generosity *Freigebigkeit, f.; Grossmut, f.* (magnanimity).
generous *großzügig.*

genius *Genie, n.*
genteel *fein, vornehm.*
gentle *artig, vornehm, sanft.*
gentleman *Herr, m.*
gentleness *Sanftheit, f.*
genuine *echt.*
geographical *geographisch.*
geography *Geographie, f.*
germ *Keim, m.; Bakterien* (us. pl.); *Bazillus, m.*
German *Deutsche(r)* (noun) *m.; deutsch* (adj.).
gesture *Gebärde, f.*
get (to) *bekommen, erwerben, holen* (fetch); *werden* (become).
   get down *hinunterkommen.*
   get off *absteigen.*
   get up *aufstehen.*
ghastly *grässlich.*
ghost *Geist, m.*
giant *Riese, m.*
gift *Geschenk, n.*
gifted *begabt.*
girl *Mädchen, n.*
give (to) *geben.*
   to give back *zurückgeben.*
glad *froh.*
gladly *gern.*
glance *Blick, m.*
glass *Glas, n.*
glasses (eyeglasses) *Brille, f.*
gleam *Schein, m.; Schimmer, m.*
gleam (to) *scheinen, glänzen*
glitter *Glanz, m.; Glitzern, n.*
globe *Kugel, f.; Globus, m.*
gloomy *düster.*
glorious *glorreich.*
glory *Ruhm, m.*
glove *Handschuh, m.*
glow *Glut, f.; Glühen, n.*
glue *Leim, m.*
go (to) *gehen.*
   to go away *weggehen, fortgehen.*
   to go back *zurückgehen.*
   to go in *hineingehen.*
   to go out *herausgehen, ausgehen.*
   to go to bed *zu Bett gehen.*
God *Gott, m.*
godchild *Patenkind, n.*
godfather *Pate, m.*
godmother *Patin, f.*
gold *Gold, n.*
golden *golden.*
golf *Golf* (spiel), *n.*
good *gut.*
   Good afternoon! *Guten Tag!*
   Good evening! *Guten Abend!*
   Good morning! *Guten Morgen!*
   Good night! *Gute Nacht!*
good-bye *Auf Wiedersehen!*
good-looking *gut aussehend.*

goodness *Güte, f.*
goods *Waren, pl.*
goodwill *guter Wille, m.*
goose *Gans, f.*
gossip *Klatsch, m.; Geschwätz, n.*
gossip (to) *klatschen.*
govern (to) *regieren.*
grace *Gnade, f.; Anmut, f.* (charm).
graceful *anmutig, hold, graziös.*
grade *Grad, m.*
grain *Korn, n.; Getreide, n.; Körnchen, n.*
    (sand).
grammar *Grammatik, f.*
grand *großartig.*
grandchild *Enkelkind, n.*
granddaughter *Enkelin, f.*
grandfather *Großvater, m.*
grandmother *Großmutter, f.*
grandson *Enkel, m.*
grant *Bewilligung, f.; Schenkung, f.*
grant (to) *bewilligen, gestatten.*
grape *Weintraube, f.*
grapefruit *Pampelmuse, f.*
grasp *Griff, m.*
grasp (to) *greifen, fassen, begreifen.*
grass *Gras, n.*
grateful *dankbar.*
gratitude *Dankbarkeit, f.*
grave *Grab* (noun) *n.; ernst* (adj.).
gravy *Sauce, f.; (Braten) sosse, f.*
gray *grau.*
grease *Fett, n.*
great *gross, herrlich* (coll.); *wunderbar*
    (coll.).
greatness *Größe, f.*
greedy *gierig, gefräßig.*
green *grün.*
greet (to) *grüßen.*
greeting *Gruß, m.*
grief *Kummer, m.*
grieve (to) *sich grämen.*
grin (to) *grinsen.*
grind (to) *mahlen.*
groan *Stöhnen, n.*
groan (to) *stöhnen.*
grocer *Kolonialwarenhändler, m.*
grocery store *Kolonialwarenladen, m.*
gross *grob.*
ground *Boden, m.*
group *Gruppe, f.*
group (to) *gruppieren.*
grow (to) *wachsen; an (bauen)* (crops);
    züchten (animals).
growth *Gewächs, n.*
grudge *Groll, m.*
guaranteed *garantiert.*
guess *Vermutung, f.*
guess (to) *raten.*
guide *Führer, m.*

gum *Zahnfleisch, n.* (teeth).
    chewing gum *Kaugummi, n.*
gun *Gewehr, n.*
gush *Guss, m.*
gush (to) *hervorströmen.*

H

habit *Gewohnheit, f.*
habitual *gewöhnlich.*
hail *Hagel, m.*
hair *Haar, n.*
hairdo *Frisur, f.*
hairdresser *Frisör, m.; Friseuse, f.*
hairpin *Haarnadel, f.*
half *halb.*
hall *Halle, f.; Saal, m.; Diele, f.*
ham *Schinken, m.*
hammer *Hammer, m.*
hand *Hand, f.*
hand (to) *(über) reichen.*
handbag *Handtasche, f.*
handful *Handvoll, f.*
handkerchief *Taschentuch, n.*
handle *Griff, m.*
handle (to) *anfassen, behandeln.*
handsome *stattlich, hübsch, schön.*
handy *handlich.*
hang (to) *hängen.*
happen (to) *geschehen.*
happiness *Glück, n.*
happy *glücklich.*
harbor *Hafen, m.*
hard *hart.*
hard disk *Festplatte, f.*
hard drive *Festplattenlaufwerk, n.*
harden (to) *härten.*
hardly *kaum.*
hardness *Härte, f.*
hardware *Eisenwaren, pl.*
hardware store *Eisenwarengeschäft, n.*
hardy *abgehärtet, robust, kräftig.*
hare *Hase, m.*
harm *Schaden, m.*
harm (to) *schädigen.*
harmful *schädlich.*
harmless *harmlos.*
harmonious *harmonisch.*
harmony *Harmonie, f.*
harsh *rauh, hart* (touch); *sauer* (taste); *grell*
    (sound/color); *schroff.*
harvest *Ernte, f.*
haste *Eile, f.*
hasten (to) *eilen.*
hat *Hut, m.*
hate *Hass, m.*
hate (to) *hassen.*

hateful *gehässig.*

hatred *Hass, m.*

haughty *hochmutig, arrogant.*

have (to) *haben.*

haven *Hafen, m.; Zufluchtsort, m.; Asyl, n.*

hay *Heu, n.*

he *er.*

head *Kopf, m.* (of a person); *Chef, m.* (of a firm); *Haupt, n.* (of a government).

headache *Kopfschmerzen, pl.*

headphones *Kopfhörer (pl.).*

heal (to) *heilen.*

health *Gesundheit, f.*

healthy *gesund.*

heap *Haufen, m.*

heap (to) *(auf)häufen.*

hear (to) *hören.*

hearing *Gehör, n.*

heart *Herz, n.*

heaven *Himmel, m.*

heavy *schwer.*

hedge *Hecke, f.*

heel *Ferse, f.* (of the foot); *Absatz, m.* (of a shoe).

height *Höhe, f.*

heir *Erbe, m.*

hell *Hölle, f.*

helm *Ruder, n.*

help *Hilfe, f.*

help (to) *helfen.*

helpful *behilflich.*

hem *Saum, m.*

hen *Huhn, n.; Henne, f.*

her *ihr* (pers. pr., dat.; poss. adj.); *sie* (pers. pr., acc.).

herb *Kraut, n.; Gewürzkraut, n.* (culinary).

herd *Herde, f.*

here *hier.*

herewith *hiermit.*

hero *Held, m.*

heroic *heldenhaft, heroisch.*

heroine *Heldin, f.*

herring *Hering, m.*

hers *ihr(-er, -e, -es).*

herself *sie (ihr) selbst; sich.*

hesitate (to) *zögern.*

hide (to) *verstecken.*

hideous *scheußlich.*

high *hoch.*

higher *höher.*

hill *Hügel, m.*

him *ihn* (acc.); *ihm* (dat.).

himself *er (ihm, ihn) selbst; sich.*

hinder (to) *hindern.*

hint *Wink, m.*

hint (to) *andeuten.*

hip *Hüfte, f.*

hire (to) *mieten.*

his *sein* (poss. adj.); *sein(-er, -e, -es)* (pron.).

hiss (to) *zischen.*

historian *Geschichtsschreiber, m. (-in) f.*

historical *historisch.*

history *Geschichte, f.*

hoarse *heiser.*

hoe *Hacke, f.*

hold *Halt, m.*

hold (to) *halten.*

hole *Loch, n.*

holiday *Feiertag, m.*

holidays *Ferien, pl.* (vacation).

holy *heilig.*

homage *Huldigung, f.*

home *Heim, n.*

homosexual *homosexuell* (adj.); *Homosexuelle(r), m./f.*

honest *ehrlich.*

honesty *Ehrlichkeit, f.*

honey *Honig, m.*

honeymoon *Flitterwochen, pl.; Hochzeitsreise, f.* (honeymoon trip).

honor *Ehre, f.*

honor (to) *ehren.*

honorable *ehrenvoll.*

hood *Kapuze, f.; Haube n.* (car); *Verdeck, n.*

hoof *Huf, m.*

hook *Haken, m.*

hope *Hoffnung, f.*

hope (to) *hoffen.*

hopeful *hoffnungsvoll.*

hopeless *hoffnungslos.*

horizon *Horizont, m.*

horizontal *horizontal.*

horn (auto) *Hupe, f.*

horrible *schrecklich.*

horse *Pferd, n.*

horseback (on) *zu Pferde.*

hosiery *Strümpfe, f.; Strumpfwaren, pl.*

hospitable *gastfreundlich.*

hospital *Krankenhaus, n.; Hospital, n.*

host *Gastgeber, m.; Wirt, m.*

hostess *Gastgeberin, f.; Wirtin, f.*

hostile *feindlich.*

hot *heiß.*

hotel *Hotel, n.; Gasthof, m.*

hour *Stunde, f.*

house *Haus, n.*

household *Haushalt, m.*

housekeeper *Haushälterin, f.*

housemaid *Hausmädchen, n.*

how *wie*
   How are you?   *Wie geht's?*

however *dennoch, wie . . . auch immer.*

howl *Heulen, n.*

howl (to) *heulen.*

human *menschlich.*

humane *human.*

humanity *Menschlichkeit, f.*

humble *demütig.*

humid *feucht.*
humiliate *erniedrigen, demütigen.*
humility *Demut, f.*
humor *Humor, m.*
hundred *hundert.*
hundredth *hundertste.*
hunger *Hunger, m.*
hungry *hungrig.*
hunt *Jagd, f.*
hunter *Jäger, m.*
hurricane *Orkan, m.*
hurry *Eile, f.*
     Hurry up!   *Beeilen Sie sich!*
hurt (to) *verwunden; verletzen.*
husband *Mann, m.; Gatte, m.*
hush (to) *schweigen.*
hyphen *Bindestrich, m.*
hypocrite *Heuchler, m.*

I

I *ich.*
ice *Eis, n.*
ice cream *Eis, n.; Speiseeis, n.*
icy *eisig.*
idea *Idee, f.; Einfall, m.*
ideal *Ideal,* (noun) *n.; ideal* (adj.).
idealism *Idealismus, m.*
idealist *Idealist, m.*
identical *identisch.*
identity *Identität, f.*
idiot *Idiot, m.*
idle *müssig, träge, unbeschäftigt.*
idleness *Müßigkeit, f.; Faulheit, f.; Trägheit, f.*
if *wenn, ob.*
ignoble *unedel.*
ignorance *Unwissenheit, f.*
ignorant *unwissend.*
ignore (to) *ignorieren, nicht beachten.*
ill *krank.*
illegal *gesetzwidrig, ungesetzlich, illegal.*
illness *Krankheit, f.*
illusion *Täuschung, f.*
illustrate (to) *illustrieren.*
illustration *Abbildung, f.*
image *Einbildungskraft, f.; Ebenbild, n.; Bild, n.*
imagination *Fantasie, f.*
imagine (to) *sich einbilden.*
imitate (to) *nachahmen.*
imitation *Nachahmung, f.*
immediate *unmittelbar.*
immediately *sogleich, sofort.*
immigrant *Immigrant, m.*
imminent *bevorstehend, unmittelbar.*
immobility *Unbeweglichkeit, f.*
immoral *unmoralisch.*

immorality *Unsittlichkeit, f.*
immortal *unsterblich.*
immortality *Unsterblichkeit, f.*
impartial *unparteiisch.*
impassible *gefühllos.*
impatience *Ungeduld, f.*
imperfect *Vergangenheit* (noun) *f.* (in grammar); *unvollkommen* (adj.).
impertinence *Unverschämtheit, f.*
impetuosity *Ungestüm, n.*
import *Einfuhr, f.; Import, m.*
import (to) *einführen, importieren.*
important *wichtig.*
imported *importiert.*
importer *Importeur, m.*
impossible *unmöglich.*
impress (to) *Eindruck machen, beeindrucken.*
impression *Eindruck, m.*
imprison (to) *einsperren.*
improve (to) *verbessern.*
improvement *Verbesserung, f.*
improvise (to) *improvisieren.*
imprudence *Unvorsichtigkeit, f.; Unklugheit, f.*
imprudent *unklug.*
impulse *Antrieb, m. Anregung, f.*
impure *unrein.*
in *in* (dat.).
inadequate *unzulänglich, ungenügend.*
inaugurate (to) *eröffnen.*
incapable *unfähig.*
incapacity *Unfähigkeit, f.*
inch *Zoll, m.*
incident *Vorfall, m.*
include (to) *einschließen.*
included *eingeschlossen.*
income *Einkommen, n.*
income tax *Einkommensteuer, f.*
incomparable *unvergleichlich, nicht vergleichbar.*
incompatible *unvereinbar.*
incompetent *unfähig, unzulänglich.*
incomplete *unvollständig.*
inconvenient *lästig, unbequem, beschwerlich.*
incorrect *unrichtig.*
increase *Erhöhung, f.*
increase (to) *sich vermehren, erhöhen.*
incredible *unglaublich.*
indebted *verschuldet; verpflichtet.*
indecision *Unentschlossenheit, f.*
indeed *tatsächlich.*
independence *Unabhängigkeit, f.*
independent *unabhängig.*
index *Inhaltsverzeichnis, n.*
index *Register* (in a book).
index card *Karteikarte, f.*
index finger *Zeigefinger, m.*
indicate (to) *hinweisen, andeuten, bezeichnen.*
indicative *Indikativ* (noun) *m.* (in grammar); *anzeigend* (adj.); *hinweisend* (adj.).

indifference *Gleichgültigkeit, f.*
indifferent *gleichgültig.*
indigestion *Verdauungsstörung, f.*
indignant *empört.*
indignation *Entrüstung, f; Empörung, f.*
indirect *indirekt.*
indiscreet *indiskret.*
indiscretion *Unbedachtsamkeit, f.;*
    Indiskretion, f. (polit.).
indispensable *unentbehrlich.*
individual *einzeln, persönlich.*
indolent *träge.*
indoors *im Hause, zu Hause.*
induce (to) *veranlassen, verursachen.*
indulge (to) *sich hingeben.*
indulgence *Verwöhnung, f.*
indulgent *nachsichtig.*
industrial *industriell.*
industrious *fleißig.*
industry *Industrie, f.*
inefficient *unfähig.*
infancy *Kindheit, f.*
infant *kleines Kind, n.; Baby, n.; Säugling, m.*
infantry *Infanterie, f.*
infection *Infektion, f.*
inferior *minderwertig.*
infernal *höllisch.*
infinite *unendlich.*
infinity *Unendlichkeit, f.*
influence *Einfluss, m.*
influence (to) *beeinflussen.*
inform (to) *benachrichtigen.*
information *Auskunft, f.; Nachricht, f.* (news).
ingenious *geistig.*
ingenuity *Scharfsinn, m.*
inhabit (to) *bewohnen.*
inhabitant *Einwohner, m.*
inherit (to) *erben.*
inheritance *Erbgut, n.*
inhuman *unmenschlich.*
initial *Anfangsbuchstabe, m.*
initial (adj.) *anfänglich, ursprünglich.*
initiate (to) *anfangen, einleiten, einführen.*
initiative *Initiative, f.*
injection *Einspritzung, f.; Spritze, f.*
injury *Verletzung, f.*
injustice *Ungerechtigkeit, f.*
ink *Tinte, f.*
inkwell *Tintenfass, n.*
inland *Binnenland, n.; innenländisch,* (adj.).
inn *Gasthof, m.; Gasthaus, n.*
innkeeper *Gastwirt, m. (-in.) f.*
innocent *unschuldig.*
innocence *Unschuld, f.*
inquire (to) *sich erkundigen, nachfragen.*
inquiry *Erkundigung, f.; Anfrage, f.;*
    Nachfrage, f.
insane *geisteskrank.*
inscription *Inschrift, f.*

insect *Insekt, n.*
insensible *unempfindlich.*
inseparable *unzertrennlich.*
inside *drinnen.*
insight *Einsicht, f.*
insignificant *unbedeutend.*
insincere *unaufrichtig, heuchlerisch.*
insinuate (to) *andeuten.*
insist (to) *bestehen auf.*
insistence *Beharren, n.; Bestehen, n.*
inspect (to) *besichtigen, untersuchen.*
inspection *Besichtigung, f.; Untersuchung, f.*
inspiration *Inspiration, f., Begeisterung, f.*
inspire *begeistern, erwecken.*
install (to) *einstellen, installieren.*
installment *Rate, f.; Teilzahlung, f.*
instance *Beispiel, n.; Fall, m.*
instant *Augenblick, m.*
instantly *sofort.*
instead of *anstatt* (gen.).
institute (to) *einführen, gründen.*
institution *Anstalt, f.*
instruct (to) *unterrichten.*
instructor *Lehrer, m.; Erzieher, n.*
instruction *Anweisung, f.; Unterricht, m.*
    (teaching).
instrument *Instrument, n.*
insufficient *ungenügend.*
insult *Beleidigung, f.*
insult (to) *beleidigen.*
insurance *Versicherung, f.*
insure (to) *versichern.*
intact *unversehrt, unberührt.*
intellectual *intellektuell.*
intelligence *Intelligenz, f.*
intelligent *intelligent.*
intend (to) *beabsichtigen.*
intense *intensiv.*
intensity *Heftigkeit, f.*
intent *Absicht, m.; Plan, m.*
intent (adj.) *eifrig, beschäftigt (mit), gerichtet,*
    gespannt.
intention *Absicht, f.*
interest *Interesse, n.*
interesting *interessant.*
interfere (to) *sich einmischen, dazwischen*
    treten.
interior *Innere, n.*
intermediate *mittel.*
intermission *Pause, f.*
international *international.*
interpret (to) *interpretieren, übersetzen;*
    deuten (emotion), *dolmetschen.*
interpreter *Dolmetscher, m.*
interrupt (to) *unterbrechen.*
interval *Pause, f.; Zwischenzeit, f.*
interview *Interview, n.; Besprechung, f.*
intimacy *Vertrautheit, f.*
intimate *vertraut, zu verstehen geben.*

into *in* (dat. or acc.).
intolerant *unduldsam, intolerant.*
intonation *Tonfall, m.* (phonetics).
introduce (to) *vorstellen.*
introduction *Vorstellung, f.*
intuition *unmittelbare Erkenntnis, f.;*
      Anschauungsvermögen, n. (intuitive
      faculty).
invade (to) *einfallen, eindringen (in),*
      angreifen.
invent (to) *erfinden.*
invention *Erfindung, f.*
inventor *Erfinder, m. (-in) f.*
invert (to) *umkehren, umdrehen.*
invest (to) *investieren; anlegen* (money).
investment *Kapitalanlage, f.*
invisible *unsichtbar.*
invitation *Einladung, f.*
invite (to) *einladen.*
invoice *Faktura, f.; Warenrechnung, f.*
invoke (to) *anflehen, beschwören.*
involve (to) *verwickeln.*
iodine *Jod, n.*
Irish *irländisch.*
iron *Eisen, n.* (metal); *Bügeleisen, n.* (for
      ironing).
iron (to) *bügeln, plätten.*
irony *Ironie, f.*
irrefutable *unwiderlegbar.*
irregular *unregelmäßig.*
irresistible *unwiderstehlich.*
irritate (to) *reizen, ärgern.*
island *Insel, f.*
isolate (to) *absondern, isolieren.*
Israel *Israel, n.*
Israeli *israeli* (adj.), *Israeli, m./f., Israelit(in),*
      m./f.
issue *Ausgabe, f.*
it *es.*
Italian *Italiener* (noun) *m.; italienisch* (adj.).
itch (to) *jucken.*
its *sein* (poss. adj.); *sein (-er, -e, -es),* (poss.
      pron.), *dessen, deren.*
itself *selbst,* (emphatic), *sich* (refl.), *für sich*
      (by itself), *an sich* (in itself).
ivory *Elfenbein, n.*
ivy *Efeu, n.*

J

jacket *Jacke, f., Jackett, m.*
jail *Gefängnis, n.*
jam *Marmelade, f.*
January *Januar, m.*
Japanese *Japaner* (noun) *m.; japanisch* (adj.).
jar *Krug, m.*
jaw *Kiefer, m.*

jealous *eifersüchtig.*
jealousy *Eifersucht, f.*
jelly *Gelee, n.*
jewel *Juwel, m.*
jeweler *Juwelier, m.*
Jewish *jüdisch.*
job *Arbeit, f.; Stellung, f.; Posten, m.; Job, m.*
join (to) *sich anschließen an, verbinden,*
      zusammenfügen (mit).
joint *Gelenk, n.*
joke *Witz, m.; Scherz, m.; Spass, m.*
joke (to) *scherzen.*
jolly *lustig.*
journalist *Journalist, m.*
journey *Reise, f.*
joy *Freude, f.*
joyous *freudig.*
judge *Richter, m.; Schiedsrichter, m.* (sports).
judge (to) *urteilen.*
judgment *Urteil, n.; gerichtliche*
      Entscheidung, f.
judicial *gerichtlich.*
juice *Saft, m.*
July *Juli, m.*
jump *Sprung, m.; Satz, m.*
jump (to) *springen.*
June *Juni, m.*
junior *jünger.*
jungle *Dschungel, m.*
just *recht* (fair); *gerecht* (justice); *gerade*
      (recent).
justice *Gerechtigkeit, f.*
justify (to) *rechtfertigen.*

K

keen *scharf.*
keep (to) *behalten* (retain), *hindern* (hinder),
      aufbewahren.
  keep off   *abhalten.*
  keep on   *fortfahren.*
  keep up   *aufrecht erhalten.*
kernel *Kern, m.*
kettle *Kessel, m.*
key *Schlüssel, m.*
keyboard (computer) *Tastatur, f.*
kick *Fusstritt, m.*
kick (to) *ausschlagen, treten, einen Fußtritt*
      geben.
kidneys *Nieren, pl.*
kill (to) *töten.*
kin *Blutsverwandtschaft, f.*
kind *Art* (noun) *f.; gütig* (adj.).
kindly *freundlich.*
kindness *Güte, f.; Freundlichkeit, f.*
king *König, m.*
kingdom *Königreich, n.*

kiosk *kiosk, m.; Verkaufsstand, m.*
kiss *Kuss, m.*
kiss (to) *küssen.*
kitchen *Küche, f.*
kite *Drache, m.*
knee *Knie, n.*
kneel (to) *knieen.*
knife *Messer, n.*
knight *Ritter, m.*
knit (to) *stricken.*
knock *Schlag, m.; Hieb, m.* (beating);
    Klopfen, n.
knock (to) *klopfen, schlagen, hauen, stoßen;*
    anklopfen (door).
knot *Knoten, m.*
know (to) *wissen* (have knowledge of); *kennen*
    (be acquainted with).
knowledge *Kenntnis, f.*

L

label *Etikett, n.; Marke* (brand), *f.*
labor *Arbeit, f.*
laboratory *Laboratorium, n.*
laborer *Arbeiter, m. (-in) f.*
lace *Spitze, f.* (ornamental); *Senkel, m.* (of a
    shoe).
lack *Mangel, m.*
lack (to) *mangeln.*
lady *Dame, f.*
lake *See, m.*
lamb *Lamm, n.*
lame *lahm.*
lamp *Lampe, f.*
land *Land, n.*
land (to) *landen.*
landscape *Landschaft, f.*
language *Sprache, f.*
languish (to) *schmachten.*
languor *Schlaffheit, f.*
lantern *Laterne, f.*
large *groß.*
laser *Laser, m.*
laser beam *Laserstrahl, m.*
laser printer *Laserdrucker, m.*
last *letzt.*
    last year   *voriges Jahr.*
last (to) *dauern.*
lasting *dauernd.*
latch *Klinke, f.* (knob); *Drücker, m.*
late *spät.*
lately *kürzlich.*
latter *letzter.*
laugh (to) *lachen.*
laughter *Gelächter, n.*
lavish *freigebig.*
lavish (to) *überhäufen.*

law *Gesetz, n.; Recht, n.* (code).
lawful *rechtmäßig.*
lawn *Rasen, m.*
lawyer *Rechtsanwalt, m.*
lay (to) *legen.*
layer *Schicht, f.*
lazy *faul.*
lead *Blei, n.*
lead (to) *führen.*
leader *Führer, m.*
leadership *Führung, f.*
leaf *Blatt, n.*
leak *Leck, n.*
leak (to) *durchsickern.*
lean (adj.) *mager.*
lean (to) *lehnen.*
leap (to) *springen, hüpfen.*
leap *Sprung, m.*
learn (to) *lernen.*
learned *gelehrt.*
learning *Gelehrsamkeit, f.*
least *wenigste.*
    at least   *mindestens, wenigstens.*
leather *Leder, n.*
leave (to) *verlassen* (abandon); *weggehen* (on
    foot); *wegfahren* (by vehicle).
lecture *Vortrag, m.*
left *link, links.*
    to the left   *links.*
leg *Bein, n.*
    leg of lamb   *Hammelkeule, f.*
legal *gesetzmäßig, gesetzlich.*
legend *Sage, f.*
legislation *Gesetzgebung, f.*
legislator *Gesetzgeber, m.*
legitimate *legitim.*
leisure *Freizeit, f.*
lemon *Zitrone, f.*
lemonade *Limonade, f.*
lend (to) *(aus) leihen, verleihen.*
length *Länge, f.*
lengthen (to) *verlängern.*
lesbian *lesbisch* (adj.), *Lesbierin, f.*
less *weniger.*
lesson *Stunde, f.; Lektion, f.* (in book).
let (to) *lassen; gestatten* (allow); *vermieten*
    (rent).
letter *Buchstabe, m.* (alphabet); *Brief, m.*
    (correspondence).
level *Niveau, n.*
liable *haftbar.*
liar *Lügner, m.; Lügnerin, f.*
liberal *liberal.*
liberty *Freiheit, f.*
library *Bibliothek, f.*
license *Erlaubnis, f.; Führerschein, m.*
    (driver's license).
lick (to) *lecken.*
lie *Lüge, f.*

lie (to) *lügen* (falsify); *liegen* (rest).
lieutenant *Leutnant, m.*
life *Leben, n.*
lift (to) *heben, hochheben, aufheben.*
light *Licht* (noun) *n.; leicht* (adj.).
light (to) *anzünden* (match, fire).
   to light up *erleuchten.*
lighten (to) *erhellen* (brightness); *erleichtern* (weight).
lighter *Feuerzeug, n.*
lighthouse *Leuchtturm, m.*
lighting *Beleuchtung, f.*
lightning *Blitz, m.*
like *wie* (as); *ähnlich* (similar).
like (to) *gern haben, mögen, gefallen.*
   I'd like to *ich möchte.*
likely *wahrscheinlich.*
likeness *Ähnlichkeit, f.*
likewise *gleichfalls.*
liking *Vorliebe, f.*
limb *Glied, n.*
limit *Grenze, f.; Beschränkung, f.* (limitation).
limit (to) *begrenzen, beschränken.*
limp (to) *hinken, humpeln.*
line *Linie, f.*
line up (to) *sich anstellen.*
linen *Wäsche, f.* (household); *Leinwand, f.* (fabric).
linger (to) *(ver) weilen, sich lange aufhalten.*
lingerie *Damenwäsche, f.*
lining *Futter, n.*
link *Glied, n.*
link (to) *verbinden, verknüpfen.*
lion *Löwe, m.*
lip *Lippe, f.*
lipstick *Lippenstift, m.*
liquid *Flüssigkeit* (noun) *f.; flüssig* (adj.).
liquor *Alkohol, m.; Likör, m.* (liquor).
list *Liste, f.*
literary *literarisch.*
literature *Literatur, f.*
little *klein.*
   a little *ein wenig.*
live *lebend.*
live (to) *leben.*
lively *lebhaft, lebendig, munter.*
liver *Leber, f.*
load *Last, f.* (burden); *Ladung, f.* (cargo).
load (to) *laden.*
loan *(ver)leihen.*
lobby *Vorhalle, f., Foyer, n.*
local *lokal, örtlich.*
locate (to) *orientieren, finden, festlegen.*
location *Platz, m.; Lage, f.*
lock *Schloss, n.*
lock (to) *zuschließen, verschließen, abschließen.*
locomotive *Lokomotive, f.*
log *(Holz) Klotz, m.*

logic *Logik, f.*
logical *logisch.*
loneliness *Einsamkeit, f.*
lonely *einsam.*
long *lang.*
   long ago *vor langer Zeit; längst.*
   for a long time *seit langer Zeit; seit langem.*
long (to) *sehnen.*
   long for (to) *(sich) sehnen (nach)*
longer *länger.*
longing *Sehnsucht, f.*
look *Blick, m.*
look (to) *schauen; aussehen* (appear).
   Look! *Sehen Sie her!*
   Look out! *Passen Sie auf!*
   to look forward *sich freuen auf* (rejoice); *entgegensehen.*
loose *lose.*
loosen (to) *losmachen, loslassen.*
lose (to) *verlieren.*
loss *Verlust, m.; Schaden, m.*
lost *verloren, verschwunden.*
lot (à) *viel* (much).
   a lot of *eine Menge.*
loud *laut.*
love *Liebe, f.*
love (to) *lieben.*
lovely *schön, reizend.*
low *niedrig.*
lower (to) *niederlassen, herunterlassen, vermindern* (decrease).
loyal *treu.*
loyalty *Treue, f.*
luck *Glück, n.*
lucky *glücklich.*
luggage *Gepäck, n.*
luminous *leuchtend.*
lump *Klumpen, m.*
lunacy *Wahnsinn, m.*
lunch *Mittagessen, n.*
lung *Lunge, f.*
luxurious *prächtig, luxuriös.*
luxury *Luxus, m.; Aufwand, m.*

M

machine *Maschine, f.*
mad *verrückt.*
madam *gnädige Frau.*
made *gemacht.*
madness *Wahnsinn, m.*
magazine *Zeitschrift, f.*
magistrate *Magistrat, m.*
magnificent *prachtvoll, glänzend, herrlich.*
maid *Dienstmädchen, n.* (servant).
mail *Post, f.*

main *haupt-.*
  the main thing   *die Hauptsache.*
mainly *hauptsächlich.*
maintain (to) *erhalten; unterhalten* (support).
maintenance *Unterhalt, m.*
majesty *Majestät, f.*
major *Major, m.*
majority *Mehrheit, f.*
make (to) *machen.*
man *Mann, m.; Mensch, m.* (human being).
manage (to) *führen, verwalten, umzugehen*
  wissen mit (coll.).
management *Leitung, f.*
manager *Leiter, m.; Regisseur, m.* (theater);
  Manager, m.
manicure *Maniküre, f.*
mankind *Menschheit, f.*
manner *Art, f.; Weise, f.*
manners *Benehmen, n.*
manufacture *Fabrikation, f.; Herstellung, f.*
manufactured *hergestellt.*
many *viele.*
map *Landkarte, f.*
marble *Marmor, m.*
March *März, m.*
march *Marsch, m.*
march (to) *marschieren.*
margin *Rand, m.*
marine *Marine, f.*
mark *Kennzeichen, n.*
mark (to) *markieren* (score); *notieren,*
  aufschreiben.
market *Markt, m.*
marketplace *Marktplatz, m.*
marriage *Heirat, f.*
married *verheiratet.*
marry (to) *heiraten, sich verheiraten; trauen*
  (perform the ceremony).
  to marry off   *verheiraten.*
marvel *Wunder, n.*
marvel (to) *sich wundern.*
marvelous *wunderbar.*
masculine *männlich.*
mask *Maske, f.*
mask (to) *maskieren.*
mason *Maurer, m.*
mass *Masse, f.; Messe, f.* (church).
massage *Massage, f.*
master *Meister, m.*
master (to) *meistern.*
masterpiece *Meisterwerk, n.;*
  Meisterstück, n.
match *Streichholz, n.* (incendiary); *Gleiche, n.*
  (comparative).
match (to) *zusammenpassen; gewachsen sein*
  (to be a match for).
material *Material, n.*
maternal *mütterlich.*
mathematics *Mathematik, f.*

matter *Angelegenheit, f.* (affair); *Stoff, m.*
  (substance).
  What's the matter?   *Was ist los?*
mattress *Matratze, f.*
mature *erwachsen, reif.*
May *Mai, m.*
may *dürfen* (to be allowed); *mögen* (to be
  likely).
mayor *Bürgermeister, m.*
me *mich* (acc.); *mir* (dat.).
meadow *Wiese, f.*
meal *Mahl, n.*
mean *übel* (unkind), *Mittel* (Math).
mean (to) *meinen* (to be of the opinion);
  bedeuten (to signify).
  What does it mean?   *Was bedeutet*
    das?
meaning *Bedeutung, f.* (significance).
means *Mittel, n.*
meanwhile *inzwischen.*
measure *Maß, n.*
measure (to) *messen.*
meat *Fleisch, n.*
mechanic *Mechaniker, m.*
mechanical *mechanisch.*
medal *Medaille, f.* (jewel).
medical *ärztlich, medizinisch.*
medicine *Medizin, f.* (science); *Arznei, f.*
  (medication).
mediocre *mittelmäßig.*
mediocrity *Mittelmäßigkeit, f.*
meditate (to) *grübeln, sinnen,*
  nachdenken.
meditation *Nachdenken, n.*
medium *mittel.*
meet (to) *treffen.*
  Pleased to meet you.   *Sehr erfreut, Sie*
    kennenzulernen.
meeting *Versammlung, f.*
melon *Melone, f.*
melt (to) *schmelzen.*
member *Mitglied, n.*
memorize (to) *auswendig lernen.*
memory *Gedächtnis, n.*
mend (to) *reparieren.*
mental *geistig.*
mention (to) *erwähnen.*
menu *Speisekarte, f.*
merchandise *Ware, f.*
merchant *Kaufmann, m..*
merciful *barmherzig, mitleidvoll.*
merciless *unbarmherzig.*
mercury *Quecksilber, n.*
mercy *Barmherzigkeit, f.; Gnade, f.*
merit *Verdienst, n.*
merit (to) *verdienen.*
merry *fröhlich, heiter, lustig.*
message *Nachricht, f.*
messenger *Bote, m.*

metal *Metall, n.*
metallic *metallisch.*
method *Methode, f.*
Mexican *Mexikaner* (noun) *m.; mexikanisch* (adj.).
microphone *Mikrofon, n.*
microwave oven *Mikrowellengerät, n.; Mikrowellenherd, m.*
middle *Mitte, f.*
middle aged *von mittlerem Alter.*
Middle Ages *Mittelalter, n.*
midnight *Mitternacht, f.*
midway *halbwegs.*
might *Macht, f.*
mighty *mächtig.*
mild *leicht, mild, sanft.*
mildness *Milde, f.*
mile *Meile, f.*
military *militärisch.*
milk *Milch, f.*
milkman *Milchhändler, m.; Milchmann, m.*
Milky Way *Milchstraße, f.*
mill *Mühle, f.*
miller *Müller, m.; Müllerin, f.*
milliner *Modistin, f.*
million *Million, f.*
millionaire *Millionär, m.*
mind *Verstand, m.; Sinn, m.*
mind (to) *beachten* (to pay heed); *aufpassen* (watch over).
mine *Grube, f.* (coal).
mine (poss. pr.) *mein(-er, -e, -es).*
miner *Bergmann, m.*
mineral *mineralisch.*
mineral *Mineral, n.*
minister *Minister* (state), *m.; Geistliche, m.* (church).
ministry *Ministerium n.* (state); *Amt, n.* (church).
mink *Nerz, m.*
minor *Minderjährige(r), m.*
minority *Minderheit, f.*
minute *Minute, f.*
   Just a minute!   *Einen Augenblick!*
   Wait a minute!   *Warten Sie einen Augenblick!*
   Any minute now!   *Jeden Augenblick!*
miracle *Wunder, n.*
mirror *Spiegel, m.*
miscellaneous *gemischt, verschieden.*
mischief *Unfug, m.*
mischievous *spitzbübisch.*
miser *Geizhals, m.*
miserly *geizig.*
misfortune *Unglück, n.*
miss *Fräulein, n.*
miss (to) *versäumen, fehlen.*
mission *Mission, f.; Aufgabe, f.* (someone).
mist *Nebel, m.*

mistake *Fehler, m.*
mistaken *irrtümlich.*
   You are mistaken.   *Sie sind im Irrtum.*
mister *Herr, m.*
mistrust (to) *misstrauen.*
misunderstand (to) *missverstehen.*
misunderstanding *Missverständnis, n.*
misuse (to) *missbrauchen.*
mix (to) *mischen.*
mixture *Mischung, f.*
mob *Pöbel, m.*
mobile *beweglich.*
mobilization *Mobilmachung, f.* (mil.); *Mobilisierung, f.*
mobilize (to) *mobilisieren.*
mock (to) *verspotten.*
mockery *Spott, m.; Spotterei, f.*
mode *Mode, f.*
model *Modell, n.*
moderate *mäßigen.*
moderation *Mäßigkeit, f.*
modern *modern.*
modest *bescheiden.*
modesty *Bescheidenheit, f.*
modification *Veränderung, f.*
modify (to) *verändern.*
moist *feucht.*
moisten *unfeuchten.*
moment *Augenblick, m.; Moment, m.*
   just a moment   *einen Augenblick.*
monarchy *Monarchie, f.*
monastery *Kloster, n.*
Monday *Montag, m.*
money *Geld, n.*
monitor *Bildschirm, m.; Monitor, m.; Fenster, m.*
monk *Mönch, m.*
monkey *Affe, m.*
monologue *Monolog, m.*
monorail *Einschienenbahn, f.*
monotonous *eintönig.*
monotony *Eintönigkeit, f.*
monster *Ungeheuer, n.*
monstrous *ungeheuer.*
month *Monat, m.*
monthly *monatlich.*
monument *Denkmal, n.*
monumental *monumental, kolossal.*
mood *Stimmung, f.; Laune, f.* (temper).
moody *launisch.*
moon *Mond, m.*
moonlight *Mondschein, m.*
mop *Mop, m.*
moral *Moral, f.*
morality *Sittlichkeit, f.*
more *mehr.*
moreover *darüber hinaus.*
morning *Morgen, m.*

morsel *Bissen, m.; Brocken, m.*
mortal *sterblich.*
morality *Sterblichkeit, f.*
mortgage *Hypothek, f.*
mortgage (to) *verpfänden.*
mosquito *Mücke, f.*
most *am meisten.*
  most of   *die meisten.*
mostly *meistens.*
moth *Motte, f.*
mother *Mutter, f.*
mother-in-law *Schwiegermutter, f.*
motion *Bewegung, f.*
motionless *bewegungslos.*
motivate (to) *anregen, begründen,*
  motivieren.
motor *Motor, m.*
mount (to) *montieren; aufkleben* (paste);
  besteigen (horse).
mountain *Berg, m.*
mountainous *bergig.*
mourn (to) *trauern.*
mournful *traurig.*
mourning *Trauer, f.*
mouse *Maus, f.*
mouth *Mund, m.*
move (to) *bewegen.*
movement *Bewegung, f.*
movies *Kino, n.*
moving *rührend.*
much *viel*
  How much?   *Wie viel?*
mud *Schlamm, m.*
muddy *schlammig.*
mule *Maultier, n.; Maulesel, m.*
multiply (to) *multiplizieren.*
multitude *Menge, f.*
mumble (to) *murmeln.*
municipal *städtisch.*
munition *Munition, f.*
murder *Mord, m.*
murder (to) *ermorden.*
murderer *Mörder, m.*
murmur (to) *murmeln, rauschen.*
muscle *Muskel, m.*
museum *Museum, n.*
mushroom *Pilz, m.*
music *Musik, f.*
musical *musikalisch.*
musician *Musiker, m.*
must *müssen.*
mustache *Schnurrbart, m.*
mustard *Senf, m.; Mostrich, m.*
mute *stumm.*
mutton *Hammelfleisch, n.*
my *mein.*
myself *ich (mich, mir) selbst.*
mysterious *geheimnisvoll.*
mystery *Geheimnis, n.*

N

nail *Nagel, m.*
nail (to) *nageln.*
naive *harmlos, naïv.*
naked *nackt.*
name *Name, m.*
  first name   *Vorname, m.*
  last name   *Zuname, m.; Familienname*
    (family name).
  What is your name?   *Wie heißen Sie?*
namely *nämlich.*
nap *Schläfchen, n.*
napkin *Serviette, f.*
narrow *eng.*
nasty *garstig, ekelhaft.*
nation *Nation, f.*
national *national.*
nationality *Nationalität, f.*
native *Eingeborener, m.f.n.*
  native country   *Heimat, f.*
natural *natürlich.*
naturally *natürlich.*
nature *Natur, f.*
naughty *unartig.*
naval *See-.*
navy *Flotte, f.; Kriegsmarine, f.*
near *nah.*
nearly *beinahe.*
neat *nett, ordentlich.*
neatness *Niedlichkeit, f.; Sauberkeit, f.*
necessary *notwendig.*
necessity *Notwendigkeit, f.*
neck *Hals, m.*
necklace *Halsband, n.; Halskette, f.*
necktie *Krawatte, f.; Schlips, m.* (colloquial).
need *Not, f.; Bedürfnis, f.*
need (to) *brauchen.*
needle *Nadel, f.*
needless *unnötig.*
needy *dürftig, bedürftig.*
negative *Negative, m.*
neglect *Vernachlässigung, f.*
neglect (to) *vernachlässigen.*
negotiate (to) *verhandeln, abschließen*
    (treaty); *nehmen* (a curve in the road).
negotiation *Unterhandlung, f.; Verhandlung, f.*
neighbor *Nachbar, m.*
neighborhood *Nachbarschaft, f.*
neither *kein(er, -e, -es).*
  neither . . . nor   *weder . . . noch.*
nephew *Neffe, m.*
nerve *Nerv, m.*
  What a nerve!   *So eine Frechheit!*
nervous *nervös.*
nest *Nest, n.*
net *Netz, n.*
neuter *Neutrum, n.*

neutral *neutral.*
never *niemals, nie.*
   Never mind!   *Das macht nichts!*
nevertheless *trotzdem; auf alle Fälle.*
new *neu.*
news *Nachrichten, pl.*
newspaper *Zeitung, f.*
next *nächst.*
nice *nett.*
nickname *Spritzname, m.*
niece *Nichte, f.*
night *Nacht, f.*
nightgown *Nachthernd, n.*
nightmare *Alptraum, m.*
nine *neun.*
nineteen *neunzehn.*
ninety *neunzig.*
ninth *neunte.*
no *nein; kein* (adj.).
   no longer   *nicht mehr.*
   no matter   *ungeachtet* (gen.)
nobility *Adel, m.*
noble *adlig, edel* (fig).
nobody *niemand.*
noise *Geräusch, n.*
noisy *geräuschvoll.*
nominate (to) *ernennen.*
nomination *Ernennung, f.*
none *kein(-e, -er, -es).*
nonsense *Unsinn, m.*
noon *Mittag, m.*
nor *noch, auch nicht.*
normal *normal.*
north *Norden, m.*
northern *nordisch, nördlich.*
northeast *Nordosten, m.*
northwest *Nordwesten, m.*
nose *Nase, f.*
nostril *Nasenloch, n.*
not *nicht.*
note *Note, f.*
note (to) *notieren.*
notebook *Notizbuch, n.*
nothing *nichts.*
notice (to) *bemerken.*
notification *Benachrichtigung, f.*
notify (to) *benachrichtigen.*
notion *Idee, f.; Begriff, m.*
noun *Name, m.*
nourish (to) *nähren.*
nourishment *Nahrung, f.*
novel *Roman, m.*
novelty *Neuheit, f.*
November *November, m.*
now *jetzt*
   now and then.   *dann und wann;*
     manchmal.
nowadays *heutzutage.*
nowhere *nirgendwo.*

nuclear *Kern-, Atom-,*
   weapon   *Kernwaffe, f.; Atomwaffe, f.*
   fission   *Kernspaltung, f.*
   physics   *Kernphysik, f.*
nude *nackt, bloß.*
nuisance *Unfug, m.*
null *null.*
   null and void   *null und nichtig.*
numb *gefühllos.*
number *Nummer, f.*
numerous *zahlreich.*
nun *Nonne, f.*
nurse *Krankenschwester, f.* (for the sick);
     Kindermädchen (for children).
nursery *Kinderstube, f.* (children); *Gärtnerei,*
     f. (plants).
nursery rhyme *Kinderlied, n.*
nut *Nuss, f.*
nutcracker *Nussknacker, m.*

oak *Eiche, f.*
oar *Ruder, n.*
oat *Hafer, m.*
oath *Eid, m.*
obedience *Gehorsam, m.*
obedient *gehorsam.*
obey (to) *gehorchen.*
object (to) *einwenden, dagegen sein.*
objection *Einwand, m.*
objective *objektiv.*
objectively *sachlich.*
obligation *Verpflichtung, f.*
oblige (to) *verpflichten.*
obliging *gefällig.*
obscure *unklar, verborgen, unbekannt.*
obscurity *Dunkelheit, f.*
observation *Beobachtung, f.*
observatory *Sternwarte, f.*
observe (to) *beobachten.*
obstacle *Hindernis, n.*
obstinacy *Eigensinn, m.*
obstinate *eigensinnig.*
obvious *klar, offensichtlich.*
obviously *offenbar, deutlich.*
occasion *Gelegenheit, f.*
occasional *gelegentlich.*
occasionally *zuweilen, dann und wann.*
occupation *Beschäftigung, f.*
occupy (to) *besitzen; besetzen* (military);
     bewohnen (house).
occur (to) *vorkommen* (an event); *einfallen* (a
     thought), *vorfallen.*
occurrence *Vorfall, m.*
ocean *Ozean, m.*
October *Oktober, m.*

odd *ungerade* (uneven); *sonderbar* (unusual); *seltsam.*

odor *Geruch, m.*

of *von* (dat.); *aus* (dat.) (made of).

  of course   *natürlich.*

off *fort, weg.*

  off and on   *ab und zu.*

offend (to) *beleidigen.*

offense *Beleidigung, f.*

offensive *beleidigend.*

offer (to) *anbieten, (dar) bieten.*

offering *Angebot, n.*

office *Büro, n.*

official *offiziell.*

often *oft, oftmals, öfters, häufig.*

oil *Öl, n.*

old *alt.*

olive *Olive, f.*

olive oil *Olivenöl, n.*

on *auf* (dat. or acc.); *an* (dat. or acc.) (date).

once *einmal; vormals, einst* (formerly).

  at once   *sofort.*

  once and for all   *ein für allemal.*

  once in a while   *manchmal.*

  once more   *noch einmal.*

one *eins* (number), *ein(-er, -e).*

one (pr.) *man.*

oneself *sich, sich selbst.*

onion *Zwiebel, f.*

only *nur.*

open *offen.*

open (to) *öffnen.*

opener *Öffner, m.*

opening *Öffnung, f.*

opera *Oper, f.*

operate (to) *operieren* (med.); *betätigen; funktionieren, wirken.*

operation *Operation, f.*

opinion *Meinung, f.*

opponent *Gegner, m.*

opportune *gelegen, günstig.*

opportunity *Gelegenheit, f.*

oppose (to) *sich widersetzen gegen, gegenüber stehen.*

opposite *gegenüber.*

opposition *Widerstand, m.*

oppress (to) *unterdrücken.*

oppression *Unterdrückung, f.*

optician *Optiker, m.*

optimism *Optimismus, m.*

optimistic *optimistisch.*

or *oder.*

orange *Apfelsine, f.; Orange, f.*

orange juice *Apfelsinensaft, m.*

orator *Redner, m.*

orchard *Obstgarten, m.*

orchestra *Orchester, n.*

ordeal *Prüfung, f.; Qual, f.* (fig.).

order *Ordnung, f.* (neatness); *Bestellung, f.* (commercial); *Befehl, m.* (command); *Orden, m.* (decoration).

  out of order   *kaputt.*

  to put in order   *in Ordnung bringen.*

order (to) *ordnen* (regulate); *bestellen* (commercial); *befehlen* (command).

ordinary *gewöhnlich.*

organ *Orgel, f.* (music); *Organ, n.* (anatomy).

organization *Organisation, f.*

organize (to) *organisieren.*

Orient *Orient, m.*

oriental *orientalisch.*

origin *Ursprung, m.* (source); *Herkunft, f.* (descent).

original *original, ursprünglich.*

originality *Originalität, f.*

ornament *Ornament, n.*

orphan *Waisenkind, n.*

orthodox *orthodox.*

other *ander.*

other than *anders als, verschieden (von).*

ought (to) *sollen.*

ounce *Unze, f.*

our *unser.*

ours *unser(-er, -e, -es).*

out *aus* (dat); *hinaus, heraus.*

  out of   *ausser* (dat.)

outcome *Folge, f.; Ergebnis, n.*

outdo (to) *übertreffen.*

outdoors *im Freien.*

outer *äußer.*

outlast *überdauern.*

outlaw *Geächtete(r), m.*

outlaw (to) *ächten, verbieten.*

outlay *Auslage, f.; Ausgabe, f.*

outlet *Auslass, m.; Absatz, m.* (market).

outline *Umriss, m.*

outlook *Aussicht, f.*

output *Produktion, f.; Leistung, f.* (machine).

outrage *Unverschämtheit, f.; Schandtat, f.; Frevel, m.*

outrageous *frevelhaft, empörend, schändlich.*

outside *Außenseite* (noun) *f.; draußen* (outdoors); *außerhalb.*

oval *oval.*

oven *Ofen, m.*

over *über* (acc.); *vorbei* (finished).

  over and over   *wieder und wieder.*

overboard *über Bord.*

overcoat *Mantel, m.*

overcome (to) *überwinden.*

overflow (to) *überfließen.*

overlook (to) *übersehen.*

overrun *überrennen, überlaufen.*

overseas *nach Übersee.*

overthrow *umstürzen, stürzen* (govt.).

overwhelm (to) *überwältigen.*

owe (to) *schulden.*

owl *Eule, f.*
own *eigen.*
own (to) *besitzen* (possess); *zugeben*
    (admit).
owner *Besitzer, m.*
ox *Ochse, m.*
oxygen *Sauerstoff, m.*
oyster *Auster, f.*
ozone *ozon, n.*

P

pace *Schritt, m; Tempo, n.*
pace (to) *schreiten.*
pacific *friedlich.*
pack *Kartenspiel, n.* (cards).
pack (to) *(ein)packen, verpacken, Packung, f.*
    (cigarettes); *Rucksack, m.; Tornister, m.*
package *Paket, n.*
page *Seite, f.*
pager *Pager, m.; Beeper, m.*
pain *Schmerz, m.*
pain (to) *schmerzen.*
painful *schmerzhaft.*
painless *schmerzlos.*
paint *Farbe, f.*
paint (to) *malen* (art); *(an)streichen* (a wall);
    spritzen lassen (car).
painter *Maler, m.* (-in) f.
painting *Gemälde, n.*
pair *Paar, n.*
pajamas *Pyjama, m.*
palace *Palast, m.*
pale *blass.*
palm *Palme, f.*
pamphlet *Broschüre, f.*
pan *Pfanne, f.*
pancake *Pfannkuchen, m.*
pane *Scheibe, f.*
panic *Panik, f.*
panorama *Panorama, n.*
panties *Schlüpfer, m.*
pants *Hose, f.*
paper *Papier, n.*
parachute *Fallschirm, m.*
parade *Parade, f.*
paragraph *Paragraph, m; Absatz, m.*
parallel *parallel.*
paralysis *Lähmung, f.*
paralyzed *gelähmt.*
parcel *Paket, n.; Päckchen, n.*
pardon *Verzeihung, f; Entschuldigung, f.*
pardon (to) *vergeben, entschuldigen.*
parenthesis *Klammern, f.*
parents *Eltern, pl.*
Parisian *Pariser, m.* (-in) f.
park *Park, m.*

park (to) *parken.*
parliament *Parlament, n.*
parrot *Papagei, m.*
parsley *Petersilie, f.*
part *Teil, n.* (share); *Ersatzteil, n.*
    (replacement).
part (to) *teilen, sich trennen* (separate);
    auseinander gehen.
partial *teilweise.*
partiality *Vorliebe, f.*
particular *besonder(-er, -e, -es).*
particularly *besonders.*
partner *Partner, m.; Sozius, m.*
party (political) *Partei, f.; Gesellschaft, f.*
    (society); *Party; f.* (social).
pass *Ausweis, m.*
pass (to) *durchgehen, vorbeigehen; bestehen*
    (exam); *überholen* (overtake a car).
passage *Durchgang, m.; Überfahrt, f.* (travel).
passenger *Passagier, m.*
passion *Leidenschaft, f.*
passionately *leidenschaftlich.*
passive *Passiv, n.*
passport *Pass, m.*
past *Vergangenheit* (noun) *f.; vorbei, vorig*
    (time); *nach* (on the clock).
   ten past six   *zehn nach sechs.*
   last month   *vorigen Monat.*
   last week   *vorige Woche.*
   last year   *voriges Jahr.*
paste *Kleister, m.; Teig* (cul.).
paste (to) *kleistern, kleben.*
pastry *Gebäck, n.*
pastry shop *Konditorei, f.*
patch *Flicken, m.*
patch (to) *flicken.*
patent *Patent, n.*
paternal *väterlich.*
path *Weg, m; Pfad, m.; Bahn, f.* (elec.).
pathetic *pathetisch.*
patience *Geduld, f.*
patient *Patient* (noun) *m.; geduldig* (adj.).
patriot *Patriot, m.*
patriotic *patriotisch.*
patron *Gönner, m.; Patron, m.; Förderer, m.*
patronage *Begünstigung, f.; Schutz, m.*
patronize (to) *unterstützen.*
pattern *Muster, n.*
pause *Pause, f.*
pave (to) *pflastern.*
pavement *Pflaster, n.*
paw *Pfote, f.*
pay *Lohn, m.; Bezahlung, f.; Gehalt, n.*
pay (to) *zahlen, bezahlen.*
payment *Bezahlung, f.*
pea *Erbse, f.*
peace *Frieden, m.*
peaceful *friedlich.*
peach *Pfirsich, m.*

peak *Gipfel, n.*
peanut *Erdnuss, f.*
pear *Birne, f.*
pearl *Perle, f.*
peasant *Bauer, m.*
pebble *Kiesel(stein), m.*
peculiar *sonderbar.*
pedal *Pedal, n.*
pedantic *pedantisch.*
pedestrian *Fußgänger, m.*
peel *Rinde, f.; Schale, f.*
peel (to) *schälen.*
pen *Stift, m.*
   fountain pen   *Füllfederhalter, f.*
penalty *Strafe, f.; Todesstrafe* (death).
pencil *Bleistift, m.*
penetrate (to) *durchdringen.*
peninsula *Halbinsel, f.*
penitence *Reue, f.*
pension *Pension, f.*
people *Leute, pl.*
pepper *Pfeffer, m.*
peppermint *Pfefferminz, m.*
per *pro.*
perceive (to) *wahrnehmen.*
percentage *Prozentsatz, m.*
perfect *vollkommen.*
perfection *Volkommenheit, f.*
perfectly *gänzlich; völlig.*
perform (to) *verrichten; aufführen; vortragen*
   (theater); *durchführen.*
performance *Vorstellung, f.; Auffrührung, f.*
perfume *Parfüm, n.*
perfume (to) *parfümieren.*
perhaps *vielleicht.*
period *Periode, f.; Punkt, m.* (typ.).
periodical *periodisch; Zeitschrift, f.*
permanent *ständig.*
permission *Erlaubnis, f.*
permit *Erlaubnisschein, m.*
permit (to) *erlauben.*
peroxide *Hyperoxyd, n.; Superoxyd, n.*
perpetual *immerwährend, andauernd,*
   fortwährend.
perplex *verwirren.*
persecute (to) *verfolgen.*
persecution *Verfolgung, f.*
perseverance *Ausdauer, f.*
persist (to) *beharren.*
person *Person, f.*
personal *persönlich.*
personality *Persönlichkeit, f.*
perspective *Perspektive, f.*
perspiration *Schweiß, m.*
persuade (to) *überzeugen, überreden.*
pertaining *betreffend.*
petrol *Benzin, n.*
petticoat *Unterrock, m.*
petty *kleinlich.*

pharmacist *Apotheker, m.*
pharmacy *Apotheke, f.*
phenomenon *Phänomen, n.*
philosopher *Philosoph, m.*
philosophical *philosophisch.*
philosophy *Philosophie, f.*
phonograph *Plattenspieler, m.*
photograph *Fotografie, f.; Aufnahme, f.*
photograph (to) *aufnehmen.*
photographer *Fotograf, m.*
photostat *Photokopie, f.; Fotokopie, f.*
phrase *Frase, f.*
physical *körperlich.*
physician *Arzt, m; Doktor, m.*
piano *Klavier, n.*
pick (to) *pflücken.*
pick up (to) *aufheben, abholen.*
picnic *Picknick, n.*
picture *Bild, n.*
picturesque *malerisch.*
pie *Torte, f.*
piece *Stück, n.*
pier *kai, m.; Landungssteg, m.*
pig *Schwein, n.*
pigeon *Taube, f.*
pile *Haufen, m.; Stapel, m.*
pile (to) *aufhäufen, (auf) stapeln.*
pilgrim *Pilger, m.*
pill *Pille, f.*
pillar *Säule, f.*
pillow *Kissen, n.*
pilot *Pilot, m.*
   automatic pilot   *Steuergerät, n.*
pin *Stecknadel, f.*
pinch (to) *kneifen.*
pink *rosa.*
pious *fromm.*
pipe *Pfeife, f.* (tobacco); *Rohr, n.* (plumbing).
pirate *Seeräuber, m.; Pirat, m.*
pistol *Pistole, f.*
pitiful *mitleidig.*
pity *Mitleid, n..*
place *Platz, m.; Stelle, f.* (spot, situation); *Ort,*
   m. (locality).
   take place   *stattfinden.*
place (to) *stellen, legen, setzen.*
plain *Ebene* (noun) *f.; einfach* (adj.).
plan *Plan, m.* (project); *Entwurf, m.*
plan (to) *planen.*
plane *Flugzeug, n.*
planet *Planet, m.*
plant *Pflanze, f.*
plant (to) *pflanzen.*
plaster *Verputz, m.; Pflaster, n.* (med.).
plastic *Kunststoff* (noun) *m.; plastisch* (adj.).
plate *Teller, m.*
platform *Bahnsteig, m.* (station).
platter *Platte, f.*
play *Spiel, n.; Stück, n.* (theater).

play (to) *spielen.*
plea *Gesuch, n.; Einrede, f.*
plead (to) *plädieren* (law); *inständig bitten; anflehen.*
pleasant *angenehm.*
please *bitte.*
please (to) *gefallen.*
pleasure *Vergnügen, n.*
pledge *Pfand, n.; Versprechen, n.*
plenty *genug* (enough); *reichlich* (abundance).
plot *Verschwörung, f.* (conspiracy); *Handlung, f.* (of a story).
plot (to) *anstiften, heimlich planen.*
plow *Pflug, m.*
plow (to) *pflügen.*
plum *Pflaume, f.*
plumber *Klempner, m.*
pneumonia *Lungenentzündung, f.*
pocket *Tasche, f.*
poem *Gedicht, n.*
poet *Poet, m.; Dichter, m.*
poetic *poetisch.*
poetry *Dichtung, f.*
point *Punkt, m.; Spitze, f.*
point (to) *spitzen, hinweisen, richten auf.*
pointed *spitz(ig).*
poise *Gleichgewicht, n.; (Körper) haltung, f.*
poison *Gift, n.*
poison (to) *vergiften.*
poisonous *giftig.*
polar *polar.*
pole *Pol, m.*
police *Polizei, f.*
policeman *Schutzmann, m.; Polizist, m.*
policy *Politik, f.; Police, f.* (insurance).
Polish *polnisch.*
polish *Glanz, m., Politur, f.*
polish (to) *glänzend machen, polieren.*
polite *höflich.*
politeness *Höflichkeit, f.*
political *politisch.*
pollution *Verschmutzung, f.*
pond *Teich, m.*
pool *Schwimmbad, n.*
poor *arm.*
Pope *Papst, m.*
popular *volkstümlich; beliebt* (liked).
population *Bevölkerung, f.*
pork *Schweinefleisch, n.*
port *Hafen, m.*
porter *Träger, m.*
portrait *Bild, n.; Porträt, n.*
Portuguese *Portugiese* (noun) *m.; portugiesisch* (adj.).
position *Stellung, f.* (job); *Lage, f.* (site).
positive *bestinunt, positiv.*
possibility *Möglichkeit, f.*
possible *möglich.*
post *Post, f.; Stelle, f.* (job).

postage *Porto, n.*
postcard *Postkarte, f.*
poster *Plakat, n.*
posterity *Nachkommenschaft, f.*
post office *Postanit, n.*
pot *Topf, m.*
potato *Kartoffel, f.*
pound *Pfund, n.*
pour (to) *gießen.*
poverty *Armut, f.*
powder *Pulver, n.* (gun); *Puder, m.* (cosmetic).
powder (to) *pudern.*
power *Macht, f.; Gewalt, f.*
powerful *mächtig.*
practical *praktisch.*
practice (to) *üben.*
praise *Lob, n.*
praise (to) *loben, rühmen.*
prank *Streich, m.*
pray (to) *beten.*
prayer *Gebet, n.*
preach (to) *predigen.*
preacher *Prediger, m.*
precaution *Vorsicht, f.*
precede (to) *vorangehen.*
preceding *vorangehend.*
precept *Vorschrift, f.; Beispiel, n.* (example).
precious *kostbar, unschätzbar.*
precise *genau; steif* (formal).
precision *Genauigkeit, f.*
predecessor *Vorgänger, m.*
predict *voraussagen, vorhersagen.*
preface *Vorwort, n.*
prefer (to) *vorziehen.*
preference *Vorzug, m.*
pregnant *schwanger.*
prejudice *Vorurteil, n.*
preliminary *einleitend, vorbereitend.*
preparation *Vorbereitung, f.*
prepare (to) *vorbereiten, zubereiten.*
prepay (to) *vorauszahlen.*
prescribe (to) *verschreiben.*
prescription *Rezept, n.*
presence *Gegenwart, f.; Anwesenheit, f.*
present *Gegenwart, f.* (grammar); *Geschenk, n.* (gift); *anwesend* (adj.).
preserve (to) *erhalten; konservieren* (food); *bewahren.*
preserves *Konserven, f.; Eingemachte, n.; Konfitüren, f.* (jellies, jams).
preside (to) *präsidieren.*
president *Präsident, m.*
press *Presse, f.*
press (to) *drücken; bügeln* (clothes).
pressing *dringend.*
pressure *Druck, m.; Blutdruck* (blood-); *Drücken, n.*
prestige *Prestige, n.; Ansehen, n.*
presume (to) *vermuten.*

pretend (to) *vorgeben, vortäuschen.*
pretext *Vorwand, m.*
pretty *hübsch, nett.*
prevail (to) *vorherrschen, siegen.*
prevent (to) *verhindern.*
prevention *Verhinderung, f.*
previous *frühere.*
prey *Raub, m.*
price *Preis, m.; Beute, f.*
price-cutting *Preissenkung, f.*
price tag *Preisschild, n.*
price war *Preiskrieg, m.*
pride *Stolz, m.*
priest *Priester, m.*
prince *Prinz, m.*
principal *haupt-* (adj.); *Haupt-, n.*
principle *Grundsatz, m.; Prinzip, n.*
print (to) *drucken.*
printer *Drucker, m.*
prison *Gefängnis, n.*
prisoner *Gefangener, m.*
private *privat.*
privilege *Vorrecht, n.*
prize *Preis, m.*
prize (to) *schätzen.*
probable *wahrscheinlich.*
problem *Problem, n.; Schwierigkeit, f.*
procedure *Verfahren, n.*
proceed (to) *fortschreiten.*
process *Verfahren, n.; Prozess, m.; Verlauf, m.*
procession *Prozession, f.*
proclaim (to) *bekannt machen.*
produce (to) *erzeugen, hervorbringen, herstellen.*
production *Erzeugung, f.; Produktion, f.; Herstellung, f.; Fabrikation, f.*
productive *fruchtbar, schöpferisch, erzeugend.*
profession *Beruf, m.*
professional *beruflich, berufsmässig.*
professor *Professor, m.; Lehrer, m.* (school).
profile *Profil, n.*
profit *Gewinn, m; Profit, m.*
profit (to) *gewinnen, profitieren.*
program *Programm, n.*
progress *Fortschritt, m.*
progress (to) *vorwärts kommen, weiter kommen.*
progressive *fortschrittlich.*
prohibit (to) *verbieten.*
prohibition *Verbot, n.; Untersagung, f.*
project *Projekt, n.; Unternehmen, n.*
project (to) *hervorstehen, entwerfen.*
promise (to) *versprechen.*
prompt *schnell, sofortig.*
pronoun *Fürwort, n.*
pronounce (to) *aussprechen.*
pronunciation *Aussprache, f.*
proof *Beweis, m.*
propaganda *Propaganda, f.*

proper *passend, anständig* (decent).
property *Eigentum, n.*
proportion *Verhältnis, n.; Maß, n.*
proposal *Vorschlag, m.*
propose (to) *vorschlagen.*
prose *Prosa, f.*
prospect *Aussicht, f.* (outlook).
prosper (to) *gedeihen.*
prosperity *Wohlstand, m.*
prosperous *gedeihlich, blühend.*
protect (to) *schützen.*
protection *Schutz, m.*
protector *Beschützer, m.*
protest *Einspruch, m.; protest, m.*
protest (to) *protestieren, sich auflehnen (gegen).*
Protestant *Protestant, m.*
proud *stolz*
prove (to) *beweisen, bestätigen.*
proverb *Sprichwort, n.*
provide (to) *versorgen.*
provided that *vorausgesetzt dass.*
province *Provinz, f.*
provincial *provinziell.*
provision *Lebensmittelvorrat, m.; Beschaffung, f.; Besorgung, f.*
provoke (to) *herausfordern, reizen.*
prowl *herumschleichen, herumstreichen.*
proximity *Nähe, f.*
prudence *Vorsicht, f.*
prudent *klug, vorsichtig, umsichtig.*
prune *Backpflaume, f.*
psychological *psychologisch.*
psychology *Psychologie, f.*
public *Publikum* (noun) *n.; öffentlich* (adj.).
publication *Herausgabe, f.* (literary); *Veröffentlichung, f.* (notification).
publish (to) *herausgeben* (book); *veröffentlichen* (announcement).
publishing house *Verlag, m.*
publisher *Verleger, m.*
pull (to) *ziehen.*
pump *Pumpe, f.*
punish (to) *bestrafen.*
punishment *Strafe, f.*
pupil *Schüler, m.; Schülerin, f.*
purchase (to) *kaufen.*
purchase *Einkauf, m.*
pure *rein.*
purity *Reinheit, f.*
purple *Purpur, m.*
purpose *Absicht, f.; Zweck, m.*
purse *Geldtasche, f.; Portemonnaie, n.; Handtasche, f.*
pursue (to) *verfolgen, nachgehen.*
push (to) *stoßen.*
put (to) *legen* (lay); *setzen,* (set); *stellen* (place).
    put down   *aufschreiben.*

put off *aufschieben.*
put on *anziehen.*
put up *aufstellen.*
put into practice *einsetzen.*
put a question to someone *eine Frage
    richten an.*
puzzle *Rätsel, n.*
puzzle (to) *verwirren.*

Q

quaint *seltsam.*
qualify *befähigen, qualifizieren.*
quality *Qualität, f.*
quantity *Quantität, f.*
quarrel *Streit, m.*
quarter *Viertel, n.*
queen *Königin, f.*
queer *seltsam, eigenartig.*
quench (to) *löschen* (thirst); *auslöschen* (fire).
question *Frage, f.*
question (to) *fragen.*
quick *schnell, geschwind, rasch.*
quiet *ruhig.*
quit (to) *verlassen, aufgeben.*
quite *ganz.*
quote (to) *anführen* (a fact); *zitieren* (a
    passage).

R

rabbi *Rabbiner, m.*
rabbit *Kaninchen, n.; Hase, m.* (hare).
race *Rennen, n.* (contest); *Rasse, f.* (species).
radiate (to) *strahlen.*
radiator *Heizkörper, m.; Kühler* (motor).
radio *Radio, n; Rundfunk, m.*
rag *Lappen, m.*
rage *Wut, f.*
ragged *zerlumpt, zerfetzt.*
rail *Schiene, f.*
railroad *Eisenbahn, f.*
railroad car *Eisenbahnwagen, m.*
rain *Regen, m.*
rain (to) *regnen.*
rainbow *Regenbogen, m.*
raincoat *Regenmantel, m.*
rainy *regnerisch.*
raise (to) *erhöhen.*
raisin *Rosine, f.*
rake *Rechen, m.; Harke, f.*
rank *Rang, m.; Glied, n.* (mil.).
rapid *schnell.*
rapidly *schnell, geschwind, rasch.*
rapture *Entzücken, n.*

rash *Hautausschlag* (noun) *m.* (skin); *hastig*
    (adj.).
rat *Ratte, f.*
rate *Kurs, m.* (exchange); *Preis, m.*
rate (to) *(ab)schätzen.*
rather *ziemlich, lieber, eher.*
ration *Ration, f.*
rational *vernünftig.*
rave (to) *schwärmen.*
raw *roh.*
ray *Strahl, m.*
razor *Rasiermesser, n.*
razor blade *Rasierklinge, f.*
reach (to) *erreichen, greifen (nach).*
reach *Reichweite, f.*
react (to) *reagieren, entgegen wirken.*
read (to) *lesen.*
reading *Lesen, n.; Lektüre, f.*
ready *fertig.*
real *wirklich.*
realization *Verwirklichung, f.*
realize (to) *verwirklichen.*
really *wirklich.*
rear *Hintergrund* (noun) *m.; hinter* (adj.).
rear (to) *großziehen, aufziehen* (children);
    züchten (animals).
reason *Grund, m.* (cause); *Vernunft, f.*
    (intelligence).
it stands to reason *es versteht sich.*
reason (to) *logisch denken, vernüftig urteilen.*
reasonable *vernünftig.*
reasoning *Schlussfolgerung, f.; Urteilen, n.*
reassure (to) *beruhigen.*
rebel *Rebell, m.*
rebel (to) *sich auflehnen, rebellieren.*
rebellion *Empörung, f.; Aufstand, m.*
recall (to) *sich erinnern* (memory);
    zurückrufen (to summon back).
receipt *Quittung, f.*
receive (to) *empfangen, erhalten, bekommen.*
receiver *Empfäger, m.*
recent *neu.*
recently *neulich.*
reception *Empfang, m.*
recess *Ferien f.* (school); *Pause, f.*
reciprocal *gegenseitig.*
recite (to) *aufsagen; rezitieren* (drama).
recognize (to) *erkennen.*
recollect (to) *sich erinnern an.*
recollection *Erinnerung, f.*
recommend (to) *empfehlen.*
recommendation *Empfehlung, f.*
reconcile (to) *versöhnen.*
record *Rekord, m.* (sports).
phonograph record *(Schall)platte, f.*
recover (to) *sich erholen* (illness),
    zurückerhalten (to get back); *neu
    überziehen* (quilt, sofa).
recruit *Rekrut, m.* (mil.).

recruit (to) *rekrutieren, (an)werben.*
red *rot.*
Red Cross *Das Rote Kreuz, n.*
redeem (to) *erlösen.*
reduce (to) *herabsetzen; abnehmen* (weight).
reduction *Nachlass, m.; Verminderung, f.*
reed *Schilf, n.*
reef *Riff, n.*
refer (to) *sich beziehen.*
reference *Bezugnahme, f.*
referring (to) *mit Bezugnahme auf.*
   in reference to (corresp.)   *Betreff/Betrifft.*
refine (to) *verfeinern.*
refinement *Verfeinerung, f.*
reflect (to) *zurückstrahlen; widerspiegeln.*
reflection *Widerschein, m.* (image);
        Überlegung, f. (thoughts).
reform *Besserung, f.*
reform (to) *sich bessern, reformieren.*
refrain (to) *sich enthalten.*
refresh (to) *erfrischen.*
refreshment *Erfrischung, f.*
refrigerator *Kühlschrank, m.*
refuge *Zufluchtsort, m.*
   take refuge   *flüchten.*
refugee *Flüchtling, m.*
refund *Rückzahlung, f.*
refund (to) *zurückzahlen.*
refusal *Verweigerung, f.; Ablehnung, f.*
refuse (to) *ablehnen, verweigern.*
refute (to) *widerlegen.*
regard *Ansehen, n.*
regardless *ungeachtet; ohne Rücksicht auf.*
regime *Regime, n.*
regiment *Regiment, n.*
register (to) *eintragen* (membership);
        einschreiben (letter); *sich*
        immatrikulieren (university).
regret *Bedauern, n.; Reue, f.*
regret (to) *bedauern.*
regular *regelmäßig.*
regulate *regulieren.*
regulation *Vorschrift, f.*
rehearsal *Probe, f.*
rehearse (to) *proben.*
reign *Herrschaft, f.*
reign (to) *herrschen.*
reinforce (to) *verstärken.*
reject (to) *ablehnen.*
rejoice (to) *sich freuen.*
relapse *Rückfall, m.*
relate (to) *erzählen.*
relation *Verwandtschaft, f.*
relationship *verwandtschaftliche Beziehung,*
       f.; Verhältnis, n.
relative *Verwandte, m./f.*
relax (to) *entspannen.*
relaxation *Entspannung, f.*
release *Befreiung, f.*

release (to) *freilassen.*
reliable *zuverlässig.*
relic *Überbleibsel, n.; Relique, f.* (religious).
relief *Erleichterung, f.; Linderung, f.* (of pain).
relieve (to) *erleichtern, lindern.*
religion *Religion, f.*
religious *religiös.*
relinquish (to) *aufgeben.*
relish (to) *mit Appetit genießen.*
relish *Geschmack, m.; Genuss (an), m.*
reluctance *Widerwille, n.*
reluctant *widerwillig.*
rely (to) *sich verlassen (auf).*
remain (to) *bleiben.*
remainder *Rest, m.*
remark *Bemerkung, f.*
remark (to) *bemerken.*
remarkable *bemerkenswert.*
remedy *Arznei, f.* (medicine); *Hilfsmittel, n.*
      (cure).
remember (to) *sich erinnern (an).*
remembrance *Erinnerung, f.*
remind (about) (to) *mahnen.*
remorse *Reue, f.*
remote *entfernt* (distance); *rückständig;*
        abgelegen (distance).
removal *Beseitigung, f.*
remove (to) *entfernen.*
renew (to) *erneuern.*
renewal *Erneuerung, f.*
rent *Miete, f.*
rent (to) *mieten.*
repair *Reparatur, f.*
repay (to) *zurückzahlen.*
repeat (to) *wiederholen.*
repent (to) *bereuen.*
repetition *Wiederholung, f.*
replace *zurückerstatten* (things taken);
       ersetzen.
reply *Antwort, f.*
reply (to) *antworten.*
report *Bericht, m.; Zeugnis, n.* (report card).
report (to) *berichten.*
reporter *Reporter, m.*
represent (to) *vertreten.*
representation *Vertretung, f.*
representative *Vertreter, m.*
repress (to) *unterdrücken.*
repression *Unterdrückung, f.*
reprimand *Verweis, m; Tadel, m.*
reprimand (to) *tadeln.*
reprisal *Vergeltungsmaßnahme, f.*
reproach *Vorwurf, m.*
reproach (to) *vorwerfen.*
reproduce (to) *reproduzieren.*
reproduction *Reproduktion, f.;*
       Vervielfältigung, f.
republic *Republik, f.*
repulse *zurücktreiben, zurückschlagen.*

reputation *Ruf, m.; Ansehen; n.*
request *Bitte, f.; Ersuchen, n.*
request (to) *bitten.*
require (to) *benötigen.*
requirement *Bedarf, m.*
rescue (to) *retten.*
research *Forschung, f.*
resent (to) *verübeln.*
resentful *aufgebracht, ärgerlich.*
resentment *Verdruss, m.*
reservation *Reservation, f.*
reserve (to) *reservieren.*
reservoir *Behälter, m.*
residence *Wohnstätte, f.*
resident *Bewohner, m.*
resign (to) *aufgeben, austreten* (Aus.).
resignation *Rücktritt, m.*
resist (to) *widerstehen.*
resistance *Widerstand, m.*
resolute *entschlossen.*
resolution *Beschluss, m.*
resolve (to) *sich entschließen* (decide); *lösen; aufklären* (problem).
resort *Kurort, m.* (health); *Luftkurort, m.; Erholungsort, m.; Zuflucht, f.* (recourse); *als letzter Ausweg* (as a last resort).
resource *Hilfsmittel, n.*
respect *Achtung, f.*
respectful *ehrfürchtig, achtungsvoll.*
responsibility *Verantwortlichkeit, f.*
responsible *verantwortlich.*
rest *Ruhe, f.*
rest (to) *ruhen; sich ausruhen.*
restaurant *Restaurant, n.*
restless *unruhig.*
restoration *Wiederherstellung, f.*
restore (to) *wieder herstellen, restaurieren.*
restrain (to) *zurückhalten.*
restraint *Zurückhaltung, f.*
restrict (to) *beschränken.*
restriction *Einschränkung, f.; Beschränkung, f.*
result *Resultat, n.; Ergebnis, n.; Folge, f.*
result (to) *folgen; sich ergeben.*
resume (to) *wieder aufnehmen, wieder anfangen.*
retail *Einzelverkauf, m.; Kleinhandel, m.*
retail (to) *im Kleinhandel verkaufen.*
retain (to) *behalten.*
retaliate (to) *vergelten.*
retaliation *Vergeltung, f.*
retire (to) *sich zurückziehen, in den Ruhestand treten.*
retirement *Zurückgezogenheit, f.; Pensionierung, f.*
retract *widerrufen; zurückziehen.*
retreat *Rückzug, m.*
retreat (to) *sich zurückziehen.*
return *Rückkehr, f.*

return (to) *zurückkehren.*
reveal (to) *offenbaren, enthüllen.*
revelation *Offenbarung, f.*
revenge *Rache, f.*
revenge (to) *rächen.*
revenue *Einkommen, n.*
reverence *Ehrerbietung, f.*
reverend *ehrwürdig.*
reverse *Rückseite, f.; Kehrseite* (side of a coin).
reverse (to) *umkehren.*
review (to) *überprüfen; rezensieren* (critical); *wiederholen.*
review *Überblick, m.; Parade, f.* (army); *Revue, f.* (theater); *Rezension, f.* (book).
revise (to) *revidieren* (critique); *überarbeiten.*
revive *auffrischen, wieder zu Bewusstsein bringen.*
revival *Wiederbelebung, f.*
revoke (to) *widerrufen.*
revolt *Aufstand, m.*
revolt (to) *sich empören.*
revolution *Revolution, f.*
revolve (to) *sich drehen.*
reward *Belohnung, f.*
reward (to) *belohnen.*
rhyme *Reim, m.*
rhyme (to) *reimen.*
rib *Rippe, f.*
ribbon *Band, n.*
rice *Reis, m.*
rich *reich.*
richness *Reichtum, m.*
rid (to get) *loswerden.*
riddle *Rätsel, n.*
ride *Fahrt, f.*
ridiculous *lächerlich.*
rifle *Gewehr, n.*
right (noun) *Recht, n.*
right *richtig* (correct); *rechts* (position).
   all right   *ganz gut.*
righteous *gerecht.*
rigid *steif, fest, starr.*
rigor *Strenge, f.*
rigorous *streng, scharf, hart.*
ring *Ring, m.*
   wedding ring   *Trauring, m.*
ring (to) *ringen, läuten; schellen* (bell).
rinse (to) *spülen, ausspülen.*
riot (to) *Aufruhr, f.*
ripe *reif.*
ripen (to) *reifen.*
rise *Steigung, f.*
rise (to) *aufstehen* (get up); *steigen* (increase, mount); *aufgehen* (sun).
risk *Gefahr, f.*
risk (to) *riskieren, wagen.*
rite *Ritus, m.*
ritual *rituell.*

rival *Rivale, m.; Konkurrent, m.*
rivalry *Mitbewerbung, f.; Konkurrenz, f.*
river *Fluss, m.*
roach *Schabe, f.; Schwabe, f.*
road *Weg, m.*
roar (to) *brüllen.*
roast *Braten, m.*
roast (to) *braten.*
rob (to) *rauben.*
robber *Räuber, m.*
robbery *Diebstahl, m.*
robe *Morgenrock, m.*
robot *Roboter, n.*
robust *stark, kräftig.*
rock *Felsen, m.*
rock (to) *wiegen, schaukeln.*
rocky *felsig.*
rocket *Rakete, f.*
rod *Rute, f.; Stab, m.*
roll *Rolle, f.* (cylinder); *Brötchen, n.* (bread);
    Semmel, f. (Aust.).
roll (to) *rollen.*
Roman *Römer* (noun) *m.; römisch* (adj)
romantic *romantisch.*
roof *Dach, n.*
room *Zimmer, n.* (of a house); *Weltraum, m.*
    (space).
    There is no room.   *Da ist kein Platz.*
roomy *geräumig.*
root *Wurzel, f.*
rope *Seil, n.; Strick, m.*
rose *Rose, f.*
rot (to) *faulen; vermodern.*
rough *rauh* (coarse); *roh* (crude); *stürmisch*
    (stormy).
round *Runde* (noun) *f.; rund* (adj.).
round *um* (acc.); *herum.*
round-trip *Rundreise, f.*
rouse (to) *aufwecken; erregen* (to stir up).
routine *Routine, f.*
row *Reihe, f.*
row (to) *rudern.*
royal *königlich.*
rub (to) *reiben.*
rubber *Gummi, m.*
ruby *Rubin, m.*
rude *grob, unhöflich.*
ruffle (to) *außer Fassung bringen* (to upset);
    kräuseln.
ruin *Ruine, f.*
ruin (to) *ruinieren.*
rule *Regel, f.*
rule (to) *regieren, herrschen.*
ruler *Lineal, n.*
rum *Rum, m.*
rumor *Gerücht, n.*
run (to) *rennen, laufen.*
    run away   *weglaufen.*
rural *ländlich.*

rush (to) *Sturz, m.; Andrang, m.* (crowd).
Russian *Russe* (noun) *m.; russisch* (adj.).
rust (to) *rosten.*
rusty *rostig.*
rye *Roggen, m.*

S

sacred *heilig.*
sacrifice *Opfer, n.*
sacrifice (to) *opfern.*
sacrilege *Entweihung, f.*
sad *traurig.*
sadden (to) *betrüben.*
saddle *Sattel, m.*
sadness *Traurigkeit, f.*
safe *Schließfach* (noun) *m.* (of a bank);
    wohlbehalten (adj.) (in safekeeping);
    sicher (adj.) (secure).
safety *Sicherheit, f.*
sail (to) *segeln.*
sail *Segel, n.*
sailor *Matrose, m.*
saint *Heilige, m. & f.*
    patron saint   *Schutzheilige, m. & f.*
sake (for the . . . of) *um . . . willen.*
salad *Salat, m.*
salami *Salami, f.*
salary *Gehalt, n.*
sale *Verkauf, m.; Ausverkauf, m.* (bargain).
saleslady *Verkäuferin, f.*
salesman *Verkäufer, m.*
salmon *Lachs, m.*
salt *Salz, n.*
salute *Gruß, m.*
salute (to) *grüßen.*
salvation *Rettung, f.*
Salvation Army *Heilsarmee, f.*
same *der- (die-, das-) selbe*
    the same as   *der-, die-, dasselbe wie.*
    all the same   *es spielt keine Rolle.*
sample *Muster, n.*
sanctuary *Zufluchtsort, m.*
sand *Sand, m.*
sandal *Sandale, f.*
sandwich *belegtes Butterbrot, n.*
sandy *sandig.*
sanitary *hygienisch.*
sap *Saft, m.*
sapphire *Saphir, m.*
sarcasm *Sarkasmus, m.*
sarcastic *sarkastisch.*
sardine *Sardine, f.*
satiate (to) *sättigen.*
satin *Satin, m.*
satisfaction *Befriedigung, f.*
satisfactory *zufrieden stellend.*

satisfy (to) *befriedigen.*
saturate (to) *durchtränken, imprägnieren,*
 (chem.).
Saturday *Samstag, m.; Sonnabend, m.*
sauce *Sauce, f.; Soße, f.*
saucer *Untertasse, f.*
sausage *Wurst, f.*
savage (adj.) *wild, ungezähmt.*
save (to) *sparen* (hoard), *retten* (rescue).
saving *Ersparnis, f.*
savior *Erretter, m.*
say (to) *sagen.*
scale *Schuppe, f.; Tonleiter, f.* (music).
scales *Waage, f.*
scalp *Skalp, m.; Kopfhaut, f.*
scan (to) *flüchtig überblicken.*
scandal *Skandal, m.*
scanty *knapp, dürftig.*
scar *Narbe, f.*
scarce *knapp.*
scarcely *kaum.*
scare (to) *erschrecken.*
scarf *Schal, m.*
scarlet *scharlachrot.*
scattered *verstreut.*
schedule *Stundenplan, m.* (time); *Fahrplan*
 (train, bus).
scheme *Schema, n.; Entwurf, m.*
scholar *Gelehrte, m. & f.*
school *Schule, f.*
schoolteacher *Lehrer, m.; Lehrerin, f.*
science *Wissenschaft, f.*
scientific *wissenschaftlich.*
scientist *Wissenschaftler, m.*
scissors *Schere, f.*
scold (to) *schelten.*
scorn *Verachtung, f.*
scorn (to) *verachten.*
scornful *verächtlich, höhnisch.*
Scottish *schottisch.*
scrape (to) *kratzen; schaben* (vegetables).
scraper *Schaber, m.*
scratch *Schramme, f.; Kratzwunde, f.*
scratch (to) *kratzen.*
scream *Schrei, m.*
scream (to) *schreien.*
screen *Schirm, m., Bildschirm, m.*
 movie screen *Leinwand, f.*
screw *Schraube, f.*
scribble (to) *kritzeln.*
scruple *Skrupel, m.*
scrupulous *gewissenhaft.*
scrutinize (to) *genau prüfen.*
scuba diving *(Sport)tauchen, n.*
sculptor *Bildhauer, m.*
sculpture *Bildhauerei, f.*
sea *Meer, n.*
seal *Siegel, n.; Seehund, m.* (animal).
seal (to) *versiegeln, besiegeln (agreement).*

seam *Naht, f.*
search *Suche, f.; Untersuchung, f.* (customs).
search (to) *suchen, untersuchen.*
seashore *Seeküste, f.*
seasickness *Seekrankheit, f.*
season *Jahreszeit, f.; Saison, f.* (events).
seat *Sitz, m.*
seat (to) *setzen; Platz verschaffen.*
seat belt *Sicherheitsgurt, m.*
second *zweit(-er, -e, -es).*
secret *Geheimnis* (noun) *n.; geheim* (adj.).
secretary *Sekretär, m.; Sekretärin, f.*
sect *Sekte, f.*
section *Teil, m.*
secure *sicher.*
secure (to) *sichern.*
security *Sicherheit, f.*
see (to) *sehen.*
seed *Samen, m.*
seek (to) *suchen.*
seem (to) *scheinen.*
seize (to) *ergreifen, fassen.*
seldom *selten, rar.*
select (to) *(aus)wählen.*
selection *Auswahl, f.*
selfish *selbstsüchtig; egoistisch.*
selfishness *Selbstsucht, f.*
self-service *Selbstbedienung, f.*
sell (to) *verkaufen.*
semicolon *Semikolon, n.*
senate *Senat, m.*
senator *Senator, m.*
send (to) *senden.*
senior *Ältere(r).*
sensation *Gefühl, n.* (feeling); *Sensation, f.*
 (excitement); *Sinnesempfindung, f.*
sense *Sinn, m.*
senseless *sinnlos.*
sensibility *Vernünftigkeit, f.; Sensibilität, f.*
sensible *vernünftig, verständig.*
sensitive *empfindlich.*
sensitivity *Empfindlichkeit, f.*
sensual *sinnlich.*
sensuality *Wollust, f.; Sinnlichkeit, f.*
sentence *Urteil, n.* (legal); *Satz, m.* (grammar).
sentiment *Gefühl, n.*
sentimental *sentimental.*
sentimentality *Sentimentalität, f.*
separate *einzeln, getrennt.*
separate (to) *trennen.*
separately *besonders, getrennt.*
separation *Trennung, f.*
September *September, m.*
serene *heiter, friedlich.*
sergeant *Sergeant, m.; Unteroffizier, m.*
series *Serie, f.*
serious *ernst.*
seriousness *Ernsthaftigkeit, f.*
servant *Diener, m.*

serve (to) *dienen.*

service *Dienst, m.; Gottesdienst, m.* (church service).

session *Sitzung, f.*

set (adj.) *festgelegt.*

set *Sammlung, f.* (collection); *Untergang, m.;* (sun); *Satz, m.* (series); *Service, n.* (dishes).

set (to) *setzen; stellen* (clock).
to set the table *decken.*

settle (to) *abrechnen* (accounts); *erledigen* (conclude); *festsetzen.*
. . . in a territory *sich niederlassen.*
. . . in a place *ansässig werden.*

settlement *Begleichung, f.; Erledigung, f.; Siedlung, f.* (houses).

seven *sieben.*

seventeen *siebzehn.*

seventeenth *siebzehnte.*

seventh *siebte.*

seventieth *siebzigste.*

seventy *siebzig.*

several *mehrere.*
several times *mehrmals.*

severe *streng* (stern, rigorous); *heftig* (pain).

severity *Strenge, f.*

sew (to) *nähen.*

sewage *Kloakenwasser, n.*

sewer *Abwasserkanal, m.*

sex *Geschlecht, n.*

shabby *schäbig.*

shade *Schatten, m.*

shadow *Shatten, m.*

shady *schattig.*

shake (to) *schütteln; zittern* (tremble).
handshake *Händedruck, m.*

shallow *seicht, oberflächlich* (fig.).

shame *Schande, f.* (disgrace); *Scham, f.* (modesty).

shameful *schändlich.*

shameless *schamlos.*

shampoo *Shampoo, n.; Haarwaschmittel, m.*

shape *Form, f.*

share *Teil, m.; Anteil, m.; Aktie, f.* (stock).

share (to) *teilen, (sich) beteiligen.*

shareholder *Aktionär, m.*

sharp *scharf.*

sharpen *schärfen.*

shave (to) *sich rasieren.*

she *sie.*

shed *Hütte, f.*

shed (to) *vergießen* (spill); *abwerfen* (discard).

sheep *Schaf, n.*

sheer *rein, lauter.*

sheet *(Bett)laken, n.; Blatt, n.* (paper).

shelf *Brett, n.*

shell *Muschel, f.; Geschoss, n.* (artillery).

shelter *Unterkunft, f.; Luftschutzraum, m.* (air raids).

shelter *unterstellen* (from exposure); *schützen* (from danger); *beherbergen.*

shepherd *Schäfer, m.*

shield *Schild, n.*

shield (to) *schützen.*

shift *Schicht, f.* (workers).

shift (to) *schieben, versetzen, umstellen.*

shine (to) *scheinen; putzen* (shoes).

ship *Schiff, n.*

ship (to) *senden, verschiffen, verfrachten.*

shipment *Verladung, f.; Verschiffung, f.; Beförderung, f.* (conveyance of goods).

shirt *Hemd, n.*

shiver *Schauer, m.; Zittern, n.*

shiver (to) *(er)schauern.*

shock *Schlag, m.* (blow); *Stoß, m.*

shock (to) *anstossen* (scandalize); *erschüttern, schockieren.*

shoe *Schuh, m.*

shoemaker *Schuhmacher, m.*

shoot (to) *schießen.*

shop *Laden, m.; Geschäft, n.*

shopping center *Einkaufszentrum, n.*

short *kurz.*

shorten (to) *kürzen.*

shorthand *Kurzschrift, f.; Stenographie, f.*

shorts *Unterhosen, pl.* (men's underwear); *kurze Hosen* (short pants).

shot *Schuss, m.*

shoulder *Schulter, f.*

shout *Schrei, m.*

shout (to) *schreien.*

shovel *Schaufel, f.*

show *Vorstellung, f.* (play); *Ausstellung, f.* (exhibition).

show (to) *zeigen, aufführen, ausstellen.*

showcase *Vitrine, f.; Schaukasten, m.*

shower *Schauer, m.* (rain); *Dusche, f.* (shower-bath).

shrill *schrill, gellend.*

shrimp *Garnele, f.*

shrink (to) *einlaufen.*

shrub *Strauch, m.; Busch, m.*

shrubbery *Gebüsch, n.*

shun (to) *meiden, sich fern halten (von).*

shut *geschlossen.*

shut (to) *schließen.*

shy *schüchtern.*

sick *krank.*

sickness *Krankheit, f.*

side *Seite, f.*

sidewalk *Bürgersteig, m.*

siege *Belagerung, f.*

sigh *Seufzer, m.*

sight *Aussicht, f.; Anblick, m.*

sign (to) *seufzen, unterschreiben, unterzeichnen.*

sign *Zeichen, n.*

signal *Signal, n.*

signal (to) *signalisieren.*
signature *Unterschrift, f.*
significance *Bedeutung, f.*
significant *bezeichnend, bedeutend.*
signify (to) *bezeichnen* (indicate); *bedeuten*
    (mean).
silence *Schweigen, n.*
silent *still, schweigend, schweigsam.*
silk *Seide, f.*
silken *seiden.*
silly *dumm, albern, lächerlich.*
silver *Silber, n.*
silvery *silbern.*
similar *ähnlich.*
similarity *Ähnlichkeit, f.*
simple *einfach.*
simplicity *Einfachheit, f.*
simply *einfach, nur* (only).
simulate (to) *simulieren, vortäuschen.*
simultaneous *gleichzeitig.*
sin *Sünde, f.*
sin (to) *sündigen.*
since *seit* (dat.); *da, weil* (because).
sincere *aufrichtig; im Ernst.*
sincerity *Aufrichtigkeit, f.*
sing (to) *singen.*
singer *Sänger, m.; Sängerin, f.*
single *einzeln; ledig* (unmarried).
singular *einzigartig; seltsam* (strange).
sinister *unheilvoll, böse.*
sink *Ausguss, m.; Spüle, f.*
sink (to) *sinken.*
sinner *Sünder, m.; Sünderin, f.*
sip (to) *nippen.*
sip *Schluck, m.; Schlückchen, n.*
sir *Herr, m.*
sister *Schwester, f.*
sister-in-law *Schwägerin, f.*
sit (to) *sitzen* (be seated); *sich setzen* (sit
    down).
    to sit for an exam *sich einer Prüfung
        unterziehen.*
    to sit for a portrait *sich malen lassen.*
site *Lage, f.; Bauplatz, m.* (of a building);
    Stelle, f.
situation *Lage, f.; Umstände, pl.*
six *sechs.*
sixteen *sechzehn.*
sixteenth *sechzehnte.*
sixth *sechste.*
sixtieth *sechzigste.*
sixty *sechzig.*
size *Größe, f.*
skate *Schlittschuh, m.*
skate (to) *Schlittschuh laufen.*
skeleton *Gerippe, n.; Skelett, n.*
sketch *Skizze, f.*
sketch (to) *skizzieren.*
skill *Geschicklichkeit, f.; Fähigkeit, f.*

skillful *geschickt, kundig.*
skin *Haut, f.*
skirt *Rock, m.*
skull *Schädel, m.*
sky *Himmel, m.*
skyscraper *Wolkenkratzer, m.*
slam (to) *zuschlagen.*
slander (to) *verleumden.*
slap *Klaps, m.; Ohrfeige, f.* (in the face).
slate *Schiefer, m.; Dachschiefer.*
slaughter (to) *schlachten.*
slave *Sklave, m.; Sklavin, f.*
slavery *Sklaverei, f.*
sleep *Schlaf, m.*
sleep (to) *schlafen.*
sleeve *Ärmel, m.*
sleigh *Schlitten, m.*
slender *schlank.*
slice *Schnitte, f.; Scheibe* (bread).
slice (to) *in Scheiben schneiden.*
slide (to) *gleiten, rutschen.*
slight *gering, leichte Erkältung.*
slip (to) *(aus)rutschen, gleiten.*
    to slip on *anziehen* (clothes).
    to slip away *entschlüpfen.*
    to slip in *hineinschieben in.*
    to slip up *sich irren, im Irrtum sein.*
slip *Fehler, m.* (mistake); *Unterrock, m.*
    (lingerie).
slope *Abhang, m.*
slot *Einwurf, m.; Schlitz, m.* (mail).
slow *langsam.*
slumber *Schlummer, m.*
slumber (to) *schlummern.*
sly *schlau.*
small *klein.*
smart *elegant* (clothes); *gescheit* (clever).
smash (to) *zerschmettern.*
smear (to) *beschmieren, einreiben.*
smell *Geruch, m.*
smell (to) *riechen.*
smile *Lächeln, n.*
smile (to) *lächeln.*
smoke *Rauch, m.*
smoke (to) *rauchen.*
smooth *glatt.*
smother (to) *ersticken.*
smuggle (to) *schmuggeln.*
snail *Schnecke, f.*
snake *Schlange, f.*
snapshot *Aufnahme, f.*
snatch (to) *ergreifen.*
sneer (to) *verhöhnen.*
sneeze (to) *nießen.*
snore (to) *schnarchen.*
snow *Schnee, m.*
snowstorm *Schneesturm, m.*
so *so.*
    and so on *und so weiter.*

soak (to) *einweichen, durchnässen* (drench).

soap *Seife, f.*

sob *Schluchzen, n.*

sob (to) *schluchzen.*

sober *nüchtern.*

social *gesellschaftlich.*

society *Gesellschaft, f.*

sock *Sock, f.; kurzer Strumpf, m.*

soda *Sodawasser, n.; Sprudel, n.*

soft *weich.*

soften (to) *erweichen, aufweichen.*

software *Software, f.*

soil (to) *beschmutzen.*

soil *Erde, f.; Boden, m.*

soiled *schmutzig, beschmutzt.*

solar energy *Sonnenenergie, f.; Solarenergie, f.*

soldier *Soldat, m.*

sole *Sohle, f.*

solemn *feierlich.*

solemnity *Feierlichkeit, f.*

solicit (to) *bitten, ersuchen.*

solid *fest, solide.*

solitary *einsam* (lonely); *einzeln* (one).

solitude *Einsamkeit, f.*

solution *Lösung, f.*

solve *lösen.*

some *einige* (a few); *etwas* (partial).

somebody *jemand.*

somehow *irgendwie.*

something *etwas.*

sometimes *zuweilen, manchmal.*

somewhat *etwas, einigermaßen.*

somewhere *irgendwo.*

son *Sohn, m.*

song *Lied, n.*

son-in-law *Schwiegersohn, m.*

soon *bald.*

soot *Russ, m.*

soothe (to) *besänftigen; lindern* (pain).

sore *Geschwür* (noun) *n.; wund, schmerzhaft* (adj.); *empfindlich, verärgert* (annoyed).

    sore throat *Halsschmerzen, pl.*

sorrow *Kummer, m.*

sorry *bekümmert.*

    I am sorry. *Es tut mir Leid.*

sort *Sorte, f.; Art, f.*

sort (to) *sortieren, einordnen.*

sound *Laut, m.; Geräusch, n.*

sound (to) *lauten, läuten* (telephone).

soup *Suppe, f.*

sour *sauer.*

source *Quelle, f.* (spring); *Ursprung, m.* (origin).

south *Süden, m.*

southeast *südöstlich* (adj.); *Südosten, m.*

southern *Süd-; südlich.*

southwest *südwestlich; Südwesten, m.*

sovereign *Herrscher, m.; Herrscherin, f.; Soverän, m.*

sow (to) *säen.*

space *Raum, m.; Zwischenraum, m.* (space between).

spacious *geräumig.*

spade *Spaten, m.; Pik, n.* (cards).

Spanish *spanisch.*

spare *spärlich.*

spare (to) *entbehren, schonen.*

spark *Funke, m.*

sparkle (to) *funkeln, glänzen.*

sparrow *Sperling, Spatz, m.*

speak (to) *sprechen.*

special *besonders, extra.*

specialty *Spezialität, f.*

specific *eigen, spezifisch, genau.*

specify (to) *spezifizieren, anführen.*

spectacle *Schauspiel, n.; Schaustück, n.*

spectator *Zuschauer, m.*

speculate (to) *spekulieren.*

speech *Sprache, f.; Rede, f.*

speed *Geschwindigkeit, f.*

speedy *schnell, geschwind.*

spell *Zauber, m.* (charm).

spell (to) *buchstabieren, schreiben.*

spelling *Buchstabieren, n.*

spend (to) *ausgeben.*

sphere *Sphäre, f.*

spice *Gewürz, n.*

spice (to) *würzen.*

spicy *würzig.*

spider *Spinne, f.*

spill (to) *verschütten, vergießen.*

spin (to) *spinnen.*

spine *Rückgrat, n.; Wirbelsäude, f.*

spirit *Geist, m.*

spiritual *geistig.*

spit (to) *springen.*

spite *Bösartigkeit, f.*

    in spite of *trotz* (gen.), *trotzdem* (conj.).

splash (to) *(be)spritzen.*

splendid *prachtvoll.*

    Splendid! *Wunderbar!*

splendor *Pracht, f.; Glanz, m.*

split *Spalt, m.; Trennung, f.; Spaltung, f.*

split (to) *spalten.*

spoil (to) *verderben; verwöhnen* (child).

sponge *Schwamm, m.*

spontaneous *spontan.*

spoon *Löffel, m.*

spoonful *ein Löffel voll*

sport *Sport, m.*

spot *Fleck, m.* (stain); *Stelle, f.* (place).

spread (to) *verbreiten; bestreichen* (on bread).

spring *Frühling, m.* (season); *Sprung, m.* (jump); *Quelle, f.* (source).

spring (to) *springen.*

sprinkle *sprenkeln, bestreuen, sprengen.*

sprout *Sprössling, m.; Spross, m.*

spur *Sporn, m.*

spur (to) *anspornen.*

   on the spur of the moment   *spontan.*

spurn (to) *verschmähen* (an offer);
   zurückstoßen (a person).

spy *Spion, m.*

spy (to) *spionieren.*

squadron *Schwadron, f.; Eskadron, f.* (mil.);
   Batallion (tanks).

square *Quadrat, n.*

squeeze (to) *(aus)drücken.*

squirrel *Eichhörnchen, n.*

stabilize (to) *stabilisieren.*

stable *fest* (adj.); *stabil.*

stack *Stoss, m.* (wood), *Stapel.*

stack (to) *aufstapeln, aufhäufen.*

stadium *Stadion, n.*

staff *Stab, m.* (military); *Personal, n.*
   (business).

stage *Bühne, f.* (theater); *Stadium, n.*

stain *Fleck, m.; Färbemittel* (dye), *n.*

stain (to) *(be)flecken, färben.*

stairs *Treppe, f.*

stammer (to) *stottern, stammeln.*

stamp *Briefmarke, f.* (postage); *Stempel, m.*

stance *Haltung, f.; Stellung, f.*

stand *Stand, m.*

   stand still   *Stillstand.*

   to stand pain   *den Schmerz aushalten.*

   to stand on ceremony   *Umstände machen.*

   to stand back   *zurücktreten.*

star *Stern, m.*

starch *Stärke, f.*

stare (to) *(an)starren.*

start *Anfang, m.*

start (to) *beginnen, anfangen.*

starve (to) *(ver)hungern.*

state *Staat, m.* (country); *Zustand, m.*
   (condition).

state (to) *angeben, vorbringen, erklären.*

stately *stattlich.*

statement *Erklärung, f.; Aufstellung, f.*
   (account).

stateroom *Kabine, f.; Prunksaal, m.*

station *Bahnhof, m.* (railroad); *Stellung, f.*
   (position).

statistics *Statistik, f.*

statue *Statue, f.*

stay *Aufenthalt, m.*

stay (to) *bleiben.*

steady *fest.*

steak *Steak, n.*

steal (to) *stehlen.*

steam *Dampf, m.*

steamer *Dampfer, m.*

steel *Stahl, m.*

steep *steil.*

steer (to) *steuern.*

stem *Stengel, m.* (plant).

step *Schritt, m.; Stufe, f.* (stairs).

step (to) *schreiten.*

sterilized *sterilisiert.*

stern *ernst.*

stew *Ragout, n.; Eintopfgericht, n.*

stew (to) *schmoren, dünsten.*

steward *Steward, m.*

stick *Stock, m.*

stick (to) *stecken; ankleben* (paste).

stiff *steif.*

stiffen (to) *(ver)steifen; verstärken.*

stiffness *Steifheit, f.*

still *still, ruhig* (adj.); *jedoch, noch* (adv.).

still (to) *stillen, beruhigen.*

stimulant *Anregungsmittel, n.*

stimulate (to) *anregen.*

sting *Stich, m.*

sting (to) *stechen.*

stinginess *Geiz, m.*

stingy *geizig.*

stir (to) *rühren, bewegen.*

stirrup *Steigbügel, m.*

stitch *Stich, m.* (surgery); *Masche, f.* (sew).

stitch (to) *heften; nähen* (sew).

stock *Warenbestand, m.; Vorrat, m.*

   stocks and shares   *Aktien und Wertpapiere*
   (pl.).

stock exchange *Börse, f.*

stocking *Strumpf, m.*

stomach *Magen, m.*

stone *Stein, m.*

stool *Schemel, m.*

stop *Haltestelle, f.*

stop (to) *halten, aufhören, Halt machen.*
   Stop!   *Halt!*

store *Laden, m.; Warenhaus, n.; Geschäft, n.*

store (to) *lagern, aufbewahren; speichern* (on
   computer disk).

stork *Storch, m.*

storm *Sturm, m.*

story *Geschichte, f.; Erzählung, f.;*
   Stockwerk, n.

stove *Ofen, m.*

straight *gerade.*

   straight on   *geradeaus.*

straighten *gerade machen, aufrichten.*

strain *Anstrengung, f.*

strange *seltsam, sonderbar.*

stranger *Ausländer, m.; Fremder, m.*

strap *Riemen, m.*

straw *Stroh, n.; Strohhalm, m.* (for drinking).

strawberry *Erdbeere, f.*

stream *Strom, m.*

street *Straße, f.*

streetcar *Straßenbahn, f.*

strength *Kraft, f.*

strengthen *verstärken; kräftigen.*

strenuous *angestrengt.*

stress *Druck, m.; Betonung, f.* (accentuation).

stretch *Strecke, f.*

stretch (to) *strecken.*

strict *streng.*

stride *Schritt, m.*

string *Bindfaden, m.; Schnur* (cord), *f.*
   no strings attached   *ohne Bedingungen.*

strip (to) *abstreifen, abziehen; entkleiden* (of clothes).

stripe *Streifen, m.*

strive (to) *streben.*

stroke *Strich, m.* (of a brush, pen); *Schlaganfall, m.* (med.).

stroll *Spaziergang, m.*

stroll (to) *spazierengehen.*

strong *stark.*

structure *Bau, m.*

struggle *Kampf, m.*

struggle (to) *kämpfen.*

stubborn *hartnäckig.*

student *Schüler, m.; Schülerin, f.; Student, m.; Studentin, f.* (college, univ.).

studio *Studio, n.; Atelier, n.* (artist).

studious *lernbegierig, fleißig, arbeitsam.*

study *Studium, n.*

study (to) *studieren.*

stuff *Stoff, m.; Material, n.*

stuff (to) *stopfen, verstopfen.*

stumble (to) *stolpern.*

stump *Stumpf, m.*

stun (to) *betäuben.*

stunt *Sensation, f.; Kunststück, n.*

stupendous *fantastisch.*

stupid *dumm.*

stupidity *Dummheit, f.*

stupor *Betäubung, f.*

sturdy *kräftig.*

stutter (to) *stottern.*

style *Stil, m.*

subdue (to) *unterwerfen.*

subject *Angelegenheit, f.;* (matter) *Fach, n.* (school); *Fachgebiet, n.*

subjugate (to) *unterwerfen.*

subjunctive *Konjunktiv, m.*

sublime *erhaben.*

submission *Unterwerfung, f.*

submissive *unterwürfig.*

submit (to) *abgeben.*

subordinate *untergeordnet.*

subordination *Unterordnung, f.*

subscribe (to) *abonnieren.*

subscription *Abonnement, n.*

subsist (to) *bestehen, sich ernähren von, weiterbestehen.*

substance *Substanz, f.*

substantial *beträchtlich, wesentlich.*

substitute (to) *ersetzen.*

substitution *Ersatz, m.*

subtle *fein, raffiniert.*

subtract *abziehen.*

subtraction *Subtraktion, f.*

suburb *Vorstadt, f.*

subway *Untergrundbahn, f.*

succeed (to) *gelingen* (achieve).

success *Erfolg, m.*

successful *erfolgreich.*

succession *Nachfolge, f.*

successor *Nachfolger, m.*

such *Solch-.*
   Such a scandal!   *Solch ein Skandal!*

sudden *plötzlich.*

sue (to) *verklagen.*

suffer (to) *leiden.*

suffering *Leiden, n.*

sufficient *genügend.*

sugar *Zucker, m.*

suggest (to) *andeuten, vorschlagen.*

suggestion *Vorschlag, m.*

suicide *Selbstmord, m.*

suit *Anzug, m.; Kostüm, n.* (lady's).

suitable *passend.*

sulk (to) *schmollen, trotzen.*

sullen *mürrisch, düster.*

sum *Summe, f.*

summary *Zusammenfassung, f.*

summer *Sommer, m.*

summit *Gipfel, m.*

summon (to) *vorladen, einberufen.*

sumptuous *prächtig, kostbar.*

sum up *zusammenfassen.*

sun *Sonne, f.*

sunbeam *Sonnenstrahl, m.*

Sunday *Sonntag, m.*

sunny *sonnig.*

sunrise *Sonnenaufgang, m.*

sunset *Sonnenuntergang, m.*

sunshine *Sonnenschein, m.*

superb *herrlich, vorzüglich.*

superficial *oberflächlich.*

superfluous *überflüssig.*

superintendent *Inspektor, m.; Direktor, m.; Verwalter, m.*

superior *Vorgesetzte, m. & f.*

superiority *Überlegenheit, f.*

superstition *Aberglaube, m.*

supervise (to) *beaufsichtigen.*

supper *Abendessen, n.*

supplement *Nachtrag, m.; Anhang, m.; Beilage, f.* (of a newspaper).

supplementary *ergänzend.*

supply (to) *versorgen, beschaffen.*

support *Stütze, f.; Unterstützung, f.*

support (to) *(unter)stützen.*

suppose (to) *vermuten, annehmen.*

suppress (to) *unterdrücken.*

supreme *höchst, oberst.*

sure *gewiss, sicher.*

surety *Sicherheit, f.*

surface *Oberfläche, f.*

surgeon *Chirurg, m.*
surgery *Chirurgie, f.*
surname *Zuname, m.; Nachname, m.*
surpass *übertreffen.*
surprise *Überraschung, f.*
surprise (to) *überraschen.*
surrender *Übergabe, f.; Kapitulation, f.*
surrender (to) *aufgeben, übergeben.*
surroundings *Umgebung, f.*
survey *Übersicht, f.; Vermessung, f.*
survey (to) *besichtigen, vermessen.*
survive (to) *überleben.*
susceptibility *Empfänglichkeit, f.*
susceptible *empfänglich, empfindlich.*
suspect (to) *verdächtigen.*
suspense *Ungewissheit, f.; Spannung, f.*
suspicion *Verdacht, m.*
suspicious *verdächtig.*
sustain (to) *ernähren.*
swallow *Schluck, m.* (gulp); *Schwalbe, f.* (bird).
swallow (to) *schlucken.*
swamp *Sumpf, m.*
swan *Schwan, m.*
swear (to) *schwören.*
sweat *Schweiß, m.*
sweat (to) *schwitzen.*
sweep (to) *kehren; fegen.*
sweet *süß.*
sweetness *Süße, f.*
swell (to) *(an)schwellen.*
swift *schnell, rasch.*
swim (to) *schwimmen.*
swindle (to) *schwindeln.*
swindler *Schwindler, m.*
swing (to) *schwingen, schaukeln.*
Swiss *Schweizer* (noun) *m.; schweizerisch* (adj.).
switch *Schalter, m.*
sword *Schwert, n.*
syllable *Silbe, f.*
symbol *Symbol, n.*
symbolic *symbolisch.*
symbolize *symbolisieren.*
symmetrical *symmetrisch.*
sympathetic *mitfühlend.*
sympathize (to) *mitfühlen.*
sympathy *Sympathie, f.; Verständnis, n.*
symptom *Symptom, n.*
syrup *Sirup, m.*
system *System, n.*
systematic *systematisch, methodisch, planmäßig.*

T

table *Tisch, m.*
tablecloth *Tischtuch, n.*

tacit *stillschweigend.*
taciturn *schweigsam.*
tact *Takt, m.*
tactful *taktvoll.*
tactless *taktlos.*
tail *Schwanz, m.*
tailor *Schneider, m.*
take (to) *nehmen.*
   to take an exam   *eine Prüfung ablegen.*
   to take heart   *Mut fassen.*
   to take a vacation   *Ferien machen; Urlaub nehmen.*
   to take time   *dauern.*
   to take an oath   *einen Eid ablegen.*
   to take part   *teilnehmen (an).*
   to take place   *stattfinden.*
   to take pleasure in   *Vergnügen finden an.*
   to take one's temperature   *Fieber messen.*
   to take a walk   *einen Spaziergang machen.*
   to take over   *übernehmen.*
tale *Erzählung, f.*
talent *Talent, n.; Begabung, f.*
talk *Rede, f.; Vortrag, m.*
talk (to) *reden, plaudern, sprechen.*
talkative *gesprächig.*
tall *hoch; groß* (people).
tame *zahm.*
tame (to) *zähmen.*
tangle (to) *verwickeln.*
tank *Tank, m.*
tapestry *Wandteppich, m.*
tar *Teer, m.*
tardy *spät.*
target *Zeil, (Ziel)scheibe, f.*
tarnish (to) *trüben, anlaufen* (metal).
task *Aufgabe, f.*
taste *Geschmack, m.*
taste (to) *schmecken.*
tax *Steuer, f.*
taxi *Taxi, n.*
tea *Tee, m.*
teach (to) *unterrichten.*
teacher *Lehrer, m.; Lehrerin, f.*
team *Gruppe, f.; Mannschaft, f.* (sports).
tear *Träne, f.* (teardrop); *Riss, m.* (rip).
tear (to) *(zer)reißen.*
tease (to) *necken, ärgern.*
teaspoon *Teelöffel, m.*
technical *technisch.*
technique *Technik, f.*
technology *Technik, f.*
tedious *langweilig, ermüdend.*
telecommunications *Fernmeldewesen, n.*
telefax *Telefax, n.*
telegram *Telegramm, n.*
telegraph (to) *telegrafieren.*
telephone *Telefon, n.*
   telephone operator   *Telefonistin, f.*
telephone (to) *telefonieren, anrufen.*

tell (to) *sagen, erzählen.*
temper *Laune, f.*
temperate *gemäßig, mäßig.*
temperature *Temperatur, f.*
tempest *Sturm, m.; Gewitter, n.*
temple *Tempel, m.; Schläfe, f.* (head).
temporary *vorübergehend, vorläufig.*
tempt (to) *versuchen, verlocken.*
temptation *Versuchung, f.*
ten *zehn.*
tenacious *zäh, hartnäckig.*
tenacity *Zähigkeit, f.; Hartnäckigkeit, f.*
tenant *Mieter, m.*
tend (to) *sich neigen zu.*
tendency *Neigung, f.*
tender *zart, empfindlich.*
tennis *Tennis, n.*
tense *gespannt.*
tense *Zeitform, f.* (grammar).
tension *Spannung, f.*
tent *Zelt, n.*
tenth *Zehntel* (noun) *n.* (fraction); *zehnt-* (adj.).
tepid *lauwarm.*
term *Ausdruck* (expression), *m.; First* (time), *f.*
    to be on good terms   *auf gutem Fuß mit jemand stehen.*
terrace *Terrasse, f.*
terrible *schrecklich.*
terrify (to) *(er)schrecken.*
territory *Gebiet, n.*
terror *Schrecken, m.*
test *Prüfung, f.*
test (to) *prüfen.*
testify (to) *bezeugen.*
testimony *Zeugnis, n.*
text *Text, m.*
textbook *Lehrbuch, n.*
than *als.*
thank (to) *danken.*
    Thank you!   *Danke schön!*
thankful *dankbar.*
that *das* (demonstrative); *der, die, das, welch(-er, -e, -es)* (relative); *dass, damit* (conjunction).
thaw *Tauwetter, n.*
thaw (to) *tauen.*
the *der, die, das.* (nom.).
theater *Theater, n.*
their *ihr.*
theirs *ihr(-er, -e, -es).*
them *sie* (acc.); *ihnen* (dat.).
theme *Thema, n.*
themselves *sie (ihnen) selbst, sich.*
then *dann, damals.*
theory *Theorie, f.*
there *dort, da.*
    there is, there are   *es gibt.*
thereafter *danach.*

thereby *dadurch.*
therefore *deshalb, daher.*
thereupon *darauf.*
thermometer *Thermometer, n.*
these *diese.*
thesis *These, f.; Doktorarbeit, f.* (university).
they *sie.*
thick *dick.*
thief *Dieb, m.*
thigh *Schenkel, m.*
thimble *Fingerhut, m.*
thin *dünn.*
thing *Sache, f.; Ding, n.*
think (to) *denken.*
third *dritte.*
third world *Dritte Welt, f.*
thirst *Durst, m.*
thirteen *dreizehn.*
thirteenth *dreizehnte.*
thirtieth *dreißigste.*
thirty *dreißig.*
this *dieser(-e, -es).*
thorn *Dorn, m.*
thorough *gründlich.*
though *zwar, obwohl, obgleich.*
thought *Gedanke, m.*
thoughtful *nachdenklich.*
thoughtless *rücksichtslos.*
thousand *tausend.*
thrash (to) *dreschen.*
thread *Faden, m.*
threat *Drohung, f.*
threaten (to) *drohen.*
three *drei.*
threshold *Schwelle, f.*
thrift *Sparsamkeit, f.*
thrifty *sparsam.*
thrill *spannendes Erregnis, m.*
thrill (to) *begeistern, packen.*
thrilling *ergreifend, begeisternd.*
thrive (to) *gedeihen.*
thriving *gedeihend, blühend.*
throat *Kehle, f.; Hals, m.*
throb (to) *klopfen.*
throne *Tron, m.*
throng *Menge, f.*
through *durch* (acc.); *hindurch.*
throughout *durchaus.*
throw (to) *werfen.*
thumb *Dawmen, m.*
thunder *Donner, m.*
thunder (to) *donnern.*
Thursday *Donnerstag, m.*
thus *so, auf diese Weise.*
thwart (to) *vereiteln.*
ticket *Karte, f.; Fahrkarte, f.* (train).
ticket window *Schalter, m.*
tickle (to) *kitzeln.*
ticklish *kitzlig.*

tide *Flut, f.* (high); *Ebbe, f.* (low).
tidiness *Ordentlichkeit, f.*
tidy *ordentlich.*
tie *Band, n.* (bond); *Krawatte, f.* (necktie).
tie (to) *binden.*
tiger *Tiger, m.*
tight *eng.*
tile *Ziegel, m.* (roof); *Kachel, f.* (wall); *Fliese, f.* (kitchen).
till *bis.*
　　till now *bisher, bis jetzt.*
tilt (to) *kippen.*
timber *Bauholz, n.*
time *Zeit, f.*
　　in the nick of time *zur rechten Zeit.*
　　time of arrival *Ankunftszeit, f.*
　　time of departure *Abfahrtszeit, f.*
　　at the present time *gegenwärtig.*
　　time is up *Die Zeit ist abgelaufen.*
　　Once upon a time . . . *Es war einmal . . .*
　　to waste time *(die) Zeit verschwenden (vertreiben).*
　　for the last time *zum letzten Mal.*
　　behind the times *rückständig.*
　　from time to time *von Zeit zu Zeit.*
　　on time *pünktlich.*
　　to have a good time *sich vergnügen, sich amüsieren.*
　　what time is it? *Wie spät ist es?*
timid *furchtsam, ängstlich.*
timidity *Furchtsamkeit, f.*
tin *Zinn, n.*
tiny *winzig.*
tip *Spitze, f.* (end); *Trinkgeld, n.* (money).
tip (to) *Trinkgeld geben.*
tire *Reifen, m.*
tire (to) *ermüden.*
tired *müde.*
tireless *unermüdlich.*
tiresome *langweilig, ermüdend.*
title *Titel, m.*
to *zu* (with infinitive); *nach, zu* (dat.); *an* (dat. or acc.).
toad *Kröte, f.*
toast *Toast, m.*
tobacco *Tabak, m.*
today *heute.*
toe *Zehe, f.*
together *zusammen.*
toil (to) *schwer arbeiten.*
toilet *Toilette, f.*
token *Andenken, n.; Münze, f.* (coin).
tolerable *erträglich.*
tolerance *Toleranz, f.; Duldung, f.*
tolerant *duldsam, tolerant, geduldig* (patient).
tolerate (to) *dulden.*
toll (to) *läuten, schlagen* (hours).
tomato *Tomate, f.*
tomb *Grab, n.*

tomorrow *morgen.*
ton *Tonne, f.*
tone *Ton, m.*
tongs *Zange, f.*
tongue *Zunge, f.*
tonight *heute Abend.*
too *auch* (also); *zu* (excessive).
tool *Werkzeug, n.*
toolbox *Werkzeugkasten, m.*
tooth *Zahn, m.*
toothbrush *Zahnbürste, f.*
toothpaste *Zahnpasta, f.*
toothpick *Zahnstocher, m.*
toothpowder *Zahnpulver, n.*
top *Gipfel, m.; Oberst, n.; Spitze, f.*
topic *Gesprächsstoff, m.; Thema, n.*
torch *Fackel, f.*
torment *Qual, f.*
torment (to) *quälen.*
torture *Folter, f.*
torture (to) *foltern.*
toss (to) *werfen.*
toss *Wurf, m.*
total *Gesamtsumme, f.; gesamt* (adj.); *völlig* (adj.).
totally *gänzlich.*
touch (to) *berühren.*
touching *rührend.*
touchy *überempfindlich.*
tough *hart, zäh.*
tour *Rise, f.; Rundreise, f.; Tour, f.*
tour (to) *herumreisen, durchreisen.*
tourist *Tourist, m.*
tournament *Turnier, n.*
toward *zu, nach* (dat.); *gegen* (acc.).
towel *Handtuch, n.*
tower *Turm, m.*
town *Stadt, f.*
toy *Spielzeug, n.*
trace *Spur, f.*
trace (to) *durchzeichnen* (drawing), *(nach) zeichnen, aufspüren.*
track *Spur, f.*
trade *Handel, m.*
tradition *Tradition, f.; alter Brauch, m.*
traditional *traditionell, üblich.*
traffic *Verkehr, m.*
tragedy *Tragödie, f.*
tragic *tragisch.*
trail *Pfad, m.; Weg, m.; Fährte, f.* (hunting).
train *Zug, m.*
train (to) *erziehen, schulen* (children); *trainieren* (athletes).
training *Ausbildung, f.*
traitor *Verräter, m.*
trample (to) *niedertreten.*
tranquil *ruhig.*
tranquility *Ruhe, f., Ungestörtheit.*
transaction *Verhandlung, f.; Transaktion, f.*

transfer (to) *übertragen*
transit *Durchgang, m.*
transition *Übergang, m.; Überweisung, f.*
transitory *vergänglich.*
translate (to) *übersetzen, f.*
translation *Übersetzung, f.*
translator *Übersetzer, m.*
transmission *Übersendung, f.*
transmit (to) *übersenden, übertragen.*
transparent *durchsichtig.*
transport *Transport, m.*
transport (to) *transportieren.*
transportation *Beförderung, f.; Überführung,*
    f.; Transport, m.
trap *Falle, f.*
trap (to) *fangen, ertappen.*
trash *Abfall, m.; Auswurf, m.*
travel *Reisen, n.*
travel (to) *reisen.*
traveler *Reisende, m. & f.*
tray *Tablett, n.*
treacherous *treulos, verräterisch.*
treachery *Treulosigkeit, f.*
treason *Verrat, m.*
treasure *Schatz, m.*
treasurer *Schatzmeister, m.*
treasury *Schatzamt, n.*
treat *Hochgenuss, m.*
treat (to) *behandeln, bearbeiten,*
    spendieren.
treatment *Behandlung, f.*
treaty *Vertrag, m.*
tree *Baum, m.*
tremble (to) *zittern.*
trembling *Zittern, n.*
tremendous *ungeheuer.*
trench *Graben, m.; Schützengraben, m.*
    (military).
trend *Neigung, f.*
trial *Probe, f.; Prozess, m.* (law).
triangle *Dreieck, n.*
tribe *Stamm, m.*
tribunal *Tribunal, n.*
tribune *Tribüne, f.*
tribute *Ehrung, f.; Hochachtung, f.*
trick *Kniff, m.; Trick, m.*
trifle *Kleinigkeit, f.*
trifling *kleinlich* (petty); *gering* (minor).
trim (to) *stutzen* (hedges); *kürzen* (hair).
trimming *Verzierung, f.; Garnierung, f.*
trip *Fahrt, f.*
trip (to) *stolpern.*
triple *dreifach.*
triumph *Triumph, m.; Sieg, m.*
triumph (to) *siegen.*
trivial *geringfügig.*
trolley car *Straßenbahnwagen, m.*
troop *Truppe, f.*
trot *Trab, m.*

trot (to) *traben.*
trouble *Unannehmlichkeit, f.;*
    Schwierigkeit, f.
    to go to the trouble   *sich Umstände*
        machen.
    to save oneself the trouble   *sich die Mühe*
        ersparen.
trousers *Hose, f.*
truck *Lastwagen, m.*
true *wahr.*
truly *wahrhaftig; aufrichtig.*
    yours truly   *hochachtungsvoll.*
trump *Trumpf, m.*
trump (to) *trumpfen.*
trumpet *Trompete, f.*
trunk *Koffer, m.*
trust *Vertrauen, n.*
trust (to) *trauen.*
trustworthy *zuverlässig.*
truth *Wahrheit, f.*
truthful *wahrhaft, genau.*
truthfully *aufrichtig, ehrlich gesagt,*
    wahrhaftig.
truthfulness *Ehrlichkeit, f.; Wahrheit, f.*
try (to) *versuchen, probieren.*
tube *Rohr, n.*
tumble (to) *stürzen, stolpern.*
tumult *Getümmel, n.*
tune *Melodie, f.*
tune (to) *stimmen.*
tunnel *Tunnel, m.*
turf *Rasen, m.*
turkey *Truthahn, m.*
turmoil *Aufruhr, f.; Unruhe, f.*
turn (to) *drehen.*
    turn back   *zurückkehren.*
    Turn left.   *Biegen Sie links ein!*
    to turn around   *sich undrehen.*
    to turn pages   *umblättern.*
    to turn upside down   *auf den*
        Kopf stellen.
    It's your turn.   *Sie sind dran.*
    to turn against   *sich wenden gegen.*
turnip *weiße Rübe, f.*
twelfth *zwölfte.*
twelve *zwölf.*
twentieth *zwanzigste.*
twenty *zwanzig.*
twice *zweimal.*
twilight *Zwielicht, n.*
twin *Zwilling* (noun) *m.; doppelt* (adj.).
twist (to) *drehen, wickeln.*
two *zwei.*
type *Modell, n.; Typ, m.*
type (to) *mit der Schreibmaschine*
    schreiben.
typewriter *Schreibmaschine, f.*
tyranny *Tyrannei, f.*
tyrant *Tyrann, m.*

U

ugliness *Hässlichkeit, f.*
ugly *hässlich.*
ultimate *(aller) letzt* (time), *best*
umbrella *(Regen)schirm, m.*
umpire *Schiedsrichter, m.*
unable to *unfähig.*
unanimity *Einmütigkeit, f.; Einstimmigkeit, f.*
unanimous *einstimmig.*
unawares *unversehens.*
unbearable *unerträglich.*
unbelievable *unglaublich.*
unbutton (to) *aufknöpfen.*
uncertain *unsicher.*
uncertainty *Unsicherheit, f.*
unchangeable *unveränderlich.*
uncle *Onkel, m.*
uncomfortable *unbequem.*
uncommon *ungewöhnlich.*
unconscious *bewusstlos, unbewusst.*
unconsciousness *Ohnmacht, f.*
uncouth *ungebildet.*
uncover (to) *aufdecken; offenbaren* (feelings).
undecided *unentschieden.*
undefinable *unerklärbar, unerklärlich.*
undeniable *unleugbar, unbestreitbar.*
under *unter* (dat. or acc.).
undergo (to) *durchmachen, erleiden* (suffer).
underground *Untergrund* (noun) *n.;*
        unterirdisch (adj.); *Untergrundbahn, f.*
        (subway).
underline (to) *unterstreichen.*
underneath *unten, unterhalb.*
understand (to) *verstehen.*
understanding *Verständnis, n.*
undertake (to) *unternehmen.*
undertaker *Leichenbestatter, m.*
undertaking *Unternehmen, n.*
underwear *Unterwäsche, f.*
undesirable *unerwünscht.*
undignified *würdelos.*
undo (to) *aufmachen; auflösen* (untie).
undress (to) *sich ausziehen.*
uneasy *beunruhigt.*
uneasiness *Beunruhigung, f.*
unemployed *arbeitslos.*
unequal *ungleich.*
unequaled *unvergleichlich.*
uneven *uneben.*
uneventful *ereignislos.*
unexpected *unerwartet.*
unfair *ungerecht.*
unfaithful *untreu.*
unfavorable *ungünstig.*
unforgettable *unvergesslich.*
unfortunate *unglücklich.*
unfortunately *unglücklicherweise, leider.*

ungrateful *undankbar.*
unhappily *leider.*
unhappy *unglücklich.*
unharmed *unverletzt.*
unhealthy *ungesund.*
unheard (of) *unerhört.*
uniform *Uniform* (noun) *f.; gleichförmig* (adj.).
uniformity *Gleichförmigkeit, f.*
uniformly *gleichförmig.*
unify (to) *vereinigen.*
unimportant *unwichtig.*
unintentional *unabsichtlich.*
union *Vereinigung, f.; Verband, m.;*
        Gewerkschaft, f. (trade union).
unit cost *Stückkosten (pl.).*
universal *universal.*
universe *Weltall, n.*
university *Universität, f.*
unjust *ungerecht.*
unkind *unfreundlich.*
unknown *unbekannt.*
unlawful *ungesetzlich.*
unless *es sei denn dass; ausgenommen.*
unlike *unähnlich, anders als.*
unlikely *unwahrscheinlich.*
unlimited *unbeschränkt.*
unload (to) *abladen, ausladen.*
unluckily *unglücklicherweise.*
unnecessary *unnötig.*
unoccupied *unbesetzt; unbeschäftigt.*
unpack (to) *auspacken.*
unpleasant *unangenehm.*
unpublished *unveröffentlicht.*
unquestionably *fraglos, sicherlich.*
unravel (to) *enträtseln, auflösen.*
unreal *unwirklich.*
unreasonable *unvernünftig.*
unreliable *unzuverlässig.*
unrestrained *ungezwungen.*
unroll (to) *abwickeln, entrollen.*
unsafe *unsicher, gefährlich.*
unsatisfactory *unbefriedigend.*
unsatisfied *unbefriedigt.*
unscrupulous *bedenkenlos, skrupellos.*
unselfish *selbstlos.*
unsteady *unsicher, wackelig.*
unsuccessful *erfolglos.*
unsuitable *unpassend.*
untidy *unordentlich.*
untie (to) *aufbinden, losbinden.*
until *bis, an, zu* (dat.).
    until now *bisher.*
untrue *unwahr; untreu* (faithless).
unusual *ungewöhnlich.*
unwell *unwohl.*
unwholesome *ungesund.*
unwilling *widerwillig, unwillig.*
unwise *unklug.*
unworthy *unwürdig.*

up *auf* (dat. or acc.); *aufwärts; oben.*
uphold (to) *stützen, aufrechterhalten* (fig.).
upkeep *Instandhaltung, f.*
upon *auf, über* (dat. or acc.).
upper *ober.*
upright *aufrecht.*
uprising *Aufstand, m.*
upset *beunruhigt, aufgeregt.*
upset (to) *umkehren; aufregen* (distress).
upside down *drunter and drüber.*
upstairs *oben.*
upward *steigend, aufwärts.*
urge (to) *dringen, drängen, auffordern.*
urgent *dringend.*
us *uns.*
use *Gebrauch, m.; Verwendung, f.* (utility).
use (to) *gebrauchen; verwenden.*
used to (to be) *gewöhnt sein.*
useful *nützlich.*
useless *nutzlos.*
usual *gewöhnlich.*
utensil *Werkzeug, n.; Gerät, n.*
utility *Nützlichkeit, f.*
utilize (to) *nutzbar machen.*
utmost *äussert.*
   to the utmost *aufs Äußerste.*
utter (to) *äußern, aussprechen.*
utterly *durchaus.*

V

vacant *frei, leer, unbesetzt.*
vacation *Ferien, pl.; Urlaub* (from job).
vaccination *Impfung, f.*
vaccination certificate *Impfschein, m.*
vacuum (all purpose) *Allzwecksauger, m.; Staubsauger* (vacuum cleaner), *m.*
vaguely *unbestimmt.*
vain *eitel.*
   in vain *vergebens, umsonst.*
valiant *tapfer.*
valid *gültig.*
validity *Gültigkeit, f.*
valley *Tal, n.*
valuable *wertvoll.*
value *Wert, m.*
value (to) *schätzen.*
valued *geschätzt.*
valve *Ventil, n.*
vanilla *Vanille, f.*
vanish (to) *verschwinden.*
vanity *Eitelkeit, f.*
vanquish (to) *besiegen.*
vapor *Dampf, m.*
variable *variabel, veränderlich, wechselnd.*
variation *Abweichung, f.* (deviation), *Variation, f.*

varied *verschieden.*
variety *Abwechslung, f.; Mannigfaltigkeit, f.*
various *verschieden(e), mehrere.*
varnish (to) *lackieren.*
vary (to) *sich ändern, verschieden.*
vase *Vase, f.*
vast *ungeheuerlich (gross); weit.*
vault *Gewölbe, n.; Schatzkammer* (bank), *f.*
veal *Kalbfleisch, n.*
vegetable *Gemüse, n.*
vehicle *Fahrzeug, n.*
veil *Schleier, m.*
veil (to) *verschleiern.*
vein *Ader, f.* (body and mineral); *vene, f.*
velvet *Samt, m.*
venerable *ehrwürdig.*
venerate (to) *verehren.*
veneration *Verehrung, f.*
vengeance *Rache, f.*
ventilation *Lüftung, f.*
ventilator *Ventilator, m.; Lüftungsanlage, f.*
venture (to) *versuchen.*
verb *Zeitwort, n.*
verdict *Urteil, n.*
verge *Rand, m.*
   on the verge of *am Rand von* (gen).
verification *Bestätigung, f.*
verify (to) *bestätigen.*
verse *Vers, m.; Dichtung, f.* (poetry).
version *Version, f.;* (translation); *Darstellung, f.* (account).
very *sehr.*
vest *Weste, f.*
veterinarian *Tierarzt, m.*
VHS recorder *Videorekorder, m.*
vice *Untugend, f.*
vice president *Vizepräsident, m.*
vice versa *umgekehrt.*
vicinity *Nähe, f.; Nachbarschaft, f.*
victim *Opfer, n.*
victor *Sieger, m.*
victorious *siegreich.*
victory *Sieg, m.*
view *Aussicht, f.; Ansicht, f.* (opinion).
vigorous *kräftig.*
vile *abscheulich.*
village *Dorf, n.*
vine *Weinstock, m.; Rebe, f.*
vinegar *Essig, m.*
vineyard *Weinberg, m.*
violence *Gewalttätigkeit, f.*
violent *gewaltig.*
violet *Veilchen, n.*
violet *violett.*
violin *Geige, f.*
violinist *Geiger, m.*
virtue *Tugend, f.*
virtuous *tugendhaft.*

visible *sichtbar.*
vision *Sehen, n.; Erscheinung, f.* (ghost).
visit *Besuch, m.*
visit (to) *besuchen.*
visitor *Besucher, m.*
visualize (to) *sich vorstellen.*
vital *lebens-; vital.*
vitality *Lebenskraft, f.*
vivacious *lebhaft.*
vivacity *Lebhaftigkeit, f.*
vivid *lebendig; leuchtend* (color).
vocabulary *Wortschatz, m.*
vocal *stimmlich.*
vocation *Beruf, m.*
vogue *Mode, f.*
voice *Stimme, f.*
void *Leere* (noun) *f.; leer* (empty); *ungültig* (invalid).
volcano *Vulkan, m.*
volume *Umfang, m., Lautstärke, f.*
voluntary *freiwillig.*
vote (to) *wählen.*
vote *Stimme, f.*
vow *Gelübde, n.*
vow (to) *geloben.*
vowel *Vokal, m.*
vulgar *vulgär, gemein, niedrig.*
vulnerable *verwundbar, verletzbar.*

W

wager *Wette, f.*
wager (to) *wetten.*
wages *Lohn, m.*
waist *Taille, f.*
wait (to) *warten.*
  waiting room   *Wartezimmer, n.*
waiter *Kellner, m.; Kellnerin, f.*
wake (to) *aufwecken.*
wake up (to) *aufwachen.*
walk *Spaziergang, m.*
walk (to) *gehen.*
  take a walk   *spazierengehen, einen Spaziergang machen.*
wall *Wand, f.*
wallet *Brieftasche, f.*
walnut *Walnuss, f.*
wander (to) *wandern.*
wanderer *Wanderer, m.*
want *Mangel, m.; Not, f.* (poverty).
want (to) *wollen.*
war *Krieg, m.*
ward *Station, f.* (hospital); *Mündel, m./f.* (law).
ward off (to) *abwehren.*
wardrobe *Kleiderschrank, m.; Garderobe, f.*
ware *Ware, f.*

warehouse *Warenhaus, n.*
warm *warm.*
warm (to) *wärmen.*
warmth *Wärme, f.*
warn (to) *warnen.*
warning *Warnung, f.*
warrior *Krieger, m.*
wash (to) *waschen.*
washroom *Waschraum, m.*
waste *Verschwendung, f.*
waste (to) *verschwenden.*
watch *Uhr, f.*
watch (to) *wachen, achtgeben, aufpassen; zusehen* (to watch someone do work).
watchful *wachsam.*
water *Wasser, n.*
waterfall *Wasserfall, m.*
waterproof *wasserdicht.*
wave *Welle, f.*
wave (to) *schwenken; winken, wellen* (hair), *nicht berechnen* (fees).
wax *Wachs, n.*
way *Weg, m.* (road); *Weise, f.* (manner).
we *wir.*
weak *schwach.*
weaken (to) *schwächen.*
weakness *Schwachheit, f.; Schwäche, f.*
wealth *Reichtum, m.*
wealthy *reich.*
weapon *Waffe, f.*
wear (to) *tragen, anhaben.*
weariness *Müdigkeit, f.; Langweile, f.*
weary *müde.*
weather *Wetter, n.*
weave (to) *weben.*
wedding *Hochzeit, f.*
Wednesday *Mittwoch, m.*
weed *Unkraut, n.*
week *Woche, f.*
weekend *Wochenende, n.*
weekly *wöchentlich.*
weep (to) *weinen.*
weigh (to) *wiegen.*
weight *Gewicht, n.*
welcome *Empfang, m.* (reception); *freundliche Aufnahme, f.*
welfare *Wohlfahrt, f.*
well *gut, wohl.*
well *Brunnen, m.*
  oil well   *Ölquelle, f.*
west *westlich, Westen, m.*
westward *westwärts.*
wet *nass, feucht.*
whale *Walfisch, m.*
what *was; welch-* (-er, -e, -es) (which)
  what kind of   *was für ein.*
whatever *was auch immer.*
wheat *Weizen, m.*

wheel *Rad, n.*
when *wenn, als; wann* (interrogative).
whenever *so oft wie.*
where *wo; wohin* (whereto).
whereas *da, nun.*
wherever *überall wo.*
whether *ob.*
which *der (die, das); welch(-er, -e, -es).*
   which one *welch(-er, -e, -es).*
while *Weile* (noun) *f.; während*
   (conj.).
whim *Laune, f.; Einfall, m.*
whip *Peitsche, f.*
whisper (to) *flüstern.*
whistle *Pfeife, f.*
whistle *pfeifen.*
white *weiß.*
who *der (die, das), welch(-er, -e, -es)* (pron.);
   wer (inter. pron.).
whoever *wer auch immer.*
whole *Ganze* (noun) *n.; ganz* (adj.).
wholesale *Großhandel, m.*
wholesome *heilsam, gesund.*
whose *dessen (deren); wessen* (inter.)
why *warum.*
wicked *böse.*
wide *breit.*
widen (to) *verbreitern, erweitern.*
widow *Witwe, f.*
widower *Witwer, m.*
width *Weite, f.; Breite, f.*
wife *Frau, f.*
wig *Perücke, f.*
wild *wild.*
wilderness *Wildnis, f.*
will *Wille, m.; Testament, n.* (legal).
will (to) *werden.*
willing *gewillt.*
willingly *gern; mit Vergnügen.*
win (to) *gewinnen.*
wind *Wind, m.*
wind (to) *winden, aufwickeln.*
windbreaker *Anorak, m.*
window *Fenster, n.*
windy *windig.*
wine *Wein, m.*
wing *Flügel, m.*
wink *Blinzeln, n.; Augenzwinkern, n.*
wink (to) *blinzeln, zwinkern.*
winner *Sieger, m.*
winter *Winter, m.*
wipe (to) *wischen; ausrotten* (wipe out).
wire *Draht, m.*
wire (to) *kabeln, telegraphieren.*
wisdom *Weisheit, f.*
wise *weise.*
wish *Wunsch, m.*
wish (to) *wünschen.*
wit *Witz, m.; Geist, m.*

witch *Hexe, f.*
with *mit* (dat.)
withdraw (to) *zurückziehen; zurücknehmen*
   (statement); *abheben* (money).
wither (to) *verwelken.*
within *drinnen.*
without *ohne* (acc.).
witness *Zeuge, m.*
witness (to) *bezeugen.*
witticism *witzige Bemerkung, f.*
witty *witzig, geistreich.*
woe *Weh, n.*
wolf *Wolf, m.*
woman *Frau, f.*
wonder *Wunder, n.*
wonder (to) *sich wundern, sich fragen.*
wonderful *wunderbar, herrlich.*
wood *Holz, n.*
woods *Wald, m.*
woodwork *Holzwerk, n.*
wool *Wolle, f.*
word *Wort, n.*
   word-for-word *Wort für Wort.*
word processor *Textverarbeiter, m.*
work *Arbeit, f.*
   work of art *Kunstgegenstand, m.*
work (to) *arbeiten; sich beschäftigen.*
worker *Arbeiter, m.*
workshop *Werkstatt, f.*
world *Welt, f.*
worldly *weltlich.*
worried *besorgt.*
worry *Sorge, f.; Plage, f.*
worry (to) *besorgen; plagen.*
   Don't worry *Sorgen Sie sich nicht!*
     (Machen Sie sich keine Sorgen!)
worse *schlechter.*
worship *Gottesdienst, m.*
worship (to) *anbeten, verehren.*
worst *schlechtest.*
worth *Wert, m.*
worthless *wertlos.*
worthy *würdig.*
wound *Wunde, f.*
wound (to) *verwunden.*
wounded *verwundet.*
wrap (to) *einpacken, (ein)wickeln.*
wrath *Zorn, m.*
wreath *Kranz, m.*
wreck *Wrack, n.; Schiffbruch, m.*
wreck (to) *zertrümmern, scheitern.*
wrestle (to) *ringen; sich quälen* (with a
   problem).
wrestler *Ringkämpfer, m.*
wrestling *Ringkampf, m.*
wretched *elend, unglückselig.*
wring (to) *wringen.*
wrist *Handgelenk, n.*
write (to) *schreiben.*

writer *Schreiber, m.; Schriftsteller, m.*
writing *Schreiben, n.; Schrift, f.* (work).
  in writing   *schriftlich.*
wrong *unrecht, falsch.*
  You are wrong.   *Sie haben Unrecht.*

X

X-ray *Röntgenstrahlen (pl.).*

Y

yacht *Yacht, f.*
yard *Hof, m.* (courtyard).
yarn *Garn, n.* (textile).
yawn *Gähnen, n.*
yawn (to) *gähnen.*
year *Jahr, n.*
yearly *jährlich.*
yearn (to) *sich sehnen.*
yearning *Sehnen, n.; Sehnsucht, f.*
yeast *Hefe, f.*
yell (to) *schreien.*
yellow *gelb.*
yes *ja, doch.*
yesterday *gestern.*

yet *noch* (also besides); *doch, dennoch*
  (however).
yield (to) *aufgeben* (give up); *erzeugen*
  (produce).
yoke *Joch, n.*
yolk *(Ei) Dotter, n.* (of an egg); *Eigelb, n.*
you *Sie, du* (familiar sing.); *ihr* (familiar pl.);
         Sie, dich, euch (acc.); *ihnen, dir, euch*
         (dat.).
young *jung.*
  young lady   *junge Dame, f.; Fräulein, n.*
your *Ihr, dein, euer.*
yours *ihr(-er, -e, -es); dein(-er, -e, -es).*
yourself *Sie (ihnen) selbst; du (dich, dir)*
         selbst; ihr (euch).
youth *Jungend, f.*
yuletide *Weihnachtszeit, f.; Weihnachten, n.*

Z

zeal *Eifer, m.*
zealous *eifrig.*
zebra *Zebra, n.*
zero *Null, f.*
zipper *Reißverschluss, m.*
zone *Zone, f.*
zoo *Tierpark, m.; Zoo, m.*
zoology *Zoologie, f.*

GLOSSARY OF PROPER NAMES

Albert *Albrecht.*
Alfred *Alfred.*
Andrew *Andreas.*
Ann *Anna.*
Anthony *Anton.*
August *August.*
Barbara *Barbara.*
Bernard *Bernhard.*
Bertha *Bertha.*
Charles *Karl.*
Charlotte *Lotte.*
Edward *Eduard.*
Elisabeth *Elisabeth, Else.*
Elsie *Ilse.*
Emily *Emilie.*
Eric *Erich.*
Ernest *Ernst.*
Eugene *Eugen.*
Frances *Franziska.*
Frank *Franz.*
Frederick *Friedrich.*
Fred *Fritz.*
George *Georg.*
Gertrude *Gertrud.*
Gustave *Gustav.*
Helen *Helene.*
Henry *Heinrich.*
Jane *Johanna.*
John *Johann, Hans.*
Joseph *Josef.*
Katherine *Katharina, Kätchen, Käthe.*
Lewis *Ludwig.*
Louise *Luise.*
Margaret *Gretchen, Margareta.*
Martha *Martha.*
Mary *Maria.*
Maurice *Mortiz.*
Michael *Michael.*
Nicolas *Nikolaus, Klaus.*
Otto *Otto.*
Paul *Paul.*
Peter *Peter.*
Ralph *Rudolf, Rolf.*
Roger *Rüdiger.*
Susan *Susanne.*
Theodore *Theodor.*
Theresa *Therese.*
Thomas *Thomas.*
Walter *Walter.*
William *Wilhelm.*

GLOSSARY OF GEOGRAPHICAL NAMES

Africa *Afrika, n.*
Aix-la-Chapelle *Aachen, n.*
Alps *die Alpen, pl.*
America *Amerika, n.*
  North America *Nord-Amerika, n.*
  Central America *Zentral-Amerika, n., Mittel-Amerika, n.*
  South America *Süd-Amerika, n.*
Antwerp *Antwerpen, n.*
Arabia *Arabien, n.*
Asia *Asien, n.*
Atlantic *Atlantik, m.*
Australia *Australien, n.*
Austria *Österreich, n.*
Belgium *Belgien, n.*
Berlin *Berlin, n.*
Bonn *Bonn, n.*
Bosnia-Herzegovina *Bosnien-Herzegowina, n.*
Brazil *Brasilien, n.*
Brussels *Brüssel, n.*
Canada *Kanada, n.*
China *China, n.*
Cologne *Köln, m.*
Croatia *Kroatien, n.*
Czech Republic *Tschechische Republik f.*
Denmark *Dänemark, n.*
Egypt *Ägypten, n.*
England *England, n.*
Europe *Europa, n.*
France *Frankreich, n.*
Frankfurt on the Main *Frankfurt a.M., n.*
Germany *Deutschland, n.*
Greece *Griechenland, n.*
Hague *Den Haag, m.*
Hamburg *Hamburg, n.*
Holland *Holland, n.*
Hungary *Ungarn, n.*
India *Indien, n.*
Ireland *Irland, n.*
Israel *Israel, n.*
Italy *Italien, n.*
Japan *Japan, n.*
London *London, n.*
Madrid *Madrid, n.*
Mexico *Mexiko, n.*
Moscow *Moskau, n.*
Munich *München, n.*
Norway *Norwegen, n.*

Nuremberg   *Nüremberg, Nünberg, n.*
Pacific Ocean   *Pazifischer Ozean, m.*
Paris   *Paris, n.*
Poland   *Polen, n.*
Portugal   *Portugal, n.*
Prussia   *Preußen, n.*
Rhine   *Rhein, m.*
Rhineland   *Rheinland, n.*
Rome   *Rom, n.*
Russia   *Russland, n.*
Saar   *Saar, f.*
Saxony   *Sachsen, n.*

Scotland   *Schottland, n.*
Serbia   *Serbien, n.*
Silesia   *Schlesien, n.*
Slovakia   *Slowakei f.*
Spain   *Spanien, n.*
Sweden   *Schweden, n.*
Switzerland   *Schweiz, f.*
Turkey   *Türkei, f.*
United States (of America)   *die Vereinigten Staaten, pl.*
Vienna   *Wien, n.*
Yugoslavia   *Jugoslawien, n.*